Objectives List for System Administration for Microsoft SQL Server 6.5

Chapter 1: Server Installation and Upgrade

Objective...	Located Here...
Configure Microsoft Windows NT for SQL Server installations	*Configure Microsoft Windows NT for Installation of SQL Server*, see page **14** *Installing SQL Server on Microsoft Windows NT*, see page **18**
Configure SQL Server for various memory scenarios	*Configure Memory Options*, see page **31**
Configure SQL Executive to log on as a service	*SQL Executive Service Account Selection*, see page **25** *Configuring the SQL Executive to Run (Log On) as a Service*, see page **34**
Install client support for network protocols other than named pipes	*Installing and Configuring Client Support for SQL Server*, see page **37**
Load multiple Net Libraries	*Server-Side Network Libraries*, see page **39**
Upgrade SQL Server 4.2x to SQL Server 6.5	*Upgrading from SQL Server 4.2x to SQL Server 6.5*, see page **41**
Set up a security mode	*Setting the Security Option*, see page **46**

Chapter 2: Integration of SQL Server with Other Applications and Technologies

Objective...	Located Here...
Identify the impact of SQL Server on integrated security	*The Impact on SQL Server of Integrated Security*, see page **74**
Locate where the Windows NT Registry entries for SQL Server are stored	*Finding Registry Information about SQL Server*, see page **78**
Identify how SQL Server is integrated with Windows NT	*SQL Server Integration with Windows NT*, see page **82**
Identify capabilities of SQL Server when used with MAPI	*SQL Server and MAPI*, see page **86**

Chapter 3: Enterprise-Wide Database Administration

Objective...	Located Here...
Configure servers in the enterprise	*Modifying the SQL Server Configuration*, see page **121** *SQL Client Configuration Utility*, see page **126** *SQL Performance Monitor*, see page **142**
Manage servers in the enterprise	*Administering SQL Mail*, see page **124** *SQL Security Manager*, see page **119** *SQL Trace*, see page **140**; *ISQL/W*, see page **140**
Administer servers in the enterprise	*Distributed Management Framework*, see page **110** *SQL Enterprise Manager*, see page **112** *SQL Service Manager*, see page **119**

Chapter 4: Managing Database Storage

Objective...	Located Here...
Create a device	*How to Create Devices*, see page **172**
Create a database	*How to Create Databases*, see page **181**
Alter a database	*How to Alter the Size of a Database Using SQL Enterprise Manager*, see page **188** *How to Change the Size of a Database Using Transact-SQL*, see page **191**
Create database objects	*How to Create Database Objects*, see page **193**
Estimate space requirements	*How to Estimate Space Requirements for a Database*, see page **205**

Chapter 5: Managing User Accounts

Objective...	Located Here...
Differentiate between a SQL Server login and a SQL Server user	*SQL Server Login and User Accounts*, see page **234**
Create a login ID	*How to Create a New Login ID*, see page **248**
Add a database user	*How to Create New Database User IDs*, see page **248**
Add and drop users for a group	*How to Add Database User IDs to a Group*, see page **256** *How to Remove Database User IDs from a Group*, see page **259**

Chapter 6: Managing Permissions

Objective...	Located Here...
Grant and revoke permissions	*How to Grant or Revoke Statement Permissions*, see page **333** *How to Grant or Revoke Object Permissions*, see page **336**
Predict the outcome of a broken ownership chain	*Understanding Ownership Chains*, see page **330**
Identify system administrator functionality	*System Administrator (sa) Permissions*, see page **322**
Implement various methods of securing access to data	*System Administrator (sa) Permissions*, see page **322** *Database Owner (dbo) Permissions*, see page **323** *Database Object Owner (dboo) Permissions*, see page **325**

Chapter 7: Server Alert Processing and Task Scheduling

Objective...	Located Here...
Identify the role of the msdb database	*The msdb Database*, see page **366**
Identify the role of SQL Executive service	*The SQL Executive Service*, see page **368**
Identify conceptual relationships among the Schedule service, the msdb database, and the Windows NT event log	*SQL Alerting/Scheduling Components*, see page **365**
Set up alerts	*Defining Alerts*, see page **371**
Schedule tasks	*Adding Tasks*, see page **393**

DAVID LAFFERTY, MCSE, MCT
BRAD MCGEHEE, MCSE, MCT
CHRIS MILLER, MCSE, MCSD
WAYNE SMITH
DEANNA TOWNSEND, MCSD
STEPHEN WYNKOOP, MCSE

MCSE
TRAINING GUIDE

SQL SERVER 6.5
ADMINISTRATION

MCSE Training Guide:
SQL Server 6.5 Administration

By David Lafferty, Brad McGehee, Chris Miller, Wayne Smith, Deanna Townsend, and Stephen Wynkoop

Published by:
New Riders Publishing
201 West 103rd Street
Indianapolis, IN 46290 USA

Printed in the United States of America 2 3 4 5 6 7 8 9 0

Library of Congress Cataloging-in-Publication Data

CIP data available upon request

ISBN: 1-56205-726-X

Warning and Disclaimer

This book is designed to provide information about SQL Server 6.5 Administration and the System Administration for Microsoft SQL Server 6.5 exam, Exam 70-26. Every effort has been made to make this book as complete and as accurate as possible, but no warranty or fitness is implied.

New Riders is an independent entity from Microsoft Corporation, and not affiliated with Microsoft Corporation in any manner. This book and CD-ROM may be used in assisting students to prepare for a Microsoft Certified Professional Exam. Neither Microsoft Corporation, its designated review company, nor New Riders warrants that use of this book and CD-ROM will ensure passing the relevant Exam. Microsoft is either a registered trademark or trademark of Microsoft Corporation in the United States and/or other countries.

The information is provided on an "as is" basis. The author(s) and New Riders Publishing shall have neither liability nor responsibility to any person or entity with respect to any loss or damages arising from the information contained in this book or from the use of the discs or programs that may accompany it.

Publisher	*David Dwyer*
Marketing Manager	*Kourtnaye Sturgeon*
Executive Editor	*Mary Foote*
Managing Editor	*Sarah Kearns*

Acquisitions Editor
Stephanie Layton

Development Editor
Stacia Mellinger

Project Editor
Daryl Kessler

Copy Editors
Gina Brown
Pam Clark
Cliff Shubs

Technical Editor
Jeff Bumgardner

Software Product Developer
Steve Flatt

Software Acquisitions and Development
Dustin Sullivan

Assistant Marketing Manager
Gretchen Schlesinger

Team Coordinators
Stacey Beheler
Amy Lewis

Manufacturing Coordinator
Brook Farling

Book Designer
Glenn Larsen

Cover Designer
Dan Armstrong

Cover Production
Casey Price
Nathan Clement

Director of Production
Larry Klein

Production Team Supervisor
Laurie Casey

Graphics Image Specialists
Kevin Cliburn, Wil Cruz

Production Analysts
Dan Harris, Erich J. Richter

Production Team
Lori Cliburn, Linda Knose, Elizabeth SanMiguel, Pamela Woolf

Indexer
Chris Wilcox

About the Authors

David Lafferty graduated from DeVry Institute—Chicago, Illinois, in 1989, with a BS in computer information systems. Prior to IS consulting, he worked for one of the nation's largest insurance companies, providing implementation and support of Novell networks and Netware SAA mainframe connectivity. Since 1992, David has been an IS consultant. He is currently a managing consultant for Metamor Technologies, Ltd., in Chicago. He is responsible for project management and business development for clients engaged in large-scale desktop migration projects, and for the implementation of Microsoft BackOffice technologies. David has worked with Microsoft SQL Server for over four years. Most recently, he designed a Windows NT system architecture and database recovery methodology for a customer migrating a mainframe-based order entry system for over 400 users. David has written feature articles on SQL Server for *ENT* magazine and *Windows NT* magazine. He also publishes a monthly column titled "NT Techniques" for *Network Magazine*. David currently lives in Algonquin, Illinois, with his wife Michele and daughter Emily.

Brad McGehee is a full-time computer trainer, specializing in Microsoft Windows NT Server and Microsoft BackOffice products. He is a Microsoft Certified Trainer (MCT), a Microsoft Certified Systems Engineer (MCSE), and a Certified NetWare Engineer (CNE). He is the author or editor of four books and the author of over 100 articles on computers. He has a masters degree in business and has been involved in the computer industry since 1981.

Chris Miller was born and raised in St. Joseph, Missouri. He went to the University of Missouri at Rolla, originally as a chemical engineering major before he joined the "dark side" and graduated with a computer science degree. After three years doing consulting work ranging from Visual Basic coding to database administration and project management, Chris decided to go legit and started working at a major wireless telecommunications company as the project lead for their Microsoft System Management Server project. Chris lives in Kansas City, Missouri, with his wife Jennifer.

Wayne Smith hails from Chesapeake, Virginia, and is currently in the employ of the ADESA Corporation in Indianapolis, Indiana, where he serves as a Client/Server developer with Microsoft SQL Server and Visual Basic.

Deanna Townsend is a consultant specializing in PowerBuilder development. Her database experience includes SQL Server, Sybase, and Informix. She has received her MCSD (Microsoft Certified Solution Developer) and CPD (Certified PowerBuilder Developer) certifications. Previous to this book, she has coauthored three PowerBuilder text books for Que E & T and contributed to *JavaBeans Developers Reference* for New Riders.

Stephen Wynkoop is an author and lecturer working almost exclusively with Microsoft-based technologies. Stephen has been a regular speaker at Microsoft's TechEd conferences and has written books about SQL Server, Access, and Office 95 development technologies. He contributed to *Special Edition Using SQL Server 6.5* for Que and is working on other books regarding exciting techologies on the horizon. Stephen can be reached at swynk@pobox.com.

Trademark Acknowledgments

Dedications

Dedicated to my wife Michele and daughter Emily for putting up with me all those nights. And to my computer for waiting until the chapters were complete, before letting its ailing hard drive fail completely.

—David Lafferty

As always, to my wonderful wife Vero.

—Brad M. McGehee

This book is dedicated to my wife Jennifer, for being patient.

—Chris Miller

Acknowledgments

Thanks to New Riders's Stephanie Layton and Stacia Mellinger for their support.

—Brad McGehee

Contents at a Glance

Table of Contents

Introduction

MCSE Training Guide: SQL Server 6.5 Administration is designed for advanced end users, service technicians, and network administrators who are considering certification as Microsoft Certified Systems Engineers (MCSEs) or as a Microsoft Certified Product (MCP) Specialists. The SQL Server Administration exam (Exam 70-26: System Administration for Microsoft SQL Server 6.5) tests your ability to implement, administer, and troubleshoot information systems that incorporate SQL Server 6.5, as well as your ability to provide technical support to users of SQL Server version 6.5.

Who Should Read this Book

This book is designed to help advanced users, service technicians, and network administrators who are working for MCSE certification prepare for the MCSE System Administration for Microsoft SQL Server 6.5 exam (#70-26).

This book is your one-stop shop. Everything you need to know to pass the exam is in here, and the contents have been certified by Microsoft as approved study materials. You do not *need* to take a class in addition to buying this book to pass the exam. However, according your personal study habits, you may benefit from taking a class in addition to buying the book, or buying the book in preparation for taking a class.

This book also can help advanced users and administrators who are not studying for the MCSE exam but are looking for a single-volume reference on SQL Server administration.

How this Book Helps You

This book takes you on a self-guided tour of all the areas covered by the MCSE SQL Server Administration exam and teaches you the specific skills you need to achieve your MCSE certification. You'll also find helpful hints, tips, real-world examples, exercises, and references to additional study materials. Specifically, this book is set up to help you by offering the following:

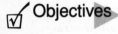
Objectives

> ▶ **Organization.** This book is organized by major exam topics (12 in all) and exam objectives. Every objective you need to know for the System Administration for Microsoft SQL Server 6.5 exam is covered in this book; we've included a margin icon, like the one in the margin here, to help you quickly locate these objectives. There are pointers at different elements to direct you to the appropriate sections in the book if you find you need to review certain topics.

> ▶ **Time-management guidance.** Pre-chapter quizzes are at the beginning of each chapter to test your knowledge of the objectives contained within that chapter. If you already know the answers to those questions, you can make a time-management decision accordingly.

> ▶ **Extensive practice test options.** Plenty of questions are at the end of each chapter to test your comprehension of material covered within that chapter. An answer list follows the questions so you can check yourself. These practice test options will help you determine what you already understand and what requires extra review on your part. The CD-ROM also contains a sample test engine that will give you an accurate idea of what the test is really like.

Note

For a complete description of the test engine, please see Appendix D, "All About TestPrep."

For a complete description of what you can find on the CD-ROM, see Appendix C, "What's on the CD-ROM."

Understanding What the System Administration for Microsoft SQL Server 6.5 Exam (#70-26) Covers

The System Administration for Microsoft SQL Server 6.5 exam (#70-26) covers 12 main topic areas, arranged in accordance with test objectives. The exam objectives, listed by topic area, are covered in the following sections.

Server Installation and Upgrade

▶ Configure Microsoft Windows NT for SQL Server installations

▶ Configure SQL Server for various memory scenarios

▶ Configure SQL Executive to log on as a service

▶ Install client support for network protocols other than named pipes

▶ Load multiple Net-Libraries

▶ Upgrade SQL Server 4.2x to SQL Server 6.5

▶ Set up a security mode

Integration of SQL Server with Other Applications and Technologies

▶ Identify the impact of SQL Server on integrated security

▶ Locate where the Windows NT Registry entries for SQL Server are stored

▶ Identify how SQL Server is integrated with Windows NT

▶ Identify capabilities of SQL Server when used with MAPI

Enterprise-Wide Database Administration

▶ Configure servers in the enterprise

▶ Manage servers in the enterprise

▶ Administer servers in the enterprise

Managing Database Storage

▶ Create a device

▶ Create a database

▶ Alter a database

▶ Create database objects

▶ Estimate space requirements

Managing User Accounts

▶ Differentiate between a SQL Server login and a SQL Server user

▶ Create a login ID

▶ Add a database user

▶ Add and drop users for a group

Managing Permissions

▶ Grant and revoke permissions

▶ Predict the outcome of a broken ownership chain

▶ Identify system administrator functionality

▶ Implement various methods of securing access to data

Server Alert Processing and Task Scheduling

▶ Identify the role of the msdb database

▶ Identify the role of SQL Executive service

▶ Identify conceptual relationships among the Schedule service, the msdb database, and the Windows NT event log

▶ Set up alerts

▶ Schedule tasks

Managing Data

▶ Identify the best uses for the dumping command and the loading command in managing data

▶ Identify the best uses for BCP when managing data

▶ Identify the appropriate replication scenario to use

▶ Identify the functionality of dynamic backup

▶ Identify how automatic recovery works

▶ Perform a database dump

▶ Perform a striped backup

▶ Create a dump device

▶ Dump a transaction log

▶ Load a database dump

Replication

- ▶ Identify prerequisites for replication

- ▶ Configure the servers used for setting up replication

- ▶ Set up various replication scenarios

- ▶ Implement replication

- ▶ Schedule a replication event

- ▶ Recognize the situations in which you must perform manual synchronization

- ▶ Identify the system tables that are used in replication

- ▶ Resolve setup problems

- ▶ Resolve fault-tolerance problems and recovery problems

Connectivity and Network Support

- ▶ Set up support for network clients by using various network protocols

- ▶ Install an extended stored procedure

Tuning and Monitoring

- ▶ Identify the benefits of installing the TempDB database in RAM

- ▶ Configure the number of worker threads

- ▶ Select the appropriate settings for read ahead

- ▶ Select the appropriate settings for locks

- ▶ Monitor log size

- ▶ Tune and monitor physical and logical I/O

- ▶ Tune and monitor memory use

- ▶ Set database options

- ▶ Update statistics

Troubleshooting

- ▶ Locate information relevant to diagnosing a problem

- ▶ Resolve network error messages

- ▶ Check object integrity

- ▶ Investigate a database that is marked suspect

- ▶ Restore a corrupted database

- ▶ Re-create a lost device

- ▶ Cancel a sleeping process

Hardware and Software Needed

As a self-paced study guide, much of this book expects you to use SQL Server and follow along through the exercises while you learn. Microsoft designed SQL Server to operate in a wide range of actual situations, and the exercises in this book encompass that range. However, the exercises require only a single stand-alone computer running SQL Server. The computer should meet the following criteria:

- ▶ Computer on the Microsoft Hardware Compatibility List

- ▶ 486DX2 66-Mhz (or better) processor for Windows NT Server

- ▶ 16 MB of RAM (minimum) for Windows NT Server

- ▶ 340 MB (or larger) hard disk for Windows NT Server

- ▶ 3.5-inch 1.44 MB floppy drive

- ▶ VGA (or Super VGA) video adapter

- ▶ VGA (or Super VGA) monitor

- ▶ Mouse or equivalent pointing device

- ▶ Two-speed (or faster) CD-ROM drive (optional)

- ▶ Network Interface Card (NIC)

- ▶ Presence on an existing network, or use of a 2-port (or more) mini-port hub to create a test network

- ▶ MS-DOS 5.0 or 6.*x* and Microsoft Windows for Workgroups 3.*x* pre-installed

- ▶ Microsoft Windows 95 (floppy version)

- ▶ Microsoft Windows NT Server (CD-ROM version)

A corporate business environment might offer the best access to the necessary computer hardware and software. It can be difficult, however, to allocate enough time within the busy workday to complete a self-study program. Most of your study time should occur after normal working hours, away from the everyday interruptions and pressures of your regular job.

Tips for the Exam

Remember the following tips as you prepare for the MCSE certification exams:

- ▶ **Read all the material.** Microsoft has been known to include material not specified in the objectives. This course has included additional information not required by the objectives in an effort to give you the best possible preparation for the examination, and for the real-world network experiences to come.

- ▶ **Complete the exercises in each chapter.** They will help you gain experience using the Microsoft product. All Microsoft exams are experienced-based and require you to have used the Microsoft product in a real networking environment. Exercises for each objective are placed at the end of each chapter.

- ▶ **Take each pre-chapter quiz to evaluate how well you know the topic of the chapter.** Each chapter opens with at least one question per exam objective covered in the chapter. Following the quiz are the answers and pointers to where in the chapter each objective is covered.

▶ **Complete all the questions in the "Review Questions" sections.** Complete the questions at the end of each chapter—they will help you remember key points. The questions are fairly simple, but be warned: some questions may have more than one answer.

Although this book is designed to prepare you to take and pass the System Administration for Microsoft SQL Server 6.5 certification exam, there are no guarantees. Study this book, work through the exercises and chapter-ending questions, and take advantage of the TestPrep test engine on the CD-ROM.

When taking the real certification exam, make sure you answer all the questions before your time limit expires. Do not spend too much time on any one question. If you are unsure about an answer, answer the question as best you can and mark it for later review when you have finished all the questions. It has been said, whether correctly or not, that any questions left unanswered will automatically cause you to fail. Good luck.

Remember, the object is not to pass the exam—it is to understand the material. Once you understand the material, passing the exam is simple. Knowledge is a pyramid; to build upward, you need a solid foundation. The Microsoft Certified System Engineer program is designed to ensure that you have that solid foundation.

Good luck!

New Riders Publishing

The staff of New Riders Publishing is committed to bringing you the very best in computer reference material. Each New Riders book is the result of months of work by authors and staff who research and refine the information contained within its covers.

As part of this commitment to you, the NRP reader, New Riders invites your input. Please let us know if you enjoy this book, if you have trouble with the information and examples presented, or if you have a suggestion for the next edition.

Please note, though: New Riders staff cannot serve as a technical resource during your preparation for the Microsoft MCSE certification exams or for questions about software- or hardware-related problems. Please refer to the documentation that accompanies SQL Server or to the applications' Help systems.

If you have a question or comment about any New Riders book, there are several ways to contact New Riders Publishing. We will respond to as many readers as we can. Your name, address, or phone number will never become part of a mailing list or be used for any purpose other than to help us continue to bring you the best books possible. You can write us at the following address:

New Riders Publishing
Attn: Publisher
201 W. 103rd Street
Indianapolis, IN 46290

If you prefer, you can fax New Riders Publishing at (317) 817-7448.

You also can send e-mail to New Riders at the following Internet address:

certification@mcp.com

If you have technical problems with the CD-ROM, contact Macmillan Computer Publishing at the following Internet address:

support@mcp.com

NRP is an imprint of Macmillan Computer Publishing. To obtain a catalog or information, or to purchase any Macmillan Computer Publishing book, call (800) 428-5331.

Thank you for selecting *MCSE Training Guide: SQL Server 6.5 Administration*!

Chapter 1

Server Installation and Upgrade

The first step in learning any product is familiarizing yourself with its installation and configuration. To install SQL Server, you will determine installation location, prepare the Windows NT computer, and make initial decisions as to how data will be stored. Configuration will include the steps necessary to configure SQL Server for a particular server; performance tuning and optimization will not be covered here.

You will also learn how to upgrade SQL Server from version 4.2x, as the exam covers in some detail the unique set of challenges associated with this conversion. Integrated Security is introduced as a setup option, but is covered in greater detail in Chapter 5, "Managing User Accounts."

Each chapter in this book begins with a list of exam objectives relating to the topic at hand, and then move on to a chapter pretest. Valuable information that directly addresses the objectives is offered, along with additional relative discussion topics. Next come exercises, chapter review questions, and finally, answers to both the chapter review questions and the chapter pretest questions.

This chapter focuses on the installation and upgrade of SQL Server, and helps you prepare for the exam by addressing and fully covering the following objectives. You will learn how to do the following:

 Objectives

▶ Configure Microsoft Windows NT for SQL Server installations

continues

▶ Configure SQL Server for various memory scenarios

▶ Configure SQL Executive to log on as a service

▶ Install client support for network protocols other than Named Pipes

▶ Load multiple Net-Libraries

▶ Upgrade SQL Server 4.2x to SQL Server 6.5

▶ Set up a security mode

Test Yourself! Before reading this chapter, test yourself to determine how much study time you will need to devote to this section.

1. What are the minimum requirements for operating system version, memory, and disk space for SQL Server?

2. A computer running Windows NT Server has 128 MB of RAM. The computer will only be used to run SQL Server. How much of this memory should be allocated to SQL Server?

3. Bill needs to change the password for his SQL Executive service account. How can he do this?

4. How is support for TCP/IP installed on a client computer without requiring the user to have a login to Windows NT?

5. The SQL Server in Mary's network needs to support users on Macintosh computers as well as the rest of the PCs, which are used primarily to access Novell Netware servers. How should Mary go about allowing SQL Server to respond to these clients?

6. Which tables does the CHKUPG65 utility modify on the SQL Server?

7. Victor needs to allow users who are not being validated by Windows NT, as well as users who are already using other domain resources, to attach to his SQL server. What security mode should Victor use on the server?

Answers are located at the end of the chapter...

Configuring Microsoft Windows NT for Installation of SQL Server

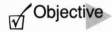**Objective** Before installation of SQL Server can begin, you must consider the setup of Windows NT, including issues such as these:

- Minimum hardware and software requirements

- Domain and security architecture

- Server name

- SQL Server installation location

Every product in the Microsoft BackOffice suite has similar considerations. Many conditions must be met to successfully run these products and maintain them in production environments.

Minimum Hardware and Software Requirements

To operate, SQL Server requires certain levels of hardware to be present. Note that, as is the case with other software packages, if the minimum hardware requirements for SQL Server are not met, while the software may run, it won't run at optimum speed, and some of the features may not be available.

Note The following section offers information on minimum hardware and software requirements. For more information—extending the discussion beyond minimum requirements to more aggressive *recommended* requirements—see Chapter 11, "Tuning and Monitoring."

First, make sure the computer that will be running SQL Server is on the Windows NT Compatibility List. This list, available from Microsoft, is the canonical guide to supported hardware. Having supported hardware can mean the difference between getting a problem resolved by Microsoft Product Support Services and giving the technician at PSS a good chuckle. SQL Server runs only on Digital Alpha, MIPS, PowerPC, and Intel systems.

SQL Server requires a system with 16 MB of RAM. If the server is going to participate in replication as a distribution server, then 32 MB of RAM is required.

Hard disk requirements vary depending on the size of the master device that is chosen, which defaults to 25 MB, and whether the Books Online package is installed locally, run from CD-ROM, or not installed. A minimum installation requires 60 MB of disk space. Books Online adds approximately another 15 MB. If this is an upgrade installation, 50 MB of disk space will be required.

Note

Although you may be tempted to run Books Online from CD-ROM to save disk space, this is not advised. The information in Books Online is critical during recovery operations, and other operations that are primarily performed while you are logged on to the server. (Digging through a desk late at night, trying to find the CD so the server can be restored before the users arrive in the morning, is not fun.) If disk space is so critical that 12 MB is not available, use compression on NTFS partitions to reduce the impact of having Books Online installed.

SQL Server can be purchased in two different packages: SQL Workstation and SQL Server. SQL Workstation is a product used by developers to develop and test software. SQL Workstation is licensed for only one user, has a maximum of 15 client connections, and includes developer tools. It runs on either Windows NT Server or Windows NT Workstation. The SQL Server package does not have any limitations on user connections.

The primary tool for the administration of SQL Server, the SQL Enterprise Manager, can be installed on any Win32 operating system, including Windows 95, Windows NT Workstation, and Windows NT Server. To install the SQL Enterprise Manager on Windows 95, run the setup program in the i386 directory on the CD-ROM. To install SQL Enterprise Manager on Windows NT systems, run Setup, but choose the Install Utilities Only option.

SQL Server supports all the major network protocols, without the need for additional software. This includes the most popular LAN protocols: TCP/IP, NetBEUI, the Novell-compatible NWLink, and many others. SQL Server also supports all the same network cards as does Windows NT.

Domain and Security Architecture

Microsoft Windows NT Server can be installed to operate as a primary domain controller, a backup domain controller, or as a standalone server. (SQL Server can also be installed on Microsoft Windows NT Workstation, but a connection limit of 15 clients is strictly enforced.)

Microsoft recommends against the installation of SQL Server on computers that are participating in the network as domain controllers. Practical experience points out that SQL Server should not be run on a domain controller in the account domain of any appreciably-sized network. If the network is using a master-domain model, and SQL Server is running on a domain controller in a resource domain, the overhead involved will be minimal. Keep in mind that the reduction of any overhead on the server is a good idea if the server is going to be approaching the limits of the hardware involved.

If users are being validated against a Windows NT Domain, then it is also possible to use SQL Server Integrated Security. The use of Integrated Security is not precluded by setting SQL Server up on Windows NT configured as a standalone server, as long as the server is participating in a domain.

Server Name

SQL Server uses the Windows NT name as its server name. However, SQL Server places some restrictions on what those names should be:

▶ The first character must be a letter or an underscore.

▶ Spaces cannot be embedded in the name.

▶ After the first character, any combination of letters, numbers, and the special characters '#', '$' or '_' can be used, but no other special characters can be used.

▶ All other restrictions for naming computers in Windows NT apply, including the 15-character limit.

In reality, the server name should follow the naming standard already set by the organization. You can choose anything from the names of your favorite science fiction authors, to combinations of letters and numbers relating to server location and function.

SQL Server Installation Location

The SQL Server setup program creates a set of directories, and installs various configuration and executable files in these directories. By default, SQL Server is installed on drive C in a directory called MSSQL. Beneath the MSSQL directory are several other directories (see table 1.1).

Table 1.1

Directory Names and Descriptions

Directory	Contents
Backup	A good directory to place backup dump files. Empty after an installation.
Bin	Client-side network libraries.
Binn	Executables and associated files. Includes the executable for SQL Server itself, and any administration tools that are loaded.
Charsets	Character sets and sort orders for different database installations.
Data	Default location for database devices.
Install	SQL Server Books Online and indexes.
Log	SQL Server error logs. Text files that are the equivalent of the Windows NT event log, but more detailed.

continues

Table 1.1   Continued

Directory	Contents
Repldata	Default location for temporary data used in replication.
Snmp	Management Information Bases (MIBs) for SQL Server.
Sqlole	Samples for using OLE automation from Visual Basic to manage SQL Server.
Symbols	Debugging symbols used by programmers.

That covers the exam's pre-installation topics. Now take a look at how to install SQL Server.

Installing SQL Server on Microsoft Windows NT

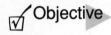 Objective   After the preparation of the Windows NT computer is complete, the next step is to run the Setup program to install SQL Server. The Setup program has three phases:

1. Option selection

2. Copying files

3. Setup verification

The Setup program, Setup.exe, is usually found in the architecture directory of the SQL Server CD-ROM (see fig. 1.1). For most users, this is the i386 directory. Run the Setup program to begin the option selection phase of setup.

Figure 1.1

Double-click on the Setup.exe icon to start the SQL Server Setup program.

Option Selection

Option selection is the most important part of setup. The fastest, easiest way to mess up an SQL Server is to install it incorrectly, and option selection is the only opportunity you have to make these crucial decisions. Option selection can be divided further, as follows:

▶ Installation type

▶ Installation location

▶ Allocation of Master Device

▶ Selection of character set and sort order

▶ Network support

▶ Startup options

▶ SQL Executive service account selection

Installation Type

The three primary types of setup are these (shown in fig. 1.2):

▶ **Install SQL Server and utilities.** Installs the SQL Server executables, necessary administration tools and, optionally, the Books Online package.

▶ **Install only the utilities.** Useful for installation on administrative workstations.

▶ **Perform an upgrade of the server from a previous version.** Covered in the later section "Upgrading from SQL Server 4.2x to SQL Server 6.5."

Figure 1.2

Choose the type of installation. (Note that some of the installation types are automatically disabled.)

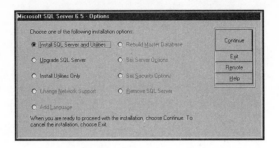

Installation Location

Setup uses this directory to store the files that are copied (see fig. 1.3). Choose a drive and directory name under which to install SQL Server.

Figure 1.3

Choose the installation path. (Note MSSQL is the default directory.)

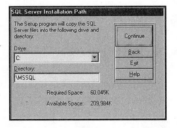

Note

The default directory name is MSSQL. It is not a good idea to stray from the default directory name, because it is one more variable that has to be explained to Microsoft Product Support Services, if technical help is needed. It's also easier to reference an installation with documentation from another source if you have left the directory names unchanged.

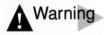Warning

Do not use a long file name in SQL Server's path. The Setup program doesn't appear like long file names—a known bug.

Usually on a Windows NT Server that is going to be a production SQL Server, the operating system and paging files are stored on the first logical partition, drive C, while the applications and data files are stored on other logical partitions.

Allocation of Master Device

The *Master device* is a file that contains databases used by SQL Server (see fig. 1.4). These include the Master, Model, Pubs, and TempDB databases. There are three boxes to fill in on this stage of setup: drive, directory, and size. The drive defaults to the drive on which you have chosen to install the MSSQL directory. The directory defaults to \MSSQL\DATA. The size defaults to 25 MB, which is the minimum size. Usually, this will be made larger to accommodate a larger Master database. A key thing to remember is that devices are easy to expand, but impossible to shrink. Experienced DBAs usually choose to make the Master device 50 MB. This provides enough room to expand databases without having to expand devices, but is still small enough that it fits on a production server.

Figure 1.4

Select the Master Device's size and location.

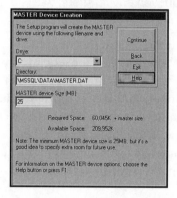

Selection of Character Set and Sort Order

Character set and sort order are two irrevocable decisions that must be made during the setup process (see fig. 1.5). The character set is the set of symbols that will be allowed in the database. This enables SQL Server to display characters from languages other than English. Sort order determines what order records are sorted in, how they are compared, and the case sensitivity of the database. Character set and sort order are configured at the same step in setup, and are closely related. Here are the details of how these options are implemented and the effects they have on the installation of SQL Server:

Figure 1.5

Choose Character Set, Sort Order, Additional Network Support, and Auto Start options.

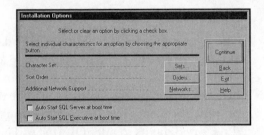

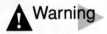**Warning**

> The most important thing to remember about the character set and sort order issue is that after the choices of character set and sort order are made, they cannot be changed. If a mistake is discovered, all the data has to be exported out of the SQL Server databases, SQL Server reinstalled, and the data read back. On any significantly-sized database, or in a production environment, this is a major ordeal.

Character set maps the value of data in the database to actual symbols. A character set contains 256 characters. The first 128 are the same from one character set to another, and include all the numbers and letters in the English alphabet, along with some common symbols. The last 128 characters are called *extended characters*. These include alphabetic characters with accent marks, characters not found in English, or other special characters, such as markers for foreign currency.

In addition to foreign character sets (see fig. 1.6), three English character sets come with SQL Server:

- ▶ The default character set, called ISO 8859-1, is compatible with all Microsoft operating systems. If no other factors effect the character set decision, use this character set.

- ▶ Code Page 850 is the default character set of SQL Server version 4.21. If interoperability with this version of SQL Server is necessary, this is most likely the character set that will be needed. Code Page 850 includes all the characters used by U.S. English, and characters used in European, North American, and South American countries.

- ▶ Code Page 437 contains all the characters used in U.S. English, and the extended characters are all graphics characters. This code page should be used if backward compatibility is desired, as it was the default code page for SQL Server 4.21; otherwise, this code page should be avoided because more modern pages are available.

Figure 1.6

Select a character set and click OK.

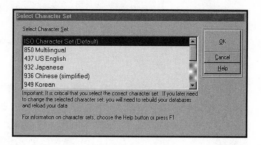

Sort orders have a direct impact on the programs that affect your database, including how character data is compared, as well as how it is ordered in a list. Sort orders have three major characteristics:

▶ **Case Sensitivity.** If the database is case sensitive, then all object names, field names, user names, and stored procedure names are also case sensitive. If a database is not case sensitive, then nothing is case sensitive. (The binary sort order is case sensitive.)

▶ **Sort Order.** Dictionary sort orders will sort uppercase before lowercase. An example list would look like A, a, B, b, C, c. Other sort orders will sort differently, either as all uppercase first (A, B, C, a, b, c) or all lowercase first.

▶ **Accent Sensitivity.** If this feature is active, any diacritical marks are considered in the comparison, but not in the sort order.

The default sort order is Dictionary order case insensitive (see fig. 1.7). This sort order is the easiest to administer and to use because it allows for sloppy typing; for example, no distinction is made between a table called "Authors" and a table called "authors." Under a case sensitive sort order, these would be considered two different objects.

Figure 1.7

*Select a sort order
and click OK.*

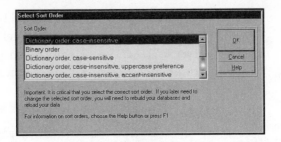

Note

The Binary sort order was the default sort order for SQL Server 4.21. and relies on the character set of the underlying operating system. It is also case sensitive. In essence, binary sort order compares two characters by determining the local value for the characters, with no consideration given to the characters' meaning.

Note

Microsoft has made claims regarding the performance benefits of using binary sort orders over other sort orders. Bear in mind, however, that the use of a binary sort order implies that all the overhead of converting to uppercase or lowercase is done in the client program. In addition, programmers find case sensitive sort orders very frustrating to work with because of the increased difficulty involved in tracking down problems when they arise.

Network Support Options

SQL Server supports many different network protocols. The Multi-Protocol and Named Pipes libraries are standard network support libraries used by SQL Server, and they support connections from TCP/IP, IPX/SPX via NWLink, and NetBEUI. Server-side network protocols are covered in a later section titled "Server-Side Network Libraries." The SQL Server Setup program can be used to modify network support after installation is complete.

Auto Start Options

SQL Server and SQL Executive are installed in Windows NT as operating system services. The SQL Executive service is used to monitor SQL Server, perform scheduled tasks, and handle alert processing. Services can be configured to automatically start at boot time. By default, services do not start automatically. For most production equipment, these options should be turned on; in case of power failure or system reboot, the services will be up and running in a minimum amount of time. However, developers or persons involved in testing machines may prefer to leave these options turned off. These options can be changed in SQL Server Setup, or by the Service applet in Control Panel.

SQL Executive Service Account Selection

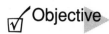 The SQL Executive service is a program that runs as a service of the Windows NT operating system, which means that the program runs in the background with no user interface and no console. Because all programs that run in the Windows NT operating system must belong to a user, all the services must belong to a user as well. For setup, use the Local System account, or select a user account (see fig. 1.8). More information on service accounts and the SQL Executive will be provided in the section, "Configuring the SQL Executive to Run (Log On) as a Service."

Figure 1.8

Enter the SQL Executive's account information. (Note that either an account can be selected, or the Local System account can be used.)

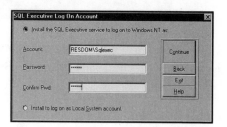

That's the last of the decisions to be made during the install process. From here on, it is time to sit back and watch the blue bar.

Copying Files

The next part of setup has two phases. Phase 1 actually copies files from the CD onto the hard drive while the installer (you) gets to watch the blue bar count from 0 percent to 100 percent. Phase 2 is the installation phase, during which SQL Server actually creates the

SQL Server devices, registers the OLE objects, and makes changes to the Registry. This part of setup takes about 10 to 15 minutes to complete, so kick back and watch the sand fill the hourglass.

Setup Verification

After setup is complete, make sure that the setup program actually installed everything it was supposed to (see fig. 1.9). Go to the Services applet in the Control Panel and make sure the SQL Executive and MSSQL Server services are in the list. If Auto Start was selected for either of these services, make sure the startup type is set to Automatic instead of Manual. If the services are not started, start them, and make sure they reach Started status.

Figure 1.9

All these icons should be in the SQL Server program group.

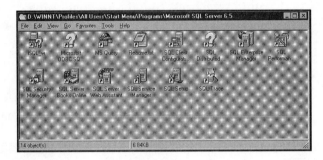

In the Microsoft SQL Server 6 program group, there should be icons for SQL Enterprise Manager, SQL Books Online, ISQL/W, SQL Security Manager, and other files (see table 1.2).

Table 1.2

Program Group Icon Descriptions

Icon Label	Program Description
ISQL_W	The SQL Query tool
Microsoft ODBC SQL	ODBC Driver Help Server Driver
MS Query	A graphical tool to help build queries
Readme.txt	The release notes for the current version of SQL Server

Icon Label	Program Description
SQL Client Configuration Utility	Configures network protocols for client programs
SQL Distributed Management Objects	Help file for the OLE object model for SQL Server
SQL Enterprise Manager	The primary tool used to manage SQL Server
SQL Performance Monitor	An environment file for Windows NT Performance Monitor that includes most of the server health counters
SQL Security Manager	The Integrated Security setup tool
SQL Server Books Online	All the paper books in electronic searchable format
SQL Server Web Assistant	Used to make web pages out of queries
SQL Service Manager	The Stoplight Application, which enables the SQL Server to be started or stopped
SQL Setup	Used to change SQL Server configuration
SQL Trace	Used to watch queries going to and from the SQL Server

Initial Configuration of SQL Server

After you have finished running the Setup program, you will need to set some options in SQL Server. These options make SQL Server fit onto the hardware, and form the first step in tuning SQL Server performance. These steps include include the following:

▶ Setting up SQL Enterprise Manager

▶ Configuring memory allocation

▶ Setting the number of user connections

Setting Up SQL Enterprise Manager

The SQL Enterprise Manager is the Graphical User Interface (GUI) used to control SQL Server, and makes many of the day to day tasks of managing SQL Server much easier. There are two ways to do almost everything in SQL Server: by using the GUI in SQL Enterprise Manager, or by typing the SQL in to a query tool. This text covers both methods of SQL management, because the exam requires knowledge of both.

The first time SQL Enterprise Manager is started by each user on a given computer, it is necessary to register the servers on which SQL Enterprise Manager will be used (see fig. 1.10).

Figure 1.10

The SQL Server registration screen.

Register servers by performing the following tasks:

1. Bring up the Register Server dialog box. If there aren't any servers registered, the box will appear when Enterprise Manager is started. Otherwise, start it by choosing Register Server from the Server menu.

2. Type in the name of the server.

3. Choose the security type. Standard Security is the default.

4. Type in the login ID and password. For a new SQL Server, the security mode is standard, the login ID is sa, and the password is blank. If Integrated Security was chosen in Step 3, then these fields will be grayed out and the logon name of the current user will be used.

The sa or System Administrator account is the default login for SQL Server, and is the account with global permissions to do anything. By default, the password is blank.

Whenever the password for the account used in registration changes, the server's registration has to be updated with the new password. Choose Server, Register Server from the menu in Enterprise Manager to edit the registration information.

After a server has been registered, the server name will appear in the window, along with a small icon that looks like a traffic light. The icon should eventually change to either a red light, yellow light, or green light. A red light means the SQL Server is stopped, a green light means the SQL Server is running, and a yellow light means the SQL Server is paused.

When a service is paused, it is still processing data for the current connections, but is not accepting any new connections. This is handy if the server needs to be brought down, but active users still have work to complete.

Take the time necessary to familiarize yourself with the interface; get used to where things are and how to expand and contract trees using the plus and minus icons (see fig. 1.11). To expand a server, click the plus sign to the left of the server's name. To modify any object, try right-clicking on the object. The right-click action usually presents options that will create a new object, modify an object, or configure an object.

Many of the examples used in this book will require you to use a *query tool*. The query tool can be accessed in one of two ways. From SQL Enterprise Manager, choose the correct database and go to Tools, SQL Query Tool on the menu. The ISQL/W program, which can be started from the SQL Server program group, can also be used.

Figure 1.11

An expanded server. One of the database names has been right-clicked to display the pop-up menu for a database.

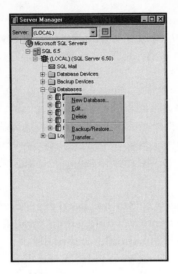

The query tool is a text entry box (see fig. 1.12). Type in the query, press the Execute button, which is the right-pointing triangle on the query window toolbar, and SQL Server returns a response. The query isn't executed until the Execute button is used. SQL Server queries are almost free-form; queries can be formatted over multiple lines for increased readability without affecting the way the query executes.

Figure 1.12

The SQL Server query tool.

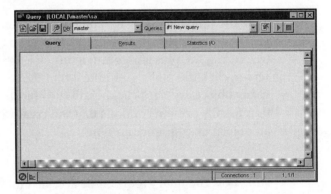

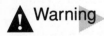 **Warning** Always make sure the database name in the text box labeled DB: is correct before you execute a query. Check the name at least twice before you use the Execute button.

Configuring Memory Options

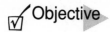 **Objective**

One of SQL Server's most important options is the Memory option. Most programs and services that run, start and allocate memory from the operating system on an as-needed basis. SQL Server requires that the amount of memory it uses be set, and when the service is started, it allocates that chunk of memory as its own. Balancing the needs of SQL Server and the Windows NT operating system make setting up memory options a challenge.

When SQL Server is installed, if the computer has less than 32 MB of RAM, the Setup program sets 8 MB of memory aside for SQL Server. If the computer has 32 MB of RAM or more, the SQL Server is given 16 MB of memory. That is the initial setup. For servers with more than 32 MB of RAM, this is not an optimal setup, and it will require additional tuning.

The purpose of fine-tuning the amount of memory given to SQL Server is this: You want SQL Server to have as much memory as possible without causing Windows NT to begin paging. To monitor paging follow these steps:

1. Start the Windows NT Performance Monitor application.

2. Choose Edit, Add to Chart.

3. In the Computer: box, type \\ and the name of the computer you want to monitor.

4. Drop-down the Object: box and select Memory.

5. In the Counter: box select Pages per Second and then select Done.

If the computer seems to be consistently paging at a certain level, SQL Server has been given too much memory, and Windows NT does not have enough. If there is sporadic paging, the balance of memory is pretty close to where it should be. If there is no paging, either the balance is right on or SQL Server does not have enough memory. Add the SQL Server Cache Hit Ratio to the Performance Monitor chart to obtain a picture of how well SQL Server is using memory:

1. Choose Edit, Add to Chart.

2. Drop-down the Object: box and select SQL Server.

3. In the Counter: box, select Cache Hit Ratio.

A good cache hit ratio for a server that has been running for a while is over 98 percent. Anything less than this and either the server needs more memory or the database needs to be restructured to fit more data on a page. For more information, see Chapter 11.

Table 1.3 illustrates good starting points for memory configuration.

Table 1.3

Memory to Allocate for SQL Server Based on Total System Memory	
Total System RAM	Memory for SQL Server
16 MB	8 MB
32 MB	16 MB
40 MB	24 MB
64 MB	40 MB
80 MB	40 MB
128 MB	88 MB
256 MB	216 MB

Note that Windows NT never gets more than 40 MB of RAM. This is usually what Windows NT will max out at in requirements for a server that is running SQL Server, and is not running any file and print services. At that point, Windows NT is capable of running without swapping, and SQL Server has the rest of the memory to use for caching data.

An interesting aspect of having many options set in SQL Server is the units that have to be used. For memory options, SQL Server has to be told how much memory to use in 2 KB pages. For example, 16 MB of RAM results in a memory setting of 8192. To check this figure, multiply 16 MB by 1024 to get the number of kilobytes in 16 MB, and then divide that by 2 to get the number of 2 Kb pages. That's the hard way. The easy way is to multiply 16×512. Always watch the units for which SQL Server is asking.

To set the Memory options using the SQL Enterprise Manager, start the SQL Enterprise Manager, expand the server, and right-click on the server name. Choose the Configure option, and then select the Configuration tab. Look for the line item that says memory and put in the setting. The settings are in alphabetical order (see fig. 1.13).

Figure 1.13

Most server options are configured on the SQL Server Configuration screen.

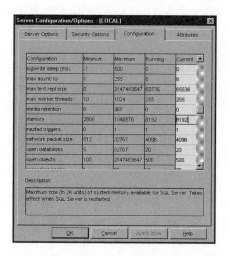

The Running value shows the value being used. The new value, entered in the Current column, must be between the values in the Minimum and Maximum column.

To use a query tool to set memory options, open up ISQL/W, connect to the server, and type the following command:

```
Sp_configure "memory", 8192
```

This example will configure the server to use 16 MB of RAM. The server can be set to use from 1000 pages, which is a little under 2 MB, up to 2 GB. After the memory configuration option has been changed, SQL Server must be stopped and restarted.

Setting the Number of User Connections

The User Connections setting in SQL Server determines how many simultaneous connections are available to users. This value is a hard limit on the number of users that SQL Server can handle at the same time. Any connection attempted when SQL Server is at the limit will fail. Although this may seem like an artificial licensing tool, it is actually an important tuning parameter. Each configured user connection uses 37 KB of the memory set aside for SQL Server. The User Connections setting defaults to 20, but can range from 5 to 32,767.

The number of user connections should be set to the number of anticipated simultaneous connections to the server, plus a safety margin of 10 to 20 percent. Setting the User Connections option is similar to setting the Memory option. In Enterprise Manager, expand the server, right-click on the server, and select the Configuration option. Then select the Configuration tab and look for an item called User Connections.

In a query tool, open up a connection to the server, and type:

```
Sp_configure "user connections", 50
```

This example will set the number of User Connections to 50. Regardless of which method is used, the SQL Server service has to be stopped and restarted (also referred to as *bounced*), for the options to take effect.

Configuring the SQL Executive to Run (Log On) as a Service

The SQL Executive is a part of the SQL Server program that executes scheduled tasks and sends notifications. It is optional, and

SQL Server will run without it. The SQL Executive is installed to run as a service. The SQL Executive's task scheduling and alert notification capabilities are covered in Chapter 7, "Server Alert Processing and Task Scheduling." Basically, it provides the DBA (database administrator) with the capability to run backups and diagnostics overnight without user intervention.

Every program in Windows NT has to run in a security context. Without a security context, the operating system doesn't know which privileges a process has. To choose a security context, select a user account to run the program by using either the SQL Server Setup program, SQL Enterprise Manager or the Services applet in the Control Panel. The choice of a security context to run the SQL Executive is critical if the tasks being executed involve other servers, or if the alerts are being sent to another server. Without a security context that is valid on both servers, these capabilities will not work.

Note

> All services can be controlled from the Control Panel by running the Services applet. This is a uniform procedure that can be used to configure any service. Most of the information in this section can be applied to any Windows NT service.

For every service, you have the option to run the service using the Local System account or another account in a locally accessible account database. The Local System account is the account the operating system uses. It essentially has administrator access to the entire local machine, but only has guest access outside the machine.

By using an account other than the Local System account, the SQL Executive service will be able to access resources on other computers. This, for example, might be necessary if the SQL Executive is being used to copy files to another server. Usually the service account is in the Domain Administrators group. All accounts that are used as service accounts have to have the special privilege to Log On as a Service. Most Setup programs will automatically assign this privilege to any account that you specify as a service account.

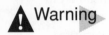 **Warning**

When it is necessary to set up a service account, give it the minimum level of privilege necessary to accomplish the tasks. Keep in mind that the SQL Executive service can run command-line programs, such as the net user command, which can be used to create accounts. This is a potential security problem.

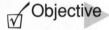 **Objective**

The service account for SQL Executive can be changed at any one of two locations. To change the account using Enterprise Manager follow these steps:

1. Start Enterprise Manager.

2. Make sure the server is registered. If it is not, register the server.

3. Expand the server by clicking on the plus sign to the left of the server name. A red lightning bolt should appear next to the server name. This means there is a connection to that server.

4. Right-click on the SQL Executive entry and choose Configure. Type in the name of the account, the password, and click OK.

To accomplish the task of changing the service account for the SQL Executive via the Windows NT Control Panel, use the following procedure:

1. Open the Control Panel.

2. Open the Services applet in Control Panel.

3. Scroll down and choose the SQL Executive Service.

4. Press the Startup button. This will display startup options: Automatic, Manual, or Disabled. Automatic will start the service when Windows NT starts. Manual requires that a user start the process after Windows NT starts. Disabled means the service cannot be activated without first changing its startup state to Manual or Automatic. Change the user name and password for the service account and then click OK.

Note The MSSQL Server service is the service that is used by SQL Server. It has the capability to use a service account.

Installing and Configuring Client Support for SQL Server

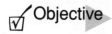 **Objective**

After configuring the server, the client software has to be installed and configured to use SQL Server. The client software has to be configured to find the correct network protocols and the correct server name so that successful network connections can be made.

For 16-bit Windows and MS-DOS clients, there is a CLIENTS directory on the CD. For the 16-bit Windows clients, there are ODBC drivers, ISQL/W, Books Online, and READPIPE. The ODBC drivers are used to connect client/server applications to SQL Server. ISQL/W is the SQL Server query tool, Windows edition. READPIPE is a program used to test Named Pipes.

For Windows 95 or Windows NT clients, run the Setup program in the i386 directory on the CD. This enables a full set of SQL Server utilities to be installed, including the SQL Enterprise Manager, ISQL/W, BCP, and Books Online.

For any of the Windows operating systems, the Setup program is W3DBVER.EXE. This program enables the network library to be selected. Choices include Named Pipes, Multi-Protocol, TCP/IP, and IPX/SPX. This is usually given the icon SQL Client Configuration Utility in the SQL Server program group. The first step is to configure the default network library by choosing the Net Library page (see fig. 1.14).

In the Net Library page of the SQL Server Client Configuration Utility dialog box, choose the default network library. You can deduce which operating system is being used, in this case Windows NT, by examining the name of the DLL used.

After the default network library has been configured, the exceptions have to be handled. If some servers on the network can't be reached using the default network library, use the Advanced page to override the default (see fig. 1.15). The most frequent use of this page occurs in TCP/IP environments that don't have DNS or WINS in use. Because name resolution isn't working, neither Named Pipes nor Multi-Protocol will work. The way around the problem is to go to the Advanced page, choose TCP/IP, and enter the IP address of the server in the Connection String text box, as described in the steps following these figures.

Figure 1.14

The SQL Server Client Configuration Utility, Net Library page.

Figure 1.15

The SQL Server Client Configuration Utility, Advanced page.

1. Install the client support utilities. For Windows NT or Windows 95, run the Setup program in the i386 directory on the CD. For other Windows clients, run the Setup program in the Clients directory on the CD.

2. Run the SQL Client Configuration Utility.

3. On the Advanced page of the SQL Server Configuration Utility, type in the name of the name of the server and choose the network protocol to be used.

4. Type in data for the Connection String. This is different for each protocol; for example, TCP/IP sockets requires the IP address of the server, and IPX/SPX requires the Novell Bindery's name for the server.

5. Press the Add/Modify button to save changes.

Any time an application requires a server name, type in the server name supplied in the Server box of the Client Configuration Utility.

 Note

When you are using network libraries other than Named Pipes, it is possible to type any correct server name into the Server Name box in the Client Configuration Utility. The client tools use only the library name and the connection string to establish the connection; the Server Name mentioned is there for the user's convenience so he doesn't have to remember IP addresses. It is recommended, however, to simply use the server name in the Server Name box.

For MS-DOS clients, only two utilities are included. ISQL is the command-line SQL Query tool, and BCP is the Bulk Copy Program. The MS-DOS clients require Named Pipes, and require a memory resident program to be loaded to handle network communications.

Server-Side Network Libraries

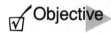 **Objective**

Unlike sort order and character set, the network support chosen during setup can be changed without necessitating any drastic measures beyond starting and stopping the SQL Server. The network support setup involves choosing which server-side libraries will be loaded. This means that SQL Server determines which protocols to listen to and where to listen to them.

After SQL Server Network has been installed, library support can be changed by running Setup and choosing the Change Network

Support option. This will often require that you insert the CD for file access, and may require that you provide additional information, depending on the library chosen.

The network libraries come in two varieties. The combined libraries, such as the Named Pipes and Multi-Protocol libraries, automatically support more than one protocol. The single protocol library, such as the TCP/IP Sockets library, supports only one protocol.

The Multi-Protocol library uses Remote Procedure Call (RPC) mechanisms built into Windows NT. The Multi-Protocol library automatically sets up connections on all the RPC-capable network protocols on the Windows NT computer. The Multi-Protocol library includes support for features such as password and data encryption, Integrated Security support, and high performance. In most situations, this is the protocol of choice.

The Named Pipes library works on systems that have the Windows NT redirector installed. The Named Pipes library works with all the same protocols that Windows NT File and Print Services work with, including NetBEUI, NWLink, and TCP/IP. Named Pipes is always installed and active.

The TCP/IP library is especially useful if the SQL Server is supporting clients that cannot use RPC. Whenever TCP/IP is added to a SQL Server, the Setup program will prompt for a port number, which will default to 1433. Port 1433 is the default port for SQL Server.

 Note For a listing of other default port numbers, consult the text file called SERVICES in the WINNT/SYSTEM32/DRIVERS/ETC directory. These are the Internet standard services and port numbers.

For clients using NetWare, the NWLink protocol is very useful. NWLink is an IPX/SPX compatible protocol used with Windows NT, and enables NetWare clients to connect to SQL Server without loading additional protocols. The Setup program will prompt for a NetWare Bindery Service Name whenever this option is added.

Banyan VINES users are supported via the VINES Sequenced Packet Protocol (SPP). This protocol is only available on the Intel platform because it requires the network protocols from Banyan, which are only available for Intel systems. The VINES SPP protocol requires the entry of a name in the form: Name@Group@Org. The Name portion of the entry must be registered with StreetTalk before the system can be used.

For systems that use Digital's Pathworks, a DECnet library is included with SQL Server. This library requires the entry of an object ID, which must be unique on the system.

Finally, there is a library for connecting AppleTalk users to SQL Server using the AppleTalk ADSP protocol. The AppleTalk Service name must be entered as part of setup for this protocol.

To add support for multiple protocols follow these steps:

1. Run Setup from the SQL Server 6.5 program group.

2. Choose Change Network Support from the Installation Type screen.

3. Add network support by choosing a network library and adding it. Each network library will require different information, as detailed in the previous descriptions.

Upgrading from SQL Server 4.2x to SQL Server 6.5

☑ Objective ▶ Use the Setup program to upgrade from SQL Server 4.2x or SQL Server 6.0 to SQL Server 6.5. Upgrades from SQL Server 1.x as well as from other products must be accomplished by exporting the data from the old database, installing SQL Server 6.5, and importing the data. The following section focuses on upgrading to 6.5 from 4.2x.

Several preparatory tasks need to be performed before the actual upgrade step. The process in its entirety includes the following:

1. Back up all the databases.

2. Make sure none of the databases have the read-only option set.

3. Run the CHKUPG65.EXE utility to check that each database is ready to upgrade.

4. Check for available disk space. At least 50 MB of free space is required on the installation drive.

5. Make sure that space is available in the *master* database.

6. Make sure all applications are closed.

7. Log in using an account in the Administrators group on the local machine.

8. Back up all the databases.

9. Run Setup.

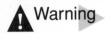 Warning

It is critically important that the databases be backed up before the upgrade. Better yet, back the database up twice, once to tape and once to another server. There is no such thing as too many backups.

Back Up All the Databases

Make sure all databases are backed up to tape. Make sure the server executables are backed up too. If the upgrade crashes, it may be necessary to completely recreate the server from backups, so do not skimp on this step.

Turn Off the Read-Only Option

SQL Server setup will modify the structures in all the databases, so the Read-Only option has to be turned off. In Enterprise

Manager, double-click on the database name and make sure that the Read-Only check box is not checked on the Options page. Using a query tool, type the following:

```
Sp_dboption pubs, "read only", 0
```

This will turn off the Read-Only attribute on the database called *pubs.*

Run the CHKUPG65.EXE Utility

The CHKUPG65.EXE utility is a read-only utility that checks a database server to make sure it is ready to be upgraded. Each version of SQL Server beginning with version 6.0 comes with a new version of CHKUPG65.EXE. This utility checks each database to make sure it is compatible with the new version of SQL Server. It does not fix problems, it just finds them.

To run CHKUPG65.EXE, insert the SQL Server CD and open a command prompt. Change to the CD-ROM drive, and then go to the appropriate directory for the hardware architecture on the system, usually i386, and then type:

```
Chkupg65 [/Usa] [/Ppassword] [/Sservername] /ofilename
```

Note

Using command-line utilities with SQL Server can get messy if a few simple rules are not followed:

- ▶ Do not put spaces between the argument type and the argument, for example, the argument should be /Usa not /U sa.

- ▶ Assume that all arguments are case sensitive. Some of them are and some are not.

- ▶ Separate arguments with spaces.

- ▶ Whenever a password is requested, it is optional. If the password isn't on the command line, the utility will prompt for it.

Send the output from CHKUPG65.EXE to an output file by using the /o option. The output file can then be read with any text editor, such as Notepad. Read the output carefully and make sure that every issue is resolved before you attempt to upgrade SQL Server or the upgrade may fail.

What does CHKUPG65.EXE look for? The first thing that CHKUPG65.EXE checks is to make sure that none of the stored procedures have had their text removed from the *syscomments* table. The text for all stored procedures is stored in the *syscomments* table. If the text isn't there, the upgrade process cannot recompile the stored procedures. If the text has been removed, it is probably best to drop the procedure and recreate it from the saved script.

Note

So why would text be missing from the *syscomments* table? If a programmer has stored proprietary procedures in a database, the programmer may have removed those procedures to keep the code a secret. SQL Server 6.0 and up provides encryption options, so this practice is no longer necessary.

CHKUPG65.EXE also checks for the use of keywords as object names. A *keyword* is a word that cannot be used as an object name, and includes words such as CURRENT_DATE or CURRENT_TIME. In the output file, some of the keyword problems may be marked as SQL-92 keywords. Any words marked as such are not keywords that are used by SQL Server; they are just reserved for future use. The current upgrade will still work, but upgrades to future versions of SQL Server may not work.

Remember that the CHKUPG65.EXE utility is a Read-Only utility. It finds all the problems that will prevent an upgrade, but does not attempt to fix anything. CHKUPG65.EXE merely reads through the databases and makes sure they are ready to upgrade.

As part of the upgrade process, SQL Server Setup runs the CHKUPG65.EXE utility, and if it discovers any problems, setup will terminate. Your best course of action is to run the utility by itself first to make sure you encounter no surprises during setup.

Check for Available Disk Space

To install SQL Server 6.5 on a server that already has SQL Server 6.0 installed requires 20 MB of free disk space. Upgrading from version 4.21 requires 65 MB of available space. This space must be available on the drive where the SQL Server executables are installed.

Check for Available Database Space

Upgrades from SQL Server 6.0 to SQL Server 6.5 require 2 MB of space in the master database. Upgrading from SQL Server 4.21 requires 9 MB of disk space. If the space is not available, the Setup program will allocate the space it needs. However, it's still a good idea to handle this issue before setup just to make sure you don't run into any unnecessary problems.

Close All Other Applications

Make sure all other applications are closed. Also make sure no users are using the database over the network. All instances of performance monitoring should also be stopped to prevent any conflicts.

Log In Using an Account in the Administrators Group

Some of the Registry keys have security set so that they cannot be changed except by an administrator. In addition, if Integrated Security is turned on, the Administrator will automatically be validated as an sa, thereby preventing any permission problems.

Back Up All the Databases

Dump the databases out to disk and copy the files across the network onto another machine. Although this may sound a bit paranoid considering the backups performed earlier, being paranoid saves data.

Run Setup

Running setup for an upgrade greatly resembles running setup for an installation. Choose Upgrade from the initial menu screen. From there, setup will copy files, and then upgrade the databases. Upgrading may take a long time depending on how large the databases are, and if the CHKUPG65.EXE utility runs cleanly. Setup runs automatically, so start the process and call out for pizza if the databases are big or the servers are slow.

Setting the Security Option

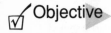 Objective

To access data stored in SQL Server, users have to be authenticated. When a user is authenticated, SQL Server determines to which objects the user should be permitted to access. If the users are already being authenticated by a Windows NT domain, then it is possible to use a security system integrated with Windows NT. If the users are not authenticating against Windows NT, then the SQL Server Standard Security mechanism can be used. If some users are authenticating against Windows NT, and some users are not, then a security system called Mixed Security can be used.

Standard Security requires that the DBA create and maintain an account, or login ID for each user. When a user needs to connect to SQL Server, he has to provide a login name and a password. This name and password are transmitted to the SQL Server, which then authenticates the user.

 Note

If the server and client are using a network library other than the Multi-Protocol library, the password is transmitted as clear text. With a relatively simple network diagnostic tool, a curious user could easily find out user names and passwords, and break into the server.

With Integrated Security, Windows NT is used to validate users. Users are placed in groups in the Windows NT security system. These groups are then added to the SQL Server by using the SQL Server Security Manager. This program creates the logins, and also creates random string passwords for the users. When a user logs in to the server, SQL Server queries Windows NT, discovers which group the user belongs to, and authenticates the user based on the group. Integrated Security only works on connections that are using the Multi-Protocol or Named Pipes communications libraries.

> If a user belongs to more than one Windows NT group that has been defined in SQL Security Manager, then the user will be placed in one group or another, but not both. Make sure that the users belong to only one group.

Mixed Security is a mix of Integrated and Standard security modes. If the user is using a Named Pipes or Multi-Protocol connection, and the user's network login matches a SQL Server login, the user is authenticated. If these conditions are not met, then Standard Security is used to authenticate the user.

The security mode can be set in two ways. First, using SQL Enterprise Manager, expand a server, right-click on it and select Configure. Then select the Security Options tab (see fig. 1.16). Alternatively, go into SQL Server setup and select Set Security Options. The dialog box is the same either way. Choose one of the three security options. If Mixed or Integrated Security is chosen, enter the default domain name. This should be the name of the domain that contains most of the user accounts. The server must be bounced after changing a security option.

Figure 1.16

The default domain determines which domain is searched first when users log in using Integrated or Mixed Security.

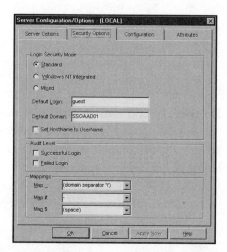

Exercises

Exercise 1.1: Configure Microsoft Windows NT for SQL Server Installation

Exercise 1.1 walks you through a list of things to check prior to installing SQL Server on Windows NT, and should take you about 20 minutes to complete.

1. Check the server name for any conflicts with the SQL Server naming rules. Remember that server names have to start with a letter and cannot contain embedded spaces. Open the Control Panel. Choose the Network icon, and look at the Computer Name: field.

2. Check the minimum software requirements. Bring up Program Manager. If you don't have a Program Manager, you're running Windows NT 4.0, and you're all set. If you are using a different version of Windows NT, choose Help, About from the Program Manager to determine what version of Windows NT you are running. You must be running version 3.51 or later.

3. Check the minimum hardware requirements. Make sure you have 16 MB of RAM, and 70 MB of hard disk space available. Make sure Windows NT runs on your system.

4. Choose an installation location. If you are running multiple drive partitions, choose a disk on which to put the SQL Server files.

For more information, refer to the section earlier in this chapter "Configuring Microsoft Windows NT for Installation of SQL Server."

Exercise 1.2: Installing SQL Server

Exercise 1.2 will step you through the installation process. It assumes that you are running setup from a CD-ROM, but the instructions will be similar if you are running it from a network share point. The exercise assumes your CD-ROM drive is D:. If it is not, substitute the correct letter. This exercise should take 30 minutes to an hour, depending on the computer you are using.

1. Insert the CD into the CD-ROM drive.

2. Open File Manager or Explorer.

3. Go to drive D:.

4. Open the architecture directory for your computer. Usually, this is the i386 directory.

5. Run the program called Setup.exe to start the setup process.

6. Press OK on the Welcome screen.

7. Enter your name and your company's name and click OK.

8. Choose Install SQL Server and Utilities and click OK.

9. Choose the install location decided on in the previous exercise and click OK.

10. Verify that the character set being used is the ISO 8859-1 character set.

11. Verify that the sort order being used is Dictionary Order Case Insensitive.

12. Verify that the Named Pipes and Multi-Protocol libraries are being installed.

13. Verify that the Auto Start SQL Server and Auto Start SQL Executive check boxes are set the way you want them. If these features are turned on, you won't have to worry about the services starting when you reboot the computer, but it will use a lot of memory. Click OK.

14. Choose the Local System account for the SQL Executive and click OK.

15. Relax, wait, and watch the sands of the hourglass fill the Q in SQL over and over again.

For more information, refer to the section in this chapter "Installing SQL Server on Microsoft Windows NT."

Exercise 1.3: Configuring SQL Enterprise Manager

You will use Enterprise Manager to perform the steps in this exercise for each server. Following these steps will enable you to use Enterprise Manager to monitor, configure, and query your server. This exercise should take about 10 minutes to complete.

1. Start SQL Enterprise Manager, located in the SQL Server 6.5 program group.

2. If no servers are registered, SQL Enterprise Manager will automatically bring up the Register Server window. If it does not, choose the Register Server entry from the Server menu.

3. Fill in the server name. In most cases, this is the Windows NT Server name for the server.

4. If the server is using Standard Security, make sure the Use Standard Security option is chosen. Enter a valid account name in the login, usually sa, and the password, which is blank by default.

5. If the server is using Integrated or Mixed Security, choose the Use Trusted Connection option. This disables the user name and password boxes.

6. Click the Register button to register the server. SQL Enterprise Manager will save the server, clear out the registration window, and enable you to continue to add new servers. If you have completed the registration process, click the Close button.

7. Your server should now appear in the Server Manager window.

For more information, refer to the section "Setting Up SQL Enterprise Manager."

Exercise 1.4: Configure SQL Server for Various Memory Scenarios

In this exercise, you will set the memory option twice, once using the SQL Enterprise Manager, and once using a query tool. This exercise requires that you know how much memory is in your computer, and should take about 20 minutes to complete.

Using SQL Enterprise Manager:

1. Start SQL Enterprise Manager from the SQL Server 6.5 program group.

2. Register your server by following the procedure outlined in Exercise 1.3.

3. Expand your server by clicking the plus sign to the left of its name.

4. Right-click on the server name and choose Configuration.

5. Go to the Configuration tab. You should see a table of options, with Minimum, Maximum, Running, and Current values.

6. Scroll down until you find the row that says Memory. Figure out how much memory you should give SQL Server based on how much memory is in your computer. See the section "Configuring Memory Options," if you need help.

7. Click OK.

Using a query tool:

8. Open the SQL Query tool. From SQL Enterprise Manger, choose Tools, SQL Query Tool, or from the SQL Server 6.5 group run ISQL/W and connect to your server.

9. Run sp_configure with no options. This will display all the current options. Verify that the memory option you chose is in the Current column.

10. Close the query window.

11. Stop and restart SQL Server. This can be done in Enterprise Manager by choosing the server, right-clicking on it and choosing Stop. Otherwise, run the SQL Service Manager

continues

from the SQL Server 6.5 group, make sure your server name is in the Server box and double-click the word Stop. When the server has stopped, choose Start.

For more information, refer to the section "Configuring Memory Options."

Exercise 1.5: Configure SQL Executive to Run (Log On) as a Service

In this exercise, you will modify how the SQL Executive Service is running. It is assumed that the service is running using the Local System account, as the procedures in Exercise 1.2 indicate, but if that isn't the case, it isn't a problem. First you'll walk through the process using SQL Enterprise Manager, and then you'll go through how you would do it by using Control Panel. Each method should take about five minutes.

Using SQL Enterprise Manager:

1. Start SQL Enterprise Manager from the SQL Server 6.5 program group.

2. Make sure your server is registered. If it isn't, register the server by following the procedures outlined in Exercise 1.3.

3. Check the icon to verify that the server is started. It may take a few minutes for all the icons to switch from all-gray to having colored lights indicating their states. If the server is showing a red light, meaning the service is not started, right-click on the server and choose Start.

4. Expand your server by clicking on the plus sign to the left of the server name.

5. Right-click on the SQL Executive entry in the outline view beneath your server. Choose the Configure option.

6. In the dialog box, you'll be able to adjust the various parameters of the SQL Executive service. You want to focus on the

Service Startup Account section. Right now, the System Account option should be selected. To change this, choose the This Account option.

7. In the This Account text box, type in the domain name of the account, a backward slash, and the name of the account. For example, to use the sqlexec account in the resdom domain, you would type **resdom\sqlexec**.

8. Type the password for the account in both the Password and Confirm Password boxes.

9. Click on the OK button to commit the change.

10. To make the change take effect, stop and restart the SQL Executive service by right-clicking on the SQL Executive, and choosing Stop. Wait a minute or so and then right-click on SQL Executive again and choose Start.

Using Control Panel:

(This procedure actually works in Control Panel as well as in Server Manager. This is the standard procedure for changing service accounts for any Windows NT Service.)

1. Start the Control Panel.

2. Start the Services applet.

3. Scroll down to the SQL Executive service. Click the Startup button.

4. Choose the This Account option to change to a service account. Type the domain name in the same way as you did in the last section, as domain name, then backward slash, and then user name.

5. When the changes are complete, stop the service and restart it, and then close the window.

For more information, see the section "Configuring the SQL Executive to Run (Log On) as a Service."

Exercise 1.6: Installing Client Support for Network Protocols Other than Named Pipes

In Exercise 1.6 you will configure the network protocols for Windows clients that connect through SQL Server. This exercise will take about 10 minutes.

1. Start the SQL Client Configuration Utility in the SQL Server 6.5 program group.

2. Read the DBLibrary window to find out which versions of network libraries are currently being used by your system.

3. Choose the Net Library tab to change the default protocol from Named Pipes. Choose the Done button to commit the change. This is all you have to do to change the client protocol to something other than Named Pipes.

For more information, see the section "Installing and Configuring Client Support for SQL Server."

Exercise 1.7: Advanced Configuration of Client Support for Network Protocols

Exercise 1.6 is usually all there is to configuring protocols on the client. But if you have chosen, for example, TCP/IP Sockets, you will need to have some method of changing server names into IP addresses, such as WINS, DNS, LMHOSTS, or HOSTS. If you don't have any of these, the Advanced tab still enables you to connect to SQL Server. This exercise will take about 15 minutes.

1. Start the SQL Client Configuration Utility.

2. Choose the Advanced tab.

3. This is where the interface gets a little tricky. Type in the name of the server, drop down the list, choose the library you want to use, and then type in the connection string. Always choose the library name by dropping down the list or it will not work the way you expect it to. The connection string varies depending on which network protocol you have chosen. For TCP/IP Sockets, the connection string is the IP address of the server.

4. Choose Add, Remove to add the server to the list. If you accidentally choose Done instead of Add, Remove you will have to go in, type in all the information again, and then choose Add, Remove.

5. Choose Done when you are finished.

For more information, see the section "Installing and Configuring Client Support for SQL Server."

Exercise 1.8: Loading Multiple Network Libraries on the Server

If your server will be supplying data to computers that are using multiple network protocols, you will need to configure the server to comply with those protocols. Failure to follow this step will cause the clients not to be serviced. This exercise will take about 30 minutes to complete.

1. Install Windows NT support for the protocol. This step will vary from protocol to protocol, but usually works something like this:

A. Open the Control Panel.

B. Open the Networks applet.

C. Choose Add Software.

D. Choose the protocol you want to add, or put in a disk from another manufacturer, (for example, Digital for Pathworks Support.)

E. Click the OK button. Windows NT will install the protocols, and will usually bring up an window full of items you will need to configure. Configure them.

F. Choose OK to close the Network applet and reboot.

2. After the system comes back up, start the SQL Setup program from the SQL Server 6.5 program group. You can also run the Setup program from CD.

continues

Exercise 1.8: Continued

3. Choose the Continue button until you reach the window that is captioned Microsoft SQL Server 6.5-Options. Choose the Change Network Support option and click Continue.

4. Choose the network protocols the server should support by placing a check in the check box next to them.

5. Choose OK when you have finished adding network protocols.

6. For each chosen network protocol, there is a configuration screen. On most screens you will accept the defaults, but on some you may have to customize the protocol to fit your installation.

7. Stop and start SQL Server to make the changes take effect.

For more information, see the section "Server-Side Network Libraries."

Exercise 1.9: Running the CHKUPG65.EXE Utility

The CHKUPG65.EXE utility is included with SQL Server 6.5, and is designed to be run against other versions of SQL Server to ensure smooth upgrades. This utility is also a focal point of the exam questions on upgrading. The following exercise will take about 10 minutes to complete.

1. Copy the CHKUPG65.EXE utility from the SQL Server 6.5 CD-ROM to a computer on your network, or onto the server which is to be upgraded.

2. Start a command prompt.

3. Use the CD command to go to the directory where the CHKUPG65.EXE utility is installed.

4. Run the following command:

```
chkupg65 /Sserver /Uloginid /Ppassword /Ooutputfilepath
```

Usually the login ID will be sa and the password may be blank. The Output File is a text file, so you should give it the extension .TXT so that it can be easily read by Notepad.

5. Examine the output file for any problems that could cause the upgrade to fail.

For more information, see the section "Upgrading from SQL Server 4.2x to SQL Server 6.5."

Exercise 1.10:   Setting the Security Mode

SQL Server has three security modes. This exercise will walk you through two different ways to select a security mode, and will take about 20 minutes to complete.

Using SQL Enterprise Manager:

1. Start SQL Enterprise Manager.

2. Verify that your server is registered. If it is not, register it by following the steps listed in Exercise 1.3.

3. Right-click on your server's name and choose Configure to bring up the Server Configuration/Options window.

4. Choose the Security Options tab.

5. In the Login Security Mode frame, choose the desired security mode.

6. If you chose Integrated or Mixed Security, you will need to set a default domain name and a default login. The default domain should be set to the domain that contains the most user accounts. The default login is usually set to guest.

7. Click the OK button to commit your changes.

8. Stop and restart the SQL Server to make the changes take effect.

continues

Exercise 1.10: Continued

Using SQL Setup:

1. Start SQL Setup.

2. Choose Continue until you reach the Microsoft SQL Server 6.5-Options window.

3. Choose the Set Security Options option and choose Continue.

4. Choose your security option.

5. If you chose Integrated or Mixed Security, you will need to set a default domain and a default login. The default domain should be set to the domain that contains the most user accounts. The default login is usually set to guest.

6. Click Continue to change your security options.

7. Stop and restart SQL Server to make the changes take effect.

For more information, see the section "Setting the Security Option."

Review Questions

The following questions will test your knowledge of the information in this chapter.

1. Which of the following types of Windows NT installation can SQL server be installed on?

    A. Windows NT Server, installed as a Primary Domain Controller

    B. Windows NT Server, installed as a Backup Domain Controller.

    C. Windows NT Server, installed as a Standalone Server, not as a member of the domain

    D. Windows NT Server, installed as a Standalone Server and member of a domain

2. Julio needs to modify the character set of his database so it can contain characters special to the Portuguese alphabet. How can he accomplish this task?

    A. Character sets cannot be changed, so this is not possible.

    B. Manually edit the *syscharsets* table to reflect the change in character set.

    C. Dump the database, reinstall SQL Server, and load the database.

    D. Export each individual object in the database to a text file, reinstall SQL Server, and then import each individual object.

3. After installing SQL Server on a Windows NT Server computer with 128 MB of RAM, Denise notices that the server is running slowly for a computer with that amount of memory. Which of the following choices is the likely source of the problem?

    A. SQL Server has not been allocated enough memory.

    B. SQL Server needs to be reinstalled.

    C. Windows NT needs to be reinstalled.

    D. The disk drives are too slow.

4. James just executed the following command in a query window in SQL Enterprise Manager:

```
sp_configure "memory", 16384
```

How much memory did James just allocate to SQL Server?

   A. 16 MB

   B. 16 KB

   C. 8 MB

   D. 32 MB

5. Sandra wants to change the security on her SQL Server to Integrated Security. Unfortunately, the Integrated option on her system is grayed out. Why?

   A. The SQL Server is not participating in domain security, so there is no source for account information.

   B. The SQL Server is not installed on a Primary or Backup Domain Controller, so Integrated Security cannot be used.

   C. The *sysdomains* table does not contain the name of the domain to be accessed.

   D. The trust relationships in the resource domain are not correct.

6. After using SQL Enterprise Manager for a time, suddenly Biff can no longer attach to his server. The SQL Enterprise Manager keeps putting up the following message:

```
A connection could not be established to BIFFSERV -
[SQL Server] Login Failed
```

What is a likely cause of this problem?

A. A network-related problem is preventing communication with the server BIFFSERV.

B. The TCP/IP protocol is not allowing a connection to the server BIFFSERV.

C. Biff changed the password for his account and has not edited the registration with his new password.

D. Biff is accessing the server from an untrusted domain.

7. Sam has changed the configuration of the clients on his system to use TCP/IP sockets. What else does he need to change so his clients can start using TCP/IP connections to the server?

A. Each client workstation must have TCP/IP loaded.

B. Windows NT on the SQL Server computer must have TCP/IP loaded.

C. The server must have a registered list of all the client computers' IP addresses in the SQL Server database.

D. TCP/IP must be configured as a network library by SQL Server.

8. Which of the following is true about the Dictionary Order Case Insensitive sort order?

A. Lowercase letters sort before uppercase letters.

B. Uppercase letters sort before lowercase letters.

C. Only the standard character set can be chosen.

D. It is the same as a Binary sort order.

9. The CHKUPG65.EXE utility is run against a SQL Server 4.21 database. The output file shows that the keyword ADD was used in several columns of tables in the database. What action should be taken to correct the problem?

  A. The database cannot be upgraded.

  B. The column names will have to be changed prior to the upgrade.

  C. The CHKUPG65.EXE utility repairs all of the problems, so no special steps need to be taken.

  D. The database should be backed-up to tape. The upgrade can then proceed. After the upgrade, restore the database.

10. Bart has a Windows NT server with 256 MB of RAM that will be dedicated to running SQL Server. How much of the memory should Bart leave for Windows NT to use?

  A. None. It will use virtual memory.

  B. 40 MB

  C. 128 MB

  D. It does not matter, SQL Server will take what it needs.

11. Which of the following commands can be used in a query tool to change the number of available user connections from 15 to 100?

  A. `sp_configure "users", 100`

  B. `sp_config "users", 100`

  C. `sp_configure "user connections", 100`

  D. `sp_configure "user connections", 15, 100`

12. After changing the number of connected users successfully by using the sp_configure command, Maggie keeps getting phone calls that users cannot use the database. Which of the following is the most likely cause?

    A. The SQL Server needs to be stopped and started.

    B. The Windows NT Server needs to be shutdown and restarted.

    C. Each client machine needs to reboot.

    D. There is a network problem.

13. The SQL Executive account is currently running using the Local System account. Milhaus wants to change the service so it is using a service account. Which of the following procedures will *not* accomplish that task?

    A. Log on to the server. Start Control Panel, Services, click the Startup button, and change the account.

    B. Log on to any Windows NT Server, use Server Manager, find the server, and choose the Services item from the Computer menu. Click the Startup button, and change the account.

    C. Open the SQL Server query tool and execute the following command:

    ```
    sp_configure "SQL Executive Account",
    "resdom\sqlexec"
    ```

    D. Open the SQL Enterprise Manager, expand the server, right-click on the SQL Executive, choose Configure and change the account.

14. Apu has a server he wants to upgrade from SQL Server 4.21 to SQL Server 6.5. Unfortunately, the developer who created the system wanted to keep the stored procedures a secret, so he erased the contents of the *syscomments* table. How can Apu upgrade the server?

    A. The upgrade will not work while entries are missing from the *syscomments* table.

    B. Run the CHKUPG65.EXE utility to fix the problem.

    C. Call the developer and have him manually enter the data into the *syscomments* table.

    D. Upgrade to SQL Server 6.0 first, and then upgrade to SQL Server 6.5.

15. After adding memory to the server, what action has to take place to for SQL Server receive any benefit?

    A. The memory has to be configured as parity memory.

    B. The SQL Server needs to be informed of the new memory upgrade using the sp_configure stored procedure or through configuration in SQL Enterprise Manager.

    C. Reinstall SQL Server so it will find the new memory.

    D. All the client computers need to reboot.

16. What is the first step to be taken in the process of upgrading a server from SQL Server 6.0 to SQL Server 6.5?

    A. Back up the database.

    B. Run the CHKUPG65.EXE utility to repair the database.

    C. Install SQL Server 6.5.

    D. Copy all the DLL files from the upgrade directory on the CD to the MSSQL directory.

17. In SQL Enterprise Manager, one of the servers has a yellow light in the stoplight icon. What does this signify?

    A. The server is in caution mode and is ready to fail.

    B. The server is paused and not accepting any new connections.

    C. The server is completing processing and is about to shut down.

    D. The server is almost at capacity.

18. Barney is getting ready to install SQL Server Workstation Edition on his Windows NT workstation. Which two of the following statements are true?

    A. There will be a limit of 15 simultaneous connections to the database.

    B. There will be a limit of 15 simultaneous network connections to the database.

    C. Barney will have a suite of developer tools not found in a normal SQL Server installation.

    D. There will not be any connections allowed from outside the current workstation.

19. Which of the following is a valid name for a Windows NT computer that will be running SQL Server?

    A. #1Computer

    B. Computer_1

    C. Computer One

    D. _Computer

20. Moe needs to install the SQL Enteprise Manager on his Windows 95 PC. Which procedure should he follow?

    A. SQL Enterprise Manager can't be installed on Windows 95. Upgrade to Windows NT workstation first, and then install on Windows NT.

    B. Run the SETUP.EXE program in the \CLIENTS\WIN95 directory on the CD-ROM.

    C. Run the SETUP.EXE program in the \WIN95 directory on the CD-ROM.

    D. Run the SETUP.EXE program in the \I386 directory on the CD-ROM.

21. Ernesto has a scheduled job in SQL Enterprise Manager that continually fails. Part of the job requires a file to be copied from one Windows NT Server to another. Which two of the following are possible reasons for the failure?

    A. The SQL Server service is running low on virtual memory.

    B. The SQL Executive Service is configured to log on as Local System instead of as a user.

    C. The destination server does not allow the user specified as the SQL Executive service account to access the destination directory.

    D. The SQL Executive service is not installed.

22. Jay needs to have the client computers on his network connect to SQL Server using the TCP/IP protocol. There are no WINS or DNS servers on the network, and the client machines do not have host definition files. How is Jay going to get the clients to attach to the server?

    A. Install the TCP/IP network library on the clients, and specify TCP/IP as the default network library.

    B. Install the TCP/IP network library on the clients, and use the Advanced tab to set the hostname of the SQL Server.

    C. Install the TCP/IP network library on the clients, and use the Advanced tab to set the TCP/IP address of the SQL Server.

    D. Install the IPX/SPX network library.

23. Julia needs to have SQL Server monitor for both TCP/IP and IPX/SPX traffic. The Windows NT Server running SQL Server already has the necessary protocols and services installed. What needs to be done to make SQL Server process these requests so the clients do not have to validate against Windows NT?

    A. Install both the TCP/IP and IPX/SPX libraries.

    B. Install the Multi-Protocol library.

    C. Install the Named Pipes library.

    D. SQL Server can only listen to one protocol at a time, so Julia cannot meet her objective.

24. Which of the following is an advantage of using Standard Security?

    A. Encrypted passwords.

    B. Clients don't need to validate against Windows NT.

    C. Password aging.

    D. Minimum password length enforcement.

25. Which of the following cannot be done with the SQL Client Configuration Utility?

    A. Enforcement of minimum password length

    B. Designation of a default network library

    C. Specify IP addresses for servers

    D. Find out the version numbers of various network libraries

26. What is the minimum operating system version required by SQL Server 6.5?

    A. Windows 95

    B. Windows NT Version 3.51

    C. Windows NT Version 3.5

    D. Windows NT Version 4.0

27. What does the Multi-Protocol network library require?

    A. The user must be running multiple protocols.

    B. The user must be running a 32 bit operating system.

    C. The user must be running NetBEUI.

    D. The user must be validated by Windows NT.

Review Answers

1. A, B, C, D

2. D

3. A

4. D

5. A

6. C

7. A, B, D

8. B

9. B

10. B

11. C

12. A

13. C

14. A

15. B

16. A

17. B

18. B, C

19. B

20. D

21. B, C

22. C

23. A

24. B

25. A

26. B

27. D

Answers to Test Yourself Questions at Beginning of Chapter

1. SQL Server 6.5 requires Windows NT 3.51 or later, 16 MB of RAM, and a minimum of 60 MB of disk space. See the section "Minimum Hardware and Software Requirements," for more information.

2. With 128 MB of RAM on a computer dedicated to SQL Server, 88 MB of RAM can be dedicated to SQL Server, with the remaining 40 MB going to Windows NT. See the section titled "Configuring Memory Options" for the full details.

3. Bill can change the SQL Server service account via Control Panel, Services, or by using the SQL Enterprise Manager and right-clicking on the SQL Executive icon for the server. Check out the section called "Configure the SQL Executive to Run (Log On) as a Service."

4. Support for TCP/IP can be installed on the client computer by using the SQL Client Configuration Utility, and installing the TCP/IP Sockets network library. Using either Named Pipes or Multi-Protocol network libraries will require validation by Windows NT.

5. SQL Server will need to have the IPX/SPX network library installed, and the Windows NT computer running SQL Server will need to have NWLink installed. See the section "Server-Side Network Libraries" for more information.

6. CHKGUPG65.EXE is a read-only utility. It does not modify any tables or fix any problems. See the section "Upgrading from SQL Server 4.2x to SQLibraries Server 6.5," for more information.

7. Victor should use the Mixed Security mode to provide painless access to users already being validated by Windows NT, but still allow manual validation by SQL Server. This topic is covered in the section "Setting the Security Option."

C h a p t e r

2

Integration of SQL Server with Other Applications and Technologies

To truly understand how to administer SQL Server, you must understand how SQL Server integrates with its environment. You need to have a thorough understanding of how SQL Server integrates with the operating system services, specifically services that involve security. In this chapter, you will learn about the integration of Windows NT security services on SQL Server, examine the Windows NT Registry, find the SQL Server keys, and scope out the integration of SQL Server with Windows NT from the perspective of memory and thread management. In addition, many new features have been added to the most recent upgrade that enable SQL Server to interface with electronic mail systems.

As with each chapter in this book, Chapter 2 commences with a list of the exam objectives relating to the topic at hand, and then moves on to the chapter pretest. Valuable information is presented that directly addresses the objectives, along with additional related discussion topics. The chapter continues with exercises and chapter review questions. Finally, answers to both the chapter review questions and the chapter pretest questions are provided.

This chapter focuses on the integration of SQL Server with other applications and technologies. You will learn how to achieve the following objectives:

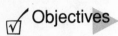 **Objectives**

▶ Identify the impact on SQL Server of Integrated Security

▶ Locate where the Windows NT Registry entries for SQL Server are stored

▶ Identify how SQL Server integrates with Windows NT

▶ Identify capabilities of SQL Server when it is used with MAPI

Test Yourself! Before reading this chapter, test yourself to determine how much study time you will need to devote to this section.

1. Which server security options enable the use of trusted connections?

2. Server MySQLServer is set up to use Standard Security and the TCP/IP Sockets network library. The guest account is not enabled. Assuming her network configuration is correct, does Jane have to log in to a Windows NT account to use the server?

3. Where are service control entries for SQL Server stored in the Registry?

4. Explain the difference between the SQL Server Error Log and the Windows NT Event Log.

5. What is an extended stored procedure?

6. Which extended stored procedures are used to start and stop mail services?

Answers are located at the end of the chapter...

Integrated Security's Impact on SQL Server

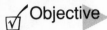 Objective

Integrated Security enables Windows NT user accounts to access SQL Server. Windows NT has a great capacity for handling user accounts, aging passwords, and forcing minimum password lengths. SQL Server using Standard Security is not as robust in how it handles user accounts, providing only users, groups, and passwords. Many of the features that are important to security of a system are not available using SQL Server without Integrated Security (see fig. 2.1)

Figure 2.1

The Windows NT Account Policy screen is part of the User Manager utility.

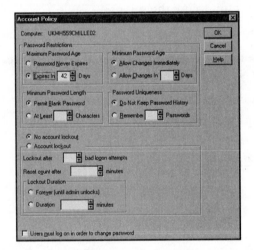

Notice in figure 2.1 the wealth of options for management of user accounts and password security.

When SQL Server is set up to use Standard Security, and a user attempts to open a connection with SQL Server, the software he is using will prompt him for a user name and password. If, for example, the user is using ISQL/W, a SQL Server query tool, he must provide a server name, user name, and password. ISQL/W sends the user name and password to the appropriate server, which validates the response and either grants the connection or causes the connection attempt to fail.

When Integrated Security is in use, the behind-the-scenes action is a little more complex, but much less is demanded of the user. On a SQL Server using Integrated Security and ISQL/W, the user fills in the server name, but can leave the user name and password blank. When SQL Server is in Integrated Security mode and receives a request for a user name or password, SQL Server asks Windows NT which user started the connection. Windows NT provides the information to SQL Server, which then validates the user or fails the connection attempt. When a user connects to a SQL Server that is using Integrated Security, the connection is called a *trusted connection*. Integrated Security works when the client is connecting to SQL Server using either Named Pipes or the Multi-Protocol network library. The Multi-Protocol library supports clients who are using Novell's IPX/SPX network protocols. When a client who is not logged in with a Windows NT user account attempts to make a connection to the SQL Server using the Multi-Protocol network library, the user is prompted by his network software to log on to Windows NT. The client would be required to have both Novell and Windows NT network software loaded and configured to be fully functional.

For SQL Server to use Integrated Security, the Windows NT server that is hosting SQL Server must be participating in a domain as a primary domain controller, a backup domain controller, or a member of the domain. If the server is not participating in a domain, Windows NT has no source for domain security information.

Standard Security, Windows NT, and Network Libraries

To make a connection using either the Named Pipes or Multi-Protocol libraries, the user must be validated by Windows NT regardless of the security mode. This can be done in one of two ways: create a user account for the user, or enable the guest account. If the decision is made to create a user account for each user who will be

connecting to the server, consider implementing either Integrated or Mixed Security mode. The groundwork of creating user accounts and groups will still be required.

The guest account enables a user to access defined network resources without his having a specific Windows

continues

NT login. Enabling the guest account does not provide users with free reign over the server. Users logged in as guest can have access only to the objects that have the guest account enabled, including Named Pipes. Because the guest account defaults to disabled when Windows NT is installed, you will have to enable it. To enable the guest account:

1. Start User Manager.

2. Go down the list of users to the Guest account.

3. Choose File, Properties from the menu.

4. Uncheck the Account Disabled box.

If neither of these options are desired, consider using a different network library, such as TCP/IP or the IPX/SPX libraries, along with Standard Security. Neither of these protocols require a Windows NT account. They will, of course, still require a SQL Server account.

For more information on Integrated Security and logging into the SQL Server, refer to Chapter 5, "Managing User Accounts." To set up Integrated Security on SQL Server, see the section "Setting the Security Mode" in Chapter 1, "Server Installation and Upgrade."

Locate Where Windows NT Registry Entries for SQL Server Are Stored

The Windows NT operating system maintains the Registry, which is a database of configuration information. Settings for the operating system as well as most applications are stored in the Registry. The Registry contains all the information needed to start the operating system, as well as the user preference information for different applications.

Exploring the Registry

The Windows NT Registry contains the information used by the operating system and programs written to the Win32 API. The Registry provides a place to store information on configuration and startup for each application. Before getting into the SQL

Server-specific pieces of the Windows NT Registry, take a look at the following review of the Registry structure.

Registry Organization

The Registry is a hierarchical database, and is divided into *hives*. The hives are divided into *keys*. Each key can contain other keys or can contain values. A *value* is a configuration setting, such as "Name = Lisa Stewart." In this case, the value would be *Name* and it is set to the data Lisa Stewart. Two hives contain the information pertinent to SQL Server. The HKEY_LOCAL_MACHINE hive contains all the information that is needed regardless of which user is logged on. The HKEY_CURRENT_USER hive contains the settings specific to a given user. As a user logs on to Windows NT, the HKEY_CURRENT_USER hive points to the configuration information of the current user only.

Editing and Viewing the Registry

Editing and viewing the Registry is important to understanding how SQL Server starts. In this section you will learn how the Registry editing tools work, and how to use them.

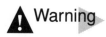 **Warning**

> The Registry is a useful tool for diagnosing and fixing problems. The Registry is also the single fastest way to completely destroy an installation of Windows NT. The rule for Registry editing is simple: Don't guess. If you don't know what it is, don't change it.

To edit the Registry in Windows NT 3.51, use the REGEDT32 application, which can be started from the File, Run command in Program Manager. For Windows NT 4.0 systems, use Start, Run and run REGEDIT. REGEDIT has a much more powerful search engine than the previous version (see fig. 2.2). The Registry is examined by expanding keys. Use the plus signs next to the keys, or double-click on the key itself. Follow the path down the hierarchy to the specific entry. To search, use the Find command, located on the Edit menu in Windows NT 4.0, or on the View menu in Windows NT 3.51.

Figure 2.2

The Windows NT 4.0 Registry Editor.

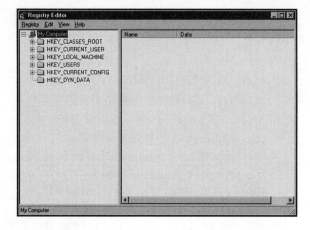

Finding Registry Information About SQL Server

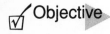 Objective

All the information on how SQL Server is started is stored in the Registry. This includes any service account names, parameters, and the location of the Master database and the output log files. All this information is required by SQL Server when it starts. After SQL Server is started, all the configuration information is stored in the Master database. This includes the names and locations of all of the database devices, and other parameters that are needed as the server starts.

Client information is also stored in the Registry, along with selected connection settings and protocols for SQL Server Enterprise Manager and ISQL/W. Registered servers are not stored in the Registry, so each user will need to register servers on his own.

Service Startup Information in the Registry

Any operating system service in Windows NT has service startup information stored in the Registry. This is information such as the security context to use, and the startup type. The same entry format is used for each service in Windows NT.

The HKEY_LOCAL_MACHINE\CurrentControlSet\Services\ MSSQLServer key contains the startup information for SQL Server service, and three other keys (see fig. 2.3).

Figure 2.3

The Service Control keys in REGEDIT on Windows NT 4.0.

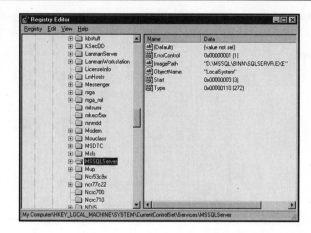

The important Registry keys used during SQL Server service start-up are outlined in table 2.1.

Table 2.1

SQL Server Service Control Keys

Value Name	Use	Typical Value
ImagePath	Location of SQLSERVR.EXE	C:\MSSQL\BINN\ SQLSERVER.EXE
Object Name	Identification of service account	LocalSystem
Start	Startup Type	3 (manual) or 2 (automatic)
Performance	Location of the perform-ance monitoring library for this service	SQLCTR60.dll
Security	Password for the service account, encrypted	Random numbers

SQL Server Parameter Keys

The key under CurrentControlSet, discussed in the previous section, is the minimum requirement for Windows NT to start the SQL Server service. The rest of the information to complete the startup is actually stored in the HKEY_LOCAL_MACHINE\ Software\Microsoft\MSSQLServer\MSSqlServer key (see fig. 2.4).

Figure 2.4

*The
MSSQLServer
keys.*

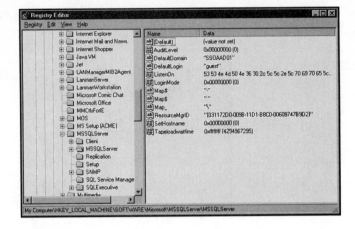

After the service is started, SQL Server requires certain parameters so that it can find the startup databases, figure out where to log error messages, and where to keep special settings called *trace flags*. These keys are stored within the MSSQLServer key in the Registry.

The important keys for starting SQL Server are outlined in table 2.2.

Table 2.2

SQL Server Startup Parameters

Value Name	Use	Typical Value
Audit Level	Determines what types of login attempts are logged: successful, unsuccessful, none.	0 (none)
Default Domain	Domain used by trusted connections for validation.	AccountDom
LoginMode	Login Security Mode	0 (standard) 1 (Integrated) 2 (Mixed)
CurrentVersion	Registration Information	

Value Name	Use	Typical Value
Parameters\ SQLArg0	Command Line Parameter for SQL Server,–d denotes this is the Master device name.	–d D:\MSSql\Data\ Master.Dat
Parameters\ SQLArg1	Command line parameter for SQL Server, –e denotes this is the name of the file to which to write the SQL Server log.	–e D:\MSSQL\ DATA\errorlog

If additional arguments for SQL Server are needed, they can be added as SQLArg2, SQLArg3, and so on. If trace flags are needed by SQL Server, they can be added as startup parameters.

What Is a Trace Flag?

A *trace flag* is a way of modifying how SQL Server runs. Most trace flags change the information in the SQL Server error log, and are useful for troubleshooting. Other trace flags are used to modify how SQL Server works. Trace flags are turned on with the –T parameter at startup, or by using the DBCC TRACEON (<number>) or DBCC TRACEOFF (<number>) commands in query tool. If the DBCC commands are used, then the trace flag will only apply to the current connection unless the trace flag –1 is set. Some trace flags include the following:

▶ 1204 Enhanced deadlock reporting to the error log

▶ 1205 Which commands caused a deadlock

▶ 3205 Disable hardware compression for tape drives

▶ 3604 Send trace log output to the client software

▶ 3605 Send trace log output to the error log

Many more trace flags exist and most are documented in SQL Server Books Online. Some undocumented trace flags circulate in newsgroups or in knowledge base articles. Undocumented trace flags may not be available in the next version of SQL Server, so do not plan on their future availability.

Client Information in the Registry

In addition to the information used by SQL Server as the services start, information used by the various client utilities that come with SQL Server is also placed in the Registry. The important key to remember in this case is the SQLEW key, which contains the list of registered servers for SQL Enterprise Manager, and is located in HKEY_CURRENT_USER.

SQL Server Integration with Windows NT

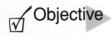

So far, the use of Windows NT security and Registry functionality have been discussed. SQL Server is integrated with Windows NT in other ways as well, and uses it to provide the following services:

- ▶ Security

- ▶ Network protocol support

- ▶ Event logging

- ▶ File and tape services

- ▶ Extended stored procedures

- ▶ SNMP support

- ▶ Service control

Security integration was discussed in the first section of this chapter, so it's time to move on to network protocol support.

Network Protocol Support

Windows NT supports a great selection of network protocols, and this provides SQL Server with a great deal of flexibility. Much of this flexibility comes through support for the Named Pipes and Multi-Protocol libraries. Named Pipes is essentially a way of using the file system support built in to Windows NT as a network

communications mechanism. This provides any client that can
connect to Windows NT with a mechanism to connect to SQL
Server, regardless of which network protocol is being used.

The Multi-Protocol library uses RPC (Remote Procedure Calls) to
communicate between SQL Server and client software. Because
Windows NT controls RPC, any network protocol that can support
RPC can be used with SQL Server, and maintain network inde-
pendence.

Other network libraries have to be installed to support other protocols, but the network libraries are not the same as the protocols.
The network libraries of SQL Server only provide Windows NT
with a place to send the incoming requests. That means that any
new protocols that evolve can be supported by adding the protocol to Windows NT, and adding a network library to SQL Server.

This level of integration also separates SQL Server from the un-
derlying network hardware. No configuration exists to change
SQL Server subnet masks, server names, or network addresses.
Windows NT takes care of those services.

Event Logging

One of the key features of Windows NT that makes it superior to
any other operating system is its capability to log errors in a central location. Although, to the inexperienced, this may sound like
a trivial feature, it is in fact a valuable diagnostic tool because error messages are logged in only one place.

SQL Server uses a combination of the event logging features in
Windows NT (see fig. 2.5) along with its own error log. The Event
Log records all the critical errors, startup, and shutdown information for SQL Server and related services. If a critical error is
found in the Event Log, the SQL Server Error Log can be consult-
ed for more detailed information on what happened. The SQL
Server Error Log is a plain text file located in the \MSSQL\LOG
directory.

Figure 2.5

*The Windows NT
4.0 Event Viewer.*

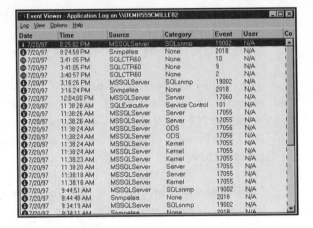

File and Tape Services

SQL Server uses Windows NT file services to store files. SQL Server needs to know only the location of the file that contains its data, and does not have any dependency on which file system is being used.

Tape services can be crucial to successful backup of SQL Server. When the Windows NT tape services are used, there is no reliance on hardware in SQL Server. Set tape drives up with Windows NT and SQL Server will be able to access them without the need for any additional drivers.

Extended Stored Procedures

Extended stored procedures enable SQL Server to execute tasks that interact with the outside world, including the operating system. Extended stored procedures are written using ODS (Open Data Services) libraries. Extended stored procedures are usually written in C or C++ programming languages, and are always compiled into DLL (Dynamic Link Library) files. These DLLs are then linked into the SQL Server environment.

Table 2.3

Some Examples of Extended Stored Procedures	
Extended Stored Procedures	Descriptions
xp_startmail, xp_stopmail, xp_sendmail, xp_deletemail, xp_readmail	These procedures handle the MAPI integration functionality, covered later in this chapter.
xp_cmdshell	Starts an operating system shell and runs the specified command.
xp_logevent	Logs an event to the Windows NT Event Log

All these stored procedures are linked into the Master database. Stored procedures run in the same security context as SQL Server, so you may choose to use a service account other than LocalSystem if the stored procedure has to interface with other computers. In addition, extended stored procedures are protected from the rest of SQL Server if they are executed in their own thread, so that if an extended stored procedure causes an access violation, SQL Server continues to run, and logs an error.

SNMP Support

SNMP (Simple Network Management Protocol) is used by network management software such as HP OpenView to monitor different processes, servers, and workstations on the network. SQL Server can use SNMP to send error messages, called *traps*, to specified computers.

For SNMP support to function, TCP/IP must be installed on the Windows NT computer, along with the simple TCP/IP services. This fully initializes the SNMP support. If SQL Server has already been installed, run the SQL Setup application, choose Set Server Options and enable SNMP support.

Note   A known bug exists in SQL Server 6.5 with regard to SNMP support. The DLL that starts the service logs a number of extraneous error messages to the Windows NT Event Log (see fig. 2.6). These log entries can be ignored.

Figure 2.6

One of the erroneous event messages.

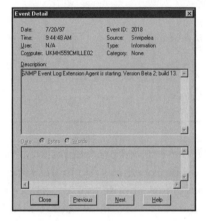

Service Control

Windows NT provides easy-to-administer support for programs that run independent of the logged-on user. These operating system services are controlled by using Control Panel, Services, and can be easily stopped, started, and configured. SQL Server runs as a service of Windows NT, so SQL Server can be started and stopped like any other service.

SQL Server and MAPI

 **Objective**   Microsoft Exchange and Microsoft Mail can both be integrated with SQL Server to provide feedback for administrative purposes, as well as providing support for mailed-in queries. The handling of electronic messages is accomplished via MAPI (Messaging Application Programming Interface). This interface has the capability to receive queries from the client processes, process the queries, and return results. In addition, SQL Server can be set up to send error messages to administrators when the server generates certain system messages. The integration of MAPI with SQL Server is

also called *SQL Mail.* Integration with tasks and alerts is covered in Chapter 7, "Server Alert Processing and Task Scheduling." The next section focuses on the remaining exam topics that relate to SQL Server integration:

▶ Installation and configuration of SQL Mail

▶ Using SQL Mail to process messages

▶ Using SQL Mail to send messages

Installation and Configuration of SQL Mail

To install and use SQL Mail, you have to do a few things. First, client software for the mail system has to be installed on the server. Usually, this is the Microsoft Exchange client, the Microsoft Mail client, or Microsoft Outlook. Prior to configuring SQL Mail, verify that the proper client software is installed; be sure to test it by sending and receiving mail.

For the Microsoft Mail client, use the following procedure:

1. Install and configure the Microsoft Mail client software on the server.

2. If the SQL Server and the Microsoft Mail post office are on different servers, run the MSSQLServer service using a service account that has access to the post office. You can accomplish this by using Control Panel, Services, as described in Chapter 1. If this is not done, the Microsoft Mail client software, which runs in the same security context as the SQL Server service, will not be able to attach to the post office.

3. Run the Microsoft Mail client software. Log in using the same mailbox that SQL Server should use.

4. From the SQL Server 6.5 program group, start the SQL Setup program.

5. Choose Next until the window titled Microsoft SQL Server 6.5-Options that contains the setup options appears (see fig. 2.7).

6. Choose Set Server Options and click the OK button. The Select Server Options window will appear (figure 2.8).

7. Click the Auto Start Mail Client option to automatically start the Mail client, if you want.

8. Click the Mail Login button.

Figure 2.7

The SQL Setup option window.

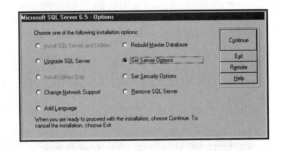

Figure 2.8

Setting server options.

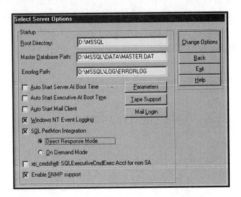

9. Enter the mailbox name and password that should be used to connect to Microsoft Mail.

10. Make sure the Copy SQL Mail Configuration from Current User Account box is checked and click Continue.

11. Choose Change Settings to commit the changes.

12. Exit Setup.

Installation of SQL Server via the Exchange client is very similar. The primary difference is that SQL Mail can make direct use of Exchange profiles to handle Mail setup. The following instructions will also work for Microsoft Outlook:

1. Make sure that SQL Server is running using a service account. For more information, follow the procedures outlines in Chapter 1 for the handling of service accounts.

2. Create an Exchange mailbox on the Microsoft Exchange Server that uses the service account as its Windows NT account.

3. Using the service account, log on to the Windows NT computer that is running SQL Server.

4. Install the Exchange Client software.

5. After the Exchange Client is installed, set up a profile by starting the Exchange Client. Accept the defaults for the name of the Personal Address book and Personal Storage files. At the prompt for server name, insert the name of the Exchange server that hosts the mailbox.

6. When the profile creation process is completed, go to the Control Panel, and open Mail and Fax.

7. Choose the Show Profiles button. Choose Copy. This will create a new profile and enable a real name to be assigned to the profile. Give the profile the same name as the service account. Although this step is not strictly necessary, it's a lot easier to type in a profile name that is manually entered than it is to use the default name.

8. Close the Mail and Fax application.

9. Start SQL Setup. Press Next until the screen with setup options appears.

10. Choose Set Server Options and then Next (refer to figure 2.7).

11. Click the Auto Start Mail Client option to automatically start the Mail client, if you want to do so (refer to figure 2.8).

12. Click the Mail Login button.

13. Type in the profile name specified in Step 7.

14. Choose Change Settings to commit the changes.

15. Exit the setup program.

After the SQL Mail client is installed, run a test. Open a SQL Server query window, use the Master database, and run xp_startmail. This process attempts to start the Mail client software. If xp_startmail succeeds, it will return a SQL Mail Session Started message. If it fails, the error is most likely caused by a login script problem.

Troubleshooting SQL Mail Problems

SQL Mail problems are usually caused by one of three problem areas:

▶ Windows NT login

▶ Mailbox connection/security

▶ Service restart

If you are faced with a Windows NT login problems, log on using the service account at the server. Start the Mail client; send and receive mail to make sure the connection to the server is working and the security is okay.

If a Mailbox connection/security problem exists, make sure that the service account has user rights and that Exchange Mailbox is being used. For Microsoft Mail, check that the Mail client can be started with the password specified in the SQL Mail setup.

If all else fails, restart the SQL Server and SQL Executive services.

Using SQL Mail to Process Messages

SQL Server has the capability to receive mail messages, perform queries contained in the messages, and send the results back to the user via SQL Mail. This is done by executing the stored procedure *sp_processmail*. This procedure in turn calls the extended stored procedures *xp_findnextmsg*, *xp_readmail*, and *xp_deletemail* to receive an incoming query. The query should be in the body of the message, and should include exactly one query. Then the *xp_sendmail* query runs to send the results of the query back to the user. The procedure does not run automatically when mail is received, so usually the *sp_processmail* stored procedure is scheduled to run at a specified interval. Use the scheduled tasks facility in the SQL Enterprise Manager to set up this schedule.

The *sp_processmail* stored procedure uses the following syntax:

```
sp_processmail [@subject = subject] [[,] @filetype = filetype]
[[,] @separator = separator] [[,] @set_user = user] [[,] @dbuse =
dbname]
```

The *subject* argument enables different subjects to be picked up by different processes. If, for example, the procedure needs to run against the Pubs and Production databases, the subject line could be set to "pubs" for mail that needs to process against the Pubs database. Multiple calls to *sp_processmail* would then have to be scheduled.

The *filetype* argument enables different file types to be sent out. The normal arguments are TXT and CSV. The TXT argument sends out a file with the extension TXT, and is a column-delimited text file. The CSV extension sends out comma-delimited data.

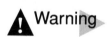 **Warning**

> Be very careful when using the comma-delimited options for output. Make sure the data being exported does not contain any commas, or the data will not be correctly parsed.

The *separator* argument specifies what to use to separate fields in the text file. Use a character that does not appear in the data. The *user* option specifies which security context should be used to execute the query. If this option is omitted, the query is run using the guest login id. Take note that this may cause problems with permissions. Finally, the *dbname* parameter determines which database is used to execute the query.

Stored Procedure Parameters

Stored procedures use parameters to set variables inside the procedure. These parameters are either required parameters or optional parameters. There are two calling conventions for specifying parameters in a call to a stored procedure. Here's a sample stored procedure to illustrate the two calling conventions:

sp_testproc @argument1=1, @argument2=2, @argument3=3

If the stored procedure is being run, and only arguments *@argument1* and *@argument2* are used, the stored procedure can be called like this:

sp_testproc 1, 2

If the stored procedure is being run and arguments *@argument1* and *@argument3* are needed, the call should look like this:

sp_testproc @argument1=1, @argument3=3

Notice that because *@argument2* was left out, the argument names had to be specified. Using a blank between commas or just using two commas doesn't work:

sp_testproc 1, , 3

...and neither will this:

sp_testproc 1,,3

That's why all the stored procedures are specified with the parameter names.

Using SQL Server and SQL Mail to Send Messages

SQL Server can send status or error messages to any user at any time by using the *xp_sendmail* procedure, part of SQL Mail. Refer to Chapter 7 for an in-depth look at how to send error messages.

The best example of how to send a status message is the following one, which deals with inventory shortage. A table made up of rows that contain the name of an item, the current stock level, and the minimum stock level, includes a trigger. Whenever the row is updated, the trigger checks to see if the current stock level has fallen below the minimum stock level for the updated item; if it has, a message is sent to the purchasing department to inform them of the shortage.

The *xp_sendmail* procedure uses this syntax:

```
xp_sendmail @recipient = recipient [; recipient2; [...;
recipientn]]
        [, @message = message]
        [, @query = query]
        [, @attachments = attachments]
        [, @copy_recipients = recipient [; recipient2; [...;
recipientn]]]
        [, @blind_copy_recipients = recipient [; recipient2;
[...; recipientn]]]
        [, @subject = subject]
        [, @type = type]
        [, @attach_results = {'true' ¦ 'false'}]
        [, @no_output = {'true' ¦ 'false'}]
        [, @no_header = {'true' ¦ 'false'}]
        [, @width = width]
        [, @separator = separator]
        [, @echo_error = {'true' ¦ 'false'}]
        [, @set_user = user]
        [, @dbuse = dbname]
```

Most of these arguments are self-explanatory. Keep in mind that the *recipient [; recipient2; [...; recipientn]]* should be a semicolon-delimited list of names that is completely contained in quotes, for example:

"John Doe;Lisa Smith;Bart Jordan"

The list can contain distribution lists, names, public folders, or any other registered recipient in the mail system.

The *query* parameter is used if it is desirable to return a query result to the user. In the cited example, the message body, specified in the *message* parameter, will provide enough information in a friendly format.

The *type* parameter is used to set a message type. This will normally be blank, but can be used to cause different actions to happen on messages when they are received. For more information, refer to the documentation on the mail system being used.

Exercises

Exercise 2.1: Examining the SQL Server Registry Entries

Now for a look at the Registry. This exercise will assume that you are running Windows NT 4.0, but Windows NT 3.51 will be fairly close. Remember that in Windows NT 3.51, the program for Registry editing is called REGEDT32. You'll be looking at the service control entries and the startup parameters, and will need only about five minutes to complete this exercise.

1. Start the REGEDIT program. The fastest way is to click the Start button, choose Run and type **REGEDIT** into the box.

2. Open the HKEY_LOCAL_MACHINE hive by clicking the plus sign to the left.

3. Open SYSTEM, CurrentControlSet, and Services on the way down the tree.

4. Under the Services entry, find the MSSQLServer key.

5. Read through the entries here. Notice that these entries are similar from one service to another. The Start value is simply the value used to handle the service startup type, which will be 1, 2, or 3 (for Disabled, Automatic, and Manual).

6. Close the Services key, and notice that this makes the list in the left-hand window pane a lot shorter.

7. Open the Software key under the HKEY_LOCAL_MACHINE hive.

8. Open Microsoft and MSSQLServer.

9. Compare the values here to the values in the service control section of the Registry (Step 5). The values in the SOFT-WARE key are used by SQL Server while the service is starting. The values in the service control section of the Registry are used by Windows NT to start SQL Server.

10. Close REGEDIT.

For more information, see the section "Finding Registry Information About SQL Server" found earlier in this chapter.

Exercise 2.2:   Viewing the Event Log and Error Log

SQL Server error messages are kept in two different places. It is
important to know which types of messages are stored in which
place. One place is the Windows NT Event Log. The Event Log
contains all the events that happen in Windows NT, including the
SQL Server events. The Error Log is a text file that contains detailed information on what SQL Server is doing. Start by opening
the Event Viewer, and then examining the Error Log. This exercise should take approximately 20 minutes.

1. Open the Event Viewer, which is located in the Administrative Tools program group.

2. Go to Log, Application to find the Application Event Log.
   The Application Event Log handles all the events associated
   with SQL Server. The System Event Log is useful for diagnosing operating system problems. The Security Log is used for
   auditing security events.

3. In the Application Event Log, look through the Source column. This column tells you where the event originated. SQL
   Server events usually come from the SQLExecutive, SNMPE-
   LEA, MSDTC, or MSSQLSERVER sources. The SQLExecutive source is usually events related to scheuled tasks or
   alerts. The SNMPELEA source is the SNMP Event Log Extension Agent service, which handles SNMP integration with
   SQL Server. The MSDTC messages are from the Distributed
   Transaction Coordinator, and are usually normal system
   startup messages. The MSSQLServer source is source of most
   of the error messages in SQL Server.

4. Open one of the MSSQLServer messages. Read through
   them until you find a message that begins with Mesg 17162.
   This is the first startup message from SQL Server, and it tells
   you how SQL Server is running.

continues

Exercise 2.2:   Continued

5. Cycle through the error messages by using the Previous button. There will be a series of Mesg 18109 events, which are caused by SQL Server recovering the databases. These are normal messages, and mean that SQL Server is re-attaching to each database.

6. Following these messages will be a series of Mesg 17026 messages, which provide valuable information on various DLL's being loaded by SQL Server.

7. Notice that there is a mixture of different services represented in the Windows NT Event Log.

8. Start Notepad, which is located in the Accessories group.

9. Open the errorlog file. Choose File, Open. Set the file type to All Files. Go to the C:\MSSQL\LOG directory. Notice that there is a series of files here, named errorlog errorlog.1 errorlog.2 and so on up to errorlog.6 assuming SQL Server has been started seven times. These files are created when SQL Server starts. The file named "errorlog" is the most recent, followed by "errorlog.1" and so on.

10. The SQL Server Error Log is a plain text file. Each line contains the date and time of the event, the user who caused the event, and the event text. Notice that there is a lot more information in here about startup than there was in the Windows NT Event Log. When you are debugging problems in SQL Server, the Windows NT Event Log helps track down major problems, but more detailed information can be found in the SQL Server Error Log. In addition, the SQL Server Error Log contains only SQL Server events.

For more information, see the section "Event Logging" found earlier in this chapter.

Exercise 2.3: Extended Stored Procedures

Exercise 2.3 will focus on extended stored procedures. Now you will run a couple of extended stored procedures and examine how they are linked into the SQL Server environment. This exercise should take about 10 minutes to complete.

1. Start a query tool. You may use either the SQL Enterprise Manager query tool, or go to the SQL Server 6.5 group and run ISQL/W.

2. Make sure the database is set on Master.

3. Type *xp_cmdshell "dir"*. Click the Execute button on the toolbar—it's the one that looks like a VCR's Play button. The keyboard shortcut, or hotkey, is Ctrl+E.

4. The result should be a directory listing, probably of the c:\winnt directory on the SQL Server. Any command can be run from this prompt. Keep in mind that by default, commands executed run in the context of the MSSQLServer service.

5. Run the following command in a query window:

   ```
   xp_logevent 60000, "this is a test", informational
   ```

6. Check the Application Log in the Windows NT Event Log. There should be a new event there that was entered by the extended stored procedure.

7. In a query window, run the following command:

   ```
   sp_helpextendedproc xp_logevent
   ```

8. The output should tell you the name of the extended stored procedure, and the name of the DLL from which the procedure came.

For more information, see the section "Extended Stored Procedures" found earlier in this chapter.

To investigate SQL Mail, first set up SQL Mail following the directions in the section, "Installation and Configuration of SQL Mail." First you'll test to make sure that SQL Mail is working, and then you'll set up SQL Mail to receive, process, and send mail. Each part of the exercise will take about 15 minutes. Be sure to allow enough time for the mail that is sent to be processed and returned. This can take 5 to 10 minutes, depending on the mail system used, system topography, polling intervals, and a number of other factors.

Testing SQL Mail:

1. The first test is to start SQL Mail. Start a query tool and connect to the Master database. Run *xp_startmail.* If this returns successfully, then SQL Mail is up and running.

2. Use *xp_sendmail* to send a message to another mailbox. Use the following command, substituting the mailbox name in the first argument:

```
xp_sendmail "<mailbox name>", "This is a test", @subject =
"SQL Server Mail Test"
```

If both of these tests worked, then SQL Mail is up and running on your server. If either one failed, follow the procedures in the sidebar titled "Troubleshooting SQL Mail Problems" found in the section "Installation and Configuration of SQL Mail."

Processing Mail with SQL Mail:

1. From another mail account, send a piece of mail to the address for SQL Server. In the body of the message, type the following query:

   "Select * from Authors"

2. Make sure SQLMail is running on the server. To check, run *xp_startmail* in a query tool. If it is already running, the error message will say so.

3. After waiting a few minutes for the mail to be delivered, run *sp_processmail* so it will run the query in the Pubs database:

```
sp_processmail @dbuse=pubs
```

4. Monitor the mailbox that sent in the query. It should receive the results back from the server.

For more information, see the section "Using SQL Mail to Process Messages" found earlier in this chapter.

Review Questions

The following questions will test your knowledge of the information in this chapter.

1. SQL Server Integrated Security works over which two of the following network libraries?

    A. Named Pipes

    B. TCP/IP Sockets

    C. Multi-Protocol

    D. IPX/SPX

2. Judy wants to use Integrated Security on her SQL Server. Her organization runs primarily Novell Netware for file and print services. Which three of the following statements are true?

    A. The Windows NT Server will need to have NWLINK loaded.

    B. The SQL Server needs to have the IPX/SPX network library loaded.

    C. The SQL Server needs to have the Multi-Protocol network library loaded.

    D. The Windows NT computer has to participate in a Windows NT domain.

3. Where can information on starting SQL Server services be found?

    A. The SQLSERVR.INI file in the \WINNT35 directory

    B. In the HKEY_LOCAL_MACHINE hive in the Registry, under Control/CurrentControlSet/Services/MSSqlServer

C. In the SYSTEM.INI in the \WINNT directory

D. In the Registry under HKEY_LOCAL_MACHINE\
SOFTWARE\MICROSOFT\SQLSERVER

4. Tom wants to change the way SQL Server starts from Manual to Automatic. What's the best way to do this?

A. Control Panel, Services.

B. Edit the Registry, change the Start value to 2.

C. Use the SQL Client Configuration Utility.

D. Edit the WIN.INI so the driver is loaded at boot time.

5. Which of the following server-side libraries require that users be validated by Windows NT?

A. The Multi-Protocol Library

B. TCP/IP sockets

C. IPX/SPX

D. The Named Pipes Library

6. Amanda is having a problem with her SQL Server, and wants detailed information about events affecting just the SQL Server service. Where should she look to find this information?

A. The *log* table in the Master database

B. C:\MSSQL\LOG\ERRORLOG

C. The Windows NT Event Log

D. C:\WINNT\SQLLOG.TXT

7. Billy needs to log an event to the Windows NT Event Log whenever a value in the inventory table falls below a certain level. Which of the following techniques is best for accomplishing this task?

   A. Call the xp_logevent extended stored procedure from within a trigger on the table.

   B. Make a Win32 API call using the stored procedures sp_callWin32.

   C. Periodically scan the table, and if a value is found, write it directly to the file "c:\mssql\log\errorlog".

8. SQL Server can be integrated with which of the following mail standards?

   A. MAPI

   B. VIM

   C. X.400

   D. SMTP

9. The SQL Mail service is started in which two of the following ways?

   A. Control Panel, Services

   B. SQL Enterprise Manager

   C. Net Start SQLMail at the command line

   D. *xp_startmail* extended stored procedure

10. When integrating SQL Server with Microsoft Exchange, which of the following steps must be completed?

    A. Microsoft Exchange Server must be installed on the same computer as SQL Server.

    B. The Microsoft Exchange Client Software must be installed.

C. The Microsoft Exchange SQL Server integration package must be installed.

D. The Mail=1 Registry entry must be added to the MSSQLServer Registry entry.

11. Barclay needs to install mail services on his SQL Server. He is using a Microsoft Mail system. How does he need to log on to Microsoft Mail to successfully configure SQL Mail?

A. Barclay should log on as himself.

B. Barclay should log on as the account from which SQL Server will be sending mail.

C. It doesn't matter how Barclay is logged on, as long as the mail client is set up.

D. The configuration will not work if Barclay is logged on. He should completely exit the Mail client before configuration.

12. Joe wants to send mail to three different people using the SQL Server extended procedure *xp_sendmail.* Here are the people and how their mailboxes are set up:

Mailbox	Name
jsmith	John Smith
sspade	Sam Spade
jdaniels	Joe Daniels

How should the list of people be specified?

A. "John Smith, Sam Spade, Joe Daniels"

B. "John Smith; Sam Spade; Joe Daniels"

C. "jsmith;sspade;jdaniels"

D. "jsmith,sspade,jdaniels"

13. Which security context does SQL Server use to run?

    A. The context of the currently logged in user

    B. The context of the administrator

    C. The context of the installer

    D. The context of the service as specified in Control Panel, Services, Startup

14. Integrated Security runs using which of the following network libraries?

    A. Named Pipes

    B. TCP/IP

    C. Multi-Protocol

    D. NetBEUI

15. The Windows NT Registry contains which two of the following?

    A. Information on how to start the SQL Server service

    B. Which security mode SQL Server should use

    C. Where all the user databases are stored

    D. How big the backup devices are allowed to become

16. What is the best place to look for problems that are logged by SQL Server and Windows NT?

    A. The SQL Server Error Log

    B. The ERRORS.INI file

    C. The Windows NT Registry

    D. The Windows NT Event Log

17. Steve needs to use SQL Server functionality to receive queries using Microsoft Exchange and return values back to the sender. Which two of the following will Steve be using to implement this functionality?

    A. SQL Server task scheduling

    B. SQL Mail integration

    C. Custom applications to read mail and send responses

    D. Third-party mail routing software

18. Bill needs to log events to the Windows NT Event Log whenever an inventory falls below a certain level. What functionality will enable Bill to accomplish this goal?

    A. A trigger and the *xp_logevent* extended stored procedure.

    B. A trigger and custom ODS software.

    C. This behavior is automatic and does not require any additional functionality or setup.

    D. A rule and the *xp_logevent* extended stored procedure.

Review Answers

1. A, C

2. A, C, D

3. B

4. A

5. A, D

6. B

7. A

8. A

9. B, D

10. B

11. B

12. B

13. D

14. A, C

15. A, B

16. D

17. A, B

18. A

Answers to Test Yourself Questions at Beginning of the Chapter

1. Integrated or Mixed Security both enable the use of trusted connections. Trusted connections are covered in the section "Integrated Security's Impact on SQL Server."

2. No. If the server were using Multi-Protocol or Named Pipes, a login to the Windows NT computer would be mandatory. This topic is covered in the section "Integrated Security's Impact on SQL Server."

3. All service control entries are stored in the Registry under HKEY_LOCAL_MACHINE\SYSTEM\CurrentControlSet\Services\MSSQLServer. It is important to realize that the entry is MSSQLServer, not SQLServer. The use of the Registry is discussed in "Exploring the Registry."

4. The Windows NT Event Log contains events that relate to all services running under Windows NT, as well as operating system events. The SQL Server Error Log provides more detailed information just about SQL Server. This topic is covered in the section "Event Logging."

5. An extended stored procedure is a link into a DLL and is used to provide SQL Server with an interface to the operating system. This topic is covered in the section "Extended Stored Procedures."

6. The extended stored procedure *xp_startmail* starts the SQL Mail system. The extended stored procedure *xp_stopmail* stops the SQL Mail system. This topic is covered in "Installation and Configuration of SQL Mail."

Chapter

Enterprise-Wide Database Administration

3

Server administration and configuration (that is, enterprise-wide database administration) is accomplished with a number of tools that provide centralized methods by which various aspects of a SQL Server can be controlled. This chapter will focus on the use of each of these tools and their respective functions. Specifically, this chapter covers the following:

▶ Distributed Management Framework (DMF)

▶ SQL Enterprise Manager

▶ SQL Service Manager

▶ SQL Client Configuration Utility

▶ SQL Security Manager

▶ SQL Setup

▶ SQL Trace

▶ SQL Performance Monitor

▶ SQL/W

As always, this chapter begins with a list of the exam objectives relating to the topic at hand, moves on to the chapter pretest, offers valuable information directly addressing the objectives and additional relative discussion topics, and finishes with exercises, chapter review questions, and answers to both the chapter review questions and the chapter pretest questions.

This chapter focuses on enterprise-wide database administration. It helps you prepare for the exam by addressing and fully covering the following objectives:

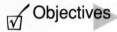 **Objectives**

- ▶ Configure Servers in the Enterprise

- ▶ Manage Servers in the Enterprise

- ▶ Administer Servers in the Enterprise

Since the objectives for this portion of the exam are somewhat high-level, this chapter instead focuses on how the objectives of server management and administration are accomplished. To do this, the content highlights the tools and utilities included with SQL Server that are used to perform common administrative tasks such as database creation, client connectivity configuration, modifying security options, or alert management.

Rather than being organized around the three exam objectives, this chapter is structured by each SQL Server management and administrative utility. The sections are presented in no specific order other than to try to establish a foundation for server management prior to exploring a particular utility in greater detail. All utilities are presented with the exception of the SQL Server Web Assistant; this tool relates more to advanced server functionality rather than server administration, and thus is outside the scope of this chapter.

Test Yourself! Before reading this chapter, test yourself to determine how much study time you will need to devote to this section.

1. What are three methods that can be used to stop SQL Server?

2. How can I increase the amount of memory SQL Server allocates upon startup?

3. How can the SQL Server security mode be modified?

4. How can Windows NT Security be integrated with SQL Server?

Answers are located at the end of the chapter...

Distributed Management Framework (DMF)

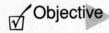 **Objective**

With the release of SQL Server 6.0, and now version 6.5, Microsoft introduced the *Distributed Management Framework*, or *DMF*, as the primary means of SQL Server administration. DMF is comprised of a set of methods, services, and components that expose functionality of SQL Server and its related services through common interfaces and applications (see fig. 3.1).

Essentially, DMF provides *OLE (Object Linking and Embedding)* interfaces to SQL services for use by the included administration tools, as well as any user-written VB 4.0 or even MS Excel VB application. These OLE objects are referred to as *Distributed Management Objects*, or *DMOs*. SQL system files that provide this functionality are illustrated in table 3.1.

Table 3.1

System Files that Comprise the SQL Server Distributed Management Framework	
File Name	Description
SQLOLE.REG	This file contains the required Windows NT Registry Entries for OLE functionality to SQL Server.
SQLOLE65.TLB	This OLE Type Library file is used by Visual Basic Applications.
SQLOLE65.SQL	This file contains Transact-SQL statements required for the execution of SQL stored procedures utilizing DMO functions. It is installed by default during SQL Server setup.
SQLOLE.HLP	This Primary help file contains information on available DMO methods and properties.

Figure 3.1

The SQL Distributed Management Framework exposes common server functions to administrative applications.

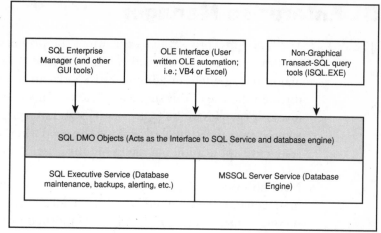

SQL-DMF contains over 60 objects (*Database Management Objects*, or *DMO*) and 1000 methods and properties. Microsoft publishes a number of books on SQL Server Programming through DMO. Note that sample Visual Basic code and Excel 5.0 modules are included in the SQL Server installation. Complete descriptions of these files and their functions can be found by viewing the README.TXT file located in the MSSQL\SQLOLE\SAMPLES directory.

The Distributed Management Framework is important because it is the basis for all tools that are used in SQL Server Management and Administration. Prior to DMF, only tools and utilities supplied with SQL Server could be used in its administration. This restriction made it difficult for end users to customize tools for specific uses or functions. DMF provides increased flexibility; server administration and management can be accomplished with either the supplied tools, or via user-defined applications that take advantage of the DMF framework.

One of the primary advantages of DMF is that it enables the automation many common administrative tasks such as database backup and alerting. The basis of almost all functionality within the SQL Enterprise Manager, the primary SQL Server administrative tool (see next section), is through the use of SQL-DMF.

SQL Enterprise Manager

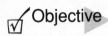

The SQL Enterprise Manager provides the primary interface used to administer multiple servers within the enterprise. Almost every major management or administrative task can be accomplished through the use of this single application. In some cases, such as invoking queries to the SQL Server, SQL Enterprise Manager actually uses the same tool as would be used when invoking the respective application manually—in this case, ISQL/W.

Not only does Enterprise Manager centralize administration and management, it also allows centralized administration of multiple servers in the enterprise. This is accomplished by registering a SQL Server in the Enterprise Manager. After a server is registered, it's possible to administer just about any SQL Server function, such as the following:

- ▶ Starting and stopping SQL services

- ▶ Viewing the SQL error log

- ▶ Modifying the SQL Server configuration

- ▶ Administering SQL mail

- ▶ Creating databases and devices

- ▶ Adding/modifying logins

- ▶ Setting up scheduled tasks and alerts

- ▶ Administering SQL replication

- ▶ Setting up database maintenance

These tasks represent the most common SQL Server management and administrative requirements.Before this can be accomplished using Enterprise Manager, however, the application must know about each server that will be managed. This is accomplished by registering servers, which is explored next. From this point, you learn how each of the above administrative tasks is accomplished.

Registering Servers

Before a server can be administered using SQL Enterprise Manager, it must be registered. This allows the administrator to define multiple servers, quite possibly in multiple NT domains, to be administered from single location.

A server is registered by using the following steps:

1. Start the SQL Enterprise Manager by double-clicking the SQL Enterprise Manager icon in the Microsoft SQL Server program group. If no servers have been registered previously, the Register Server window will be displayed. Otherwise, the application will already indicate previously registered servers in the Server Display window. A server can also be registered by right-clicking on the default SQL 6.5 server group and selecting the Register Server option from the pop-up window.

2. In the Register Server window, enter the required server name in the Server field. This is usually the NT computer name for the SQL Server.

3. In the Login Information area, select the login method to be used. The Use Trusted Connection option is available only when SQL Server is configured for Integrated Security mode, relying on NT user account information to grant access to SQL Server. Standard Security is the default login method when using Standard or Mixed Security mode, where SQL Server logins are maintained separately from NT.

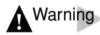Warning

If a server has been registered using Standard Security, requiring the sa account password, this information is retained in the NT Registry. This means that anyone can obtain unauthorized access to the SQL Server if he is able to access SQL Enterprise Manager on the given computer.

4. Enter the login ID and password to be used by SQL Enterprise Manager. This must be the *sa (system administrator)* account for the given server. Trusted connections do not require login account information.

5. In the Server Group window, the default group of SQL6.5 is displayed. This is where the server will be added when displayed in the Explorer style tree in the Server window of Enterprise Manager.

6. Click the Register button to complete the server registration. The server should now be visible within the SQL 6.5 structure in the Server window. If the server isn't immediately visible, it may be necessary to expand the tree by clicking the + sign next to the SQL 6.5 group.

To manage and administer the server, click the + sign next to the server name to expand its available functions. Each aspect of the server's configuration is now displayed.

 Tip

Keep in mind that server registration information is maintained in the Windows NT Registry under the SQL Server software key. This means that the information is available when starting Enterprise Manager only on the workstation on which the server was registered. It might be helpful to designate certain machines that will be used for SQL Administration and register the appropriate servers from these machines. This would ensure that all servers could be accessed from a single location or multiple centralized locations. Additionally, registering each server on its own local console aids administration in that Enterprise Manager can easily be used when logging on to the local SQL Server.

Defining Server Groups

Server groups allow various SQL Servers to be presented in logical groupings within SQL Enterprise Manager to aid in administration (see fig. 3.2). For example, suppose you are responsible for administering SQL Servers in each region of the United States: Northeast, Southeast, Midwest, Northwest, and Southwest. Using Enterprise Manager, you could define corresponding server groups so that it's easy to identify the servers within each geographical region. Another method of grouping might be to identify servers for various departments within the enterprise.

Server groups are defined by selecting Server Groups from the
Server menu in Enterprise Manager or by right-clicking on the
default SQL 6.5 Server group and selecting New Server Group
from the pop-up menu. Either of these two methods will display
the Manage Server Groups window, as shown in figure 3.3. When
adding a server group, you must determine whether the group
will be a top-level group, or a sub-group within an already existing
group. You determine the level by selecting the appropriate Level
option. Enter the desired group name and click the Add button.
This will add the new group to the server list in Enterprise Manager. Server groups can be renamed or removed by accessing the
Manage Server Groups window and right-clicking on the required
group name.

Figure 3.2

*Server groups
can help organize
SQL Servers to
aid administration
of multiple
servers.*

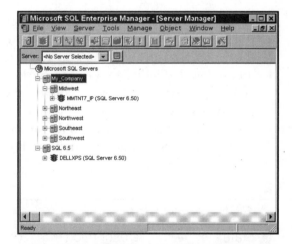

Figure 3.3

*The Manage
Server Groups
window is used to
organize SQL
servers within the
organization.*

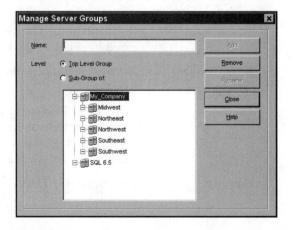

After the appropriate server groups have been defined, servers can be assigned to various groups simply by highlighting the required server and dragging it to the group.

Starting and Stopping Servers

One of the most common administrative tasks is that of starting and stopping SQL servers, which is often required when invoking server configuration changes or, in some cases, to allow the SQL Server database files to be backed up while SQL Server is off-line. This can be accomplished by using a number of methods, both from within SQL Enterprise Manager, as well as with other SQL Server tools.

From within Enterprise Manager, SQL Servers can be started and stopped by highlighting and right-clicking the desired server in the Server Manager window. This action displays the Server pop-up window that indicates the available control commands for the SQL Server service. The same command window can also be displayed by selecting SQL Server from the Server menu option in Enterprise Manager. The available commands to control the "state" of SQL Server are detailed in table 3.2.

Table 3.2

SQL Server States

State	Description
Stop (or Stopped)	The service is stopped, making SQL Server non-functional. The server cannot be recognized by client workstations.
Start (Started)	Normal operation—the server is fully functional.
Pause	SQL Server is started and active, but no further user connections are possible after it has been paused. Existing users continue to operate and the SQL Server is visible on the network.
Continue	Deactivates the Paused state, resuming normal operation.

The current state of the server determines which actions can be taken to control it. For example, when right-clicking on an active server, the Start option will be grayed out. A server's state is indicated by its associated icon in the Server Display window. The icon uses a stoplight metaphor: a green light indicates a running server, a yellow light indicates a paused server, and a red light indicates a stopped server.

 Tip

Enterprise Manager makes extensive use of icons not only to indicate the status of a given server, but also to indicate various database objects and related services. To quickly view the meaning of each icon, display the legend by using the Toggle Legend option from the File menu. Just as with a map, the legend provides a floating window that can be used to quickly reference the meaning of various icons within Enterprise Manager. You can also use the display legend toolbar button located next to the Server field in the Server Display window.

Starting and Stopping Related Services

In addition to controlling the SQL Server itself through Enterprise Manager, you can start or stop supplemental SQL services by using the similar methods: either by right-clicking on the desired service in the Server Display window, or by selecting the appropriate option from the Server menu.

Supplemental services are those that provide additional functionality to SQL Server, but are not part of the core database engine (SQLSERVR.EXE). For example, the SQL Executive Service is used to process server alerts and scheduled tasks (see Chapter 7, "Server Alert Processing and Task Scheduling"). Without this service, alert and task processing is not possible; however, the database engine is still functional and able to process user requests. In this case, the SQL Executive is a supplemental service.

These services follow:

▶ The SQL Executive

▶ SQL Distributed Transaction Coordinator (DTC)

▶ The SQL Mail Service

Figure 3.4 illustrates these services.

Figure 3.4

Supplemental SQL Services can be controlled by using Enterprise Manager.

SQL supplemental services are started or stopped using the following steps:

1. Highlight the desired server in the Server Display window. (Note that this may require that a server group be expanded by clicking the + sign next to the group name.)

2. Verify that the desired SQL Server state is active by noting the green stoplight shown in the server's icon. The SQL Server must be active in order to control its supplemental services.

3. Click the + sign next to the server to expand the server's properties. The first three items shown are the supplemental services.

4. Highlight the required service—SQL Mail, for example—
   and right-click it. The server pop-up window will be displayed along with the available states for that service.

5. Select the desired state (Start or Stop) to control the service.

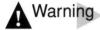

Warning

Some SQL Services such as SQL Mail and SQL DTC require specific configuration settings before they can be started successfully. Other than SQL Executive, which is required for alerting and scheduled database maintenance, don't start services such as SQL Mail or DTC unless you require the specific functionality provided by these services.

Supplemental SQL services are dependent on SQL Server, meaning that they can be started only if SQL Server is already started.

SQL Service Manager

Objective Another tool that can be used to start and stop SQL Services is the
SQL Service Manager. The Service Manager tool provides an interface to control SQL Server services on any connected server in
the enterprise. This capability is required in order to easily administer multiple servers in the enterprise.

The Service Manager makes it possible to easily control any SQL
server in the network, without the need to invoke SQL Enterprise
Manager. This is especially useful in situations where administrative personnel must start and stop servers, but are not responsible
for additional configuration items that are performed by using
Enterprise Manager.

Tip

The SQL Server and SQL Executive services can also be directly controlled using the Windows NT Control Panel's Services applet. Note that SQL Server is listed as the MSSQLServer service.

The SQL Service Manager controls the SQL Server and the SQL Executive services of local or remote servers (see fig. 3.5). SQL Mail and SQL DTC services can be controlled only by using Enterprise Manager.

Figure 3.5

The SQL Service Manager controls the SQL Server and SQL Executive services.

Stopping the SQL Server service on a can be accomplished by following these steps:

1. Start the SQL Service Manager by double-clicking the SQL Service Manager icon in the SQL Server program group. In the Server field, enter the name of the local SQL server. When connecting to remote servers, enter the server name and click the Connect button.

2. In the Service field, verify that either the SQL Server or SQL Executive service is indicated. Use the pull-down menu to select the appropriate choice for the service you are administering.

3. Double-click the stoplight icon for the action being performed. For example, double-clicking the red light will stop the selected service. Double-clicking the green light will start the service.

The bottom portion of the SQL Service Manager window indicates the current state of the selected service. Possible states follow:

▶ The Service is Starting

▶ The Service is Running

▶ The Service is Stopping

▶ The Service is Stopped

▶ The Service is Paused

Noting the server state is useful to verify when an operation has been completed. Servers maintaining large databases or with high user activity can sometimes take several minutes to complete a shutdown or startup request.

 Tip

Clicking the system icon in the upper-left corner of the SQL Service Manager window displays the System Menu. By using options on the system menu, you can modify behavior of the application. By selecting the option Remote Control, the Server field will not be displayed; this prevents SQL Service Manager from administering remote servers. The Action Verify option will prompt for verification when starting or stopping services. Use the Polling Interval option to control the frequency at which SQL Service Manager will poll the service to determine its current state. Foreground Polling Interval is used when the application is active on the desktop. Background Polling Interval determines the frequency of updates when SQL Service Manager is minimized.

Modifying the SQL Server Configuration

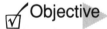 Objective

Another common SQL management task is to modify the server's configuration. For example, suppose you want to increase the number of concurrent user connections supported by a given SQL server. Modify the User Connections system parameter, which is part of its overall configuration. SQL system parameters are modified by using the SQL server, Configure option from the Server menu in Enterprise Manager (see fig. 3.6).

Figure 3.6

SQL Server configuration parameters.

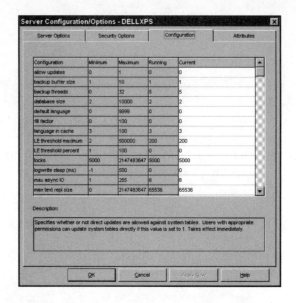

Because SQL Server allocates memory from Windows NT when it is started, it's essential that the server's "working set" portion of memory is allocated properly. Many configuration options allocate additional memory from the operating system based on how they are configured. Although many SQL operational settings almost never require modification, many common settings come into play often. Following are some examples of these settings:

▶ **User Connections.** Controls the maximum number of user connections the server will accept.

▶ **Memory.** Determines the total amount of memory SQL Server will allocate for its use upon startup.

▶ **Open Databases.** Determines the maximum number of simultaneous open databases.

▶ **Open Objects.** Determines the maximum number of open database objects for the given server.

To modify the SQL server configuration, use the following steps:

1. Start the SQL Enterprise Manager. Select the required local or remote server in the Server Display window.

2. From the Server menu, select SQL Server and then select Configure from the pop-up window. The Server Configuration Options window appears. (Note that many of the Server options on the first tab can also be controlled using the SQL Setup program.)

3. Click the Configuration tab to access the Server configuration information. This window indicates each configuration option and its minimum, maximum, running, and current values.

4. Highlight the required server option and enter a new value. Note that the value must be within the minimum and maximum range for that setting.

5. Click the Apply Now button to put the change into effect. Depending on which option was changed, this action affects only the current value and not the running value for the configuration option; most configuration options require a restart in order to be put into effect.

6. Click the OK button to return to the Server Display window.

 Tip

By highlighting a configuration option, you can view the amount of memory allocated to it, as well as additional details about its use, in the Description field at the bottom of the Configuration window.

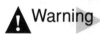 **Warning**

Use caution when changing SQL configuration options; incorrectly setting items like Memory can prevent the SQL Server from starting. If this happens, use the SQL Setup program to add the -f startup option to the server, which causes SQL Server to start in a minimal configuration, essentially ignoring the offending configuration option settings. Correct the required settings and restart SQL Server without the -f startup option, to again return to normal operation.

Administering SQL Mail

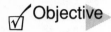Objective The SQL Mail service allows SQL Server to send query results as e-mail messages, and accept query requests from user-submitted e-mail messages. SQL Mail also plays a critical role in the capability of SQL Server to forward messages based on events and alerts. Suppose you are responsible for ensuring that when errors are encountered within a given database, notification is sent to the application developer. SQL Mail interacts with SQL Server to forward e-mail messages when data errors are encountered in the database.

To be fair, SQL Mail relies heavily on the ability of the messaging software (Microsoft Exchange or an NT post office) to obtain its configuration information. The configuration requirements for SQL Mail basically consist of providing the proper mail login ID and password, or an Exchange user profile name.

Understanding how to enable and configure SQL Mail plays a vital role in Database Server management. The SQL Mail service can really be considered part of the server's overall configuration. Briefly explore how to configure this capability in the following section.

Configuring SQL Mail

To use SQL Mail, it is essential that Microsoft Exchange Server software first be installed and functional on the SQL Server. The Exchange installation will modify NT Registry parameters, which affects the information displayed when configuring SQL Mail from the SQL Setup program or SQL Enterprise Manager. Follow these steps to configure SQL Mail:

1. In Enterprise Manager, highlight the SQL Mail service on the desired server and right-click it to display the Service pop-up window. Select the Configure option to configure the service. (Alternatively, select the SQL Mail service from the Server menu in Enterprise Manager.)

2. The Exchange Profile box is displayed. Enter the name of the Exchange user profile to be used with SQL Server. Click OK to return to the Server Display window.

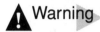

The Exchange user profile for SQL Mail must be set up using the same account that the MSSQLServer is started with in the Windows NT Control Panel. A good practice is to start MSSQLServer with a valid NT domain account, rather than with the NT LocalSystem unique account. This will not only facilitate SQL Mail, but is vital for additional SQL domain operations, such as replication and database backup/restore to network locations.

Starting SQL Mail

To start SQL Mail, highlight the service, right-click it, and select the Start option. If SQL Mail is properly configured, the icon will change from red to green. If an error message appears when you start the service, consult the SQL Server error log for additional details (use the Error Log menu option from the Enterprise Manager Server menu).

You can also start SQL Mail by executing the XP_STARTMAIL command from ISQL/W or from the SQL Query Tool in the Tools menu of Enterprise Manager.

Stopping SQL Mail

Stopping SQL Mail is accomplished in much the same way as starting the service: right-click the icon in the Server Display window and select Stop from the Service pop-up window.

You can also execute the XP_STOPMAIL command from ISQL/W or from the SQL Query Tool in the Tools menu of Enterprise Manager, to stop the SQL Mail Service.

SQL Client Configuration Utility

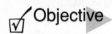 One of SQL Server's strengths lies in its capability to be integrated into almost any environment, regardless of the network protocols that are in place, such as TCP/IP or IPX/SPX. In order to provide this functionality, it is necessary to understand how to configure client workstations for the required connectivity method or transport that the SQL Server is supporting. This is accomplished by using the SQL Client Configuration Utility.

The SQL Client Configuration Utility determines the Network Library, or *Net Library* or *Net Lib*, that the NT Workstation or Server will use to communicate with SQL Server. The designated Net Library is dependent on the installed network protocol to provide connectivity to SQL Server. In this way, SQL Server can be integrated in many different network environments.

SQL Server Network Library Types

Prior to understanding how to change a client's Network Library, it is beneficial to review some background information about the available Network Libraries and the best situations for their use.

SQL Server Net Libraries determine which network transport clients are used in connection with the SQL Server. Depending on the Net Library used, certain SQL functionality may or may not be available. Table 3.3 describes each Net Library and its characteristics.

Table 3.3

Defining SQL Server Network Library Types	
Net Library	Description
Named Pipes	The default communication method for SQL Server, Named Pipes requires no additional configuration changes to the client or server. Named Pipes must be used to take advantage of integrated NT and SQL Security. This Net Library is common in pure Microsoft networking environments, and is always available on the server, regardless of additional Net Libraries that may be in use.

Net Library	Description
Multi-Protocol	This Net Library uses *RPCs (Remote Procedure Calls)* to communicate with SQL Server and does not require additional configuration parameters. Multi-Protocol clients can take advantage of encryption and integrated security with any installed protocol, such as Novell clients using IPXODI or SPX.
NWLink IPX/SPX	The NWLink Net Library utilizes the SPX network protocol to communicate with SQL Server. It is most commonly used in Novell Netware environments so that workstations can communicate with SQL Server without additional network transports being installed. Be sure to install the IPX/NWLink transport on the NT Server first.
TCP/IP Sockets	Clients using this Net Lib communicate with SQL by using native TCP/IP socket connections. By default, SQL Server listens for TCP/IP connections on Port 1433. This Net Lib is ideal for mixed environments or those requiring SQL connectivity with the Internet. Note that integrated NT/SQL security cannot be used with TCP/IP Sockets clients.
Banyan VINES	The VINES Net Lib enables clients to connect to SQL Server by using the VINES *SPP (Sequenced Packet Protocol).* To use this Net Library, you must install the VINES protocol on both the SQL server and the client workstation.

Advanced Client Options

To use Net Library communication methods other than Named Pipes, support for the appropriate communication method must be installed on the server using the SQL Setup program. Depending on the Net Library used, both SQL Server and the client workstation might require that specific network protocols be installed. After the required protocols are installed, it may be necessary to set up an alias for the client to use in connecting to SQL Server using the alternative communication method.

For a client to use TCP/IP Sockets, for example, the SQL server's DNS name would be referenced in the alias configuration. The following steps illustrate how to set up a client to use TCP/IP Sockets:

1. Start the SQL Client Configuration Utility. The DB-Library tab appears.

2. Select the Advanced tab to access the advanced client options (see fig. 3.7).

3. In the Client Configuration section, enter a server name in the Server field. (The pull-down option is used for modifying existing entries only.) This is the server name that is used to connect to the server using the alternative Net Library.

4. In the DLL Name field, select the appropriate Net Library. For the purposes of this example, the Net Library would be TCP/IP Sockets.

5. In the Connection String field, enter the required connection information. This information will vary depending on the chosen Net Library. For TCP/IP connections, the format is the IP address (or DNS Name) for the SQL Server followed by the port number: My_DNSServername, 1433.

6. Click the Done button to complete the configuration and add the entry to the Current Entries section.

To modify existing entries, highlight the appropriate entry in the Current Entries section and change the Net Library information as required. When the edits are complete, click the Add/Modify button to modify the existing entry.

Note

The name entered in the Server Name field is a logical definition used to reference the SQL server. This value can be anything you want; however, you should avoid using the NT computer name, if possible, to eliminate confusion in situations in which NT clients can connect by using either Named Pipes or TCP/IP. A good practice is to make the name unique to the given Net Library, such as Servername_IP or Servername_IPX.

Figure 3.7

The SQL Client Configuration Utility shows an alias for a TCP/IP Sockets Connection.

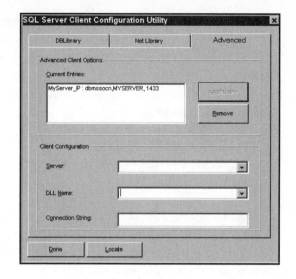

Changing the Default Net Library

By using the Client Configuration Utility, you can choose which Net Library method the workstation will use by default. The default automatically substitutes the correct *.DLL file for the required communication method. This automatic substitution is useful in environments in which the default method of Named Pipes is not possible. For connections to SQL Server in a Novell Netware environment, for example, NwLink IPX/SPX will most likely be the method of choice. To change the default Net Library, follow these steps:

1. Start the SQL Client Configuration Utility.

2. Select the Net Library tab to display the Net Library configuration. Use the pull-down box in the Default Network field to highlight the desired Net Library.

3. Press the Done button to complete the Default Network change.

SQL Security Manager

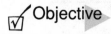Objective ▶

The SQL Security Manager is used to administer the selected SQL Server security mode (see fig. 3.8). In short, SQL Server security can be integrated with already-established security in NT domain user accounts, or it can be maintained separately, providing greater flexibility for application development and security integration. It is important to understand the implications that each method brings to the table. More importantly, when managing multiple servers in the enterprise, each SQL server can be configured to support different security configurations.

This section details the available security methods and how the SQL Security Manager utility can be used to modify the server security configuration.

SQL Server provides the capability to support multiple methods for login and security. Different security methods enable SQL Server to integrate tightly with existing Windows NT security, or to maintain its own separate security mechanisms for database login. Table 3.4 outlines each of the SQL Security modes and situations in which each might be used.

Table 3.4

SQL Server Security Modes	
Mode	Description
Standard	SQL Server user accounts are maintained separately from existing Windows NT domain accounts. This is the default mode, which is desirable for applications that require specific security settings or environments in which access to Windows NT resources is not desired.
Integrated	In Integrated mode, SQL Server dynamically maps SQL user IDs to NT domain accounts. After an NT account is created, no additional action is required on the SQL Server for the user to obtain access. This mode is useful for minimizing NT and SQL account administration.
Mixed	Mixed security mode is a combination of Standard and Integrated modes. It is useful in mixed environments where some client workstations are unable to take advantage of Windows NT security.

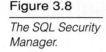

Figure 3.8

The SQL Security Manager.

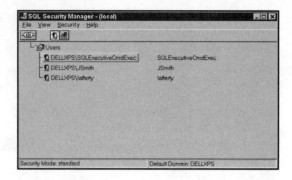

Although SQL security administration is accomplished by using the SQL Security Manager, selecting the supported security mode is accomplished through the use of the SQL Setup Program, which is discussed later in this chapter.

Using SQL Security Manager, NT user accounts can be defined as either SQL user accounts or SQL *sa (system administrator)* accounts. The Security Manager then creates an account that maps back to the specified NT user account. Understanding how to grant account privileges is crucial, especially when the server is configured for Integrated security mode. For example, support personnel utilizing an NT domain account are members of the Administrators group. Although these personnel require administrative access to the NT Server for system maintenance and support, it may not be desirable that these personnel gain access to SQL server databases with SQL sa authority. By controlling how account privileges are granted, these situations can be better managed and controlled.

Figure 3.9 indicates three NT user accounts and their corresponding SQL server logins.

NT accounts can be defined as SQL logins by using the following steps:

1. Start the SQL Security Manager and log in to the desired server. The Security Manager's User Privilege screen appears, showing NT accounts that currently have user-level logins in SQL Server.

Figure 3.9

The SQL Security Manager integrates NT domain accounts with SQL logins.

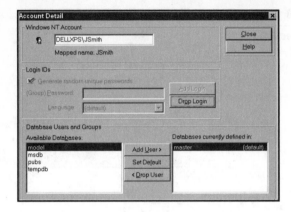

2. If user accounts are currently defined, the Users group button appears. Click the Users button to expand its detail.

3. From the Security menu, select the Grant New option. This will display the Grant User Privilege window. Select a local or domain user group and click the Grant button. Make sure the Add Login IDS for Group Members option is selected. This will create a SQL login for each NT user account within the selected group.

sa level accounts are added in a similar manner. After starting SQL Security Manager, select the SA Privilege option from the View menu.

 Tip

Double-clicking an account in SQL Security Manager displays the account details. Using the account details, user privileges can be controlled to access specific databases, as well as change the default database that users are connected to, after login to SQL Server.

SQL Setup

Within NT domains, many server administrative changes can be made centrally, and applied to all NT Servers within a domain. One example is adding user accounts. Because NT centralizes account information into a single domain security database, centralized changes can be accomplished.

With SQL Server, however, each server within an enterprise must be managed separately, even when the servers are located within a single NT domain. For this reason, it is necessary that certain configuration and management tasks be performed on each SQL server. One tool that is used for this purpose is the SQL Setup Program. The SQL Setup program is one administrative tool that really serves multiple purposes. Unlike many other setup programs, which are used solely for installation of the application, the SQL Setup program is vital for ongoing server administrative needs. The SQL Setup program is used to perform the following administrative tasks:

- ▶ Upgrade the SQL Server software

- ▶ Change the installed network support

- ▶ Add optional foreign language support to the server

- ▶ Rebuild the Master database in the event of a catastrophic software failure

- ▶ Modify various SQL Server options

- ▶ Change the security mode of the SQL Server

Explore each of these activities further in the following sections.

Upgrading SQL Server

Subsequent SQL Server software upgrades are performed using the Setup program (SETUP.EXE). Upgrades can be performed with the installed SQL Setup program, or with the SQL Setup program that comes with the new SQL installation software in the I386 directory for Intel-based machines or in the ALPHA directory for Digital Alpha based servers. Using the latterSetup program is the more common of the two methods. Prior to starting an upgrade to SQL 6.5 from a previous version, it is essential to run the CHKUPG65.EXE utility located in the MSSQL\BINN installation directory. This ensures that no keyword conflict or other conflicts exist in the installed databases prior to the upgrade.

To perform an upgrade, simply start the SQL Setup program. The program will detect the fact that a prior installation of SQL Server has been installed and will prompt to verify that an upgrade is desired. The Setup program will then prompt to verify the Master database configuration, server options, and network support. In short, the upgrade process is similar the installation process, with the exception that Setup will upgrade the existing user database as required, depending on the version of SQL Server that is being upgraded.

For additional information on installing/upgrading SQL Server, refer to Chapter 1, "Server Installation and Upgrade."

Changing Installed Network Support

By using the Setup program, SQL Server can be configured to integrate with various network types. This determines the transport and Net Library that client workstations must use when connecting to SQL Server. By default, SQL Server will accept client connections via the Named Pipes Net Library. To accept additional Net Library connection types such as TCP/IP Sockets (see fig. 3.10), support must be enabled using the setup program.

Figure 3.10

Additional network support is added using the SQL Setup program.

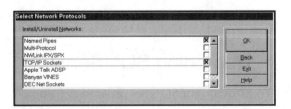

To enable additional network support, the following steps can be used:

1. Start the SQL Setup program from the icon in the Microsoft SQL 6.5 program group to launch the installed setup program located in the MSSQL\BINN installation directory.

2. The Setup program will verify that SQL Server is already installed. Click the Continue button to display the setup options screen.

3. Select the Change Network Support option and press the Continue button. The Select Network Protocols screen appears.

4. As mentioned earlier, the Named Pipes option is enabled by default. To enable additional network support, click the check box next to the desired option and then click the OK button.

5. The Setup program will now prompt for specific configuration information for each of the installed network support options. The default ListenOn Pipe for Named Pipe connections will be displayed, for example. If TCP/IP support was selected, the setup program will then prompt to verify or change the TCP/IP port number that SQL Server uses to listen for TCP/IP connections (the default is 1433).

6. Click Continue until all installed options have been verified. The Setup program will now prompt to Exit to Windows NT. Note that any network support options that were changed will not be effected until SQL Server is restarted.

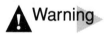 **Warning**

Modifying the default Named Pipe definition \\.\pipe\sql\query in the SQL Setup program is not usually recommended because the modification can adversely affect NT client connectivity, and may interfere with scheduled database maintenance tasks.

Adding Foreign Language Support

SQL Server supports both the U.S. English language and various localized languages such as German and French. This enables SQL Server to display system messages and present date/time formats not only in English, but also in the installed local language. Additional language support is installed using the Setup program, without the need to reinstall the SQL Server.

Foreign language support is installed by starting the Setup program and selecting Add Language from the SQL 6.5 Setup

Options screen. The Select Language window appears, in which the required language can be entered along with the SQL Server sa account password (see fig. 3.11). Similar to the addition of network support options, SQL Server requires a restart before the changes are put into effect.

Figure 3.11

Use the Setup program to add support for foreign languages.

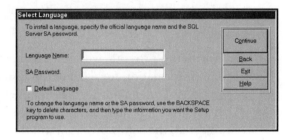

Rebuilding the Master Database

In certain failure situations, it is necessary to rebuild the Master database. SQL Server stores its own configuration information, as well as information on each user-installed database in the Master database. Because rebuilding this database essentially resets all information back to the system default, user-added information about databases, logins, permissions, and so on, is lost. Rebuilding the Master database, therefore, is somewhat less desirable than restoring the required database from a system backup.

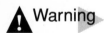 **Warning**

Rebuilding the Master database will destroy all previously stored user configuration data. Ensure that all user databases and the existing Master database are properly backed up prior to the rebuild.

Certain aspects of the SQL Server configuration require that the database be rebuilt; this is true when changing the installed sort order or code page. The *sort order* is the algorithm SQL server uses to perform sorting activity of data. A number of methods are available at installation time, each carrying its own performance implications. A *code page* determines the character sets that SQL Server will support.

Normally the sort order and code page are selected at installation time and cannot be changed. In the event that it is necessary to change these options via a database rebuild, however, the follow these steps:

1. Start the SQL Setup program. Select Rebuild Master Database from the Server Options window. A verification notice appears, indicating that all previously stored data in the Master database will be lost. Click Resume to continue the rebuild process.

2. The Rebuild Options window appears. Change the sort order or code page options here as required and click Continue.

3. The SQL Server Installation Path window now appears. Verify that the correct directory location for the existing SQL Server installation is displayed and click Continue.

4. The Rebuild Master Device window appears, which enables a different directory location to be specified for the newly rebuilt Master database. Additionally, the size for the newly rebuilt Master database device (or file) can be modified. Select the directory location and size as required and click Continue.

SQL Server now begins the rebuild process. Depending on the size specified for the Master database and the server hardware configuration, this process may take a few minutes. After the process is complete, you must restart the SQL Server. Note that when the server is restarted, all previously stored user information will not be present.

Modifying SQL Server Options

Static configuration options for SQL Server are modified by using the Setup program. Each of these options require that SQL be restarted before they are put into effect. To change static options, start the SQL Setup program and select Set Server Options from the SQL 6.5 Options window (see fig. 3.12).

Figure 3.12

Static configuration options modified by using the SQL Setup Program.

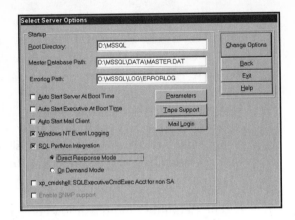

Table 3.5 describes the available options and typical uses for modifying each.

Table 3.5

Static SQL Server Configuration Options	
Option	Description/Typical Use
Root Directory	Determines the location of SQL Server System Files. This option is useful for specifying an alternative file location for troubleshooting or debugging purposes. Note that NT Registry changes might also be required to complete the location change configuration.
Master Database Path	Determines location of SQL Server installed Master database. This option is helpful in situations where an alternative Master database file may need to be temporarily referenced without disturbing the original SQL database configuration.
Auto Start Server At Boot Time	Controls whether the SQL Server service will automatically start when the NT Server is started or rebooted. This option is useful in situations in which SQL Server availability is required in a short timeframe after the NT Server restart.
Parameters Button	Controls SQL Server command line startup parameters. This option is most commonly used to specify troubleshooting or debugging parameters that are required when SQL Server is started.

Option	Description/Typical Use
Auto Start SQL Executive at Time	Similar to the Auto Start Server option— it allows the SQL Executive service to be Boot started automatically when the NT Server is restarted.
Tape Support Button	This option controls how SQL Server handles database backups directly to tape—for example, how long SQL Server will retry attempts to back up to a tape that hasn't been loaded before it aborts the backup. This option is only a factor in environments backing up databases directly to tape.
Auto Start Mail Client	Controls whether SQL Mail capability is available automatically upon startup of SQL Server. This option might be useful when strict control over user's SQL Mail capability is required.
Mail Login	Determines the mail (or MS Exchange) account that the SQL Mail service will use to process SQL Mail messages.
Windows NT Event Logging	Allows SQL Server system messages to be displayed in the NT Event Log, in addition to the SQL Server Error Log. This option is enabled by default in SQL 6.5. Using NT Event Logging allows server application messages to be consolidated into a single logging mechanism, easing SQL Server administration.
SQL PerfMon Integration	This option makes SQL Server performance data available to the Windows NT Performance Monitor. When enabled, the Integration mode must also be determined. Direct Response mode provides better response time in the NT Performance Monitor; however, the actual data displayed is actually one refresh interval behind. On Demand mode provides a slower response time, although the information displayed is the most current SQL performance data.

continues

Table 3.5 Continued

Option	Description/Typical Use
XP_CMDSHELL Impersonates Client	XP_CMDSHELL is an extended stored procedure that enables SQL Server to directly interact with the NT operating system. Because of the powerful nature of this procedure, enabling this option restricts XP_CMDSHELL use to only system administrators (SQL sa account), or members of the local NT Administrators group on Servers supporting Integrated security.
Enable SNMP Support	This option is available only on NT Servers with SNMP (System Network Management Protocol) support installed. Selecting this option enables SQL system messages to be available as SNMP alerts. This is useful in environments in which SNMP management tools are in use.

SQL Trace

 Objective

The SQL Trace Utility, new in SQL 6.5, provides the primary means by which specific user connections and server processes can be monitored. This utility enables the administrator to obtain detailed information on the actual SQL database queries that a user executes from a given application. SQL Trace becomes an important tool in managing server performance as well as in troubleshooting. For example, suppose that users complain of poor SQL performance every day at around the same time. SQL Trace could help determine what condition or user request is contributing to the poor performance.

By using SQL Trace, filters that monitor connection information for a given user, or for all users on the SQL Server, can be defined. Additionally, a filter can be built to monitor connections on a single server or multiple SQL Servers on the network. SQL Trace filters can redirect output in one of several ways (see table 3.6).

Table 3.6

SQL Trace Output Options	
Output Type	Description/Use
Screen File	The Screen File option redirects trace output to the filter display screen in SQL Trace. This method is best suited for online monitoring and ad-hoc query debugging (see fig. 3.13).
Script File	This method is helpful because trace commands are formatted for explicit Transact-SQL execution. Script output also allows performance data to be incorporated (see fig. 3.14).
Log File	Log File output provides good audit trail information of subsequent connection activity (see fig. 3.15).

Figure 3.13

SQL Trace Screen File Output.

Figure 3.14

SQL Trace Script File Output.

Figure 3.15

SQL Trace Log File Output.

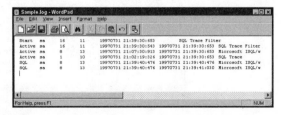

Tip

SQL Trace functionality can also be initiated from the command line by using the XP_SQLTRACE extended stored procedure. In fact, the SQL Trace application simply provides a graphical interface to use much of this procedure's existing functionality.

SQL Trace also provides the option of including performance information when filtering results of a given trace. This option is helpful for identifying potential performance problems caused by poor query design or database structure. SQL Trace performance data incorporates the following statistics:

▶ The duration of the SQL event

▶ CPU utilization for the SQL event

▶ Number of disk reads

▶ Number of synchronous writes for the SQL event

SQL Performance Monitor

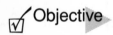 **Objective**

While the SQL Trace tool provides information about SQL connections, the SQL Performance Monitor provides information about all metrics of SQL Server's operation (see fig. 3.16). When SQL Server is installed, additional performance counters are configured in the NT Registry that are specific to SQL Server Operation. This makes SQL Server performance data available to the Windows NT Performance Monitor.

Figure 3.16

The SQL Performance Monitor.

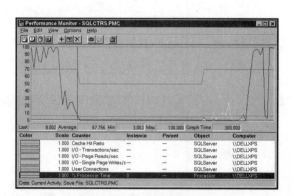

SQL Performance Monitor utilizes the capability of the Windows NT Performance Monitor (PERFMON.EXE) to save custom chart settings in a *.PMC file. This chart settings file (SQLCTRS.PMC) is located in the MSSQL\BINN installation directory, and contains the most common SQL Server Performance Monitor Counters.

SQL Performance Monitor provides a centralized means to monitor multiple SQL servers in the network. Multiple servers can be monitored by using the following steps:

1. Start SQL Performance Monitor using the Performance Monitor icon in the SQL 6.5 Program Group. This action will launch the Performance Monitor with the common counters for the local SQL Server displayed.

2. Click the + tool button to add additional performance counters. The Add to Chart window appears.

3. In the Computer field, enter a remote SQL Server name or click the Browse button (located next to the field) to select the required server.

4. Click the Object field to select the SQL Server object on the given server. After the SQL Server object is selected, the available counters are displayed in the Counters field.

5. Choose the counters that are to be monitored and click the Add button. After all the required counters have been added, click the Done button to return to the Performance Monitor display. This makes it possible to view performance data for each server in a single chart display.

 Tip

Keep in mind that SQL Performance Monitor is nothing more than presaved settings for the Windows NT Performance Monitor. This means that the original SQLCTRS.PMC file can be modified to suit your given environment by using the File, Save menu option.

ISQL/W

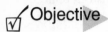 Objective ▶ The ISQL/W Tool is the interface to the SQL Server query engine. Its primary use is to execute explicit Transact-SQL commands on the SQL Server. Although it is not used extensively for managing servers within the enterprise, many system-related SQL commands can be invoked using ISQL/W. This provides direct access to many of the same procedures that are used by other SQL tools for server management activity. Table 3.7 illustrates some common ISQL/W alternatives for server administration.

Table 3.7

Common ISQL/W Alternatives for Server Management

Command/ Procedure	Description
SHUTDOWN	This command can be invoked to shut down a SQL Server. After the server has been stopped, however, the connection to ISQL/W is broken and the server will have to be restarted using Enterprise Manager or the SQL Service Manager.
XP_SQLTRACE	This is the extended stored procedure that provides identical functionality to the SQL Trace tool. It provides a command-line method to trace user connection output to a log or *.SQL file.
sp_configure	This is the stored procedure used to configure SQL Server operation parameters. It provides the same functionality as the Configure Servers menu option in SQL Enterprise Manager.
sp_who	This command displays a list of user connection activity. Similar in function to the Current Activity display in Enterprise Manager.
xp_startmail	This command starts the SQL Mail Service.
xp_Stopmail	This command stops the SQL Mail Service.

Exercises

Exercise 3.1: Registering Servers By Using SQL Enterprise Manager

In this exercise, you will register a SQL Server so that it can be administered using the Enterprise Manager. This allows all aspects of the server's configuration to be remotely modified and controlled. This exercise can be used to register a SQL server by using Standard SQL security. This is a rather simple exercise that should take no more than 10 minutes.

1. Start the SQL Enterprise Manager from the Microsoft SQL Server program group.

2. If no servers were previously registered, the Register Server window is displayed. Enter the server name in the Server field or click the Servers button to display a list of active SQL servers.

3. In the Login Information section, highlight the option for Standard Security. This will require a valid SQL login ID and password.

4. Enter **sa** for the account name and the required password.

5. Click the Register button to complete the server registration.

6. Click the Close button to return to the Server Display window. The newly added server should now be visible in the default SQL 6.5 Server group.

For more information, consult the "Registering Servers" section, earlier in this chapter.

Exercise 3.2: Creating Server Groups in Enterprise Manager

This exercise demonstrates how to create server groups in the SQL Enterprise Manager. Server groups are used to logically arrange multiple servers within the enterprise to ease administration. This exercise should take approximately five minutes.

continues

Exercise 3.2: Continued

1. Start the SQL Enterprise Manager. If no servers have been registered, register at least a single server now. (Refer to Exercise 3.1.)

2. In the Server Display window, highlight the default SQL 6.5 global group.

3. Click the right mouse button and select the New Server Group option. This will display the Manage Server Groups window.

4. Enter a group name and select the Top Level option. This will create a top-level group as a peer to the default SQL 6.5 group.

5. Click the Add button and then click Close to complete the group definition and return to the Server Display window.

Subgroups can be created in the same manner by selecting the Subgroup option from the Manage Server Groups window.

For more information, refer to the earlier "Defining Server Groups" section.

Exercise 3.3: Starting and Stopping Servers

In this exercise you'll start and stop servers by using the SQL Service Manager. This represents just one method that can be used to start and stop servers. The required time to complete this exercise is approximately five minutes.

1. Start the SQL Service Manager from the Microsoft SQL Server Program group.

2. Ensure that the desired SQL Server name appears in the Server field. If not, highlight the server and enter the required server name.

3. From the Services pull-down menu, select the MSSQL Server service.

4. Double-click the red light on the stoplight icon to stop the SQL service. The status line at the bottom of the window will indicate when the service has been completely stopped.

5. Double-click the green light on the stoplight icon to start the SQL Server service. The status line will indicate that the service is running after startup is complete.

The SQL Executive service and SQL DTC services can be controlled in the same manner simply by selecting the appropriate service from the pull-down menu in the SQL Service Manager.

For more information on stopping and starting servers, see the sections titled "SQL Service Manager" and "Starting and Stopping Servers" earlier in chapter.

Exercise 3.4: Modifying the SQL Server Configuration

In this exercise, you'll modify the server configuration to increase the number of simultaneous user connections that the server will accept. This is a common administrative function that can be completed by using the SQL Enterprise Manager. This exercise will take approximately 10 minutes to complete.

1. Start the SQL Enterprise Manager. Click the + sign next to the Server icon to expand its object list and ensure connectivity to the correct server for configuration.

2. From the Server menu, select SQL Server and Configure. This will display the SQL Configuration/Options window.

3. Click the Configuration tab and scroll down the list of options until the User Connections option is displayed.

4. In the Current column, increase the number of simultaneous user connections by ten (10). The current configuration value can be obtained by viewing the value in the Running column. For example, if the running value is 10, enter 20 in the Current column.

continues

Exercise 3.4: Continued

4. Click the Apply Now button to save the configuration option change. Click the OK button to return to the Server Display window.

5. In order to put the configuration change into effect, it is necessary to restart the SQL Server. Can you remember one of the methods that can be used to accomplish this?

Refer to the earlier section "Modifying the SQL Server Configuration" for additional information.

Exercise 3.5: Using the SQL Server Setup Program

The SQL Server Setup program is used to modify various aspects of the SQL Server installation. In this exercise, you'll use the setup program to disable Windows NT event logging and configure SQL Server to start automatically when the NT Server is started. This exercise should take approximately five minutes to complete.

1. From the Microsoft SQL Server program group, start the SQL Setup program.

2. Click the Continue button twice to display the SQL Server Options window.

3. Select Set Server Options and click the Continue button.

4. Select the Auto Start Server at Boot Time.

5. Deselect Windows NT Event Logging.

6. Click the Change Options button to save the configuration changes to the NT Registry and put them into effect for SQL Server.

7. Click Exit to quit the setup program and return to Windows NT.

8. Be sure to restart SQL Server to put the configuration changes into effect.

For more information on using the SQL Setup program, see the section titled "SQL Setup."

Exercise 3.6:   Using SQL Trace

The SQL Trace tool is useful for monitoring specific information on a given user session or all sessions with the SQL Server. In this exercise, you set up an onscreen filter to capture all information for the sa user account when accessing SQL Server with the ISQL/W query tool. Allow approximately 10 to 15 minutes to complete this exercise.

1. From the SQL Server Program group, start the SQL Trace application.

2. When prompted for login, log in to the server with the sa user account and password.

3. From the File menu, select the New Filter option.

4. Enter a name for the new filter, such as SA Active Trace.

5. Press the Browse button next to the Login Name field to display available SQL Server logins.

6. Highlight the sa account and press OK.

7. Click the Browse button next to the Application field and select Microsoft ISQL/W from the list of applications. Click the OK button.

8. Make sure <All> is displayed in the Host Name field to ensure that sa user activity from ISQL/W on any client workstation is filtered.

9. In the SQL Scripts section, ensure that the View on Screen option is selected.

10. Click OK to complete the filter configuration. You will be prompted to start the filter if it is not currently running.

11. Click Yes to start the filter. The SQL Trace Filter output screen will appear, verifying that the filter has been successfully defined and is running.

Refer to the section titled "SQL Trace" for additional information.

Review Questions

The following questions will test your knowledge of the information in this chapter.

1. Name three tools that can be used to stop SQL Server.

    A. SQL Enterprise Manager, SQL Setup Program, SQL Service Manager

    B. SQL Enterprise Manager, SQL Service Manager, Windows NT Control Panel

    C. SQL Service Manager, SQL Performance Monitor, SQL Trace

    D. SQL Enterprise Manager, ISQL/W, SQL Performance Monitor

2. The foundation for SQL Server administration is through the use of SQL-DMF. What does DMF stand for?

    A. Distributed Monitoring Facility

    B. Distributed Monitoring Foundation

    C. Dynamic Management Facility

    D. Distributed Management Framework

3. Which single utility is used to stop SQL Server and all of its related services?

    A. SQL Service Manager

    B. SQL Setup Program

    C. SQL Security Manager

    D. None of the above

4. You want to configure the SQL Server so that it must be started manually after the NT Server is started, rather than starting automatically upon boot. Which administration tool is used to perform this change?

    A. SQL Setup Program

    B. SQL Enterprise Manager

    C. SQL Service Manager

    D. ISQL/W

5. Name the ISQL command that can be used to stop the SQL Mail service using the ISQL/W tool.

    A. SHUTDOWN SQL_MAIL

    B. XP_STOPMAIL

    C. EXEC SQL_MAIL(STOP)

    D. NET STOP SQLMAIL

6. What two (2) methods can be used to configure SQL Server to stop accepting new user connections, while still maintaining existing connections?

    A. Using SQL Service Manager, click the yellow light in the stoplight icon.

    B. Start the SQL Setup program. Select the option Disallow Future Logins from the Server Options window.

    C. Using the SQL Security Manager, select Paused Connections from the View menu.

    D. Right-click the SQL Server icon in the SQL Enterprise Manager Server Display window. Select Pause from the pop-up menu.

7. What is the default Net Library for SQL Server?

    A. Named Pipes

    B. RPC

    C. IPX/SPX

    D. TCP/IP

8. Which Security mode enables SQL Server to integrate SQL user logins with NT domain user accounts?

 A. Standard

 B. Mixed

 C. Integrated

 D. B and C

9. A server's configuration can be modified by using the SQL Enterprise Manager, and selecting the SQL Server, Configure option from the Server menu. What Transact-SQL command can be used in ISQL/W to accomplish the same function?

 A. EXEC sys.configs

 B. SELECT options FROM sysoptions

 C. XP_CONFIG

 D. sp_configure

10. You are implementing SQL Server in a Netware 4.1 environment. Which of the following configurations must be made in order for Novell client workstations to access SQL Server? (Choose one answer.)

 A. Enable GSNW (Gateway Services for Netware) on the NT/SQL Server. Enable the IPX/SPX Net Lib in the SQL Server Setup program.

 B. No special configuration is required.

 C. Install the IPX/NWLink protocol on the NT Server.

 D. Install the IPX/NWLink protocol on the NT Server. Enable the IPX/SPX Net Lib in the SQL Setup program.

11. Which of the following is true of the SQL Performance Monitor?

A. It is really a Chart Settings file of common SQL counters.

B. It cannot be used if SQL Enterprise Manager is stopped.

C. It is a special version of Performance Monitor that can only be used with SQL Server.

D. It cannot monitor multiple SQL Servers concurrently.

12. How can NT Event logging for SQL Server messages be disabled?

A. This feature cannot be disabled.

B. Choose the Error Log option from the Server menu in SQL Enterprise Manager and select the Disable option.

C. Start the SQL Setup program and deselect the NT Event Logging option from the Server Options window.

D. Using the SQL Setup program, reinstall SQL Server and select the NT Event Logging option when the Server Options window is displayed.

13. Which two (2) SQL Server Security modes enable SQL user logins to be integrated with NT domain security?

A. Integrated mode

B. Standard (default) mode

C. RPC Security mode

D. Mixed Security mode

14. Which of the following tools is used to collect performance information about SQL user connections?

A. SQL Performance Monitor

B. SQL Enterprise Manager

C. SQL Trace

D. SQL Connection Manager

15. The SQL Setup program is used to modify which of the following?

   A. Static SQL configuration parameters

   B. SQL Security mode

   C. Server registration status

   D. A and B

16. SQL Mail is controlled by using which of the following tools?

   A. The SQL Enterprise Manager

   B. SQL Trace

   C. ISQL/W

   D. SQL Service Manager

17. Before a SQL Server can be administered by using Enterprise Manager, what must first be done to the server?

   A. SQL Server must be added to the SQL Remote Server list in the Enterprise Manager Server Display window.

   B. SQL Server must be registered.

   C. No special actions are required prior to using Enterprise Manager.

   D. The SA must first attach to a network driver on the server before SQL Server can be administered.

18. Which Net Library does not support integrated NT/SQL Security?

   A. RPC

   B. Named Pipes

   C. IPX/SPX

   D. TCP/IP

19. Which two (2) of the following files are components of the SQL Distributed Management Framework?

    A. SQLDMF.DLL

    B. SQLOLE65.SQL

    C. SQLOLE.REG

    D. SQLOLE65.TLB

20. The SQL Security Manager can be used to perform which of the following tasks?

    A. Grant SQL sa authority to NT Domain Administrator accounts.

    B. Prevent unauthorized users from accessing a given database.

    C. Add NT domain accounts using SQL Server.

    D. None of the above.

21. What is the name of the extended stored procedure that can be executed via ISQL/W to provide similar functionality to the SQL Trace tool?

    A. XP_SQLTRACE

    B. DBCC(SQLTRACE)

    C. sp_configure trace, 'on'

    D. sp_SQL_TRACE

22. Which tool is used to enable SNMP alerting for SQL Server?

    A. SQL Client Configuration Utility

    B. SQL Enterprise Manager

    C. SQL Trace

    D. SQL Setup Program

23. Which of the following is true using the L Setup program?

    A. The server must be completely reinstalled in order to install foreign language support.

    B. Foreign language support can be installed using the SQL Setup program without reinstalling the server.

    C. Foreign language support cannot be managed using the SQL Setup program.

    D. Foreign language support is automatically installed when running the SQL Setup program.

24. What are Server groups in SQL Enterprise Manager?

    A. A logical display of servers presented in groupings to aid in administration.

    B. SQL Servers within a domain that are configured to use the same security mode.

    C. NT domain user accounts that have the required privileges to access SQL Server.

    D. SQL Server user logins that are classified by their respective privilege levels.

25. Which of the following statements is true regarding SQL memory allocation?

    A. SQL Server allocates its memory "working set" from Windows NT when SQL Server is started.

    B. SQL Server memory allocation can only be modified by reinstalling the server.

    C. SQL Server allocates its memory "working set" dynamically, based on load.

    D. None of the above.

Review Answers

1. B

2. D

3. D

4. A

5. B

6. A, D

7. A

8. D

9. D

10. D

11. A

12. C

13. A, D

14. C

15. D

16. A

17. B

18. D

19. B, C, D

20. A

21. A

22. D

23. B

24. A

25. A

Answers to Test Yourself Questions at Beginning of the Chapter

1. SQL Server can be stopped using the SQL Service Manager tool. Select the SQL Server service and double-click the red light on the stoplight icon. Another method is to use the Windows NT Control Panel to access the MSSQLServer service. Click the Stop button to stop the server. SQL Server can also be stopped by right-clicking the SQL Server in the Server display window of the SQL Enterprise Manager and then selecting Stop from the Service pop-up window. Refer to the section titled "Starting and Stopping Servers."

2. To increase SQL memory allocation, use the Configure option from the Server, SQL Server menu in the Enterprise Manager. Access the Configuration tab from the Server Option window and modify the Memory setting. Configuration parameters are also modified using the sp_configure Transact-SQL command in ISQL/W. Refer to the section titled "Modifying the SQL Server Configuration" for details on modifying the server's configuration.

3. The SQL Server Security mode is modified using the SQL Security Manager utility. For more information on this utility, refer to the "SQL Security Manager" section.

4. Windows NT Security is integrated with SQL Server by using the SQL Setup program to set the server to use either Mixed or Integrated Security mode. Windows NT domain accounts can be customized with various SQL Server account privileges by using the SQL Security Manager application. This is discussed in greater detail in the "SQL Security Manager" section.

Chapter

Managing Database Storage

One of the most important topics for the *database administrator (DBA)* to master is how to manage database storage. Not only is it a heavily tested subject on the certification test, it is one of the most common tasks a DBA performs. Not only will you need to learn how to manage database storage using SQL Enterprise Manager, you will also need to understand how to perform these same tasks using Transact-SQL statements and stored procedures.

This chapter begins by introducing you to some preliminary topics you need to thoroughly understand before proceeding to the sections on managing database storage. These include an introduction to database objects, database storage structures, and transaction logs. Next, you will be presented with all the information you need to know to perform day-to-day database storage management. The topics included not only cover the test objectives listed in the next section, but includes additional information you need to round out your knowledge of database storage management, such as how to create databases on removable media.

As always, this chapter begins with a list of the exam objectives relating to the topic at hand, moves on to the chapter pretest, offers valuable information directly addressing the objectives, as well as additional relative discussion topics, and finishes with exercises, chapter review questions, and, finally, answers to both the chapter review questions and the chapter pretest questions.

This chapter focuses on the database storage management. It helps you prepare for the exam by covering the following objectives:

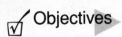 **Objectives**

▶ Creating a device

▶ Creating a database

▶ Altering a database

▶ Creating database objects

▶ Estimating space requirements

Test Yourself! Before reading this chapter, test yourself to determine how much study time you will need to devote to this section.

1. What are the two types of devices used by SQL Server, what is each type used for, and what are the two ways you can create new devices with SQL Server?

2. What is a database, who can create a database, and what are the two ways you can create a new database with SQL Server?

3. How do you expand or reduce the size of a database?

4. List all the types of objects you can create in a database, along with how they can be created with SQL Server.

5. What is an allocation unit, an extent, and a page, and how can they be used to help estimate the space requirements of a database?

Answers are located at the end of the chapter...

SQL Server Storage Management Fundamentals

Before beginning the discussion on managing database storage, you need a solid foundation in SQL Server storage management terminology and architecture. This section covers the following:

▶ Database objects

▶ Database storage structures (devices, databases)

▶ Transaction logs

SQL Server Database Objects

SQL Server databases include both database objects and data. *Database objects* are used either to contain data (an object such as a table) or to interact with data (an object such as a stored procedure). In essence, everything managed by SQL Server is an object, which includes every SQL database and everything each database contains. The various objects that can be included in a database include tables, views, indexes, datatypes, defaults, rules, stored procedures, triggers, and constraints.

Tables

Tables are the most important objects within a database because this is where data is stored. Tables are made up of rows (records) and columns (fields) (see fig. 4.1).

Views

Views are created to provide alternate ways to view data stored in tables. Views can be created to display a subset of data from a single table, or two or more tables can be linked and combined to create a view (see fig. 4.2). Views themselves do not contain data, they only point to selected data in tables and present it visually.

Figure 4.1

Tables are the most important database object.

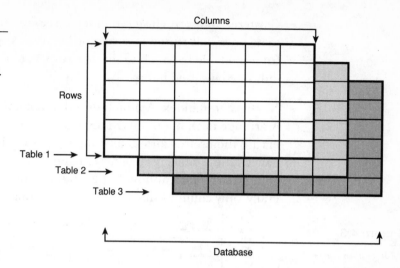

Figure 4.2

Views do not store data, only present it visually.

staff Table

staff_id	f_name	l_name	title	pager_number	hire_date

cert_attained Table

certification	staff_id

View (Combines columns from the above two tables)

staff_id	f_name	l_name	title	pager_number	certification	hire_date

Indexes

Indexes are database objects used to speed up data access. Indexes contain ordered pointers that point to data stored in tables, enabling SQL Server to quickly locate data. Without indexes, SQL Server would have to search every row in a table to find a particular piece of data. Indexes, likes indexes in a book, enable SQL Server to locate data in a table quickly. SQL Server uses two different types of indexes (see fig. 4.3):

▶ **Clustered index.** A clustered index forces the rows in a table to be physically stored in sorted order, using one column from the table by which to sort the rows. A table may have only one clustered index.

▶ **Nonclustered index.** A nonclustered index does not physically arrange data, but points to the data in a table. The pointers are themselves sorted, making it easy to quickly locate data within a table. A table may include an index for every column in a table, although this would be uncommon. Generally, only columns that benefit from sorting have indexes.

Figure 4.3

SQL Server supports clustered and nonclustered indexes.

staff Table Sorted with a Clustered Index

staff_id	f_name	l_name	title	pager_number	hire_date
537	Kristin	Shurley	Tech 1	4823	6-1-95
574	Veronica	Rodriguez	Manager	4887	2-5-95
663	Gail	Jenner	Tech 2	4830	12-1-97
779	Walter	Neil	Tech 2	4811	1-2-95
839	Brett	Marie	Tech 1	4883	4-3-96

In a clustered index, the data is physically sorted. Here, the table is physically sorted by the *staff_id* column.

staff Table

staff_id	f_name	l_name	title	pager_number	hire_date	physical location
574	Veronica	Rodriguez	Manager	4887	2-5-95	bbb
839	Brett	Marie	Tech 1	4883	4-3-96	ddd
537	Kristin	Shurley	Tech 1	4823	6-1-95	aaa
779	Walter	Neil	Tech 2	4811	1-2-95	ppp
663	Gail	Jenner	Tech 2	4830	12-1-97	nnn

Not a table column.

Nonclustered Index

staff_id	pointer
537	aaa
574	bbb
663	nnn
779	ppp
839	ddd

A nonclustered index is an object separate from a table. The table remains in the same physical order as it was created. Above, the nonclustered index is sorted by staff_id. The pointer column points to the physical location in the database where the row is stored, so it can be located quickly.

Datatypes

Datatypes define or describe the type of data that can be entered into a column and how it is stored by SQL Server. A datatype must be specified for every column in a table. A column with the numeric datatype, for example, is designated to store numbers, not letters. Datatypes are often used by database designers to prevent data-entry workers from entering the wrong type of data into a particular column of a row. SQL Server includes many standard datatypes, and custom datatypes can also be created to meet special needs. If you are interested in learning how to create custom datatypes (this subject is not included on the certification test), refer to the Transact-SQL Books Online.

Defaults

Defaults are values that are automatically entered into columns when no values are entered into them during data entry. Defaults can be assigned to any column in a table. Defaults are generally added to a table to reduce the amount of keying a data-entry operator needs to perform. If, for example, most of an organization's sales orders are from the state of California, then the letters "CA" may be added as the default for the state column for the sales table. This way, the data-entry operator would not need to enter the state abbreviation for orders from California because these letters are automatically entered into the state column. But if orders are not from California, then the data-entry operator would have to replace the "CA" with the appropriate state abbreviation. Overall, this should save the data-entry operator some keystrokes.

Rules

Rules are database objects used to control which data can be entered into a table. Database designers use them to help prevent bad data from being entered into a table. A database developer, for example, could create a rule that verifies that the value entered into a particular column was within an acceptable range, and if it were not, the data-entry operator could be notified with a message that the data was incorrect and needs to be corrected. A specific example of this is an age column. A rule might be written that says that if any age younger than 18 or older than 115 is entered, the data-entry operator should be notified to correct the problem.

Stored Procedures

Stored Procedures are powerful and flexible database objects that enable you to automate many tasks. They are made up of precompiled Transact-SQL statements that carry out a predetermined task or series of tasks. SQL Server includes many predefined stored procedures, and Transact-SQL developers can write their own. All built-in stored procedures begin with the characters "sp_" and are stored in the Master database. An example of a built-in stored procedure is sp_help. If this stored procedure is entered from the SQL Query tool (or ISQL/W), then it would be executed, and help information on the databases managed by SQL Server would be displayed. Stored procedures written by database developers can be used to perform any task SQL Server can perform, including inserting, updating, and deleting records.

Triggers

Triggers are a special type of stored procedure that execute whenever specific events occur to a table. Whenever data in a table is inserted, updated, or deleted, for example, a trigger can automatically fire, executing a series of Transact-SQL statements contained within the trigger, performing virtually any task SQL Server is able to perform. Triggers are often used by Transact-SQL developers to help ensure data integrity and perform other tasks. If, for example, a customer master record is to be deleted from the customer sales database, it is important that all the individual customer sales records also be deleted at the same time; otherwise, there would be sales records stored in the database without a corresponding master record. This would result in a loss of database integrity. One way to prevent this from happening is for a database developer to write a trigger that automatically deletes all the individual customer sales records whenever a customer master record is deleted.

Constraints

Constraints are used to enforce data integrity. In many ways, they are like datatypes, defaults, rules, and triggers, which all are also used to enforce data integrity. Constraints are more flexible than these other database objects and are easier to use.

Database Storage Architecture

To be able to manipulate large quantities of data in a reasonable amount of time, SQL Server stores data on physical media in a specific way. This section introduces the SQL Server database storage architecture and introduces the following related terms:

▶ Device

▶ SQL Server database

▶ Page

▶ Extent

▶ Allocation unit

▶ Transaction log

What Is a Device?

The two types of devices are database devices (used to store databases and transaction logs) and dump devices (used to store database backups). This chapter focuses on database devices.

A database *device* is an NTFS or FAT file stored on physical media, such as a hard disk, and is used to preallocate physical storage space to be used by a database or transaction log. Before a SQL Server database or transaction log can be created, a device must first be created. A single device may hold one or more SQL Server databases, or a single SQL Server database may exist on one or more devices.

How SQL Server Stores Data in a Database

After one or more devices have been created, the DBA can create a database. Databases have to be created before any data or objects can be stored in them. In a sense, a database is just a preallocated portion of a device that will be used to store database objects and data. When a database is created, SQL Server allocates space within the database in a fixed way using special data structures (units of measurement). These include the page, extent, and allocation unit (see fig. 4.4).

Figure 4.4

Databases are made up of pages, extents, and allocation units.

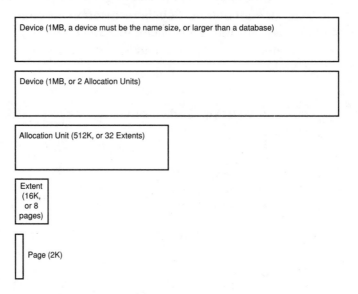

Device (1MB, a device must be the name size, or larger than a database)

Device (1MB, or 2 Allocation Units)

Allocation Unit (512K, or 32 Extents)

Extent (16K, or 8 pages)

Page (2K)

What Is a Page?

All information in SQL Server is stored on a *page*, which is the smallest data structure used in a database. Each page stores 2 KB (2,048 bytes) of information. All pages include a 32-byte page header, leaving 2,016 bytes to store data. The header is used by SQL Server to uniquely identify the data stored on the page. SQL Server has five different pages types:

▶ **Allocation Pages.** Used to control the allocation of pages to tables and indexes within a database.

▶ **Data and Log Pages.** Used to store database data and transaction log data. Data stored on each page is stored in data rows. Each page can store up to 256 rows, and the maximum size on one row is 1962 bytes. SQL Server does not allow rows to cross pages.

▶ **Index Pages.** Used to store database indexing information.

▶ **Distribution Pages.** Used to store information about the indexes in a database.

▶ **Text/Image Pages.** Used to store large amounts of text or binary large objects (BLOBs).

What Is an Extent?

An *extent* is a data structure made up of eight contiguous pages (8×2 KB = 16 KB). SQL Server automatically allocates an extent whenever a new database object, such as a table, is created. Each extent can include only one database object.

What Is an Allocation Unit?

An *allocation unit* is a data structure made up of 32 extents (32×16 KB = 512 KB), or 256 pages. Whenever a new database is created, space is allocated in multiple allocation units of 512 KB each. Because a database object takes up at least one extent (as described previously), a single allocation unit can contain up to 32 objects.

Transaction Logs

Whenever a database is created by using SQL Server, a transaction log is created at the same time. A *transaction log* is a reserved storage area on a device used to automatically record all changes made to database objects, before the changes are actually written to the database. This is an important fault-tolerant feature of SQL Server that helps prevent a database from becoming corrupted.

Where Transaction Logs Are Created

When a database is created, a device must be specified on which to create it. The same is true for transaction logs. When a database is created, the location of the device used to store the transaction log must also be specified. Although it is possible to store both a database and its transaction log on the same device, this is not recommended.

Some of the benefits of creating a transaction log on a device separate from its database include the following:

▶ The transaction log can be backed up separately from the database.

▶ Up-to-date recovery is made possible in the event of server failure.

▶ The transaction log does not compete with the database for device space.

▶ Transaction log space can be easily monitored.

▶ The contention between writes to the database and transaction log is reduced, which can increase performance.

None of these benefits are available if the database and transaction log occupy the same device.

How Do Transaction Logs Provide Fault Tolerance?

SQL Server considers a *transaction* as a set of operations (Transact-SQL statements that change a database) that are to be completed at one time, as if they were a single operation. To maintain data integrity, transactions must either be completed fully or not performed at all. If for some reason, such as a server failure, a transaction is partially applied to a database, the database has become corrupted.

SQL Servers uses a database's transaction log to prevent incomplete transactions from corrupting data. The following is how SQL Server uses a transaction log to prevent data corruption:

▶ A user performs a task at the client (front-end of the database) that modifies an object, such as a table, within the database (on the SQL Server).

▶ When a transaction begins, as above, a "begin transaction" marker is recorded in the transaction log, not directly in the database. Following this marker is a before and after image of the object being changed. This is followed by a commit transaction marker in the transaction log. The transaction log records every transaction in this same way.

▶ Periodically, a *checkpoint* process occurs, and all completed transactions recorded in the transaction log are applied to the database. This process also creates a checkpoint marker in the transaction log, which is used during the recovery process to determine which transactions have and have not been applied to the database.

▶ A transaction log will continue to grow, retaining all transactions, until it is backed up. At that point the transactions are removed (truncated), making room for more transactions.

Should a server fail between the time a transaction is entered and stored in the transaction log, and the time it is applied to the database, or if the server should fail at the exact moment the transaction log is being applied to the database, the database does not become corrupted. When the server is brought back up, SQL Server begins a recovery process. It examines the database and transaction log, looking for transactions that were not applied and for transactions that were partially applied, but not complete. If transactions in the transaction log are found that were not applied, they are applied at this time (rolled forward). If partial transactions are found to have been made and not completed, then these are removed from the database (rolled back). The recovery process is automatic, and all the information necessary to maintain a database's integrity is maintained in the transaction log. This capability substantially increases SQL Server's fault tolerance.

Now that you have a basic foundation in SQL Server storage terminology and architecture, it is time to introduce you to the specific objectives covered by the System Administration for Microsoft SQL Server test.

How to Create Devices

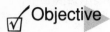 Objective

Before a SQL Server database can be created, one or more devices must be created. *Devices* are physical files that reside on a server's hard disk that act as preallocated storage areas for databases and transactions logs. Normally, you create two devices for every database you create. One device, called the *database device*, is used to store one or more databases. The other device, *transaction log device*, is used to store one or more database transaction logs. This section introduces you to rules for creating devices, covers how to create devices by using SQL Enterprise Manager, and shows how to create devices by using Transact-SQL statements. It also touches on how to manipulate the size of a device.

Rules for Creating Devices

Devices are easy to create if you keep the following in mind:

▶ Before any new database and transaction log can be created, one or more devices must be created.

▶ A single device can hold a single database or transaction log or it may hold multiple databases and transaction logs. Generally, for ease of administration, a separate device is created for each database and transaction log.

▶ Only an system administrator can create and manage devices. This capability cannot be delegated to anyone else.

▶ The minimum size of a device is 1 MB.

▶ Whenever a new device is created, its information is stored in the *sysdevices* table in the Master database.

▶ When creating a device, it must be assigned both a logical and physical name. The logical name is how the device is known to SQL Server and the SA. The physical name is how the device is known to the operating system.

▶ Device logical names must follow these rules:

1. They can range from 1 to 30 characters.

2. The first character of the name must be a letter or one of the following symbols: _, @, or #.

3. Characters after the first character can include letters, numbers, or the symbols _, @, or #

4. Names must not have any spaces, unless the name is surrounded by quotes, which is not recommended.

▶ Device physical names follow the rules of the operating system being used.

▶ Devices must be created on the local physical server's hard disks. Devices may not be created on devices accessed over a network.

▶ Before creating any devices, be sure than any fault-tolerant measures have been implemented, tested, and are ready for use.

▶ When a device is created (or later by using the sp_diskdefault stored procedure), it can be specified as a default device. If a device has been specified as the default, the SQL Server can automatically use it should the SA (system administrator) create a new database and not specify a specific device to use for the new database. Default devices are automatically used for databases in alphabetical order of their name. When SQL Server is first installed, the Master device is automatically a default device. You will want to change this because you do not want anyone to accidentally create a database on the Master device. Normally, an SA assigns a specific database to a specific device because this is easier to administer, which means that specifying a device as a default device is not required.

▶ Device size can be increased, but not reduced.

Should You Use SQL Enterprise Manager or Transact-SQL Statements to Manage SQL Server?

Although most DBAs will want to manage SQL Server by using SQL Enterprise Manager, some prefer to use Transact-SQL statements instead. SQL Enterprise Manager is commonly used because it is easy to use and the interface is graphical. The disadvantage is that most tasks, such as creating a new device or database, cannot be automated. The advantage of using Transact-SQL statements instead of using SQL Enterprise Manager to perform the same task is that the task can be automated by creating a SQL script. A *SQL script* is a collection of Transact-SQL statements that can be played back over and over again, saving many keystrokes. Of course, the script has to be created in the first place. The topic of how to create scripts is beyond the scope of this book (and is not discussed on the test), but you can look up more information on this topic in the Transact-SQL Books Online.

The following sections describe how to perform many database management tasks using both SQL Enterprise Manager and Transact-SQL. Both are included, even though you may never use both, because you need to know how to use both methods for the certification test.

How to Create Devices Using SQL Enterprise Manager

The steps necessary to create devices by using SQL Enterprise Manager follow:

1. From the SQL Enterprise Manager's Server Manager window, select a SQL Server and open its folder by clicking the plus sign. Various SQL Server folders display.

2. Open the Database Devices folder by clicking the plus sign next to it. A list of all the current database devices for this SQL Server is display (see fig. 4.5).

3. Right-click on the Database Devices folder and select New Device from the menu. The New Database Device dialog box appears (see fig. 4.6).

Figure 4.5

All SQL Server database devices can be viewed from this screen.

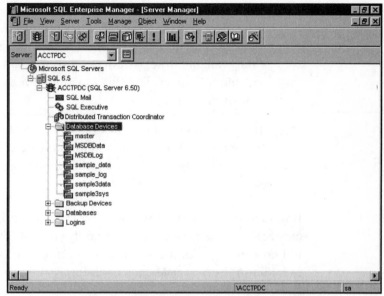

Figure 4.6

New devices are created from this dialog box.

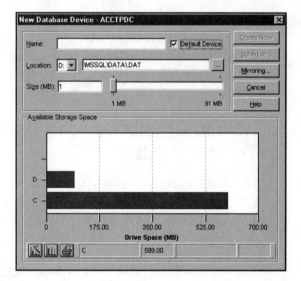

4. In the Name box, enter the logical name of the database device, following the logical naming rules described previously.

5. In the Location boxes, select the disk drive, full pathname, and physical name of the database device. SQL Server fills these boxes with default values; you may leave the defaults or change them to meet your needs.

6. In the Size box, enter in MB the size of the new database device. You also can drag the slider button to select the desired size. The bottom part of the screen is a graphical view of the available storage devices on your computer, with the available free space. Use this as a guide for sizing and locating your devices.

7. After you have finished, click the Create Now button to create the device. If you do not want to create the device now but want to schedule it for another time, you can do so by selecting the Schedule button.

If you chose Create Now, the device is created, and you receive a message that the device was successfully created. The new device will now appear with the other devices under the Database Devices folder in the Server Manager window.

 Tip

When you create a new device, it is a good idea to create two devices, one after another. One will be used to store a new database, and the other will be used to store the transaction log for the new database.

How to Create Devices Using Transact-SQL

The Transact-SQL statement to create a new device is the DISK INIT statement. This Transact-SQL statement, like all Transact-SQL statements, can be entered using the SQL Query tool, or by using some similar tool, such as ISQL/W.

The syntax for the DISK INIT Transact-SQL statement is

```
DISK INIT
    NAME = 'logical_name',
    PHYSNAME = 'physical_name',
    VDEVNO = virtual_device_number,
    SIZE = number_of_2 KB _blocks
```

where:

logical_name = The logical name assigned to the device.

physical_name = The physical name and location of the physical file that is the device. Includes the full path name.

virtual_device_number = The virtual number is used to uniquely identify the device. Each device must have a unique virtual number from 0 through 255. Device number 0 is reserved for the Master device. If you do not know which virtual device numbers have already been used, you can use the sp_helpdevice stored procedure to tell you. You can assign any virtual device number from 0 through 255 that is not currently being used. When creating a device with SQL Enterprise Manager, you do not need to specify a virtual device number because it will select an appropriate number for you.

number_of_2 KB _blocks = The number of 2 KB blocks needed to equal the total space you want allocated to the device. The minimum size is 512 2 KB blocks.

Example:

```
DISK INIT
    NAME = 'acct_data',
    PHYSNAME = 'c:\mssql\data\acct_data.dat',
    VDEVNO = 100,
    SIZE = 2560
```

To create a new device by using Transact-SQL, follow these steps:

1. Load the SQL Query tool (or similar tool). Be sure the Query tab is selected.

2. Select the Master database from the DB drop-down menu. New devices must be created from the Master database.

3. Enter the Transact-SQL statement.

4. Execute the statement. The Results window appears with the message:

```
"This command did not return data, and it did not return
any rows."
```

The device has been created. The new device will not be displayed in the Database Devices folder until you refresh the screen by selecting View, Refresh from the drop-down menu.

How to Increase the Size of a Device by Using SQL Enterprise Manager

If you discover that you need to increase the size of a device to provide more room for a database or transaction log, you can increase it at any time by using SQL Enterprise Manager or Transact-SQL. Database devices may not be reduced in size.

Following are the steps required to increase the size of a device with SQL Enterprise Manager:

1. From the SQL Enterprise Manager's Server Manager window, select a SQL Server and open its folder by clicking the plus sign. Various SQL Server folders are displayed.

2. Open the Database Devices folder by clicking the plus sign next to it. A list of all the current database devices for this SQL Server are displayed.

3. Right-click the database device you want to increase in size, then select Edit. The Edit Database Device dialog box appears (see fig. 4.7).

4. The Size box will contain the current size of the device. Change this number to the new size you want. If the current size is 4 MB and you want to double its size, for example, change the 4 to an 8.

5. After you have entered the new size, click the Change Now button, and the device size will be increased. You will receive no message telling you what happened. To verify that the size was increased, right-click the device, select Edit, and view the new size from the Edit Database Device dialog box.

Figure 4.7

A device's size can be increased in the Edit Database Device dialog box.

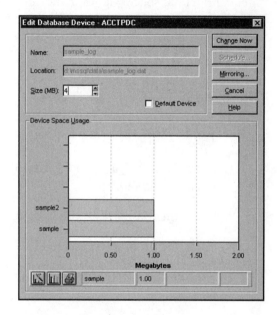

How to Increase the Size of a Device by Using Transact-SQL

The Transact-SQL statement to increase the size of a device is DISK RESIZE. Like all Transact-SQL statements, this Transact-SQL statement can be entered by using the SQL Query tool or a similar tool, such as ISQL/W.

The syntax for the DISK RESIZE Transact-SQL statement is

```
DISK RESIZE
     NAME = 'logical_name',
     SIZE = number_of_2 KB _blocks
```

where:

logical_name = The logical name assigned to the device.

number_of_2 KB _blocks = The number of 2 KB blocks needed to equal the total space you want allocated to the device.

Example:

```
DISK RESIZE
    NAME = 'acct_data',
    SIZE = 12560
```

To expand a device by using Transact-SQL, follow these steps:

1. Load the SQL Query tool (or similar tool). Be sure the Query tab is selected.

2. Select the Master database from the DB drop-down menu.

3. Enter the Transact-SQL statement.

4. Execute the statement. The Results window appears with the message:

   ```
   "This command did not return data, and it did not return
   any rows."
   ```

The device has been expanded. The newly sized device will not be reflected in the Server Manager window until it has been refreshed by choosing View, Refresh from the drop-down window.

Although a device cannot be directly reduced in size, there are ways to accomplish the same effect. The easiest way to reclaim wasted disk space due to an overly large device is to create a new device of the appropriate size, use SQL Server's Transfer Manager to make a copy of the old database onto the new device, and then delete the old device and database.

How to Create Databases

 Objective

After the database and transaction log devices have been created, a database can be created. When you create a database, what you are really doing is allocating space on a device to store database objects and data, and you are also creating the system tables that exist in all SQL Server databases. After the database is created, you can add the necessary tables, views, indexes, and other objects that will make up your database.

When you create a database, you specify where the transaction log will be located. If you do not specify a specific device for the transaction log, then it is placed on the same device as the database itself. As was mentioned previously, it is highly recommended that a database and its transaction log be placed on separate devices.

Whenever a new database is created, SQL Server uses the Model database as a template. The Model database, which is automatically created when SQL Server is installed, contains all the system tables necessary to track and manage all the objects stored in a database. Because the Model database is 1 MB in size, any database you create also has to be at least 1 MB in size.

If you want every new database you create to have specific objects, database user IDs, or permissions, you can directly modify the Model database to include them. After doing this, every time you create a new database, the new database has these same features (because Model is used as the basis for all new databases).

The upcoming sections discuss the act of creating databases in greater detail.

Tips for Creating New Databases

Keep the following in mind when creating new databases:

▶ By default, only the SA can create a new database, although the SA may delegate this responsibility to others by issuing a specific statement permission.

▶ The name assigned to a database follows the same rules as were described previously for the logical name for a device. A database does not have a physical name.

▶ All new databases are copies of the Model database, which means that a new database cannot be any smaller than the current size of Model.

▶ Whenever a database is created, a transaction log is automatically created. By default, a transaction log is created on the same device as the database. A transaction log may also be stored on a separate device of its own, if specified during database creation. Also, a transaction log originally created on the same device as the database can be moved at any time to a separate device of its own.

▶ A single database may be stored on a single device or spread over multiple devices.

▶ A database can both be expanded and reduced in size.

▶ Whenever a new database is created, SQL Server automatically updates the *sysdatabases* and *sysusages* tables in the Master database.

▶ The "For Load" option can be set when creating a new database. This option is only selected if you intend to create a new database, then populate it by restoring a database backup to the new database. Otherwise, do not choose this option.

How to Create a Database Using SQL Enterprise Manager

Below are the steps necessary to create a database when using SQL Enterprise Manager:

1. From the SQL Enterprise Manager's Server Manager window, select a SQL Server and open its folder by clicking the plus sign. Various SQL Server folders display.

2. Open the Database Devices folder by clicking the plus sign next to it. A list of all the current databases for this SQL Server displays (see fig. 4.8).

Figure 4.8

All SQL Server database can be viewed from this screen.

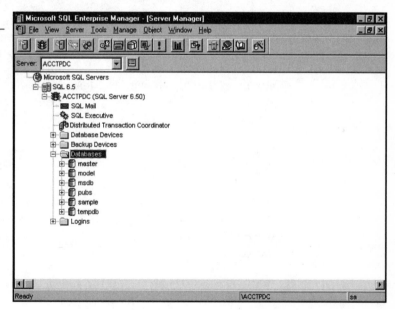

3. Right-click the Database folder, and then select New Database from the menu. The New Database dialog box appears (see fig. 4.9).

4. In the Name box, enter the name of the new database.

Figure 4.9

New databases are created in the New Database dialog box.

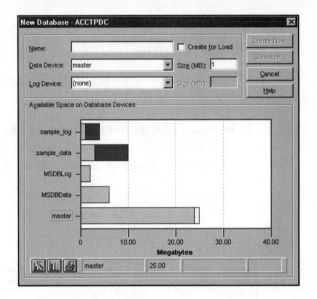

5. In the Data Device box, select the appropriate database device from the drop-down box. The available devices are listed at the bottom of the screen, along with the free space available on each device.

6. In the Size box, enter the size of the new database in megabytes.

7. In the Log Device box, select the appropriate database device from the drop-down box. This assumes you want to place the transaction log on a separate device than the database.

8. In the Size box, enter in MB the size of the new transaction log.

9. To create the new database now, click the Create Now button. If you want to schedule the creation of this database for another time, you can do so by clicking the Schedule button.

If you selected Create Now, the database is created immediately, and you receive no feedback from SQL Server telling you the database was created. To verify its creation, view it under the Databases folder in the Server Manager window.

Whenever you create or alter the size of a database, you should document all your steps. If you should ever have to re-create the database and restore a database backup to it, you will have to re-create the database following the exact same steps you used to create the original database. If you do not have these steps documented, you may not be able to restore your database from a backup.

How to Create Databases Using Transact-SQL

The Transact-SQL statement to create a new database is the CREATE DATABASE statement. This Transact-SQL statement, like all Transact-SQL statements, can be entered by using the SQL Query tool or a similar tool, such as ISQL/W.

The syntax for the CREATE DATABASE Transact-SQL statement is

```
CREATE DATABASE database_name
    ON database_device = size, database_device = size, . . .
    LOG ON database_device = size, . . .
```

where:

database_name = the name assigned to the new database to be created.

database_device = the logical name of the device used to contain the newly created database.

size = the size, in megabytes, of the database and its transaction log.

Example:

```
CREATE DATABASE acct
    ON acct_data = 5
    LOG ON acct_log = 1
```

To create the database:

1. Load the SQL Query tool (or similar tool). Be sure the Query tab is selected.

2. Select the Master database from the DB drop-down menu. New databases must be created from the Master database.

3. Enter the Transact-SQL statement.

4. Execute the statement. The Results window appears with these messages, "CREATE DATABASE: allocating *x* pages on disk '*device_name*'" and "CREATE DATABASE: allocating *x* pages on disk '*device_name*'".

The database has been created. The new database will not be reflected in the Server Manager window until it has been refreshed by choosing View, Refresh from the drop-down window.

Setting Database Options

Every database has a variety of database options that must be changed to perform certain database tasks. These options can be changed from SQL Enterprise Manager or by using the sp_dboption stored procedure. Each database's option setting is separate from all other databases on a SQL Server. The following offers a brief look at the various database options:

▶ **Select Into/Bulk Copy.** This option must be set before any non-logged operation can be performed to a database. A *non-logged operation* is one that bypasses the transaction log and directly alters a database. Examples of non-logged operations include a fast bcp, WRITETEXT, and SELECT INTO Transact-SQL statements. This option is off by default.

▶ **DBO Use Only.** This option configures the database so that only the DBO (database owner) can access the database. If turned on while users are accessing the database, they are not logged out, but no new users can log in. DBO Use Only is often used when performing a bcp out from the database, and this is the setting made to a new database when it is created with the FOR LOAD option. This option is off by default.

▶ **No Checkpoint on Recovery.** Normally, when SQL Server starts, it performs an automatic recovery, whether one is required or not. This process adds a checkpoint record to the transaction log, which tells SQL Server at which point the last automatic recovery was made. This option, which prevents SQL Server from adding a checkpoint record to the transaction log, is often used when an SA performs manual online mirroring between a production and standby server. By default, this option is set to off.

▶ **Read Only.** This option sets the database so that it is read-only and that no user can alter any record in the database. Read Only is used whenever you want to make a database read-only. By default, this option is set to off.

▶ **Single User.** This option sets the database so that only one user can access it at a time. It is most often used whenever you want to prevent users from accessing a database, such as when you run the DBCC SHRINKDB, DBCC CHECKAL-LOC, or DBCC UPDATEUSAGE commands. By default, this option is set to off.

▶ **Columns Null by Default.** This option determines whether columns in a table are set to NULL or NOT NULL by default. Turning this option on makes SQL Server comply with the ANSI standard for SQL Databases. The default is off.

▶ **Truncate Log on Checkpoint.** This options tells SQL Server to automatically truncate a database's transaction log every time a checkpoint is executed. Normally, a transaction log is only truncated when it is manually truncated or when a backup is made of the transaction log. This option is sometimes set when a database is under development, and there exists the possibility that the transaction may become full before it is manually truncated, or truncated when a backup of the transaction log is made. By default this option is set to off.

▶ **Offline.** This option appears on databases that have been marked for distribution onto removable media. When set to offline, a database cannot be accessed. By default this option does not appear with a normal database.

▶ **Published.** This option appears on databases that have been marked for publication in a replication scenario and indicates that its tables can be published. By default this option does not appear with a normal database.

▶ **Subscribed.** This option appears on databases that have been marked as a subscriber in a replication scenario and indicates that the database can be subscribed. By default this option does not appear with a normal database.

To change any of these settings from SQL Enterprise Manager, follow these steps:

1. From the SQL Enterprise Manager's Server Manager window, select a SQL Server and open its folder by clicking the plus sign. Various SQL Server folders display.

2. Open the Database folder by clicking the plus sign next to it. A list of all the current database for this SQL Server displays.

3. Right-click the database whose size you want to change, and then select Edit. The Edit Database dialog box appears.

4. Click the Options tab at the top of the Edit Database dialog box to display the database options. You can change them by clicking the appropriate check box.

How to Alter the Size of a Database Using SQL Enterprise Manager

 Objective

Unlike a device, a database may be increased and reduced in size. The next two sections take a look at how to change the size of a database by using either SQL Enterprise Manager or Transact-SQL.

Following are the steps required to increase (and decrease) the size of a device by using SQL Enterprise Manager:

1. From the SQL Enterprise Manager's Server Manager window, select a SQL Server and open its folder by clicking the plus sign. Various SQL Server folders display.

2. Open the Database folder by clicking the plus sign. A list of all the current databases for this SQL Server displays.

3. Right-click on the database you want to change in size and select Edit. The Edit Database dialog box appears (see fig. 4.10).

Figure 4.10

Databases can be expanded or shrunk by using the Edit Database dialog box.

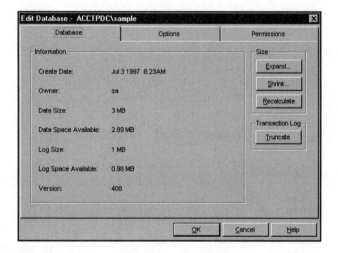

4. To expand a database, click the Expand button, and the Expand Database dialog box appears (see fig. 4.11).

5. From the Data Device drop-down box, select the database device on which you want to expand the database and then enter in megabytes the size you want. If you want to expand the database by 5 additional megabytes, for example, enter a 5 in the Size box. The bar charts indicate which devices are available, along with the amount of free space on each, which can be used for database expansion.

Figure 4.11

Both a database and its transaction log can be expanded by using the Expand Database dialog box.

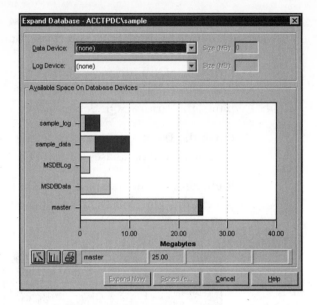

6. If appropriate, from the Log Device drop-down box, select the database device you want to expand the transaction log on. Enter in the Size box the size (in MB) by which you want to expand the transaction log.

7. After you have specified all the appropriate information, click on the Expand Now button, and the database (or transaction log or both) will be increased in size.

8. To shrink the size of a database, choose the Shrink button from the Edit Database dialog box, which displays the message:

   ```
   "The database must be set to single user mode for the
   duration of this dialog. Continue?"
   ```

   To shrink a database, the database will automatically be put into single user mode, which means that no one can access the database during this process. Click on Yes to continue. The Shrink Database dialog box appears (see fig. 4.12).

Figure 4.12

*Databases are
reduced with the
Shrink Database
dialog box.*

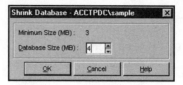

9. The dialog box tells you the smallest you can shrink the database and its current size. To reduce the size, enter in megabytes the final size you want the database to be, without exceeding the minimum possible size.

10. After you are done, click the OK button, and the database is shrunk.

How to Change the Size of a Database Using Transact-SQL

 Objective

The Transact-SQL statement to increase the size of a database is ALTER DATABASE. To reduce the size of a database, use the DBCC SHRINKDB command. This Transact-SQL statement, like all Transact-SQL statements, can be entered by using the SQL Query tool or a similar tool, such as ISQL/W.

The syntax for the ALTER DATABASE Transact-SQL statement is

```
ALTER DATABASE database_name
     On device_name = size, device_name = size, . . .
```

where:

database_name = the name of the database to be expanded.

device_name = the logical name assigned to the device where the database is to be expanded.

size = the number in megabytes of the amount you want to expand the database from its current size. If you want to increase the database by 5 MB, enter a 5 for size.

Example:

```
ALTER DATABASE acct
     ON acct_data = 5
```

The syntax for the DBCC SHRINKDB Transact-SQL statement is

```
DBCC SHRINKDB (database_name, size)
```

where:

database_name = the name of the database to be shrunk.

size = the new size, in 2 KB pages, you want the database to be.

Example:

```
DBCC SHRINKDB (acct, 2048)
```

To change the size of a database using Transact-SQL, follow these steps:

1. Load the SQL Query tool (or similar tool). Be sure the Query tab is selected.

2. Select the name of the database to be changed from the DB drop-down menu.

3. Enter the Transact-SQL statement.

4. Execute the statement.

The size of the database has been changed. The newly sized device will not be reflected in the Server Manager window until it has been refreshed by choosing View, Refresh from the drop-down window.

 Note

Sometimes when you shrink a database, you are not able to shrink it as small as you would like. The minimum size as stated by SQL Enterprise Manager, for example, may be larger than it can actually be shrunk. If you know that a database can be made smaller than as indicated by SQL Enterprise Manager, you can use another method to reduce the size of the database. Use the Transfer Manager program to copy the database to a new device. This enables you to reclaim lost space. After the database has been successfully copied, the old one can be dropped.

How to Drop Databases and Devices

Whenever you are finished using a database or device, they can be dropped (deleted) from SQL Server. Both can be dropped using either SQL Enterprise Manager or Transact-SQL (DROP DATA-BASE, sp_dropdevice).

To drop a database or device by using SQL Enterprise Manager, right-click the database or device you want to drop and select delete. You will receive a warning message that you are about to delete something. Click the Yes button to accept the deletion.

You will be reminded if you delete a device that contains one or more active databases. If you choose to delete the device, SQL Server will also delete any databases currently on the device.

SQL Server does not automatically delete the physical file that represents a device from your computer's hard disk. You will have to remove the physical file manually by using NT Explorer.

How to Create Database Objects

Although database objects are most often created by database developers, it is important that the DBA understand how they are created. The following sections take a look at how to create several database objects, including tables, views, and indexes, by using Transact-SQL statements. You will need to know how to create objects for the test, but you will not have to remember the exact syntax of the examples provided here. *The most important thing to remember is the process of how objects in general are created in a database.*

How to Create a Table

Generally after creating a database, the next step is to add the necessary tables to store data. Tables are created with the CREATE TABLE Transact-SQL statement. By default, only the SA, or the DBO of a database can create a new table. This task can be granted to others by the SA or the DBO of the database.

Before you create a table, you need to define the columns (fields) that will make up each table. You also need to determine each column's datatype and width. *Datatypes* are used to specify the type of data that will be stored in each column, such as text, numbers, dates, and so forth. The width specifies how may characters may be entered into a column. Table 4.1 illustrates the SQL Server standard datatypes.

Table 4.1

Standard Datatypes	
Data Type	Transact-SQL Name
Approximate Numbers	float(n), real
Binary	binary(n), varbinary(n)
Character	char(n), varchar(n)
Date & Time	datetime, smalldatetime
Dollars & Cents	money, smallmoney
Exact Numbers	decimal, numeric
Integers	int, smallint, tinyint
Special	bit, timestamp, user-defined
Text & Images	text, image

n = number of characters

The syntax for the CREATE TABLE Transact-SQL statement is

```
CREATE TABLE table_name
    ( column_name column_properties,
    . . .
    column_name column_properties )
```

where:

table_name = the name assigned to the new table to be created.

column_name = the name of the column.

column_properties = the datatype and width of the column.

Example:

```
CREATE TABLE employees
    ( employee_id int,
    f_name char(20),
    l_name char(35),
    title char(25),
    pager_number char(10),
    hire_date smalldatetime )
```

To create a new table object:

1. Load the SQL Query tool (or similar tool). Be sure the Query tab is selected.

2. Select the name of the database from the DB drop-down menu where you want to create a new table. Tables must be created in the databases where they belong.

3. Enter the Transact-SQL statement as given previously.

4. Execute the statement. The Results window appears with the message:

   ```
   "This command did not return data, and it did not return
   any rows."
   ```

The table was created. This can be verified by opening the Tables folder of the database where the table was created.

How to Create a View

After one or more tables have been created in a database, views can be created using the CREATE VIEW Transact-SQL statement.

Views are database objects that enable you to view data in one or more tables in an alternate way you specify.

Views are not tables and do not include data. They are special objects that enable you to view data in preexisting tables. Views are virtual tables that only exist when displayed.

Views can be used instead of tables to query, view, insert, update, and delete data in tables. Views can also be used to define queries. For example, instead of typing in the same query again and again, a query can be assigned to a view, and when the view is displayed, the query is automatically run, and the view displays the results of the query. This includes queries run on a single table, and on multiple tables.

Views are also used to help ensure security—only displaying data from columns that a user is permitted to view—and they are also used to create derived columns, often used in calculations. For the most part, view creation is left up to the database developer. The DBA generally does not create views on a regular basis.

The syntax for the CREATE VIEW Transact-SQL statement is

```
CREATE VIEW view_name
AS
SELECT column_name, . . column_name
FROM table_name
```

where:

view_name = the name assigned to the new view to be created.

column_name = the name of the column(s) to be included in the view.

table_name = the name of the table on which the view is based.

Example:

```
CREATE VIEW employee_view
AS
SELECT employee_id, f_name, l_name, title, pager_number
From employee
```

To create a view:

1. Load the SQL Query tool (or similar tool). Be sure the Query tab is selected.

2. Select the name of the database where you want to create the view from the DB drop-down menu. Views must be created in the databases where they belong.

3. Enter the CREATE VIEW Transact-SQL statement as given previously.

4. Execute the statement. The Results window appears with the message:

```
"This command did not return data, and it did not return
any rows."
```

The view was created. This can be verified by opening the Views folder of the database where the view was created.

How to Create an Index

Most tables in a database need one or more indexes, which are created using the CREATE INDEX Transact-SQL statement. Indexes are used to both enforce the uniqueness of rows in a table and to speed data retrieval during queries. Indexes are database objects, just like tables and views.

SQL Server enables you to create two types of indexes:

▶ **Clustered index.** Forces all the rows in a table to be physically stored in sorted order, using one column from the table by which to sort the rows. A table may only have one clustered index.

▶ **Unclustered index.** Does not physically arrange data, but instead points to the data in a table. The pointers are themselves sorted, making it easy to locate data within a table quickly. A nonclustered index exists as an object separate from the table. Virtually any column of a table can have its own index.

Although most indexes are created by the database developer, the DBA often gets involved with indexes after the fact because indexes play a significant part in how a database is optimized for speed.

The syntax for the CREATE INDEX Transact-SQL statement is

```
CREATE [UNIQUE] [CLUSTERED¦NONCLUSTERED] INDEX index_name
ON table_name (column_name, . . column_name)
```

where:

UNIQUE = if used, specifies that the index to be created is to be unique. If not specified, the index will not be unique.

CLUSTERED|NONCLUSTERED = used to specify the type of index to be created. Use CLUSTERED to create a clustered index and use NONCLUSTERED to create a nonclustered index. Only one or the other may be used.

index_name = the name assigned to the new index to be created.

table_name = the name of the table for which the index is being created.

column_name = the name of the column(s) to be included in the index.

Example:

```
CREATE CLUSTERED INDEX employee_id_idx
ON employee (employee_id)
```

To create an index:

1. Load the SQL Query tool (or similar tool). Be sure the Query tab is selected.

2. Select the name of the database where you want to create an index from the DB drop-down menu. Indexes must be created in the databases where they belong.

3. Enter the CREATE INDEX Transact-SQL statements as given previously.

4. Execute the statement. The Results window appears with the message:

```
"This command did not return data, and it did not return
any rows."
```

The index is created.

How to Create Databases on Removable Media

SQL Server includes the capability to copy a database from a SQL Server to virtually any form of removable media, to move the database to another SQL Server, and then to install it. The reproduced database is read-only.

This capability provides an easy way to move information from one SQL Server to any other SQL Server in the world. Although SQL Server replication can provide the same benefit, replication sometimes is not feasible (the required dedicated connection is too expensive or not available, for example), and moving a SQL database from one server to another using removable media is the only way to easily and inexpensively move data.

The removable media can include diskettes, CD-ROMs, writable optical disks, zip drives, and virtually any type of removable media that is available to all the servers involved in the distribution of data.

Using removable media to share data between SQL Servers is a multi-step process, including the following:

▶ Preparing the original database to be reproduced onto removable media

▶ Reproducing the database

▶ Installing the database onto the new SQL Server

▶ If appropriate, removing the database from the new server

Only an SA can perform these steps. These steps cannot be performed from SQL Enterprise Manager, and they must be performed by using Transact-SQL statements.

The rest of this section covers how to perform these steps.

How to Prepare a SQL Server Database for Distribution

A SQL database that is to be shared via removable media is similar to any other SQL Server database. When creating and populating a database to be shared, keep the following in mind:

▶ All the objects created in the database must be owned by the SA or DBO.

▶ Specific database user IDs must not be created in the database, nor should any permissions be assigned to individual database user IDs. Use the guest database user ID and the public group to allow access into the database, if required.

▶ The database must be created on one device, the transaction log must be created on another device, and the system catalog tables for the database must be created on a third device. This can be performed for you automatically, as described in the following text.

To create a new database that will be used for distribution, the stored procedure sp_create_removable must be used. The syntax is

```
sp_create_removable dbname,
syslogical, 'sysphysical', syssize,
loglogical, 'logphysical', logsize,
datalogical, 'dataphysical', datasize, . . .
```

where:

dbname = the name of the database that will be created for use on the removable media.

syslogical = the logical name of the device that will contain the system catalog tables.

sysphysical = the physical name, including path, of the device that will hold the system catalog tables.

syssize = the size, in megabytes, of the device that will hold the system catalog tables.

loglogical = the logical name of the device that will contain the transaction log.

logphysical = the physical name, including path, of the device that will contain the transaction log.

logsize = the size, in megabytes, of the device that will contain the transaction log.

datalogical = the logical name of a device that will contain the data tables.

dataphysical = the physical name, including path, of a device that will contain the data tables.

datasize = the size, in megabytes, of a device that will contain the data tables.

Example:

```
sp_create_removable acctcopy,
acctsys, 'c:\mssql\data\acctsys.dat', 2,
acctlog, 'c:\mssql\data\acctlog.dat', 2,
acctdata, 'c:\mssql\data\acctdata.dat', 5
```

When this stored procedure is executed, the following occurs:

1. The database is copied onto three new devices, divided into three pieces.

2. One device includes the system catalog tables, one device contains the transaction log, and one contains the data tables.

The database has now been created as required. The next job is to populate the database with data.

After the database has been populated with data and is ready for distribution, another stored procedure, sp_certify_removable, which acts on the newly copied database, must be executed on the three new devices. This stored procedure prepares the populated database for distribution.

The syntax for sp_certify_removable is

```
sp_certify_removable dbname[, AUTO]
```

where:

dbname = the name of the database to be verified.

AUTO = if required, gives ownership of the database and all database objects to the SA, and drops any user-created database users and any assigned permissions.

Example:

```
sp_certify_removable acctcopy
```

The following happens when this stored procedure is executed:

1. The database is checked to ensure that no user-created database objects exist, that no permissions are assigned, that the SA is the DBO of the database and all database objects, and that all device fragments are contiguous and in order.

2. The transaction log is truncated and moved to the system device, and the transaction log device is dropped.

3. The database is set to offline.

4. Verification information is written to a text file in the directory c:\mssql\log under the name of CertifyR_*database_name*.txt. This information is required later when the database is installed onto another SQL Server.

How to Reproduce the Database

After the database has been prepared as described, the two remaining devices (the one that holds the system tables and transaction log, and the one that holds the data tables) can be physically copied by using standard operating system commands onto the appropriate removable data for reproduction and transportation to other physical servers.

How to Install a Removable Database onto a New SQL Server

When installing a removable database onto a new server, you have two choices about how to copy the two devices from the removable media to a hard disk on the new SQL Server. At the very least, you must copy the device that contains the system tables and transaction log onto the SQL Server's hard disk because these files need to be on read-write media in order to be installed into SQL Server. The data device can remain on the removable media or it can also be copied to a hard disk on the new SQL Server. In either event, the data remains read-only. If you want maximum speed, copy the data device to the SQL Server's hard disk. If speed is not an issue or if you do not have room to copy the data device to the SQL Server's hard disk, it can remain on the removable media.

After one or both devices are copied to the hard disk of the SQL Server, the sp_dbinstall stored procedure must be run for each device. The stored procedure must be run for each separate device to update the SQL Server about the characteristics of each device, and this must be done one device at a time. The syntax is

```
sp_dbinstall database_name,
logical_dev_name, 'physical_dev_name', size,
'devtype' [,'location']
```

where:

database_name = the name of the removable media database being installed.

logical_dev_name = the logical name of the device being installed.

physical_dev_name = the physical name, including the path, of the device being installed. The path is to the device on the distribution media.

size = the size, in 1-MB blocks, of the device being installed.

devtype = [SYSTEM|DATA] This indicates the type of device being installed, whether it is the device that contains the system tables and transaction log, or the device that contains the data.

location = the destination location to which the device will be copied from the distribution media. A location is required for the system device but is optional for the data device because it can remain on the removable media.

Example:

```
sp_dbinstall acct,
acct_data, 'e:\acct_data.dat', 5, 'data'
```

This stored procedure will have to be repeated for both devices, and you can gain much of the information required for the stored procedure's parameters by examining the text file that was generated when the sp_certify_removable stored procedure was run.

The next step after the database has been installed is to place the database online by using SQL Enterprise Manager or the sp_dboption stored procedure.

At this point, the database is ready for use. The SA will probably want to add one or more database user IDs to the database, along with the appropriate permissions so people can access the data.

How to Uninstall a Removable Database

If you need to uninstall and remove a removable database from a SQL Server, you must run the following stored procedure: sp_dbremove. The syntax is

```
sp_dbremove database_name [,dropdev]
```

where:

database_name = name of database to be dropped.

dropdev = an option that automatically drops all the devices that made up the database being dropped. The physical files that represent the devices must be deleted manually.

Example:

```
sp_dbremove acct, dropdev
```

After this command is run and the device files deleted, the removable database is completely removed.

How to Estimate Space Requirements for a Database

✓Objective ▶   As a DBA, one of your many tasks will be to create new devices and databases, each of which must have a specified size. It is your responsibility to be able to accurately estimate the proper sizes in order not to waste unnecessary resources or not to run out of space due to growing data needs.

As was discussed earlier in this chapter, SQL Server uses three units of measure (page, extent, and allocation unit). You need to become familiar with them to help you better estimate the size of databases you create.

How Space Is Allocated in a Database

The most basic unit of SQL Server data storage is the *page*, which represents 2,048 (2 KB) bytes of data. Each page can hold up to 2,016 byte of actual data, with the remaining 32 bytes reserved for overhead. A page can hold many database rows, but a database row cannot exceed the size of one page.

The next unit of measurement is the *extent*, which is made of eight pages, which is a total of 16 KB. Every time a new database object is created, the space allocated to it is allocated in extents. Even if an object is less than 16 KB in size when first created, an entire extent is reserved for its use. And whenever the extent fills up, another entire extent is allocated for the object's use, even if not all the space in the extent will be used by the object. An extent cannot hold more than one database object.

The allocation unit is the largest storage unit, and it consists of 32 extents (512 KB) or a total of 256 pages. Whenever a database is created, it must be created in an even number of allocation units.

What to Consider When Estimating the Size of a Database

Many factors affect the final size of a database. You will need to consider them all when estimating database size. Some of the most important factors include:

▶ **The size of each row.** Every row is made up of one or more columns of data, each contributing to the size of each row. You will have to get the size of each column from the database developer or by examining each table in the database yourself.

▶ **The number of rows.** The number of rows in a table may be static, or may vary considerably. The database developer will have to tell you how many rows are expected in each of the tables.

▶ **The number of tables.** Some databases have a few tables, others have hundreds. You can view the number of tables yourself through the use of SQL Enterprise Manager.

▶ **The number of indexes.** Each table may have one or more indexes, either clustered or nonclustered. Each nonclustered index takes up additional space in a database.

▶ **The size of each index.** The size of an index is a function of the size of the column used for the index, the number of rows in the index, and the index's FILLFACTOR. A FILL-FACTOR of 100 means that no space is wasted in the index object when it is created. A FILLFACTOR of 50 means than half of the space in an index object is empty space. The larger the FILLFACTOR, the larger the space occupied by the index objects.

▶ **The number of other database objects.** Databases include many objects, such as triggers, views, and stored procedures, among others. Some of these, such as stored procedures, can occupy large amounts of space. The database developer should be able to tell you the approximate size of all a databases' objects.

▶ **The size of the transaction log.** The size of a transaction log can vary widely, depending on many factors, such as how often data is changed in the database. Most transaction logs start at 10 to 25 pecent of the database size and is adjusted after the database is put into production and monitored.

▶ **The projected growth of the database.** Some databases never grow, whereas others grow a lot every day. You will need to find growth estimates for each of the tables in the database for you to come up with an overall projected growth figure.

Most of these numbers do not come easily. You will have to work closely with the database developers to determine these numbers and to estimate the size. When estimating, be conservative—overestimate your needs, which is usually less of a problem than underestimating your storage needs.

Although you can always increase the size of a database later, the more accurately you do it up front, the less surprises you will face and the easier your job as the DBA will be.

Exercises

Exercise 4.1: Creating a Device Using SQL Enterprise Manager

Exercise 4.1 steps you through the process of creating a new database device by using SQL Enterprise Manager. The device you are creating is used in later exercises. *These exercises are cumulative and should be done in order.* This exercise should take less than five minutes to complete.

1. From the SQL Enterprise Manager's Server Manager window, select your SQL Server and open its folder by clicking the plus sign. Various SQL Server folders display.

2. Open the Database Devices folder by clicking the plus sign next to it. A list of all the current database devices for this SQL Server displays.

3. Right-click the Database Devices folder and select New Device from the menu. The New Database Device dialog box appears.

4. In the Name box, enter **sample_dat**.

5. In the Location boxes, leave the default values.

6. In the Size box, enter **10**.

7. After you have finished, click the Create Now button to create the device.

8. Return to the Server Manager window to see the new device listed with all the other devices for this SQL Server.

For more information, refer to section "How to Create Devices Using SQL Enterprise Manager," earlier in the chapter.

Exercise 4.2: Creating a Device Using Transact-SQL

Exercise 4.2 steps you through the process of creating a new database device using Transact-SQL statements. The device you are creating is used in later exercises. This exercise should take less than five minutes to complete.

1. Load the SQL Query tool. Be sure the Query tab is selected.

2. Select the Master database from the DB drop-down menu.

3. Enter the following Transact-SQL statement:

```
DISK INIT
      NAME = 'sample_log',
      PHYSNAME = 'c:\mssql\data\sample_log.dat',
      VDEVNO = 100,
      SIZE = 2048
```

4. Execute the statement. The Results window appears with the message "This command did not return data, and it did not return any rows." The device has been created. The new device will not be displayed in the Database Devices folder until you refresh the screen by selecting View, Refresh from the drop-down menu.

For more information, refer to the section "How to Create Devices Using Transact-SQL," earlier in chapter.

Exercise 4.3: Creating a Database Using SQL Enterprise Manager

Exercise 4.3 steps you through the process of creating a new database using SQL Enterprise Manager. You will be placing the database on the sample_data device and the transaction log on the sample_log device. This exercise should take less than five minutes.

1. From the SQL Enterprise Manager's Server Manager window, select a SQL Server and open its folder by clicking the plus sign. Various SQL Server folders display.

2. Open the Database folder by clicking the plus sign next. A list of all the current databases for this SQL Server displays.

3. Right-click on the Database folder and select New Database from the menu. The New Database dialog box appears.

4. In the Name box, type **sample1**.

continues

5. In the Data Device box, select the "sample_data" database device from the drop-down box.

6. In the Size box, enter **2**.

7. In the Log Device box, select the "sample_log" database device from the drop-down box.

8. In the Size box, type **1**.

9. To create the new database, click the Create Now button. The database and transaction log are created immediately, and you receive no feedback from SQL Server telling they were created. To verify the creation of the new database, view it under the Databases folder in the Server Manager window.

For more information, refer to the section "How to Create a Database Using SQL Enterprise Manager," earlier in chapter.

Exercise 4.4: Creating a Database Using Transact-SQL

Exercise 4.4 steps you through the process of creating a new database using Transact-SQL. You will be creating a database on the sample_data device and its transaction log on the sample_log device. This exercise should take less than five minutes to complete.

1. Load the SQL Query tool. Be sure the Query tab is selected.

2. Select the Master database from the DB drop-down menu.

3. Enter the following Transact-SQL statement:

```
CREATE DATABASE sample2
    ON sample_data = 2
    LOG ON sample_log = 1
```

4. Execute the statement. The Results window appears with the messages "CREATE DATABASE: allocating 1,024 pages on

disk 'sample_data'" and "CREATE DATABASE: allocating 512 pages on disk 'sample_log'." The database has been created. The new database will not be reflected in the Server Manager window until it has been refreshed by choosing View, Refresh from the drop-down window.

For more information, refer to the section "How to Create a Database Using Transact-SQL," earlier in chapter.

Exercise 4.5: Altering a Database Using SQL Enterprise Manager

Exercise 4.5 steps you through the process of expanding the sample database by 1 MB by using SQL Enterprise Manager. This exercise should take less than five minutes.

1. From the SQL Enterprise Manager's Server Manager window, select a SQL Server and open its folder by clicking the plus sign. Various SQL Server folders display.

2. Open the Database folder by clicking the plus sign. A list of all the current database for this SQL Server displays.

3. Right-click on the sample1 database, then select Edit. The Edit Database dialog box appears.

4. Click the Expand button, and the Expand Database dialog box appears.

5. From the Data Device drop-down box, select the sample_data device and type **1** in the box to indicate how much you want to expand the database.

6. After you have specified all the appropriate information, click the Expand Now button, and the database will be increased in size by 1 MB.

For more information, refer to the section "How to Alter the Size of a Database Using SQL Enterprise Manager," earlier in chapter.

Exercise 4.6: Altering a Database Using Transact-SQL

Exercise 4.6 steps you through the process of expanding the *sample2* database by 1 MB using Transact-SQL. This exercise should take less than five minutes.

1. Load the SQL Query tool. Be sure the Query tab is selected.

2. Select Master from the DB drop-down menu.

3. Enter the following Transact-SQL statement:

```
ALTER DATABASE sample2
    ON sample_data = 1
```

4. Execute the statement. The Results window appears with the message "Extending database by 512 pages on disk sample_data." The size of the database has been changed.

For more information, refer to the section "How to Change the Size of a Database Using Transact-SQL," earlier in chapter.

Exercise 4.7: Creating Database Objects Using Transact-SQL

Exercise 4.7 steps you through the process of creating a new table in the *sample* database using Transact-SQL. This exercise should take less than 10 minutes to complete.

1. Load the SQL Query tool. Be sure the Query tab is selected.

2. Select the *sample1* database from the DB drop-down menu.

3. Enter the Transact-SQL statement as given previously.

```
CREATE TABLE employees
    ( staff_id int,
    f_name char(20),
    l_name char(35),
    title char(25),
    pager_number char(10),
    hire_date smalldatetime )
```

4. Execute the statement. The Results window appears with the message "This command did not return data, and it did not return any rows." The table was created. This can be verified by opening the Tables folder of the database where the table was created.

For more information, refer to the section "How to Create a Table," earlier in chapter.

Review Questions

The following questions will test your knowledge of the information in this chapter.

1. Which of the following is a pre-allocated file used to store databases, transaction logs, and backups?

   A. DBCC

   B. dump

   C. device

   D. default

2. Who has the ability to create a new database or backup device?

   A. NT Administrator (not an SA)

   B. SA

   C. DBO

   D. DBOO

3. Whenever a new device is created, which Master system table is automatically updated?

   A. sysdevices

   B. sysusages

   C. sysdatabases

   D. systransactions

4. The SA is attempting to create a new device by using the following DISK INIT Transact-SQL statement:

```
DISK INIT
      NAME = 'data_device1'
      PHYSNAME = 'c:\mssql\data\data_device1.dat'
      VDEVNO = 5
      SIZE = 256
```

Every time this statement is executed, an error is returned. What is the SA doing wrong?

   A. The logical name of the device cannot contain a number.

   B. The extension used for the physical file is incorrect.

   C. The virtual device number must be over 127.

   D. The size of the device is too small.

5. The SA is attempting to create a new device by using the following DISK INIT Transact-SQL statement:

```
DISK INIT
      NAME = 'data_device'
      PHYSNAME = '\\server1\mssql\data\data_device.dat'
      VDEVNO = 170
      SIZE = 1024
```

Every time this statement is executed, an error is returned. What is the SA doing wrong?

   A. The physical file name has an incorrect extension.

   B. The physical file name is pointed to a non-local device.

   C. The size of the device is too small.

   D. The size of the device is too large.

6. Every time the SA creates a new database, by default it is created on the Master device. Unfortunately, this is not what the SA wants to accomplish. What advice would you give the SA to prevent this from reoccurring?

    A. Tell her that she has no choice, and that databases are always created by default on the Master device.

    B. Tell her to specify a remote device to create the database on, which will circumvent this problem.

    C. Tell her to create at least one new device, and then designate it as a default device. She should then remove the default status from the Master device.

    D. Tell her to create all new databases by using Transact-SQL statements instead of SQL Enterprise Manager; this will enable her to resolve the problem

7. Recently, you created a device 2 GB in size and created a 1 GB database on this same device. You then decided you wanted to reclaim some of the unused space on the device by shrinking the device. Unfortunately, your attempts to shrink the device by using SQL Enterprise Manager fail. What other way can be used to shrink the size of a device?

    A. Devices can only be shrunk by using Transact-SQL statements, not SQL Enterprise Manager.

    B. Before the device can be shrunk, the database on the device must first be removed.

    C. Devices cannot be shrunk in SQL Server.

    D. The only way to shrink the device is to use the sp_shrinkdevice stored procedure.

8. Which of the following device names are legal? Select two.

    A. _datadevice

    B. data-device

    C. data device

    D. datadevice1

9. You want to create a new device by using the DISK INIT Transact-SQL statement, but you do not know what the available virtual device numbers are. How can you find out which virtual device numbers are currently being used by SQL Server?

    A. sp_help.

    B. sp_helpdevice.

    C. sp_helpdatabase.

    D. Use the SQL Books Online.

10. Who has the ability to create a new database? Choose two.

    A. SA

    B. DBO

    C. DBOO

    D. Anyone duly authorized by the SA

11. Currently, there are two devices already created on your SQL Server. Device1 has 1 GB of free space, and device2 has 2 GB of free space. Given only these two devices, is it possible to create a 3-GB database?

    A. Yes.

    B. Yes, but only if these two devices have been designated as default devices.

    C. No.

    D. No, but it would be possible if device1 were expanded to 3 GB.

12. As the SA, you commonly want to create new databases to meet new company projects, but you are tired of having to create new database user IDs for each database and then setting the appropriate permissions every time. Is there any way to create a new database without having to constantly re-enter common information?

   A. No, each database is separate and distinct from each other.

   B. No, because each database is created on a separate device.

   C. Yes, if the common information is stored in the Model database.

   D. Yes, if each newly created database is created by using Transact-SQL statements instead of SQL Enterprise Manager.

13. Which of the following Transact-SQL statements are used to create a transaction log?

   A. sp_create_tlog

   B. CREATE TRANSACTION_LOG

   C. sp_create_database

   D. CREATE DATABASE

14. Where can a database's transaction log be physically stored? Select the best two choices.

   A. On the same device as the database.

   B. On a different device as the database.

   C. On the Master device.

   D. Transaction logs are not stored on devices; they are actually a part of the database's system table.

15. Which of the following scenarios are legally possible under SQL Server? Select all that are legal.

    A. Database_A is stored on device1, device2, device3, and device4.

    B. Database_X is stored on device5 and device6, and the database's transaction log is stored on device9.

    C. Database_T, database_W, and database_F are stored on device59.

    D. Database_P and its transaction log are stored on device14. Later, the transaction log is expanded and moved to device13.

16. After you create a new database, you immediately intend to populate the new database using a previously created database backup. How should you create the database so that it is more rapidly created?

    A. Create for Load

    B. Set for DBO Use Only

    C. Set for a Non-logged operation

    D. Create for Backup

17. Whenever a new database is created, which two systems tables in the Master database are modified?

    A. sysdatabases

    B. sysdevices

    C. sysusages

    D. syslogs

18. The SA attempts to create a new database using the following Transact-SQL statement:

```
CREATE DATABASE MARKETING
ON DEVICE_1 = 5
LOG ON DEVICE_2 = 2
```

When the statement is executed, it fails. What is the most likely cause of the problem?

    A. The name of the database does not follow SQL Server naming rules.

    B. One or both of the devices do not currently exist.

    C. The size of the device is too small.

    D. You cannot create a transaction log on a device separate from the database.

19. The SA attempts to create a new database using the following Transact-SQL statement:

```
CREATE DATABASE MARKETING_DATABASE
ON DEVICE_1 = 5, DEVICE_6 = 10, DEVICE_2 = 10
LOG ON DEVICE_1 = 2, DEVICE_6 = 2, DEVICE_2 = 2
```

When the statement is executed, it fails. What is the most likely cause of the problem?

    A. Databases must be created on consecutive devices.

    B. Transaction logs cannot all be the same size.

    C. Transaction logs cannot exist on more than one device.

    D. Use semicolons, not commas, to separate each parameter above.

20. Why is it important to thoroughly document the exact sequence in which you create all of your database devices and databases?

    A. It is not important to document this information because it can easily be retrieved from the Master database.

B. You must document your steps so you can ensure that you never reuse a virtual device number when creating a new database device.

C. You should document your steps in case you ever have to re-create the databases and then populate them with a previously made database dump.

D. You should document your steps in case you ever need to re-create the same devices on a new server when upgrading from one version of SQL server to another.

21. After creating and configuring a database, you notice that the database's transaction log virtually never grows, even when you enter many rows of new data. You want to back up the transaction log as part of an incremental backup plan, but there is no data to back up. When you check the database, all the data you have entered is there. What could be causing this problem?

A. The database is set to "No Checkpoint on Recovery."

B. The database is set to "Truncate Log on Checkpoint."

C. The transaction log is on a separate device than the database.

D. The database may be corrupt. Run the appropriate DBCC commands to correct the problem.

22. You want to fast bcp data into a database. Which of the following database configuration options must be set to true to accomplish this goal?

A. Select Into/Bulk Copy

B. DBO Use Only

C. Truncate Log on Checkpoint

D. Single User

23. Which stored procedure is used to configure a database option?

    A. sp_changeoption

    B. sp_dboption

    C. sp_configuration

    D. sp_options

24. What is an advantage of placing databases and their transaction logs on separate devices?

    A. Saves disk space

    B. Easier to create

    C. Enables the transaction log to be backed up separately

    D. Makes it easier and faster to restore both the database and transaction log from backups

25. What is the DISK RESIZE Transact-SQL statement used for?

    A. To alter the size of a database

    B. To alter the partition size of a hard disk

    C. To increase the size of a database device

    D. To reduce the size of a database device

26. Currently, your SQL Server has three database devices. Device1 has 1 GB of free space, device2 has 1 GB of free space, and device3 has 2 GB of free space. Currently on device1 is the marketing database, which is currently 4 GB in size. You need to increase the size of the marketing database. What is the maximum size you can make the marketing database, given the current database devices?

    A. 4 GB because databases cannot be increased.

    B. 5 GB because a database can only be expanded on a single device.

    C. 8 GB because a database can be expanded to any free space on any device on the same SQL Server.

    D. 12 GB because a database can be expanded to any free space on any device on the same SQL Server.

27. Which one of the following Transact-SQL statements can be used to increase the size of a database?

    A. CHANGE DATABASE ON DEVICE DEVICE1 = 3

    B. CHANGE DATABASE ON DATABASE1 ON DEVICE1 = 3, DEVICE2 = 3

    C. ALTER DATABASE ON DEVICE DEVICE1 = 3

    D. ALTER DATABASE DATABASE1 ON DEVICE1 = 3, DEVICE2 = 3

28. The SA attempts to drop a device by using the sp_dropdevice stored procedure, but receives an error message. What is the most likely cause of this message?

    A. The SA is using the wrong stored procedure.

    B. Devices can only be dropped using SQL Enterprise Manager.

    C. The device contains one or more databases.

    D. The device is a backup device and cannot be dropped.

29. After the SA drops a device using SQL Enterprise Manager, he notices that the physical file representing the device still exists on the hard drive. What did the SA do incorrectly?

   A. The SA should have used a stored procedure instead.

   B. The SA did nothing wrong. After a device is dropped by SQL Enterprise Manager, the file has to be manually deleted.

   C. The SA forgot to select the drop file option when deleting the device.

   D. The SA did not actually drop the device, as indicated by the file still being on the hard disk. He needs to try again, using the proper method.

30. The SA wants to drop the Model database because it has grown too large. The SA uses the drop database Transact-SQL statement to drop it, but receives an error message. What is the most likely cause of the error message?

   A. The Model database cannot be dropped.

   B. The SA must use the sp_dropdevice stored procedure instead.

   C. Only the DBO of Model can delete the database.

   D. The SA must first drop Master before model can be dropped.

31. The SA wants to create a new 5 MB database. How many pages will be included in this database?

   A. 1,250

   B. 2,000

   C. 2,500

   D. 5,000

32. The SA creates two new objects in a database. At the very minimum, how many pages will these two new objects take?

    A. 2

    B. 4

    C. 8

    D. 16

33. The SA want to create a new database that has eight allocation units. How many megabytes will the SA allocate to this new database?

    A. 4

    B. 8

    C. 16

    D. 32

34. Which one of the following is not a factor to consider when estimating the size of a new database?

    A. The number of users who will be accessing the database simultaneously

    B. The amount of actual data to be stored in the database

    C. The size of the transaction log

    D. The size and number of indexes to be included in the database

35. Assuming a row of data in a table always takes 252 bytes, how many rows of data can be stored in one data page?

    A. 2

    B. 4

    C. 8

    D. 16

36. Which one of the following is not a contributing factor to the physical size of a nonclustered index?

    A. FILLFACTOR setting

    B. Number of rows in the table

    C. Number of index levels

    D. PAGESIZE setting

37. Which stored procedure is used to prepare a database for eventual distribution on removable media?

    A. sp_create_removable

    B. sp_create_device

    C. sp_certify_removable

    D. sp_certify_device

38. Which two stored procedures are used to install and configure a database on removable media?

    A. sp_dbinstall

    B. sp_dboption

    C. sp_add_device

    D. sp_dbremove

39. When installing and configuring a database on removable media on a new SQL Server, which two of the following must be copies to read/write media?

    A. System catalog tables

    B. Transaction log

    C. Database device

    D. Create removable text file

Review Answers

1. C

2. B

3. A

4. D

5. B

6. C

7. C

8. A, D

9. B

10. A, D

11. A

12. D

13. D

14. A, B

15. A, B, C, D

16. A

17. A, C

18. B

19. C

20. C

21. B

22. A

23. B

24. C

25. C

26. C

27. D

28. C

29. B

30. A

31. C

32. D

33. A

34. A

35. C

36. D

37. A

38. A, B

39. A, B

Answers to Test Yourself Questions at Beginning of the Chapter

1. Two types of devices are used by SQL Server: database and backup devices. Database devices are used to contain databases and transaction logs. Backup devices are used to store backups of databases or transaction logs. Devices can be created by using either SQL Enterprise Manager or Transact-SQL statements (see "How to Create Devices").

2. A database is a collection of data and database objects used to manage data in SQL Server. By default, only the SA can create a new database, although the SA can assign this task to others by assigning the appropriate statement permission. Databases are created using either SQL Enterprise Manager or Transact-SQL statements (see "How to Create Databases").

3. Databases can be expanded or shrunk by using SQL Enterprise Manager or by using the ALTER DATABASE or the DBCC SHRINKDB Transact-SQL statements (see "How to Alter the Size of a Database Using SQL Enterprise Manager").

4. Database objects include tables, views, indexes, datatypes, defaults, rules, stored procedures, triggers, and constraints. Database objects can be created using SQL Enterprise Manager or by using Transact-SQL statements (see "SQL Server Database Objects" and "How to Create Database Objects").

5. A *page* is the smallest storage unit in SQL Server and is 2 KB (2,048 bytes) in size. An *extent* is a data structure made up of 8 contiguous pages (8 × 2 KB = 16 KB). SQL Server automatically allocates an extent whenever a new database object, such as a table, is created. An *allocation unit* is a data structure made up of 32 extents (32 × 16 KB = 512 KB), or 256 pages. Whenever a new database is created, space is allocated in multiple allocation units of 512 KB each. Knowing the size of these data structures can assist you in estimating the size of database you want to create (see "How to Estimate Space Requirements for a Database").

Chapter 5

Managing User Accounts

One of the most common tasks of the database administrator (DBA) is the routine creation of login IDs, database user IDs, groups, and the addition and deletion of group users. These tasks are closely related, and are covered extensively in this chapter. In almost all cases, these tasks can be performed from either SQL Enterprise Manager or by using stored procedures. In order to prepare for Microsoft's SQL Server 6.5 Database Administration exam, you need to learn how to perform each of these tasks using either method.

This chapter also includes the topic of Integrated Security. While security modes are also covered in Chapter 1, "Server Installation and Upgrade," Standard, Integrated, and Mixed security modes will be discussed in greater depth in this chapter, with special emphasis on Integrated Security. Integrated Security is the preferred security mode, but it is also the most complicated to set up. Before you take the exam, you need to understand how using the Integrated Security mode affects the creation and management of user accounts.

As always, this chapter begins with a list of exam objectives that relate to the topic at hand. Next comes the chapter pretest, along with valuable information that directly addresses the objectives, as well as additional related discussion topics. Exercises and chapter review questions follow, and answers to both the chapter review questions and the chapter pretest questions are provided.

This chapter, which focuses on the management of user accounts, addresses and fully covers how to perform the following:

 **Objectives**

> ▶ Differentiate between an SQL Server login and an SQL Server user
>
> ▶ Create a login ID
>
> ▶ Add a database user
>
> ▶ Add and drop users for a group

Test Yourself! Before reading this chapter, test yourself to determine how much study time you will need to devote to this section.

1. You have just been made the DBA of your organization's three SQL Servers, which have been set up to use the SQL Server Standard Security mode. Your first task is to create the necessary accounts to allow Veronica, a new employee, to access the marketing database on SQL Server One, to access the accounting database on SQL Server Two, and to access both the production and inventory databases on SQL Server Three. Based on this scenario, how many accounts, and what kind of accounts, must be created to enable Veronica to access the various databases?

2. You want to create a new login ID on Server A for the new user Veronica. What two SQL Server methods are available to create this new login ID?

3. When creating a new login ID, what are some of the rules to which you must adhere?

4. You want to create two database user IDs for the new user Veronica on SQL Server Three. Which two SQL Server methods are available to create these new database user IDs?

5. When creating database user ID accounts with SQL Enterprise Manager, which three other related tasks can you perform at the same time from the same dialog box?

6. Using SQL Enterprise Manager, how do you add the database user ID you created for the new user Veronica to the marketing group? Later, if you decide to remove Veronica from the marketing group, how do you perform this task?

Answers are located at the end of the chapter...

SQL Server Login and User Accounts

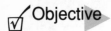 Objective

One of the main functions of the DBA is to manage SQL Server accounts, which includes creating new accounts, changing accounts, and dropping accounts as needed.

SQL Server uses two types of accounts:

▶ **Login ID.** This is the name used by SQL Server to identify users. For example, if a user wants to access a database on SQL Server, the user must first log in to SQL Server by providing an appropriate login ID and password (see fig. 5.1). After a user has logged in to SQL Server, this does not mean the user can automatically access data in a database managed by SQL Server. The user still must have an appropriate database user ID.

▶ **Database User ID.** After a user has successfully logged in to SQL Server, the user must also have an appropriate database user ID for each database the user wants to access (see fig. 5.1). If the SQL Server manages 10 databases, and a logged-in user only has database user IDs in two of the databases, then the user only has access to those two databases.

 Note

Login ID is also sometimes referred to as login name. Additionally, you may see database user ID referred to as user or user name.

Before you learn how to create SQL Server accounts, you must learn everything there is to know about account types the sometimes subtle differences between them. In this section, you will learn about the various roles each type of account can play, along with how these types are used in the context of SQL Server security. In later sections, you will learn how to create accounts and apply them to real-world situations.

Figure 5.1

Both a login ID and database user ID are required before a user can access any given SQL Server database.

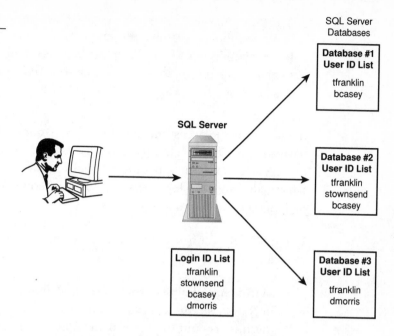

Based on the above login IDs and database user IDs, user tfranklin has the ability to log into the SQL Server and to access all three databases. User stownsend has the ability to log into the SQL Server, but can be only access database #2. User bcasey can log into the SQL Server, but can only access databases #1 and #2. User dmorris can log into the SQL Database, but can only access database #3.

Login ID Accounts

Whenever a user wants to access a SQL Server database, the user must first log in to SQL Server using a login ID. If SQL Server is set up for Integrated Security, SQL Server automatically logs the user in using the user's NT Server user account name and password. If SQL Server is set up to use Standard Security, then the user must type in both the SQL Server login ID and password.

 Note

How a user logs in to SQL Server depends on the type of security mode being used by SQL Server. SQL Server offers three security modes: Standard, Integrated, and Mixed. Standard Security is handled 100% by SQL Server, and all the login account information is stored in the *master* database.

continues

> Integrated Security uses the security provided by NT Server. Mixed security uses both Standard and Integrated security methods. Security modes are discussed in more depth later in this chapter.

If a user wants to access more than one SQL Server, the user must have a login ID for each separate SQL Server. For ease of management, you can use the same login ID and password for each SQL Server, although the login IDs must be created separately for each SQL Server the user wants to access.

When SQL Server is installed, several default login IDs are automatically created. They are as follows:

▶ **sa (System Administrator).** Like the administrator's account in NT Server, the sa account enables anyone logging in under this account to perform any function using SQL Server. The system administrator (SA) also has full privileges inside every database managed by SQL Server.

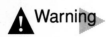

> Only the DBA should use the sa login ID. Do not allow other users, including developers, to use the sa account. Always create a separate login ID for each user. Inappropriate use of the sa login ID can corrupt a database.

▶ **probe.** This is a special login ID reserved for use by some applications that need to access SQL Server. For example, NT Server's Performance Monitor tool uses this ID in order to log in to SQL Server and gain access to SQL Server Performance Monitor objects. Probe is also used between servers to manage two-phase commit activities. This login ID is only necessary if SQL Server is using Standard Security. If SQL Server is set up for Integrated Security, then the sa login account is used instead.

▶ **repl_publisher.** This login ID is used only if SQL Server has been set up to participate as a publisher in SQL Server replication. This account enables various replication processes to log in to SQL Servers participating in replication.

▶ **repl_subscriber.** This login ID is used only if SQL Server has been set up to participate as a subscriber in SQL Server replication. This account enables various replication processes to log in to SQL Servers participating in replication.

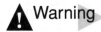 **Warning**

> When SQL Server is first installed, the sa account has no password. Make it a point to assign the sa account a password immediately upon installation. One of the first things a hacker tries when attempting to hack an SQL Server database is to log in as the SA without a password. Why? Because hackers know that it is relatively common for DBA's to forget to add a password to the sa account.

The DBA is responsible for creating login IDs for every user who needs access to SQL Server. This is done manually for SQL Servers with Standard Security. If the SQL Server uses Integrated Security, NT user names are added to SQL Server using the SQL Server Security Tool. Later in this chapter, you will learn how to perform both of these tasks.

How Is Data Protected from Unauthorized Access?

Before a user can access data in an SQL Database, the user must successfully cross four levels of security. These levels include the following:

▶ **Operating System Security.** The first barrier to accessing SQL Server data is the operating system itself. NT Server provides very good network security, and all SQL Server users must have an NT user account as a first step to accessing SQL Server database information.

▶ **SQL Server Login ID Security.** Just because a user can log in to NT Server does not mean that the user can access SQL Server data. Each person who wants to access SQL Server data must have a login ID, which enables him to log in to a specific SQL Server. If a user needs access to more than one SQL Server, then the user must have a login ID for each SQL Server involved.

continues

> ▶ **SQL Server Database User ID Security.** Just because a user can log in to SQL does not automatically mean the user has the ability to access data. The user also needs a database user ID for each database the user wants to access.

> ▶ **Database Object Security.** Last of all, just because a user has a database user ID does not mean the user can access the data contained therein. Each user must also be given permission to access any object in a database, and this permission is given to a user object by object. Even then, individual users may have different levels of access to an object. A user may be allowed only to read the data in one object, but he may be given permission to add data in another object. Permissions are discussed in Chapter 6, "Managing Permissions."

Database User IDs

After a user has successfully logged in to an SQL Server, the user may not access any databases managed by the SQL Server unless the user has a registered database user ID. Because of this requirement, a single SQL Server can manage many different databases, while at the same time preventing unauthorized access.

Fortunately, SQL Server does not require a user to enter a database user ID before being permitted to access a database. Database user IDs are associated with a user's login ID. When a user accesses a database after logging in to SQL Server, the system automatically checks to see if there is a database user ID associated with the user's login ID. If there is a match, then the user has access to the database. A single login ID can be associated with as many databases as needed.

While it is not required, most database user IDs use the same name as their associated login IDs, and use the same database user IDs for every database they have access to. This makes user management much easier for the DBA.

Database user IDs can be divided into three types:

▶ **dbo (Database Owner).** This special database user ID is the designated owner of a database, with full privileges inside the database. Whoever creates a database becomes its DBO, and there can only be one DBO per database. The database owner is known by the name dbo when inside the database, but when inside databases that are not owned, the user must be known by another database that user ID. A database owner may only be known to the database it owns as the dbo, and have no other database user ID in the same database. By default, the SA is the DBO of all databases, and the SA has the capability to assign database ownership to other users.

▶ **guest.** The guest database user ID enables anyone with a legal login ID to access a database, even without a user ID for the database. The guest database user ID is not created by default; it must be created by the DBA in those databases to which the DBA wants to permit guest access.

▶ **Database User IDs.** Database user IDs are created by either the SA or the DBO, and must be added to each database managed by SQL Server that a user needs to access.

 Tip

> If you want a guest account in every database you create, add the guest database user account to the model database. Remember, the model database is used as a template for all new databases, and any changes you make to the model database are reflected in new databases. See Chapter 4, "Managing Database Storage," for more information on the model database.

Database User Aliases

Normally, each login ID is associated with one or more database user IDs. Because of this feature, a user with a single login ID can access one or more databases managed by SQL Server. Occasionally it is useful, however, for a single database user ID to be associated with one or more login IDs (the reasons for which will be discussed in a moment). An *alias* is a database user ID that can be shared among two or more login IDs (see fig. 5.2).

Figure 5.2

An alias enables one or more login IDs to access a database using the same database user ID.

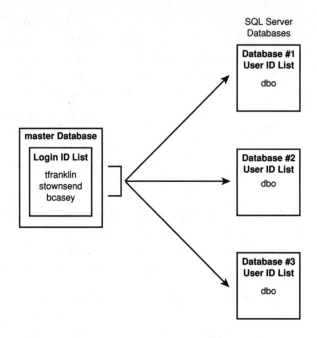

By creating aliases, any of the three login IDs in the Login ID List can access any of the three SQL Server databases using the dbo database user ID.

Aliases are generally used for a very specific reason. Aliases enable different SQL developers to create objects in a database, while maintaining the same ownership for all objects created, no matter which developer created them. Whenever an object is created in a database, it belongs to the user who created it. If one developer created a table while logged in under his database user ID, and another logs in later and creates another table using her database user ID, then the two objects have different owners. Because of this, setting permissions can become fairly complex. To prevent different objects in the same database from having different owners, developers can log in to a database using the same alias, which is generally the dbo. Any object created by any developer will have the same owner, and the DBA's task of setting permissions is greatly simplified. After a database is ready for production, the aliases can be removed.

When you set out to create an alias, keep the following in mind:

▶ Any database user ID can be an alias.

▶ Any user who has been aliased to a database cannot also have a database user ID in the same database.

Database User Groups

A database user group is similar to an NT Server global group, and is used to group users who need similar database permissions to access a database. Any member belonging to a group has all the permissions that have been assigned to that group.

Every SQL Server database includes one predefined group called public. By default, every database user is a member of the public group and cannot be removed from this group. The public group is similar to the Everyone group in NT Server, which also includes all users.

Additional groups can be defined in each database to meet the varied needs of users. Unfortunately, a significant limitation exists: a database user can belong to only one group in addition to the public group.

Assume, for instance, that a database has five database users (see fig. 5.3). By default, all five belong to the public group. In addition, each user may belong to only one other group. This limitation requires the DBA to do some careful planning when creating groups and setting permissions.

Figure 5.3

All database user IDs belong to the public group, and each one can belong to only one additional group.

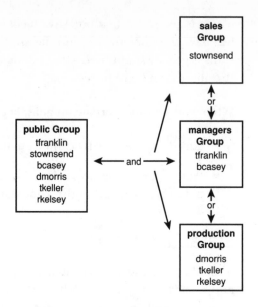

Planning a SQL Server User Account Strategy

Before you begin creating login IDs and database user IDs, you will want to take some time to create a user account strategy. Here are some suggestions on how to create such a strategy:

- ▶ Begin by determining the various tasks that the database users will be performing in the database, such as querying data, entering new data, modifying data, and so on.

- ▶ Based on the tasks determined above, group the users who will be performing each set of tasks. This grouping will act as a basis for the creation of groups to which you will assign permissions (see Chapter 6).

- ▶ The next step is to create the necessary groups in the database. When creating groups, choose group names that are easy to remember, and representative of the type of tasks the people in the group will perform. For example, data entry operators might be put into a group called data_entry.

- ▶ After the groups are created, the next job is to create the login ID for each user who needs to access the database. If this particular SQL Server application requires more than one SQL Server, then a login ID for each SQL Server needs to be created. When you create a login ID, you will also want to assign a default database, which is the database the user will use most frequently. Whenever a user logs in to SQL Server with a login ID, the user automatically accesses this database.

▶ Develop a common naming convention for login IDs and database user IDs. In order to be consistent, you may want to follow the same naming convention used to create NT Server account names.

▶ After all the login IDs have been created, the next job is to create a database user ID in the databases the user needs to access. If you desire, the guest database user ID can be used to enable a user to access a database without the necessity of creating a database user ID.

▶ The next step, if required, is to create any aliases needed by the users to access the database.

▶ Next, assign each database user ID to a group created earlier, as appropriate.

▶ And last, assign permissions to each group or user, as required (again, refer to Chapter 6 for more on permissions).

Now that you have a good foundation on SQL Server accounts and their roles, it is time to find out how to implement them in SQL Server. The next section takes a look at how to create login IDs and database user IDs using SQL Enterprise Manager and stored procedures.

Managing SQL Server Login IDs and Database User IDs

SQL Server login IDs are created for a specific SQL Server, and database user IDs are created for each database to which a user must have access. The login ID is created first, and then the database user ID is created and associated with a login ID.

Server login IDs and database user IDs can be managed from SQL Enterprise Manager, or from the SQL Query tool (or a similar tool, such as ISQL/W) using stored procedures.

The upcoming sections begin with a list of some basic rules, and continue with more hands-on instruction concerning the specifics of managing login IDs and database user IDs.

Some Basic Rules

Keep the following in mind when managing login IDs:

▶ Login IDs can only be created by the SA, are specific to a single SQL Server, and must be unique to that server.

▶ Login IDs can be up to 30 alphanumeric characters long, but the first character must be a letter or the symbols # or "_". Login IDs are not case sensitive.

▶ Login ID passwords can contain up to 30 characters, and are case sensitive. Passwords that include characters other than the letters A–Z and a–z, or that begin with 0–9, must be enclosed in quotation marks. Because of this, you should only assign passwords that begin with a letter, and do not include any characters other than those specified in the preceding description. If you do not assign a password, then the default password is NULL, which means that the login ID has no password.

▶ Only an SA can drop a login ID.

▶ A login ID cannot be dropped if it is associated with a database user ID that owns any objects in the database. Before the login ID can be dropped, any objects owned by its database user IDs must be dropped. After all the owned objects are dropped, along with the database user ID, then the login ID can be dropped.

Keep the following in mind when managing database IDs:

▶ Database user IDs can only be created by the SA or DBO, are specific to a single database, and must be unique to each database.

▶ Database user IDs can be up to 30 alphanumeric characters long, but the first character must be a letter, or the symbols or "_". Database user IDs are not case sensitive. Although it is not a requirement, most database user IDs match their associated login IDs.

▶ The SA can drop any database user ID, but the DBO is only able to drop database user IDs from the database the DBO owns.

▶ A database user ID cannot be dropped if it owns any objects in the database. Before the database user ID can be dropped, any objects owned by the database user ID must be dropped. After all the owned objects are dropped, then the database user ID can be dropped.

▶ Database ownership can be transferred only by an SA. The SA can transfer ownership of any database, except Master.

▶ Before the SA can make a login ID the owner of a database, the login ID must be set up, and the login ID must not have a database user ID or alias in the database.

 Tip

To eliminate the need to drop a database object before a database user ID is dropped, always alias all users who create database objects as the DBO. Because the DBO has ownership of all database objects, this problem does not arise. But what if you have not followed this advice, and find yourself in a situation where, in order to drop a database user ID, you must first drop a database object that you really need? Before you drop the object, create a script for the object, drop the object, and then as DBO use the script to recreate the object.

Note   The procedures for creating new login IDs discussed in the following section assume that SQL Server is set up for Standard Security. If Integrated Security is used instead, then the SQL Server Security Manager is used to add new login IDs. To learn how to use the SQL Server Security Manager, refer to the section on Integrated Security later in this chapter.

How to Create a New Login ID

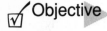

Objective   To create a new login ID using SQL Enterprise Manager, follow these steps:

1. From the Server Manager window, select a server, and open it by clicking on the plus sign to the left of the server name.

2. Choose Manage, Logins from the drop-down menu, or right-click on the Logins folder, and choose New Login. The Manage Logins dialog box appears (see fig. 5.4).

3. Type the name of the new login ID in the Login Name drop-down box. If the drop-down box is not blank, choose <New Login> from the drop-down box; this clears the box.

4. Type a password for this login ID. The password is displayed as asterisks as it is entered.

5. Select a language for the user from the Default Language drop-down box. The default language is US English.

6. At this point, everything that is required to create a login ID has been entered. If the Add button is clicked, then the login ID will be added to the selected SQL Server, and the login ID will be assigned the Master database as its default login database. If you assigned a password to this login ID, you will also get a confirmation box for the password.

   If you wish, the database user IDs that are to be associated with this login ID can be created now, before clicking Add, or they can be created at any time after the login ID is created. See the following section on how to add database user IDs to a login ID.

Figure 5.4

*Login IDs are
created in the
Manage Logins
dialog box.*

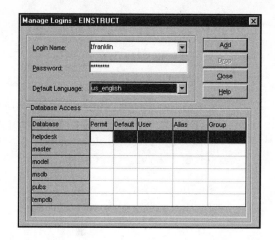

To create a new login ID using stored procedures, follow these
steps:

1. From the SQL Query Tool, type

   sp_addlogin *login_id [,password [,defdb [,deflanguage]]]*

   where

   login_id is the name of the new login ID.

   password is the password for the new login ID.

   defdb is the default database for the new login ID.

   deflanguage is the default language for the new login ID.

   Example: sp_addlogin tfranklin, greenslime, *pubs*, us_english

2. Execute the query, and the login ID is added. The new login
   ID will not appear in the Server Manager window of SQL
   Enterprise Manager until you refresh the window by right-
   clicking on the Logins folder and selecting Refresh.

How to Drop a Login ID

To drop a Login ID using SQL Enterprise Manager, follow these steps:

1. From the Server Manager window, select a server, and open it by clicking on the plus sign to the left of the server name. Open the Logins folder by clicking on the plus sign to the left of the folder name.

2. Right-click on a login id, and then select Drop. A dialog box appears, asking you `Are you sure you want to remove this Login?`.

3. Click on Yes, and the login ID is dropped from SQL Server.

To drop a login ID using a stored procedure, follow these steps:

1. From the SQL Query tool, or a similar tool, type

   sp_droplogin *login_id*

   where

   login_id is the login ID.

   Example: sp_droplogin tfranklin

2. Execute the query, and the login ID is dropped from SQL Server. The login ID will not disappear from the Server Manager window of SQL Enterprise Manager until you refresh the window by right-clicking on the Logins folder and selecting Refresh.

How to Create New Database User IDs

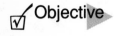 Objective

To create a new database user ID and associate it with a login ID using SQL Enterprise Manager, follow these steps:

1. From the Server Manager window, select a server, and open it by clicking on the plus sign next to the left of the server name.

2. Choose Manage, Logins from the drop-down menu, or click on the plus sign to the left of the Logins folder. All the current login IDs are displayed.

3. Right-click on a login ID that you want to associate with a database user ID, and then select Edit. The Manage Logins dialog box is displayed.

4. If the login ID you want to associate with a new database user ID is not displayed in the Login Name drop-down box, click the drop-down box and select a login ID from the list.

5. The Database Access area of the Manage Logins dialog box is used to create new database user IDs and associate them with the current login ID (see fig. 5.5). All the databases managed by this SQL Server are displayed, and sorted alphabetically in this window. To create a new database user ID, click on the empty box under the Permit column, next to the database for which you want to create a new database user ID.

After clicking the empty box, a blue check mark appears in the Permit column, along with the login ID in the box under the User column, and the group name public under the Group column (see fig. 5.5).

Figure 5.5

Database user IDs are created in the Database Access section of the Manage Logins dialog box.

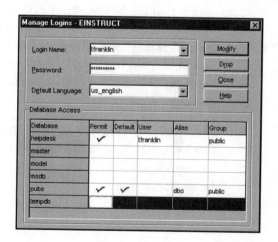

The blue check in the Permit column indicates that the current login ID has been permitted to access this particular database. The login ID in the User column is the default database user ID for this login ID in this database. Most DBA's assign the same database user ID to every login ID to make user management a little easier. If you do not want to use the same database user ID as the login ID, you can change it by selecting the box with the database user ID in it and typing a new database user ID.

The group name public, in the Group column, tells you that the database user name has been added to the public group. Remember, all database user IDs must belong to the public group.

If you want to assign this login ID a specific default database that the login ID is automatically logged in to when the user first logs in to SQL Server, you can indicate this by clicking on the box under the Default column, on the row for the database. It is good practice to not allow any login ID to use the Master database as the default database. Instead, select the database the login ID will most often access.

If you want to assign this login ID an alias for any of the databases it is permitted to access, the alias can be added by clicking on the box under the Alias column that corresponds to the database where you want the alias created. Remember, a login ID may have either a database user ID, or an alias for a database, but not both. If you have already entered a database user ID, and then add an alias, the database user ID will be automatically removed.

6. After you have created one or more database user IDs for this login ID, click on Modify and the database user IDs along with any other changes you made to this login ID will be saved.

Tip

The Manage Logins dialog box can be used anytime to change any of the settings for a login ID, including the password, default language, permitted databases, default database, database user names, aliases, and group memberships.

To add a new database user ID to a database and associate it with a login ID using stored procedures, follow these steps:

1. From the SQL Query tool, or a similar tool, select the database in which you want to create the new database user ID.

2. Then type

   sp_adduser *login_id [,user_name [,group_name]]*

   where

   login_id is the name of the login ID to be associated with the new database user ID.

   user_name is the database user ID.

   group_name is the group the new database user ID should belong to, if any.

   Example: sp_adduser tfranklin, tfranklin, managers

3. Execute the query, and the database user ID is added to the database and associated with the login ID. The new database user ID will not appear in the Server Manager window of SQL Enterprise Manager until you refresh the window by right-clicking on the Groups/Users folder and selecting Refresh.

Using the Guest Database User ID

The guest database user ID is a special database user ID that has a very specific purpose. If a guest database user ID is added to any database, then anyone with a login ID to SQL Server can access the database without having his own database user ID. This feature reduces the user management load of the DBA by enabling large groups of people to access a database without the DBA having to create an explicit database user ID for each visitor.

When a user with a login ID tries to access a database, SQL Server checks to see if the user has a database user ID or alias in the database he is attempting to access. If the user does, then he is allowed to access the database. But if he does not have a database user ID or alias in the database, SQL Server then checks to see if the guest account exists in the database. If it does, then the user is granted access to the database; otherwise he is denied access.

Keep the following in mind when creating the guest account:

▶ The guest account is always a member of the public group.

▶ By default, when databases are created, they do not contain the guest database user ID, which must be explicitly added by the DBA.

▶ When SQL Server is installed, it adds the guest account to the Master and Pubs databases. The guest account cannot be dropped from the Master database.

▶ If a user accesses a database under the guest database user ID, the user has only the permissions that have been assigned by the DBA to the guest database user ID.

How to Drop a Database User ID

To drop a database user ID using SQL Enterprise Manager, follow these steps:

1. From the Server Manager window, select a server, and open it by clicking on the plus sign to the left of the server name. Then click on the plus sign next to the Databases folder to display the databases managed on the server.

2. Click on the plus sign next to the database from which the database user ID is to be dropped. The Groups/Users and Objects folders are displayed.

3. Click on the plus sign next to the Group/Users folder. All the database groups are displayed.

4. Click on the group which contains the database user ID you want to drop. All the database user IDs belonging to this group are displayed.

5. To drop a database user ID, right-click on the database user ID, then choose Delete. A warning message appears that asks `Are you sure you want to remove this User?`.

6. Click on Yes to drop the database user ID.

To drop a database user ID from a database using a stored procedure, follow these steps:

1. From the SQL Query Tool, or similar tool, select from the DB drop-down box the database that contains the database user ID you want to drop.

2. Type

   sp_dropuser *user_name*

   where

   user_name is the database user ID.

   Example: sp_dropuser tfranklin

3. Execute the query, and the database user ID is dropped from the database. The database user ID will not disappear from the Server Manager window of SQL Enterprise Manager until you refresh the window by right-clicking on the folder of the database and selecting Refresh.

Managing SQL Server Database Groups

If you are going to use database groups to manage databases users, you will usually create the groups when the database is first created, and before any database user IDs are created. Even though groups and database user IDs can be created at any time, creating the groups before the users forces you to plan how you will handle permissions in the database. This tactic will simplify your task of managing specific user and group permissions later on.

Groups can be managed from the SQL Enterprise Manager or from the SQL Query tool using stored procedures.

The upcoming sections begin with a list of some basic rules, and continue with more hands-on instruction concerning the specifics of managing SQL Server database groups.

Some Basic Rules

Keep the following in mind when managing groups:

- ▶ Groups can only be added or dropped by the SA, or by the DBO of the database where the groups exist.

- ▶ Group names must be unique within a database.

- ▶ A group name can have up to 30 characters. Characters may be numbers or letters, but the first letter of the name must begin with a letter, or the symbols # and "_".

- ▶ Users may be added to or dropped from a group at any time.

- ▶ All users belong to the group public. This is true, even though you will not see all the database users as part of the group in the Manage Groups dialog box. The only database user IDs that are shown under public in SQL Enterprise Manager are those that do not also belong to another group.

- ▶ Database users cannot be removed from the public group.

▶ If a database user belongs to one group, and then you add that same user to another group, the user is automatically removed from the previous group when added to the new one.

▶ When you drop a group, the group is deleted, but the users are not deleted. They remain in the public group.

How to Create a New Group

To create a new group using SQL Enterprise Manager, follow these steps:

1. From the Server Manager window, select a server, and open it by clicking on the plus sign to the left of the server name. Then click on the plus sign next to the Databases folder to display the databases managed by the server.

2. Open the Database folder where you want to create the new group by clicking on the plus sign next to the database's name, then choose Manage, Groups from the drop down menu. You can also right-click on the Groups/Users folder and select New Group. The Manage Groups dialog appears (see fig. 5.6).

3. Type the name of the new group in the drop-down box. If the drop-down box is not blank, choose <New Group> from the drop-down box to clear the box.

4. Click on the Add button, and the group is added.

Figure 5.6

The Manage Groups dialog box is used to create new groups.

To create a new group using a stored procedure, follow these steps:

1. Using the SQL Query tool, or a similar tool, select the database where you want to create the new group from the DB drop-down box.

2. Then type

   sp_addgroup *group_name*

   where

   group_name is the name of the new group.

   Example: sp_addgroup managers

3. Execute the query, and the group is added. The new group will not appear in the Server Manager window of SQL Enterprise Manager until you refresh the window by right-clicking on the Groups/Users folder and selecting Refresh.

How to Add Database User IDs to a Group

 To add database user IDs to a group using SQL Enterprise Manager, follow these steps:

1. From the Server Manager window, select a server, and open it by clicking on the plus sign to the left of the server name. Then click on the plus sign next to the Databases folder to display the databases managed by the server.

2. Open the database that contains the group to which you want to add a database user ID by clicking on the plus sign next to the database's name. This action displays the Groups/Users and Objects folders.

3. Click on the plus sign next to the Groups/Users folder to display all the groups for this database.

4. Right-click on the group to which you want to add a new user and select Edit. The Manage Groups dialog box appears.

5. To add any current database user ID to a group, click on a database user ID and then click on Add. This moves the database user ID from the Users side of the window to the Users in Group side (see fig. 5.7).

Figure 5.7

The database user ID has been added to the group.

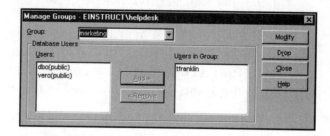

To add a user to a group using a stored procedure, follow these steps:

1. Using the SQL Query tool, or a similar tool, select the database in which you want to create the new group from the DB drop-down box.

2. Then type

   sp_changegroup *group_name, user_name*

   where

   group_name is the name of the group.

   user_name is the database user ID to be added to the group.

   Example: sp_addgroup managers, tfranklin

3. Execute the query, and the database user ID is added to the group. The database user ID will not appear as a part of the group in the Server Manager window of SQL Enterprise Manager until you refresh the window by right-clicking on the group folder and selecting Refresh.

How to Move Database User IDs from One Group to Another

To move database user IDs from one group to another using SQL Enterprise Manager, follow these steps:

1. From the Server Manager window, select a server, and open it by clicking on the plus sign to the left of the server name. Then click on the plus sign next to the Databases folder to display the databases managed by the server.

2. Click on the plus sign next to the database whose group membership you want to change. The Groups/Users and Objects folders are displayed.

3. Click on the plus sign next to the Groups/Users folder to display all the groups for this database.

4. Right-click on the group that contains the database user ID you want to move and select Edit. The Manage Groups dialog box appears.

5. To move a database user from another group to this group, click on a database user ID that is on the Users side of the dialog box, and then click on Add. (Database user IDs on the Users side of the dialog box currently do not belong to this group; instead, they belong to other groups.) This will move the database user ID from the Users side (and from the other group) to the Users in Group side, thus adding the database user ID to this group (see fig. 5.8).

Figure 5.8

The database user has been moved to the new group.

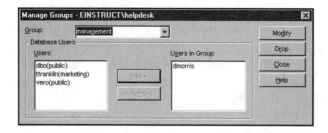

To move a database user ID from one group to another using a stored procedure, follow these steps:

1. Using the SQL Query tool, or a similar tool, select the database that contains the group that has the database user ID you want to change.

2. Then type

   sp_changegroup *group_name, user_name*

   where

   group_name is the name of the group to which the database user ID is to be added.

   user_name is the database user ID to be added to the group.

   Example: sp_changegroup managers, tfranklin

3. Execute the query, and the database user ID is moved from the old group to the new group. The database user ID will not appear as a part of the group in the Server Manager window of SQL Enterprise Manager until you refresh the window by right-clicking on the group folder and selecting Refresh.

How to Remove Database User IDs from a Group

 Objective

To remove database user IDs from a group using SQL Enterprise Manager, follow these steps:

1. From the Server Manager window, select a server, and open it by clicking on the plus sign to the left of the server name. Then click on the plus sign next to the Databases folder to display the databases managed by the server.

2. Click on the plus sign next to the database that contains the group that includes the database user ID you want to remove. The Groups/Users and Objects folders are displayed.

3. Click on the plus sign next to the Groups/Users folder to display all the groups for this database.

4. Right-click on the group which contains the database user ID that you want to remove and select Edit. The Manage Groups dialog box is displayed.

5. To remove a database user from a group, click on a database user ID listed on the Users in Group side, and then click on Remove. This will move the database user ID from the Users in Group side to the Users side (see fig. 5.9).

Note that the database user ID is not deleted, only removed from the group, and that it is still a member of the public group.

Figure 5.9

The database user ID is dropped from the group when Remove is clicked.

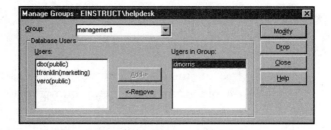

A database user ID cannot be directly dropped from a group by use of a stored procedure, but the same effect can be obtained by moving a database user ID from one group to another. To remove a user from a group and add it to another using a stored procedure, follow these steps:

1. Using the SQL Query tool, or a similar tool, select the database that contains the group that includes the database user ID you want to remove.

2. Then type

   sp_changegroup *group_name, user_name*

   where

   group_name is the name of the group.

   user_name is the database user ID to be added to the group.

   Example: sp_changegroup managers, tfranklin

3. Execute the query, and the database user ID is moved from one group to another. The database user ID will not appear as a part of the new group in the Server Manager window of SQL Enterprise Manager until you refresh the window by right-clicking on the group folder and selecting Refresh.

How to Drop a Group

To drop a group using SQL Enterprise Manager, follow these steps:

1. From the Server Manager window, select a server and open it by clicking on the plus sign to the left of the server name. Then click on the plus sign next to the Databases folder to display the databases managed by the server.

2. Click on the plus sign next to the database that contains the group you want to drop. This displays the Groups/Users and Objects folders.

3. Click on the Groups/Users folder to display all the groups for this database.

4. Right-click on the group you want to drop, and select Drop. This message is displayed: `Are you sure you want to re-move this Group?`.

5. Click on Yes to drop the group. Note that the database user IDs that belonged to the group are not dropped, only the group. These database user IDs still belong to the public group.

To drop a group using a stored procedure, follow these steps:

1. Using the SQL Query tool, or a similar tool, select the database from which you want to drop a group.

2. Then type

   sp_dropgroup *group_name*

where

group_name is the name of the group to be dropped.

Example: sp_dropgroup managers

3. Execute the query, and the group is dropped. The Server Manager window of SQL Enterprise Manager will not reflect the dropped group until you refresh the window by right-clicking on the Group/Users folder and selecting Refresh.

Some Common Login Error Messages

On occasion, a user will get an error message when attempting to log in to SQL Server and the user's default database. This section lists some of the possible error messages, and offers suggestions for repairing each problem:

▶ **Error 905**. Unable to allocate a DBTABLE descriptor to open database 'database name.' Another database must be closed or dropped before opening this one.

Most likely, SQL Server's *open databases* setting is limiting the number of databases that can be concurrently open. Either this setting can be changed, or a current database needs to be closed to enable a new database to be opened by SQL Server.

▶ **Message 916.** Server user ID *x* is not a valid user in database 'database name.'

Most likely, the user trying to access the database does not have an appropriate database user ID. If the user needs to access this database, add a database user ID for this login ID to this database.

▶ **Msg 927, Level 14, State 1.** Database 'database name' cannot be opened—it is in the middle of a load.

Most likely, the accessed database is currently being restored from a backup. Wait until the restore is complete before again trying to access the database.

Managing SQL Server Security Modes

One of the first decisions the DBA must make when installing and configuring SQL Server is the selection of the most appropriate security mode. A *security mode* refers to how SQL Server authenticates login IDs when a user logs in to SQL Server. SQL Server offers three security modes:

► Standard

► Integrated

► Mixed

The *Standard Security mode* relies entirely on SQL Server to authenticate users, and is the default security mode for SQL Server. The *Integrated Security mode* uses NT Server security to authenticate users. The *Mixed Security mode* offers the best of both worlds by enableing either SQL Server or NT Server to authenticate users. The following sections examine the implementation of each of these three security modes.

Standard Security

SQL Server's default security mode is Standard Security, whereby SQL Server takes full responsibility for authenticating any users who want to access SQL Server. Whenever a user accesses SQL Server, the user is prompted to enter a login ID and password. SQL Server verifies that the user is a legitimate user and allows the user access, or it denies access if the user does not have the proper credentials. Logins authenticated by Standard Security are referred to as *nontrusted connections*. A nontrusted connection is a network connection that cannot use NT Server security to authenticate users. Standard Security is compatible with all types of network configurations.

Standard Security is not integrated with NT Server security. If a user is connecting to SQL Server via an NT Server network, the user will first have to log in to NT Server and be authenticated by it. After a user has passed this security barrier, the user has to log in to SQL Server. This, of course, requires users to log in twice.

Normally, if SQL Server users are going to access SQL Server via an NT Server network, SQL Server should be set up to use SQL Server's Integrated Security mode. By using this technique, users only have to log in once, not twice as required with Standard Security.

You may be wondering why SQL Server even offers a Standard Security mode if NT Server security can be used instead. There are two reasons why the Standard Security mode is available. First, it provides backward compatibility with previous versions of SQL Server. Hopefully, all of your SQL Servers have been upgraded to the most recent version, and this problem will not arise. However, some organizations are slow to upgrade.

Second, Standard Security enables SQL Server to be accessed by non-Windows networking clients, such as those running the Banyan VINES operating system. Non-Windows networking clients, however, cannot use NT Server Security to be authenticated. Instead, they are authenticated by their own operating systems. Because of this, Integrated Security will not work with these clients. By using Standard Security, a non-Windows client can access an SQL Server over a network. So, one of the main reasons Standard Security exists is to enable non-Windows networking clients to access SQL Server.

How a User is Authenticated Using Standard Security

Here is how a user is authenticated by SQL Server when the Standard Security mode is used:

▶ The client software used to access SQL Server prompts the user for a SQL Server login ID and password.

▶ The login ID and password are sent to SQL Server, where they are compared with the entries in a system table.

▶ If the login ID and password match one of the entries in the system table, a message is sent back to the client software, permitting access to SQL Server.

> ▶ If the login ID and password do not match any of the entries in the system table, a message is sent back to the client software, denying access to SQL Server.

How to Implement Standard Security

When SQL Server is installed, it automatically defaults to the Standard Security mode. You do not have to take any special steps to use Standard Security. This section takes a look at the Standard Security configuration, and how it is verified. Later sections will show you how to change from the Standard Security mode to one of the two other security modes.

To verify the Standard Security mode configuration, follow these steps:

1. From the Server Manager window of SQL Enterprise Manager, right-click on the SQL Server whose security mode you want to view and choose Configure. The Server Configuration/Options dialog box appears.

2. Click on the Security Options tab. The Security Options screen appears (see fig. 5.10)

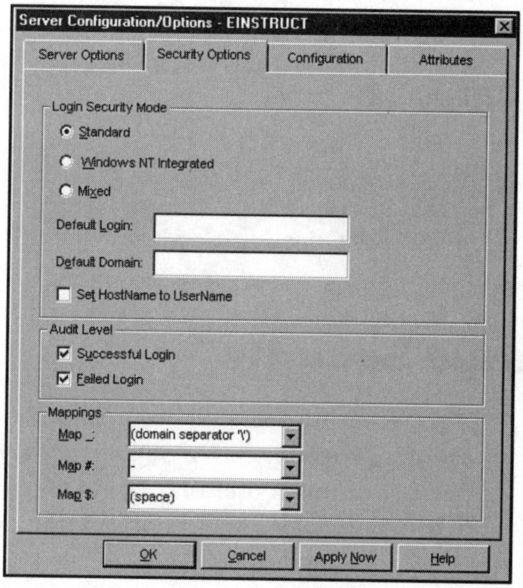

Figure 5.10

Security options are set from the Security Options tab.

Tip Another way to reach the Security Options screen is to choose Server, SQL Server, Configure from the Server drop-down menu in SQL Enterprise Manager.

Although this screen displays many options, there are only two that affect an SQL Server operating under Standard Security mode. The first is the Login Security mode section of the screen, which should be set to Standard for Standard Security.

The next portion of this screen that affects SQL Servers using Standard Security is the Audit Level. By default, these two options, Successful Login and Failed Login, are not selected. Selecting either of these turns on SQL Server login auditing. For example, if the Successful Login option is selected, and a user successfully logs in to SQL Server, the event is written to SQL Server's error log. If it is configured, it is also written to NT Server's Event Viewer Application log, or, if the Failed Login option is selected, and a user unsuccessfully attempts to log in to SQL Server, the event is written to SQL Server's error log. If it is configured, it is also written to NT Server's Event View Application log. Turn on this feature if security is an important issue for your organization.

The rest of the settings on this screen are not used by SQL Server's Standard Security mode. However, they will be described in the following sections when Integrated and Mixed Security are discussed.

Note SQL Server security modes can also be changed from the Set Security Options dialog box in the SQL Server Setup program.

Integrated Security

SQL Server's Integrated Security mode uses NT Server's authentication process instead of SQL Server's built-in security system. Because of this, a user only has to log in once, not twice, to access SQL Server. When an authorized user accesses SQL Server after logging in to NT Server, the user does not have to enter a login ID and password, as is required when SQL Server's Standard Security mode is used. This is because NT Server Accounts are associated with SQL Server login IDs, much as a database user ID is associated with a login ID. A login authenticated by NT Server is referred to as a *trusted connection.* A trusted connection is a connection that can be used by NT Server's authentication process to authenticate an NT Server account name.

Integrated Security mode provides you with all the advantages that NT Server security offers, including encrypted passwords, password aging, password uniqueness, password lockout, and domain-wide access to accounts.

Integrated Security is a great convenience for both the users and the DBA; users memorize one less ID and password, and the DBA does not have to create individual login Ids. The DBA does have some preliminary setup work, however, which is described in the following section. Integrated Security should be used in NT networking environments where all the clients accessing SQL Server are using Windows networking clients, such as Windows for Workgroups, Windows 95, or NT Workstation.

How a User Is Authenticated Using Integrated Security

Here is how a user is authenticated by SQL Server when the Integrated Security mode is used:

▶ The user must first log in to NT Server as he normally does, using his NT Server account names and passwords. If the NT network has more than one domain, the user will be authenticated by the account domain where the user account resides.

▶ The client software used to access SQL Server may or may not prompt the user for a SQL Server login ID and password, depending on how the software is designed. If a login ID and password are requested, this screen can be ignored.

▶ The user's NT Server account name is passed from NT Server to SQL Server. The password is not passed to SQL Server because it is not used to authenticate the user. All that is required is for the NT Server account name to be in a system table of SQL Server.

▶ SQL Server then compares the NT Server account name with entries in the system table and looks for a match.

▶ If there is a match, then the user is authenticated and logged in to SQL Server and the user's default database.

▶ If there is no match, then SQL Server checks if a guest login ID exists in the system table. If there is, then the user is logged in to SQL Server using the guest login ID. Remember, this login ID does not exist by default and must be created by the DBA, if it is needed (more on this special guest login ID later in this section).

▶ If there is no match and no guest login ID, the next step SQL Server takes is to determine whether or not the NT user account being used to log in to SQL Server has NT Server administrative rights. If it does, the user is logged in to SQL server using the sa user account. By default, all NT Server administrators have sa privileges on SQL Server.

▶ Finally, if there is no match, no guest login ID, and the NT user account is not an administrative account, a message is sent back to the client software and access to SQL Server is denied.

How to Prepare SQL Server for Integrated Security

In order to use SQL Server's Integrated Security mode, both SQL Server and any clients accessing SQL Server over a network must use a trusted connection. You will recall that a trusted connection is a special type of network connection that supports NT Server's authentication method to ensure security. Trusted connections are only possible if both SQL Server and SQL Server clients use either the Named Pipes or Multi-Protocol Net Libraries to communicate over a network.

Before you can configure SQL Server to use Integrated Security, you must ensure that either the Named Pipes or Multi-Protocol Net Libraries are installed on SQL Server and the clients who will access SQL Server over the network.

To verify whether or not SQL Server is configured to use the Named Pipes or Multi-Protocol Net Libraries, use SQL Server's Setup program. To verify whether or not the SQL Server client software is configured for the correct Net Libraries, use SQL Server's Client Configuration Utility.

If you currently do not have the proper Net Libraries on both SQL Server and its clients, you will need to add them before continuing with the following steps on how to configure SQL Server for Integrated Security.

If you are not able to use either the Named Pipes or Multi-Protocol Net Libraries for both SQL Server and all of its clients, you may not use Integrated Security. Instead, you must use either Standard or Mixed Security.

Note

In order for SQL Server to communicate to SQL Server clients, a common communications protocol must be used. The protocol is used to send network packets between SQL Server and a client. SQL Server can use a variety of communication protocols, referred to as *Net Libraries*. Net Libraries are dynamic link libraries (DDLs) used to implement various network protocols. Of the seven Net Libraries supported by SQL Server, only two support the trusted connection required for Integrated Security. These include the Named Pipes and Multi-Protocol Net Libraries.

Integrated Security Configuration Overview

Configuring SQL Server for Integrated Security is a multi-step process. The steps include the following:

▶ Setting SQL Server to use Integrated Security

▶ Creating NT Server Groups and Accounts

▶ Authorizing NT Server Groups and Accounts to access SQL Server

Setting SQL Server to Use Integrated Security

After you have verified that the proper Net Libraries have been loaded on both SQL Server and its clients, and that trusted connections are thereby enabled, you are ready to configure SQL Server to use Integrated Security. Follow these steps to configure SQL Server for Integrated Security:

1. From the Server Manager window of SQL Enterprise Manager, right-click on the SQL Server whose security mode you want to change and choose Configure. The Server Configuration/Options dialog box appears.

2. Click on the Security Options tab. The Security Options screen appears (see fig. 5.11).

3. Under Login Security Mode, click on the Windows NT Integrated box.

Figure 5.11

Security options are set from the Security Options tab.

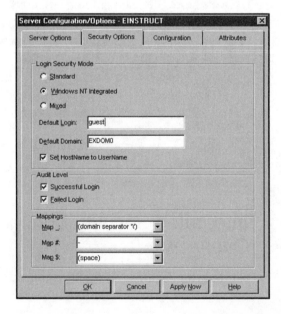

4. In the Default Login box, you may optionally enter a default SQL Server login ID that can be used by any NT Server account to log in to SQL, even if an NT Server account name does not have an explicit SQL Server login ID. If you leave this box blank, only SQL Server accounts with explicit permission will be able to log in to SQL Server. This last method ensures the best security.

   If you choose to use this option, enter a login ID, such as guest, to be used as a default login ID. Now, if an NT Server account tries to log in to SQL Server, and if it does not have an explicit SQL Server login ID, the NT user is automatically logged in to SQL Server under the guest login ID, and will be able to access those databases to which the "guest" login ID has explicit access. The guest login ID must be manually created in SQL Server; it is not automatically created when guest is entered into this box.

   In this case, the guest login ID differs from the guest database user ID used to automatically access databases that contain this database user ID.

5. In the Default Domain box, enter the name of the NT Server accounts' domain where the majority of the SQL Server users have their NT Server accounts. If the SQL Server does not belong to a domain, then enter the NetBIOS name of the computer that is running SQL Server.

   SQL Server uses the default domain name to distinguish between NT Server accounts of the same name that exist in different domains. There might be one NT Server account named jnelson in domain1, for example, and another NT Server account named jnelson in domain2. In order to differentiate between these two identical NT Server accounts, SQL Server will append the name of the domain, along with an underscore, to all NT Server accounts. For example, assuming domain1 is the default domain, then jnelson in domain2 would be renamed domain2_jnelson by SQL Server when it is mapped to SQL Server. (Although SQL Server is able to differentiate between identical NT Server account names coming from multiple domains, it is never a good practice to use the same NT Server account name within the same enterprise. Duplication can lead to NT permission-related problems, and even result in the circumvention of NT security.)

6. You will want to check the Set HostName to UserName box if it is not already checked. Doing this enables you to use the sp_who stored procedure to view the NT Server account name of those users logged in to SQL Server using trusted connections.

7. Under Audit Level, choose whether or not you want to log successful or unsuccessful logins. By default these two options, Successful Login and Failed Login, are not selected. If you select either of these, SQL Server login auditing is turned on. For example, if the Successful Login option is selected, and a user successfully logs in to SQL Server, the event is written to SQL Server's error log and, if configured, to NT Server's Event Viewer Application log. If the Failed Login option is selected, and a user unsuccessfully attempts to log in to SQL Server, the event is written to SQL Server's error log and, if configured, to NT Server's Event View Application log.

8. The Mappings section is only used if you use NT Server account names that include characters that are not valid in SQL Server login IDs. If you do, you will have to map these illegal characters to legal characters. Ideally, it is best not to use illegal SQL Server characters in NT Account names.

9. After you have made all the appropriate changes to this screen, click on OK, and the changes are saved by SQL Server, and SQL Server now begins using the Integrated Security mode.

 Note

SQL Server security modes can also be changed from the Set Security Options dialog box in the SQL Server Setup Program.

How to Map Illegal SQL Server Characters to Legal Characters

When Integrated Security is used in SQL Server, NT Server account names and passwords are used to authenticate users. Unfortunately, NT Server account names can include characters that are illegal in SQL Server login IDs. This is a problem because SQL Server uses the NT Server account name as the user's login ID in a system table. In order to use an NT Server account name that includes illegal characters as an SQL Server login ID, the illegal characters must be changed, or mapped, to legal characters.

The characters SQL Server considers illegal include the following:

- ► Ampersand &
- ► At Sign @
- ► Caret ^
- ► Domain Separator \
- ► Exclamation Point !
- ► Hyphen -
- ► Percent Sign %
- ► Period .
- ► Single Quotation '
- ► Space

If any NT Server account name uses one of the above illegal characters, the character must be mapped to a legal character, such as:

- ► Dollar $
- ► Pound #
- ► Underscore _

The NT Account name j-smith, for example, could be mapped as j$smith, j#smith, or j_smith. After mapping has taken place, the j-smith NT Account name will remain the same; the entry SQL Server makes in the syslogins system table in SQL Server is changed. The newly mapped name appears in the syslogins table, instead of the name as it appears in the NT account, and which contains the illegal characters.

To map illegal characters to legal characters, use the Mappings portion of the Security Options screen.

To map an illegal character, select the illegal character from one of the drop-down boxes that matches the legal character to which you want it mapped. If you want to map "\" to "_",for example, select "\" from the drop-down box next to the "Map _:" drop-down box. You may map up to three illegal characters to legal characters.

(To avoid mapping problems, make it a policy not to include illegal SQL Server characters in NT Account names.)

Creating NT Server Groups and Accounts

Through the use of Integrated Security, SQL Server is able to use the NT Server accounts and groups created with NT Server's User Manager for Domains tool (see fig. 5.12). SQL Server does not automatically use every NT Server account or group, only those that have been mapped to a SQL Server system table to access SQL Server, as described in the following section. The use of NT Server groups can make it much simpler to associate NT Server account names with SQL Server login IDs, as described in the following list.

Figure 5.12

NT Server's User Manager for Domains is used to create groups and accounts for SQL Server.

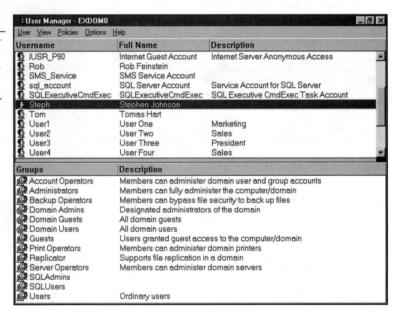

Although you have many choices how to create NT Server groups to be used with SQL Server, you may want to consider the following suggestions:

▶ Use global groups, not local groups, to organize your SQL Server users. The best practice is to use global groups to group like users, and to use local groups to assign rights and permissions.

► When naming groups, do not exceed 30 characters or use any of the illegal SQL Server characters described in the previous section.

► Keep in mind that SQL Server users may belong to only one group other than the public group. If you create NT Server groups to group like SQL Server users, a user should not be in more than one of these groups. If any user does belong to more than one group, SQL Server will enable the user to use the higher-level permissions, should the group permissions conflict.

► Create one NT Server global group for each set of SQL Server users that require the same level of permissions. For example, you might create one global group called dataentryusers for users who only need to enter data, another global group called readonlyusers for users who only need to lookup data, and another global group called managerusers who need to be able to access all the tables in a database.

► By default, all NT Administrators have sa privileges in SQL Server. If you do not want all NT Administrators to have sa privileges, then you need to create another NT Server global group called sqladministrators (or a similar name) that will include only those users who are allowed to have sa privileges in SQL Server. You will also have to manually revoke the sa privileges from the administrator groups using SQL Server Security Manager, as described in the next section. If you do create a special SQL Administrators global group, keep in mind that any user added to this group must also be a member of the NT Server Domain Administrators global group; otherwise, the individual will not be able to perform certain SQL Server administrative tasks, such as starting or stopping services.

► After all the groups have been created, place the appropriate NT Server accounts into the appropriate NT Server global groups. An NT Server account must be placed in an NT Server global group in order to have access to SQL Server. Access cannot be given to a single NT Server account, only to NT Server groups.

Authorizing NT Server Groups and Accounts to Access SQL Server

After all the necessary NT Server groups and accounts have been created, they must be associated with SQL Server login IDs in a system's table so they can access SQL Server. SQL Security Manager is used to perform this task. SQL Security Manager is a program separate from SQL Enterprise Manager and is launched from the SQL Server program group from the Start menu. To associate NT Server accounts with SQL Server login Ids, follow these steps:

1. Start the SQL Security Manager. The Connect Server dialog box appears.

2. From the Server drop-down box, select the server for which you want to authorize NT Server accounts. If no servers are listed in the drop-down box, click on the List Servers button, and select a server from this list. If you are logged in to NT Server as an administrator, you do not have to enter a login ID or password. Click on Connect.

   The SQL Security Manager window appears (see fig. 5.13). SQL Security Manager is able to assign two types of privileges to NT Server accounts that are a part of NT Server groups: either user privilege or sa privilege. Just as you might expect, user privileges are given to all NT Server accounts, except for those that need sa access.

   The SQL Security Manager can display two modes: either the user privilege (see fig. 5.13) or sa privilege view (see fig. 5.14), depending on which type of privilege you want to set at the time. To change the view, select the proper toolbar button (the one with a person is for the user privilege view, and the one with the computer and person is for the sa privilege view). You can also select the views via the View option from the drop-down menu.

3. To assign NT Server accounts user privileges, choose the user privilege view.

Figure 5.13

The user privilege view.

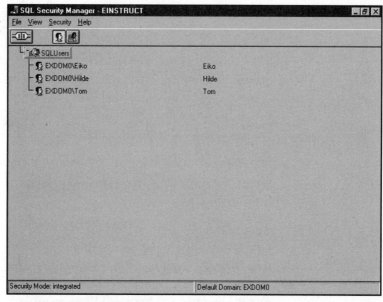

Figure 5.14

The sa privilege view.

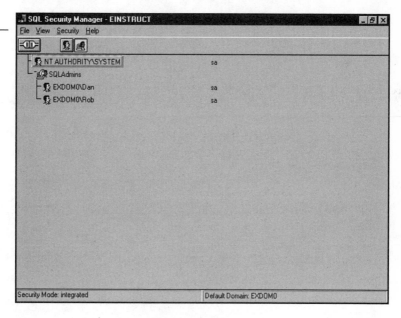

4. From the Security drop-down menu, choose Grant New.

   The Grant User Privilege dialog box appears (see fig. 5.15). The Grant Privilege window shows either local or global groups, depending on which button is selected next to Show. If Local Groups is selected, then local groups are displayed. If Groups on Default Domain is selected, then global groups are displayed.

5. Select either Local Groups or Groups on Default Domain to display the groups to which you want to grant SQL Server user privileges.

6. Be sure the box next to Add login IDs for group members is selected. Using this option automatically creates a separate user login ID in the syslogins system table for each NT Server account in the selected NT Server group, enabling anyone in the group to access SQL Server using his NT Account name. This is the step that actually maps the NT Server account name to an SQL Server login ID. If you do not check this box, an NT Server account in the selected group will not have a login ID automatically created for it, and the user will be unable to access SQL Server, unless he is accessing it under the optional guest login ID, described previously.

7. Check the Add Users to Database box. The Add Users to Database drop-down box becomes active (refer to fig. 5.15).

Figure 5.15

The Grant User Privilege dialog box.

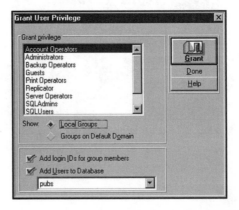

8. From the drop-down box, select a database to be the default database for all the NT Server account names that are in the group selected under Grant Privilege. The user will automatically be logged in to this database when he logs in to SQL Server. If you do not choose a default database, then the Master database will automatically become the default database for this user. It is not recommended that the Master database be the default database because a user does not usually have a database user ID for Master, and logs in under the guest account, which has no permissions other than to execute stored procedures.

9. After you have completed all the information in this dialog box, click on Grant. The Adding SQL Server Login IDs/ Users dialog box appears and displays the status of the NT Server Account names as they are added to SQL Servers syslogins system table (see fig. 5.16).

Figure 5.16

NT user accounts are automatically mapped to SQL Server.

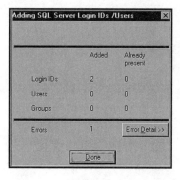

 Note

When SQL Server authorizes the NT Server Account names by placing the names in the syslogins table as login IDs, SQL Server puts in a random password at the same time. Integrated Security does not utilize this password.

10. To verify if any errors were encountered during this process, click on the Error Detail button, and an Error Detail screen is displayed. Take note of any errors, and make corrections as required. The error messages usually do a good job of describing any problems that arose during the procedure.

11. Click on Done. The Grant User Privileges dialog box reappears.

12. If you are finished, click on Done. The SQL Security Manager window reappears, and the NT Server group added appears in the SQL Security Manager window (see fig. 5.17).

Figure 5.17

The two NT user accounts (at left) are being mapped to SQL Server login IDs (at right).

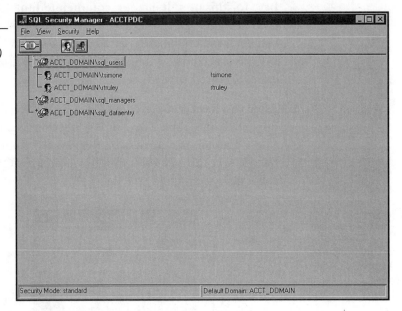

13. If you wish to view all the users in the group, double-click on the group name displayed on the screen, and all the users in the group will appear on the screen. The left column displays the NT Server account name, and the right column displays the mapped login ID, as it is entered into the syslogins system table (refer to fig. 5.17).

These NT Server accounts are now able to be used in order to log in to SQL Server using Integrated Security. (Note that if any of the NT Server account names contained illegal characters, these characters have now been mapped to legal ones.)

The preceding steps described how to configure an NT Server group for user privileges. The same steps apply when adding sa privileges to an NT Server group, the only difference being that you use the sa privilege view instead.

Note As you have already learned, all NT Server administrators receive sa privileges by default when the server is running under Integrated Security. If you want to alter these privileges, go to the sa privilege view and click on the Administrators group. To revoke sa privileges, select Security, Revoke from the Security drop-down menu and click on Yes to revoke the permission. Before you do this, however, verify that you have already created another global group in NT Server designated to group users who need the sa privilege, and that you have given the group this privilege by following the steps described previously for assigning groups privileges using SQL Security Manager.

Another feature of SQL Security Manager is its capability to perform a limited amount of login ID and database user ID management. When you double-click on any user in the user privilege view, the Account Detail dialog box appears. This box can be used to assign database user IDs to login IDs. This function and others, though, are more commonly performed through SQL Enterprise Manager.

After the SQL Server login IDs have been created for the NT Server accounts, the next step is to assign the appropriate database user IDs to the login IDs, as was explained earlier in the chapter.

Tip The SQL Security Manager is not the only tool at your disposal to grant or revoke user privileges to NT Server accounts. The xp_grantlogin extended procedure can also be used to grant user privileges, and the xp_revokelogin can be used to revoke user privileges.

Troubleshooting Integrated Security

If a client attempts to connect to an SQL Server using the Integrated Security mode, and the authentication fails, check the following possible trouble areas:

▶ Verify that the client has a good connection to the network. The problem may be as simple as a poor physical connection.

▶ Next, check to see if both SQL Server and the client attaching to the SQL Server are using either the Named Pipes or Multi-Protocol Net-Libraries. Both the SQL Server and the client must be using a trusted connection in order for Integrated Security to work.

▶ Verify that the user has both a proper NT Server Account name, and that the name has been mapped to an SQL Server system table using the SQL Security Manager.

Mixed Security

SQL Server's Mixed Security combines both SQL Server Standard and Integrated Security, and permits both trusted and nontrusted connections. When a user tries to log in to SQL Server, the system proceeds with NT Server login authentication. If authentication is unsuccessful, SQL Server Standard Security is used to verify the login. Mixed Security is best suited to environments where a mix of clients exists, some of whom are authenticated by NT Server, and some of whom are authenticated by SQL Server Standard Security. Your network, for example, may consist of a combination of NT Server and Banyan VINES. NT clients may access via Integrated Security, and Banyan VINES clients may use Standard Security.

How a User Is Authenticated Using Mixed Security

Here is what happens when a user attempts to log in to SQL Server using Mixed Security:

▶ If a user attempts to log in over a trusted connection (a connection using either the Named Pipes or Multi-Protocol Net-Libraries), SQL Server examines the login name to see if it matches the user's NT Server Account name, or if the login

ID entered is blank or contains spaces. If any of these conditions are true, SQL Server attempts to log in the user using
Integrated Security.

▶ If a user attempts to log in over a non-trusted connection, or
if the login ID entered is not the NT Server account name
(when using a trusted connection), then SQL Server attempts to log in the user using Standard Security.

How to Implement Mixed Security

Implementing SQL Server Mixed Security is much like implementing Integrated Security (with a twist of Standard Security for
variety). Because of this, the following instructions for implementing Mixed Security are abbreviated. Refer to the previous sections
on Integrated and Standard Security for more detail.

To implement Mixed Security, follow these steps:

1. Ensure that SQL Server has been set up to use trusted connections. Use the SQL Setup program to verify that either
   the Named Pipes or Multi-Protocol Net-Libraries have been
   selected.

2. From the Server Manager Window of SQL Enterprise Manager, right-click on the SQL Server whose security mode you
   want to change, and select Configure. The Server Configura-
   tion/Options dialog box appears.

3. Click on the Security Options tab.

   The Security Options screen appears (see fig. 5.18).

4. Under Login Security Mode, click on the box next to Mixed.

5. Complete the rest of the Server Configuration/Options
   screen as if you were implementing Integrated Security.

6. Using NT Server's User Manager for Domains, create the
   appropriate NT Server account names and groups for use by
   SQL Server, as you would if you were implementing Integrated Security.

Figure 5.18

Security options are set from the Security Options tab.

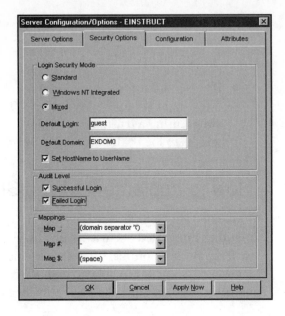

7. Use the SQL Security Manager to authorize the appropriate NT Server account and groups for use as SQL Server login IDs.

8. For those users who will be connecting to SQL Server via non-trusted connections using Standard Security, use SQL Enterprise Manager to create the necessary login IDs.

SQL Server is now set up for Mixed Security, and users can connect and be authorized by SQL Server to access any database for which they have been assigned a database user ID and the appropriate permissions.

Exercises

Exercise 5.1: Creating a Login ID Using SQL Enterprise Manager

Exercise 5.1 walks you through the process of using SQL Enterprise Manager to create a new login ID for SQL Server. You will generally use this procedure when SQL Server is running under either Standard or Mixed security. This exercise uses the Pubs sample database included with SQL Server, and should take less than five minutes to complete.

1. Load SQL Enterprise Manager.

2. From the Server Manager window, click on the plus sign next to the name of your SQL Server. The server name is highlighted, and the server's folders are displayed below the server name.

3. Choose Manage, Logins from the drop-down menu, or right-click on the Logins folder and choose New Login. The Manage Logins dialog box is displayed.

4. Type the name of a new login ID in the Login Name drop-down box. If the drop-down box is not blank, choose <New Login> from the drop-down box to clear the box.

5. Type a password for this login ID. The password is displayed as asterisks as it is entered.

6. Select a language for the user from the Default Language drop-down box. The default language is US English.

7. At this point, everything that is required to create a login ID has been entered. If the Add button is clicked on, the login ID is added to the selected SQL Server, and the login ID will be assigned the Master database as its default login database.

For more information on this topic, refer to the section "How to Create a New Login ID," earlier in this chapter.

Exercise 5.2: Creating a Login ID Using the sp_addlogin Stored Procedure

Exercise 5.2 shows you how to create a new login ID for SQL Server using the sp_addlogin stored procedure. Use the SQL Query tool from SQL Enterprise Manger to perform this exercise. Alternatively, this same exercise can be performed using ISQL/W. This procedure is generally used when SQL Server is running under either Standard or Mixed Security, and makes use of the Pubs sample database included with SQL Server. You should be able to complete this exercise in less than five minutes.

1. Load SQL Enterprise Manager.

2. Load the SQL Query tool by selecting Tools, SQL Query Tool from the drop-down menu. Be sure the default database is Master.

3. From the SQL Query tool, type

   sp_addlogin tfranklin, greenslime, *pubs*, us_english

4. Execute the query by clicking on the Execute Query button on the button bar, and the login ID is created. The preceding command creates a new login ID called tfranklin, with a password of greenslime, uses Pubs as the default database, and specifies that US English is the login ID's default language.

For more information on this procedure, refer to the section "How to Create a New Login ID," earlier in this chapter.

Exercise 5.3: Creating a Database User ID Using SQL Enterprise Manager

Exercise 5.3 steps you through the process of using SQL Enterprise Manager to create a new database user ID. The exercise uses the *pubs* sample database included with SQL Server, and should take less than 10 minutes to complete.

1. Load SQL Enterprise Manager.

2. From the Server Manager window, click on the plus sign next to the name of the SQL Server. The server name is

highlighted, and the server's folders are displayed below the server name.

3. Choose Manage, Logins from the drop-down menu, or click on the Logins folder in the Server Manager windows. All the current login IDs are displayed. Right-click on a login ID and select Edit. Whichever of the two above options you use, the Manage Logins dialog box is displayed.

4. If the login ID with which you want to associate a new database user ID is not displayed in the Login Name drop-down box, click on the drop-down box and select a login ID from the list.

5. To create a new database user ID, click on the empty box under the Permit column next to the database for which you want to create a new database user ID.

   After you click the empty box, a blue checkmark appears in the Permit column, along with the login ID in the box under the User column, and the group name public under the Group column.

   The blue check in the Permit column indicates that the current login ID has been granted permission to access this particular database. The login ID in the User column is the default database user ID for this login ID in this database. The group name public in the Group column confirms that the database user name has been added to the public group.

   If you want to assign this login ID a specific default database into which the user is automatically logged when he first accesses SQL Server, click on the box under the Default column, on the row for the appropriate database.

   If you want to assign this login ID an alias for any of the databases it is permitted to access, add the alias by clicking on the box under the Alias column that corresponds to the database for which you want the alias created, and select an alias from the drop-down box that appears.

continues

Exercise 5.3: Continued

      6. After you have created one or more database user IDs for this login ID, click Modify, and the database user Ids, along with any other changes you made to the login ID, are saved.

For more information, refer to the section "How to Create New Database User IDs," earlier in this chapter.

Exercise 5.4: Creating a Database User ID Using the sp_adduser Stored Procedure

Exercise 5.4 shows you how to create a new database user ID using the sp_adduser stored procedure. You will be using the SQL Query tool in SQL Enterprise Manager to perform this exercise. Alternatively, this same exercise can be performed using ISQL/W. The exercise uses the Pubs sample database included with SQL Server, and should take less than five minutes to complete.

      1. Load SQL Enterprise Manager.

      2. Load the SQL Query tool by choosing Tools, SQL Query Tool from the drop-down menu.

      3. Choose the Pubs database from the DB drop-down menu.

      4. From the SQL Query tool, type

         sp_adduser tfranklin, tfranklin

      5. Execute the query by clicking on the Execute Query button on the button bar, and the login ID is created. The preceding command creates a new database user ID called tfranklin for the login ID tfranklin.

For more information, refer to the section "How to Create New Database User IDs," earlier in this chapter.

Exercise 5.5: Creating a Group Using SQL Enterprise Manager

Exercise 5.5 steps you through the process of using SQL Enterprise Manager to create a new group. You must create at least one new group before completing upcoming exercises. The exercise uses the *pubs* sample database included with SQL Server, and should take less than five minutes to complete.

1. Load SQL Enterprise Manager.

2. From the Server Manager window, click on the plus sign next to the name of the SQL Server. The server name is highlighted and the server's folders are displayed below the server name.

3. Click on the plus sign next to the Databases folder to display all the current databases being managed by SQL Server.

4. Click on the plus sign next to the Pubs database so that it is highlighted and the Groups/Users and Objects folders are displayed. Select Manage, Groups from the drop-down menu, or right-click on the Groups/Users folder, and select New Group. The Manage Groups dialog appears.

5. Type the name of the new group in the Group drop-down box. If the drop-down box is not blank, choose <New Group> from the drop-down box to clear the box.

6. Click on the Add button, and the group is added.

For more information, refer to the section "How to Create a New Group," earlier in this chapter.

Exercise 5.6: Creating a Group Using the sp_addgroup Stored Procedure

Exercise 5.6 shows you how to create a new group by using the sp_addgroup stored procedure. You will be using the SQL Query tool from SQL Enterprise Manger to perform this exercise. Alternatively, this same exercise can be performed using ISQL/W. The exercise uses the Pubs sample database included with SQL Server, and should take less than five minutes to complete.

1. Load SQL Enterprise Manager.

2. Load the SQL Query tool by choosing Tools, SQL Query Tool from the drop-down menu.

continues

Exercise 5.6: Continued

3. Choose the Pubs database from the DB drop-down menu.

4. From the SQL Query tool, type:

   sp_addgroup managers

5. Execute the query by clicking on the Execute Query button on the toolbar, and the managers group is created and added to the Pubs database.

For more information, refer to the section "How to Create a New Group," earlier in this chapter.

Exercise 5.7: How to Add and Drop Users from a Group Using SQL Enterprise Manager

Exercise 5.7 steps you through the process of adding and dropping database user IDs from a group by using SQL Enterprise Manager. The exercise uses the Pubs sample database included with SQL Server, and should take less than five minutes to complete.

1. Load SQL Enterprise Manager.

2. From the Server Manager window, click on the plus sign next to the name of the SQL Server. The server name is highlighted and the server's folders are displayed below the server name.

3. From the server, click on the plus sign next to the Databases folder to display the databases managed on the server.

4. Click on the plus sign next to the Pubs database to display the Groups/Users and Objects folders.

5. Click on the plus sign next to the Groups/Users folder to display all the groups for this database.

6. Right-click on the group to which you want to add a new user, and select Edit. The Manage Groups dialog box appears.

7. To add a current database user ID to a group, click on a database user ID in the Users box, and then click on Add. This moves the database user ID from the Users side to the Users in Group side.

8. To remove a database user from a group, click on a database user ID from the Users in Group side, and then click on Remove. This will move the database user ID from the Users in Group side to the Users side.

   Note that the database user ID is not deleted, only removed from the group, and is still a member of the public group.

For more information, refer to the sections "How to Add Database User IDs to a Group" and "How to Remove Database User IDs from a Group," earlier in this chapter.

Exercise 5.8: How to Add and Drop Users from a Group Using the sp_changegroup Stored Procedure

Exercise 5.8 shows you how to add and drop a database user ID from a group by using the sp_changegroup stored procedure. You will be using the SQL Query tool from SQL Enterprise Manager to perform this exercise. Alternatively, this same exercise can be performed using ISQL/W. The exercise uses the Pubs sample database included with SQL Server, and should take less than five minutes to complete.

1. Load SQL Enterprise Manager.

2. Load the SQL Query tool by choosing Tools, SQL Query Tool from the drop-down menu.

3. Choose the Pubs database from the DB drop-down menu.

4. From the SQL Query tool, type

   sp_changegroup managers, tfranklin

5. Execute the query by clicking on the Execute Query button on the button bar, and the database user ID tfranklin is added to the managers group.

continues

Exercise 5.8: Continued

There is no way to drop a database user from a group by using a stored procedure, but the same effect can be obtained by moving a database user ID from one group (thus dropping the user from the group) to another.

For more information, refer to the sections "How to Add Database User IDs to a Group" and "How to Remove Database User IDs from a Group," earlier in this chapter.

Exercise 5.9: How to Implement SQL Server Integrated Security

Exercise 5.9 steps you through the process of changing the security mode of SQL Server from Standard Security to Integrated Security. Before you begin, be sure that SQL Server is using either the Named Pipes or Multi-Protocol Net-Libraries. The exercise should take less than 15 minutes to complete.

1. From the Server Manager window of SQL Enterprise Manager, right-click on the SQL Server whose security mode you want to change, and choose Configure. The Server Configuration/Options dialog box appears.

2. Click on the Security Options tab. The Security Options screen appears.

3. Under Login Security Mode, click on the Windows NT Integrated box.

4. In the Default Login box, you have the option of entering a default SQL Server login ID that can be used by any NT Server account to log in to SQL, even if the NT Server account name does not have an explicit SQL Server login ID.

   If you want to use this option, enter a login ID, such as guest, to be used as a default login ID.

5. In the Default Domain box, enter the name of the NT Server accounts domain in which the majority of the SQL Server users have their NT Server accounts. If the SQL Server does not belong to a domain, enter the NetBIOS name of the computer which is running SQL Server.

6. Check the Set HostName to UserName box if it is not already checked. Doing so will enable you to use the sp_who stored procedure to view the NT Server account names of those users logged in to SQL Server via trusted connections.

7. Under Audit Level, choose whether or not you want to log successful or unsuccessful logins.

8. The Mappings section is only used if you encounter NT Server account names that include illegal characters. If you do, you will have to map these illegal characters to legal characters.

9. After you have made all the appropriate changes to this screen, click on OK, and the changes are saved by SQL Server. SQL Server now begins using the Integrated Security mode.

For more information, refer to the sections "Integrated Security Configuration Overview," "Setting SQL Server to Use Integrated Security," "Creating NT Server Groups and Accounts," and "Authorizing NT Server Groups and Accounts to Access SQL Server," earlier in this chapter.

Review Questions

The following questions will test your knowledge of the information covered in this chapter.

1. Before any user can access information stored on an SQL Server using Standard Security, the user must first enter into SQL Server which one of the following types of user accounts?

    A. Database User ID.

    B. Login ID.

    C. NT user account.

    D. A separate user account is not required when using Standard Security.

2. After entering her login ID, Veronica receives the following error message: `Message 916: Server user id veronica is not a valid user in database 'marketing'`. What is the most likely cause of this message?

    A. Veronica does not have a valid login ID.

    B. Veronica does not have a valid database ID for the database marketing.

    C. The marketing database does not exist.

    D. Veronica entered an incorrect password after entering her database ID.

3. Select all of the following user names that a user has to type in when trying to access information stored in an SQL Server database when SQL Server is set up for Integrated Security?

    A. Login ID

    B. Group membership ID

    C. Database User ID

    D. NT user account

4. If Frank from the accounting department wants to access both the accounting and the marketing SQL Servers, how many login IDs does he need?

    A. 1

    B. 2

    C. 3

    D. 4

5. When SQL Server is first installed, which login IDs are automatically created?

    A. sa

    B. probe

    C. repl_publisher

    D. repl_subscriber

6. What is the default password assigned to the sa account immediately after SQL Server is installed?

    A. sa.

    B. password.

    C. The password is user-assigned.

    D. No password is automatically assigned.

7. When SQL Server is set up to use Standard Security, which role does the probe account play?

   A. Probe is not a legal login ID.

   B. Probe is only used under Integrated Security.

   C. Probe is used by some applications that need to access SQL Server under Standard Security.

   D. Probe is only required if database replication is being used.

8. Devin wants to access the production, marketing, and human resources databases stored on the company's single SQL Server. How many database user IDs must be created for Devin?

   A. None, if Devin already has a login ID

   B. 1

   C. 2

   D. 3

9. Which of the following statements about the dbo database user ID are true?

   A. The DBO of a database is the owner of the database.

   B. Whoever creates a database is the DBO of the database.

   C. The DBO may access a database she owns under more than one database user ID.

   D. A database may have more than one DBO.

10. The SA of an SQL Server wants all the users who already have login IDs to access the mail database, but he does not want to create a special database user ID for every login ID. How can the SA accomplish this task?

   A. He does not have to do anything. This occurs by default.

B. This goal is not possible. Each login ID must have an associated database user ID.

C. The SA can tell all of the users to log in to SQL Server using the guest login ID. This will automatically allow all users immediate access to the database.

D. The SA can create a database user ID called guest. After this is done, any user with a login ID can automatically access the mail database.

11. The SA of an SQL Server wants to ensure that all of the objects created in the database have the same owner. The problem is that there will be three separate database developers creating new database objects in the database, and each database developer has a different login ID and database user ID. What can the SA do to ensure that all database objects have the same owner?

A. The SA can alias each of the database developers into the database as the DBO.

B. Each of the database developers can log in using the same login ID.

C. The SA can create a special database developer database user ID.

D. The SA should not be worried about which user owns which database objects; this goal is irrelevant.

12. A database user ID that can be shared among two or more login IDs is called a(n):

A. Shared login ID.

B. Alias.

C. Shared database ID.

D. This feature is not available.

13. The SA wants to streamline the process of assigning object permissions. Which one of the following methods will help the SA accomplish this goal?

   A. Create database user groups and assign the appropriate database user IDs to each database user group.

   B. Create login ID groups and assign the appropriate database user IDs to each login ID group.

   C. Create login ID groups and assign the appropriate login IDs to each login ID group.

   D. Create NT global groups and assign to each the appropriate database user IDs.

14. The DBO of a database wants all the database user IDs already created in the database, along with all database user IDs to be created in the future, to have the same access to the *names* table object. Which group does the DBO need to create to achieve this goal?

   A. The DBO does not have to have to create any groups or make any special group assignments. The built-in public group offers this capability.

   B. The DBO can create a new group called guests. By default, all database user IDs automatically belong to the guests group.

   C. The DBO can create a new group called public, and add all of the database user IDs to this group.

   D. The DBO is not allowed to create groups. Only the SA can create a group in a database.

15. The SA wants to assign a user to three different database groups within the same database. How can the SA accomplish this objective?

   A. Use SQL Enterprise Manager to create all three groups in the database; then assign the user to all three groups.

B. Use stored procedures to create all three groups in the database; then assign the user to all three groups.

C. Use Transact-SQL statements to create all three groups in the database; then assign the user to all three groups.

D. The SA cannot reach his objective because it is against SQL Server's rules.

16. The SA wants to create a group named marketing in two different databases. How will the SA accomplish this goal?

A. The SA will create one SQL Server group named marketing.

B. The SA will create two SQL Server groups named marketing, one in each database.

C. The SA will create one database group named marketing.

D. The SA will create two database groups named marketing, one in each database.

17. The SA wants to group login IDs by departmental function. How can the SA accomplish this goal?

A. The SA will create a variety of SQL Server groups and assign the appropriate login IDs to each.

B. The SA will create a variety of database groups and assign the appropriate database user IDs to each.

C. Only the DBO of a database can create database groups, so the SA will have to ask the DBO to create the necessary groups.

D. Login IDs cannot be segregated into groups, so the SA cannot accomplish this objective.

18. Jill is setting up user accounts on a new SQL Server. In what order will she most likely create the following?

    A. Database Users IDs, Login IDs, Groups

    B. Database Users IDs, Groups, Login IDs

    C. Groups, Login IDs, Database User IDs

    D. Groups, Database User IDs, Login IDs

19. Which of the following methods can be used to create a new login ID?

    A. CREATE LOGIN_ID

    B. sp_addlogin

    C. CREATE LOGIN

    D. sp_create_login

20. Which of the following login IDs are not legal login IDs in SQL Server?

    A. _robyn

    B. 10robyn

    C. robyninthesalesdepartment

    D. robyn-cook

21. Which of the following login ID passwords are legal in SQL Server?

    A. 4ZdkkL3

    B. teLLy

    C. patient-cookie

    D. 44877690

22. Who has permission to add and drop login IDs?

    A. SA

    B. DBO

    C. Alias

    D. Probe

23. The SA attempts to drop a login ID, but gets an error message stating that the login ID cannot be dropped. What is the most likely cause of this error message?

    A. The SA does not have the necessary permission to drop the login ID.

    B. The login ID that the SA is trying to drop owns at least one database object in a database.

    C. The SQL Server service has been turned off.

    D. The SQL Server Master database has become corrupt.

24. Who is able to create a database user ID within any given database?

    A. SA.

    B. DBO.

    C. Any user who has been assigned this permission.

    D. Only the database user himself can create his own database user ID.

25. When a login ID is created from SQL Enterprise Manager, what other tasks may be completed at the same time?

    A. The database user ID can be created.

    B. The database user can be assigned to a group.

    C. The login ID can be assigned an alias.

    D. Statement permissions can be assigned to the login ID.

26. Which of the following statements can be used to drop a login ID from SQL Server?

    A. sp_droplogin

    B. drop login

    C. sp_removelogin

    D. Login IDs can only be removed with SQL Enterprise Manager.

27. When SQL Enterprise Manager is used to create a database user ID, what other tasks can the SA perform at the same time?

    A. Select a default database for the login ID.

    B. Change the database user's login ID password.

    C. Set object permissions for the database user ID.

    D. Nothing else can be done at this time.

28. Rhonda has just taken over management of an SQL Server that has been in production for over a year. She notices that every database has a guest account, but no other database user accounts. Her first thought is: how can users access a database without having a database user ID in each database they need to access? What does Rhonda have to do in order to get the SQL Server to work as she thinks it should work?

    A. Rhonda does not have to do anything. The current design of the SQL Server database user accounts is perfectly legal and desirable.

    B. Although Rhonda does not have to do anything to makes things work as they should, she should significantly limit the use of the guest account because of possible security issues. From now on, access to the database should be via database user Ids and not via the guest account to allow database access instead of only using the guest account.

   C. Rhonda needs to immediately remove the guest account and create an all-new database user ID for each login ID currently existing on this particular SQL Server.

   D. After re-evaluating the SQL Server setup, Rhonda should add a database user ID for each login ID for every database on this SQL Server, in order to significantly boost the security of the current system.

29. What is the significance of using the public group to help manage database user IDs?

   A. By default, each database user ID belongs to the public group and cannot be removed from this group, unless the ID is dropped from the database.

   B. The guest account is always a member of the public group.

   C. The public group can be dropped if necessary.

   D. Both login IDs and database user IDs can belong to the public group.

30. Which of the following techniques can be used to create or drop a group?

   A. SQL Enterprise Manager

   B. CREATE GROUP and DROP GROUP

   C. sp_addgroup and sp_dropgroup

   D. SQL Security Manager

31. Jeffrey has been assigned the task of choosing the most appropriate security mode for a new SQL Server installation. The clients who will be attaching to the SQL Server include NT Workstation, Windows 95, and Windows for Workgroups 3.11, which is using the NetWare IPX/SPX protocol stack. Which security mode is most appropriate for the SQL Server?

    A. Standard

    B. Integrated

    C. Mixed

    D. NetWare-Enhanced Standard Security

32. Jenny has implemented Integrated Security in her new SQL Server. Although most of the SQL Server clients are able to access SQL Server, several are not able to communicate. She has tested the network connection between these clients and the server, and has determined that the network is not responsible for the problem. What is the most likely cause of this problem?

    A. The clients are using an older version of NT Workstation that is not compatible with SQL Server.

    B. The users who are trying to log in to the SQL Server from these clients do not yet have login IDs.

    C. These clients' SQL Server client software is corrupt.

    D. The SQL Server clients displaying the problem are using the Banyan IP protocol stack.

33. How does a SQL Server running Standard Security authenticate users?

    A. SQL server compares the login ID and password with the login ID and password stored in NT Server's user accounts database.

    B. SQL Server compares the login ID and password with the login ID and password stored in the Master database.

    C. SQL Server compares the login ID and password with the login ID and password stored in the various user databases.

    D. SQL Servers compares the login ID and password with the login ID and password stored in the key server.

34. Betty has decided to implement Integrated Security in a new SQL Server. What should she use to create the login IDs necessary for users to access SQL Server?

    A. sp_addlogin

    B. SQL Enterprise Manager

    C. SQL Security Manager

    D. NT Server's User Manager for Domains

35. Before Sara can implement Integrated Security on a production SQL Server that has been running for over two years, what must she check to determine whether or not Integrated Security can even be implemented?

    A. She must ensure that all the SQL Server clients are running either NT Server or NT Workstation.

    B. She must ensure that all SQL Server clients have a trusted connection to the SQL Server.

    C. She must ensure that all the login IDs previously created over the past two years match the NT Server user accounts currently being used.

    D. Sara cannot implement Integrated Security on a SQL Server that has already been running Standard Security.

36. Integrated Security offers what advantages over Standard Security?

    A. Integrated Security takes advantage of NT Server's built-in security, which includes encrypted passwords, password aging, password lockout, along with many more features.

    B. Integrated Security eliminates the need for users to log in to SQL Server as a separate step.

    C. Integrated Security offers public/private key encryption of data, ensuring C-2 level security.

    D. Integrates Security enables users to access data from a SQL Server database over the Internet, but Standard Security does not.

37. Brett is using an SQL Server client to access an SQL Server that uses Integrated Security. She has already logged in to an NT Server domain and has been authenticated. When she attempts to log in to the SQL Server for the first time, she is presented with a login screen, even though Integrated Security is in place. Why is she prompted to enter a login ID and password?

    A. Even when Integrated Security is being used, a user must always log in to SQL Server using a login ID and password.

    B. The client is using a nontrusted network connection.

    C. Brett has not been assigned a login ID yet, and the SA must first create a login ID for her.

    D. There is nothing wrong. If Brett ignores the login screen, she will automatically be logged in to SQL Server.

38. Beth has just set up Integrated Security on a new SQL Server. She has also entered all of the NT user accounts into the NT domain's user accounts database by using the User Manager for Domains. Even though all the accounts and passwords have been entered correctly, none of the users are able to log in to SQL Server. What is the most likely cause of this problem?

    A. She has assigned the wrong NT NTFS permission to each of the NT user accounts.

    B. She has forgotten to use the SQL Security Manager to assign the NT User accounts to SQL Server as login IDs.

    C. She has forgotten to use SQL Enterprise Manager to map the NT user accounts to SQL Server login IDs.

    D. She is using the wrong transport protocol between SQL Server and all the clients.

39. Nathan, the SA for the company's SQL Server, has just added two new NT user accounts to the domain's user accounts database. SQL Server has been set up to use Integrated Security. Although one of the accounts works fine, the other does not work. What is the most likely cause of this problem?

    A. Nathan must use the SQL Security Manager to map the account that is not currently working.

    B. The account that is not working has an illegal character that is understood by NT, but not by SQL Server.

    C. The failing account has been given the incorrect NTFS permissions.

    D. Nathan must first assign the account a database user ID before it can be used to access SQL Server.

40. A SQL Server has just been put into production and you notice that any user with NT administrative privileges has the capability to access SQL server as an SA. This presents a security problem as you want to restrict SA privileges to a very specific group of people. How can you prevent an NT administrator from being the SA on SQL Server?

    A. It is not possible to prevent NT administrators from being an SA on SQL Server.

    B. Change the NTFS permissions using NT's Explorer.

    C. Change the permissions using SQL Enterprise Manager.

    D. Change the permissions using SQL Security Manager.

Review Answers

1. B

2. B

3. D

4. B

5. A, B

6. D

7. C

8. D

9. A, B

10. D

11. A

12. B

13. A

14. A

15. D

16. D

17. D

18. C

19. B

20. B, D

21. B

22. A

23. B

24. A, B

25. A, B, C

26. A

27. A, B

28. B

29. A

30. A, C

31. C

32. D

33. B

34. D

35. B

36. A, B

37. D

38. B

39. B

40. D

Answers to Test Yourself Questions at Beginning of Chapter

1. A separate login ID account must first be created for each of the three SQL Servers. After these are created, a database user ID account must be created for each of the four databases Veronica needs to access. To ease the burden of administration, the same name can be assigned to all of the accounts. See "SQL Server Login and User Accounts."

2. Login IDs can be created by using either SQL Enterprise Manager or the sp_addlogin stored procedure. See "How to Create a New Login ID."

3. Some of the possible correct answers include: Login IDs can only be created by the SA, are specific to a single SQL Server, and must be unique for that server. Login IDs can be up to 30 alphanumeric characters long, but the first character must be a letter or the symbols # or _. Login IDs are not case sensitive. See "Managing SQL Server Login IDs and Database User IDs."

4. Database User IDs can be created using either SQL Enterprise Manager or the sp_adduser stored procedure. See "How to Create New Database User IDs."

5. To create new database user ID accounts from SQL Enterprise Manager, go to the Manage Logins dialog box. From this box it is not only possible to create database user ID accounts, it is also possible to create new login IDs, to assign a database user ID to a group, and to assign a database user ID a variety of database permissions. See "How to Create New Database User IDs."

6. Using SQL Enterprise Manager, database user Ids can be added to or dropped from a database at any time by following this procedure:

   ▶ Select a server from the Server Manager window and open its Databases folder.

   ▶ Open the appropriate database to display the Groups/Users folder.

   ▶ Open the Groups/Users folder.

   ▶ Right-click on the appropriate group and select Edit.

   ▶ From this screen, you can either add or remove users from the selected group. See "Managing SQL Server Database Groups."

C h a p t e r

Managing Permissions

6

In the previous chapter you learned how to create login IDs in order to permit access to SQL Server, and how to create database user IDs in order to permit access to databases stored in SQL Server. Both are important first steps that must be taken before users can access data stored in an SQL Server database. There is still one more step required, however, before a user can access data: the user must be given the necessary permissions to access the data.

In this chapter, you will learn how to grant and revoke database permissions using both SQL Enterprise Manager and Transact-SQL statements. Understanding how to grant and revoke permissions using both methods is an important step in preparing for the exam. You will also learn about statement and object permissions, who is able to grant which type of permission, and the importance of properly applying permissions to database objects in order to prevent broken ownership chains.

As always, this chapter begins with a list of the exam objectives relating to the topic at hand, and then moves on to the chapter pretest. Valuable information is offered that directly addresses the objectives, and additional relative discussion topics are presented. The chapter concludes with exercises, chapter review questions, and finally, the answers to both the review questions and the chapter pretest questions.

This chapter focuses on permissions management, and helps you prepare for the exam by addressing and fully covering the listed objectives. You will learn how to achieve the following objectives:

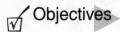 **Objectives**

▶ Identify system administrator (sa) functionality

▶ Predict the outcome of a broken ownership chain

▶ Grant and revoke permissions

▶ Implement various methods of securing access to data

Test Yourself! Before reading this chapter, test yourself to determine how much study time you will need to devote to this section.

1. What is the difference between a statement permission and an object permission?

2. By default, what permissions are assigned to the system administrator (SA), database owner (DBO), database object owner (DBOO), and every-day users?

3. Veronica, the newly appointed marketing manager needs permission to select, add, delete, and update records in the sales database. The records she needs to access are stored in the sales, inventory, and inventory tables. She already has a login ID and a database user ID. As the database administrator (DBA), what do you need to give to Veronica to give her the access she needs to the data stored in the marketing database, and how will you accomplish this task?

4. As the DBA of the organization's SQL Server, you are overseeing the creation of a new database by two database developers. Sara has been assigned a login ID and database user ID of sara, and Debbie has been assigned a login ID and database user ID of debbie. Both developers will be creating new objects in the database during the development project. Normally, each developer logs in to SQL Server using her assigned login ID and database user ID. Once the database is complete, and Sara and Debbie have completed their work, it is up to you to assign permissions to the various database objects in order to enable users to access the necessary data. Based on this scenario, will your job of assigning permissions to users be easy or difficult, and why?

5. As the DBA, you have been invited to participate in the planning of a new database. The database developers want your advice on how they can make your job as DBA easier. What suggestions might you offer them in order to make it easier for you to assign permissions to objects, while at the same time ensuring that the data is well protected?

Answers are located at the end of the chapter...

Assigning User Permissions

Permissions are used in SQL Server to specify which users are permitted to use which objects, and what they are allowed to do to with those objects. For example, a user named jknox may be given access to the sales table, in order to make changes to it (see fig. 6.1). Without the proper permissions, a user, although able to access a database, cannot access the objects in a database unless he has been granted the proper permissions.

SQL Server has two different types of permissions:

▶ Statement permissions

▶ Object permissions

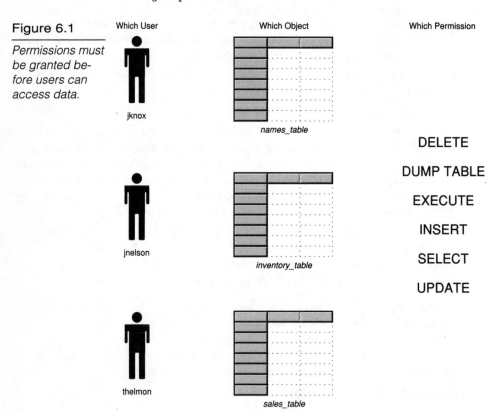

Figure 6.1

Permissions must be granted before users can access data.

Which User

jknox

Which Object

names_table

jnelson

inventory_table

thelmon

sales_table

Which Permission

DELETE

DUMP TABLE

EXECUTE

INSERT

SELECT

UPDATE

Statement permissions enable users to execute specific Transact-SQL statements that are used to create database objects, or to backup databases and transaction logs. For example, before a user can create a new table in a database, he has to be granted the necessary statement permission. *Object permissions* determine what a user may do to a preexisting database object. Before a user can view data in a specific table, for example, he has to be granted the necessary object permission.

Permissions are assigned to a user based on what the user needs to do with the data stored by SQL Server. Some users may only need to view data, others may need to query data and produce reports, others may need to change data, and so on. One of the major responsibilities of the DBA is to determine which users need access to which objects, and what permissions they need.

Before granting permissions to users, it is important for the DBA to carefully consider the users' needs. The more careful the planning, the easier it will be for the DBA to implement and manage permissions.

Permissions assigned to one database managed by SQL Server are independent of permissions assigned to another database. If a user needs access to tables in two different databases, then that user must have database user IDs in both databases, and the necessary permissions granted in each database for each object he needs to access.

Understanding Transact-SQL

An Introduction

Throughout this book, and especially in this chapter, you will encounter Transact-SQL statements. If you are new to SQL Server, you will want to read this sidebar to learn exactly what Transact-SQL is. If you are already familiar with Transact-SQL, you can skip this section.

Whenever you communicate with SQL Server, you ultimately speak to it using Transact-SQL. *Transact-SQL* is the language that SQL Server interprets. Whenever you use SQL Enterprise

continues

Manager to create or manage a database, SQL Enterprise Manager translates your request into Transact-SQL, which is in turn submitted to SQL Server for execution.

If you like, you can directly communicate with SQL Server using Transact-SQL. As a DBA, you will usually find it more convenient to manage SQL Server using SQL Enterprise Manager, or other SQL Server tools, rather than typing in Transact-SQL statements. GUI-based tools can make your job easier because you don't have to remember specific Transact-SQL statements, and you don't have to worry about making typing mistakes. There are some SQL Server tasks that can only be performed using Transact-SQL, however, such as preparing an SQL database for use on removable media. In other instances, it is more efficient to use Transact-SQL to perform some tasks, rather than using a GUI interface. This is especially the case when you create your own Transact-SQL scripts to automate routine administrative tasks. A *script* is a series of Transact-SQL statements executed together, similar to a DOS batch file.

Transact-SQL is a superset of the industry-standard ANSI-92 SQL relational database manipulation language. It was developed by Microsoft to communicate with SQL Server and includes many enhancements not included in the ANSI-92 version.

You may be wondering if Transact-SQL isn't more a subject for database developers than for DBAs. The answer is no. Although a DBA does not need to become an expert Transact-SQL programmer, he does need to know the basics. As a DBA, you need to know how to use Transact-SQL to create, manage, and query data in SQL Server databases. You also want to be able to talk intelligently with SQL developers, and that requires a basic understanding of the programming language used to create SQL Server client/server applications.

Transact-SQL Fundamentals

Unlike most programming languages, Transact-SQL is not designed to perform general tasks. For example, you cannot use it to write a spreadsheet program or to control an automated assembly line. It is a specialized language designed specifically for creating, managing, and extracting information from relational databases.

Most common programming languages are procedural in nature, meaning that the programmer specifies in the code itself how the program should execute. If a programmer wants to search through a group of records, looking for a specific piece of data, for example, the code is written in such a way as to evaluate one record at a time—field by field—until all the records have been examined. If a match is found, the results are displayed on the screen or printed in a report. The programmer is responsible for specifying exactly how the search should be conducted.

Transact-SQL is not a procedural language. Instead, the Transact-SQL programmer specifies which results are desired, then submits the request to SQL Server. It is up to SQL Server as to how to go about searching for the data. After a search method has been decided upon, it conducts the search, and then produces the results, often called a *results set* or *results output*. In addition, SQL Server does not search for data in a database record by record. Instead, SQL Server searches entire data sets (a table, for example) instead. So, SQL Server can find data quickly, even if the database is large.

Transact-SQL statements can be divided into three major categories: data definition, data manipulation, and data control. *Data definition* statements are designed for defining a database, modifying its structure after it is created, and dropping it when it is no longer needed (CREATE, DROP). *Data manipulation* statements are used for entering, changing, and extracting data (INSERT, UPDATE, DELETE, SELECT). *Data control* statements provide a way to protect a database from corruption (GRANT, REVOKE).

Transact-SQL Improves on ANSI-92 SQL

ANSI-92 SQL is very limited in that it does not include the standard control-of-flow statements commonly found in most programming languages. For example, it does not include any IF-THEN, CASE, or WHILE statements that are used to control how a program executes. Because of this limitation, ANSI-92 SQL must be used along with another programming language in order to create programs that access SQL Server data.

One of the major enhancements Microsoft has made to ANSI-92 SQL is the addition of many features that make Transact-SQL more like a standard programming language, thereby reducing the need to use another programming language to perform many tasks. Transact-SQL includes many control-of-flow statements, along with local variable, stored procedures, and triggers, none of which are available in ANSI-92 SQL. Transact-SQL can be used on its own for many applications, or it can be combined with other languages, such as Visual Basic or C++, to create very powerful client/server applications.

Transact-SQL is ANSI-92-compliant, which means that any SQL scripts

continues

written for other ANSI-92-compliant SQL database programs run unmodified in SQL Server. Keep in mind that if a developer creates a program using any Transact-SQL enhancements—ones not included in ANSI-92—these scripts will not run under non-Microsoft SQL databases. The only way to ensure portability among SQL database programs is to not use any of the neat Transact-SQL features, and stick only with ANSI-92; unfortunately, this reduces the power of SQL Server, which is no fun at all.

Using Transact-SQL

There are two ways to submit Transact-SQL statements to SQL Server for execution. The first is to use an interactive tool, such as SQL Enterprise Manager's Query tool, to enter Transact-SQL statements, one or more at a time. This enables the DBA to interact directly with SQL Server. This chapter focuses on how to use Transact-SQL by way of this interactive approach.

The other common way that Transact-SQL is used to communicate with SQL Server is via Transact-SQL scripts. A script is a collection of one or more batches of Transact-SQL statements designed to perform a specific action. A script is very similar to a standard computer program.

When a script is submitted to SQL Server, the following occurs:

- ▶ The script is parsed.
- ▶ The code is then optimized.
- ▶ The code is then compiled.
- ▶ Finally, the code is executed, statement by statement.

All of this happens automatically, very quickly, and the results, if any, are returned.

This chapter includes many examples of Transact-SQL because Transact-SQL permeates every aspect of the DBA's job, especially establishing database permissions. Although you do not have to learn Transact-SQL to do well on the System Administration for the Microsoft SQL Server 6.5 test, you will find the test to be easier if you know more about this subject.

Statement Permissions

Statement permissions can be granted to individual database user IDs or groups in order to enable them to execute the following Transact-SQL statements:

- ▶ CREATE DATABASE and ALTER DATABASE
- ▶ CREATE DEFAULT

- ▶ CREATE PROCEDURE

- ▶ CREATE RULE

- ▶ CREATE TABLE

- ▶ CREATE VIEW

- ▶ DUMP DATABASE

- ▶ DUMP TRANSACTION

The preceding database tasks can be performed using Transact-SQL statements (as shown) or by using SQL Enterprise Manager. In either case, a user must be granted explicit permissions to perform the tasks, one statement permission at a time.

Normally, statement permissions are not assigned to individual database user IDs or groups because these tasks are administrative in nature, and are usually performed by the DBA or by a database developer.

Statement permissions can only be granted to users by the SA or the DBO of a database.

Note ▶ When you compare statement permissions to object permissions, note that statement permissions affect actions that affect tasks that can be performed on a database, while object permissions affect actions that affect individual objects within a database. Statement permissions are associated with specific users, and object permissions are associated with objects.

Object Permissions

The most common type of permissions assigned to database user IDs are object permissions. Object permissions control who may access which database object, and what the user is able to do to the object. Table 6.1 lists the various Transact-SQL statements—and the objects they affect—that have object permissions associated with them.

Table 6.1

Transact-SQL Statements Defined	
Transact-SQL Statements	Objects They Affect
DELETE	Table, View
DUMP TABLE	Table
EXECUTE	Stored Procedure
INSERT	Table, View
REFERENCES	Table, Column
SELECT	Table, View, Column
UPDATE	Table, View, Column

The preceding object-related tasks can be performed using Transact-SQL statements (as shown in table 6.1), or through the use of any client front-end application that uses Transact-SQL statements to access SQL Server data. Some examples of front-end applications include Microsoft Access, Microsoft Excel, or any custom-written Visual Basic application. No matter how a user accesses objects in a database, each user must be given explicit permissions to perform a task, one object permission at a time.

Object permissions are given to individual database user IDs and groups much more frequently than are statement permissions because database users are required to access and manipulate data on a routine basis.

Only the owner of a database object may grant or revoke object permissions. In practice, the SA or DBO is the owner of all objects in a database, and they are the people who assign most, if not all, object permissions.

Understanding the SQL Server Permission Hierarchy

SQL Server automatically assigns some permissions based on a hierarchy of four different types of database roles (see fig. 6.2).

These roles include the following:

▶ **SA.** The *system administrator* has all permissions for all databases managed by SQL Server.

▶ **DBO.** The *database owner* has all permissions on the databases it owns.

▶ **DBOO.** The *database object owner* has all permissions on the objects it owns.

▶ **Users.** *Users,* by default, do not have any inherent permissions. The only permissions users have are the permissions explicitly granted to them by the SA, DBO, or DBOO. The only exception to this rule is that the built-in group *public* is granted the SELECT object permission on the system tables.

The SA, DBO, and DBOO database roles are all automatically assigned specific permissions to perform certain tasks. In certain cases, some tasks can only be performed by a certain role, and in other cases, they can be delegated to a database user. These tasks are described in upcoming sections.

Figure 6.2

SQL Server divides permissions into a hierarchy.

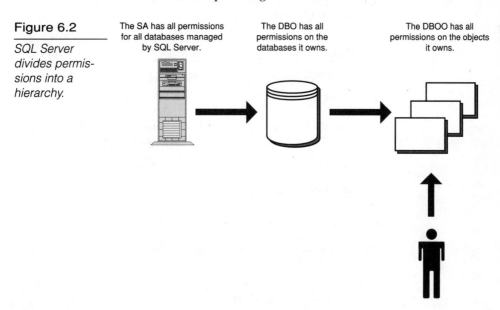

The SA has all permissions for all databases managed by SQL Server.

The DBO has all permissions on the databases it owns.

The DBOO has all permissions on the objects it owns.

System Administrator (sa) Permissions

The sa login ID is not associated with a database user ID. Anyone who logs in as the SA (using the sa password) is exempted for all SQL Server permissions, and has the capability to perform any database-related task.

> Because the sa account is allowed to perform any task in SQL Server, its use should be significantly restricted. Ideally, only the DBA (and a backup person) should use the sa account.

By default, the SA is automatically granted permission to perform the database tasks listed in the following two tables. Only the SA is granted permission to perform the database tasks in the first table. These tasks may not be delegated. The SA may grant the database task listed in the second table to others, and this applies whether the task is to be performed using Transact-SQL statements or SQL Enterprise Manager.

Tasks that cannot be delegated by the SA (that is, they belong to the SA alone) include the following:

Database Tasks	Transact-SQL Commands
Creating Devices	DISK INIT, DISK REFIT, DISK REINIT
Mirroring Devices	DISK MIRROR, DISK REMIRROR, DISK UNMIRROR
Stopping Processes	KILL
Reconfiguring SQL Server	RECONFIGURE
Shutting Down SQL Server	SHUTDOWN
Adding or Dropping Extended Stored Procedures	NA
Performing Some DBCC Commands	NA

The only task that can be delegated to others by the SA is as follows:

Database Tasks	Transact-SQL Commands
Creating Databases	CREATE DATABASE

Although the task listed in the second table can be delegated, in practice it is not, due to the fact that the responsibility for database creation and management generally falls to the SA.

Database Owner (dbo) Permissions

The DBO of a database is automatically given permission to perform any task within a given database. The DBO of one database is not automatically the DBO of another database. Each DBO is independent of the others.

Because the SA is almost always the individual who creates a database, the SA is generally the DBO of a database. Although the ownership of a database can be assigned by the SA to another user, this is not done in practice because database ownership by anyone other than the SA makes database administration more difficult than it needs to be.

Note

The SA can change the ownership of a database using the sp_changedbowner stored procedure. Use the following syntax to use this stored procedure:

sp_changedbowner *login_id* **[, true]**

where

login_id is the new owner of the current database, and *true* is optionally used to transfer aliases and their permissions to the new database owner.

Example: sp_changedbowner jnelson

Database developers (who are not SAs) are often aliased into databases as DBOs. This ensures that all newly created database objects are owned by the DBO, and not by the login ID of the developer who actually created the new object. As you will see later in this chapter, this procedure ensures the proper ownership chain.

 Tip To determine the owner of a database, either double-click on the database name from the SQL Enterprise Manager Server Manager window, or use the sp_helpdb [*database_name*] stored procedure.

By default, the DBO is automatically granted permission to perform the tasks listed in the following two tables. Only the DBO is granted permission to perform the tasks in the first table. These tasks may not be delegated. The tasks listed in the second table can be granted to others by the DBO, and this applies whether the task is performed using Transact-SQL statements or SQL Enterprise Manager.

Tasks that cannot be delegated by the DBO include the following:

Database Tasks	Transact-SQL Commands
Altering Databases	ALTER DATABASE
Deleting Databases	DROP DATABASE
Restoring Databases and Transaction Logs	LOAD DATABASE, LOAD TRANSACTION
Issuing Checkpoints	CHECKPOINT
Impersonating Database Users	SETUSER
Granting or Revoking Statement Permissions	GRANT, REVOKE
Using Most DBCC Commands	NA

Tasks that can be delegated to others by the DBO include the following:

Database Tasks	Transact-SQL Commands
Creating Objects	CREATE DEFAULT, CREATE PROCEDURE, CREATE RULE, CREATE TABLE, CREATE VIEW
Backing Up Databases	DUMP DATABASE
Backing Up Transaction Logs	DUMP TRANSACTION
Using Objects	DELETE, INSERT, SELECT, UPDATE

In practice, only the DBO of a database, or a user aliased as the DBO, creates new objects in a database. This ensures that the ownership chain is maintained.

Database Object Owner (dboo) Permissions

Any user who creates an object within a database becomes the owner of the object (the DBOO), and by default is granted all permissions on that object. Unless the DBOO grants permissions on the object to other users, other database users are not able to access the object. The SA, of course, has all permissions on all objects, but the DBO is not automatically granted permissions on the object. If the DBO wants to access an object created by the DBOO, either the DBOO must grant the DBO the necessary permissions, or the DBO can impersonate the DBOO using the SET-USER statement, which allows the DBO to access the object as if the DBO were the DBOO.

Note

The SA or DBO can use the SETUSER Transact-SQL statement to impersonate the owner of a database object. After the SETUSER statement is used, the impersonation continues until it is explicitly ended. When no user name is specified after the SETUSER statement, the original identity of the SA or DBO is re-established. The syntax is as follows:

SETUSER ['*username*' [WITH NORESET]]

where

username is the name of the user who is to be impersonated, and WITH NORESET specifies that following SETUSER statements (with a user name not specified) will not reset to the SA or DBO.

Example: SETUSER 'jnelson'

Object ownership is not transferable. If an object's ownership has to be transferred, the only option is to delete the old object and to create a new object with the new DBOO as the owner.

By default, the DBOO is automatically granted permission to perform the tasks listed in the following table on any object it owns. Only the DBOO is granted permission to perform these tasks (again, the DBOO *and* the SA or DBO who has impersonated the DBOO using SETUSER). These tasks may not be delegated. This applies to whether the task is performed using Transact-SQL statements or the SQL Enterprise Manager.

Database Tasks	Transact-SQL Commands
Altering, Dropping, or Truncating Tables	ALTER TABLE, DROP TABLE, TRUNCATE TABLE
Creating or Dropping Triggers	CREATE TRIGGER, DROP TRIGGER
Creating or Dropping Indexes	CREATE INDEX, DROP INDEX

Database Tasks	Transact-SQL Commands
Granting or Revoking Object Permissions	GRANT, REVOKE
Updating Statistics for Indexes	UPDATE STATISTICS

In practice, individual users do not create objects in a database. Instead, objects are created by the SA, DBO, or as a user aliased as the DBO, in order to ensure that all objects in a database are owned by the same user; this practice also ensures a consistent ownership chain, as well as reduces administrative tasks.

 Tip

> To find out who owns a database object, open the Objects folder from the SQL Enterprise Manager Server Manager window and then open the name of the object concerned, or use the sp_help [*object_name*] stored procedure.

Understanding Permission Precedence

Permissions can be granted to both individual database users and groups. Sometimes a user belongs to a particular group with a given permission, while at the same time this same user is given a conflicting individual permission. For example, a user may belong to a group that does not have permission to update a particular table. At the same time, this same user can be given individual permission to update the same table. Which permission wins? In SQL Server, the permission assigned to the individual user always wins over the permission assigned to the group or groups to which the user belongs (see fig. 6.3).

Figure 6.3

Individual permissions win out over group permissions.

Permission is granted to the public group to access object #1.

All members of the public group receive this same permission automatically.

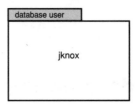

Permission is granted to the developers group to access object #2.

All members of this group receive this same permission automatically, and these are in addition to the permissions granted to them in the public group.

Permission to access object #1 is revoked.

Because individual permissions win over group permissions, this user is no longer able to access object #1, but is still able to access object #2.

When permissions are assigned to individual users and groups, you need to add the permissions in a particular order because SQL Server determines how to apply any new permissions by examining the current permissions. If you do not enter them in the correct order, SQL Server can become confused, and the permissions you think you have assigned are not the permissions SQL Server thinks you have assigned. This can happen due to the way SQL Server tracks permissions using the *sysprotects* system table. The *sysprotects* table is a system table that exists in all databases and is used to store permissions. SQL Server uses the following process to determine how to track and store permissions in the *sysprotects* table when a permission is changed:

▶ First, SQL Server examines the *sysprotects* table to see if the requested permission change already exists, as might happen if the SA is not certain of the status of the current permission, and just wants to verify.

▶ If the requested permission already exists, nothing new is written to the table, and the permission remains unchanged.

▶ If the permission does not already exist, SQL Server checks to see if the opposite permission exists in the table.

▶ If the opposite permission does exist, this permission is deleted from the table, which in effect brings about the desired permission.

▶ If the permission, or its opposite, does not exist in the table, the permission is added to the table. How it is added depends on the following:

   ▶ If a new permission is being granted for a user or group, it is entered into the table.

   ▶ If a permission that has been previously granted to the public group is being revoked from a group, SQL Server adds this information to the table.

   ▶ If a permission that has been previously granted to a group that a user belongs to is being revoked from a user, SQL Server adds this information to the table.

So what is the best way to enter permissions for a database? To ensure that there are no unexpected surprises, permissions for both users and groups should be entered in the following order:

▶ First, grant the necessary permissions to the public group. Permissions assigned to the public group affect all users, assuming there are no other conflicting group or individual user permissions. Generally, you will only want to assign permissions to the pubic group when you want to affect all database users.

▶ Second, grant the necessary permissions to other existing groups. These permissions are either more extensive than those given to the public group, or they are more restrictive. In either instance, permissions assigned to groups you create overrule permissions assigned to the public group.

▶ Third, grant the necessary permissions to individual users. These permissions are either more extensive than those given to the public group or to other groups you have created, or they are more restrictive. In either instance, permissions assigned to individual users overrule permissions assigned to groups you create, as well as those given to the public group.

As you may have noticed, you should grant permissions from the largest number of affected users (the public group), to smaller groups (the ones you create), and finally, to individual users.

Understanding Ownership Chains

 Objective ▶ Previous sections made reference to ownership chains. An *ownership chain* refers to the dependencies that one object in a database has on other objects in the same database. For example, a table might be created in a database. Next, based on the newly created table, a view might be created. Then this view might be used as part of a stored procedure. The view is dependent on the table, and the stored procedure is dependent on both the view and the table.

As you have already learned, whoever creates an object in a database becomes the DBOO of that object. In the preceding example, each of the three objects could all be owned by the same DBOO, or each of the three objects could have a different DBOO. If the same DBOO owns all the objects in the ownership chain, this is referred to as a *non-broken ownership chain*. If more than one DBOO owns the three objects, however, this is referred to as a *broken ownership chain*.

Non-Broken Ownership Chains

So how does the ownership chain affect permissions? If the ownership chain is non-broken (all the objects in the chain have the same DBOO), and if the DBOO wants to grant permissions to the highest object in the chain (the stored procedure in our example), then the DBOO only needs to grant the permission based on the highest object in the ownership chain, not to all of the objects in the chain (see figure 6.4). Separate permissions do not have to be granted to each object in the chain, even though a user has access to all of them because of the chain of ownership. This feature makes the DBA's job much easier because ownership chains are a common occurrence in all SQL Server databases.

Figure 6.4

A non-broken ownership chain.

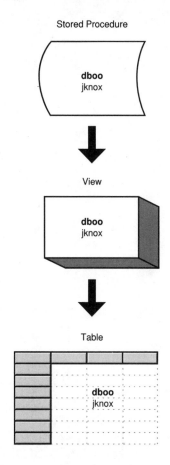

A Broken Ownership Chain
========================

What happens to permissions in a broken ownership chain? Assume for a moment that the DBOO of a stored procedure wants to grant permissions to it, but the DBOO is not the owner of the other objects in the ownership chain (see fig. 6.5). If this is the case, the DBOO of the stored procedure will first have to obtain the permission from the DBOOs of the other objects in the ownership chain. Although this is possible, it creates a lot of administrative work. After the DBOO of the stored procedure has obtained all the necessary permissions from the other DBOOs, then the DBOO of the stored procedure can grant permissions to it to others.

Figure 6.5

A broken owner-ship chain.

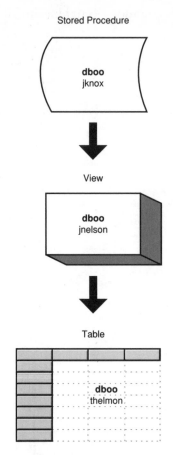

Stored Procedure

dboo
jknox

View

dboo
jnelson

Table

dboo
thelmon

How to Prevent Broken Ownership Chains

In order to prevent broken ownership chains, the same owner must own all the objects in a database. As has been repeated several times in this chapter, the best way to accomplish this goal is to not allow anyone other than the SA or DBO to create objects in a database. If various users need to create objects (database developers, for example), then the users should be aliased as the DBO whenever they create new objects. In this way, the ownership chain is preserved. When the database is finished and ready for production, the aliases can be revoked to maintain proper security. Maintaining a non-broken ownership chain can save the DBA much administrative time.

How to Grant or Revoke Statement Permissions

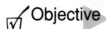 **Objective**

As you have already learned, statement permissions are assigned to specific users or groups, and they can be assigned by the appropriate database role through the use of either SQL Enterprise Manager or Transact-SQL statements. In the next section, you will learn how to use these two tools to assign statement permissions.

 Note

> Whenever a statement or object permission is granted or revoked, it happens immediately. A user does not have to log out and then log in again to be affected by a change in permissions.

Granting and Revoking Statement Permissions Using SQL Enterprise Manager

To grant a database user or group statement permissions using SQL Enterprise Manager, follow these steps:

1. Log in to SQL Server using the appropriate database role (SA, DBO, DBOO). Refer to the earlier sections of this chapter to check which database role you need to log in as in order to be able to grant statement permissions.

2. From the Server Manager window, select a server and open up the Databases folder to display the available databases.

3. Right-click on the database on which you want to change statement permissions and choose Edit. The Edit Database dialog box appears.

4. Click on the Permissions tab.

The Edit Database Permissions dialog box appears (see fig. 6.6). This dialog box lists all the database users and groups for the current database, along with the available statement permissions.

Figure 6.6

Statement permissions are set by user.

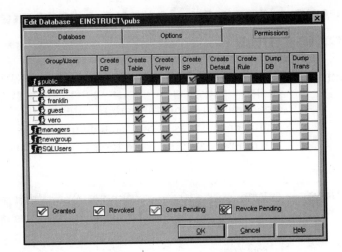

5. To grant a statement permission to an individual database user or group, click on the appropriate box. A green check appears in the box, which indicates that the granted permission is pending, and will not become effective until this dialog box is exited by clicking on the OK button. When you return to this screen, the check will turn blue, which indicates that the permission is in effect.

To revoke a statement permission from an individual database user or group, click on the appropriate box with a blue check. This produces a red circle with a slash through it, which indicates that the revoked permission is pending, and will not become effective until the OK button is clicked. When you return to this screen, the blue check and red circle disappears, and the box is empty.

Granting and Revoking Statement Permissions Using Transact-SQL

To create grant or revoke statement permissions using Transact-SQL, follow these steps:

1. Log into SQL Server using the appropriate database role (SA, DBO, DBOO). Refer to the earlier sections of this chapter to check which database role you need to log in as in order to be able to grant statement permissions.

2. From the SQL Query tool (or similar tool), select the database whose permissions you want to change.

3. To grant statement permissions, use the following syntax:

   GRANT {ALL | *statement_list*} TO {public | *name_list*}

   where

   statement_list is a list of statement permissions, where ALL refers to all possible statement permissions, where *name_list* is a list of all group names or database users to whom you want to grant statement permissions, and where public refers to the built-in public database group.

   Example: GRANT CREATE DB, CREATE TABLE TO jknox, jnelson

4. To revoke statement permissions, use the following syntax:

   REVOKE {ALL | *statement_list*} FROM {public | *name_list*}

   where

   statement_list is a list of statement permissions, where ALL refers to all possible statement permissions, where *name_list* is a list of all group names or database users from whom you want to revoke statement permissions, and where public refers to the built-in public database group.

   Example: REVOKE CREATE DB, CREATE TABLE FROM jknox, jnelson

5. Execute the query, and the specified permissions are granted or revoked.

How to Grant or Revoke Object Permissions

Object permissions are associated with specific database objects, and they can be assigned to database users by the appropriate database role using either SQL Enterprise Manager or by using Transact-SQL statements. This section shows you how to use these two methods to assign object permissions.

Although most objects are affected in their entirety by object permissions (for example, a user may be granted the object permission to delete an entire object), an exception exists. Users and groups can be assigned either the SELECT or UPDATE object permissions for either tables or views in their entirety, or on a column by column basis. For example, a user could be granted the object permission to UPDATE an entire table, or just to selected columns of a table. The same applies to views. This enables the DBA to more selectively control object security.

Granting and Revoking Object Permissions Using SQL Enterprise Manager

To grant a database user or group object permissions by using SQL Enterprise Manager, follow these steps:

1. Log in to SQL Server using the appropriate database role (SA, DBO, DBOO). Refer to the earlier sections of this chapter to check which database role you need to log in as in order to be able to grant object permissions.

2. From the Server Manager window, select a server and open up the Databases folder. The available databases are displayed.

3. Click on a database and then choose Object, Permissions from the drop-down menu.

The Object Permissions dialog box appears. This dialog box has two views: the By Object (see fig. 6.7) and the By User (see fig. 6.8) views. The By Object view is the default view. Either window may be used to perform the exact same tasks. The only different between the two windows is how the information is displayed. Choose whichever view best meets your needs. This example assumes you will be using the By Object view.

Figure 6.7

The default By Object view.

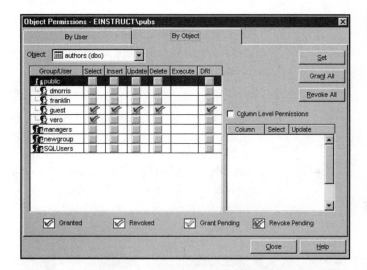

Figure 6.8

The By User view.

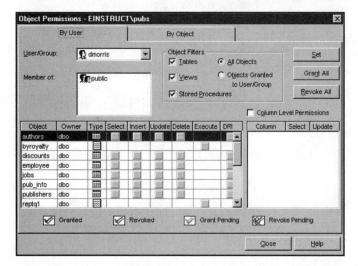

4. Select the name of the object whose permissions you want to change. To do this, click on the Object drop-down box and select the appropriate object. The current permissions for this object on a per user and group basis are displayed.

5. To grant an object permission to an individual database user or a group, click on the appropriate box. A green check in the box, indicating that the granted permission is pending, and will not become effective until the Set or Close button is selected.

   To revoke an individual object permission from an individual database user or a group, click on the appropriate box with a blue check. A red circle with a slash through it appears, indicating that the revoked permission is pending, and will not become effective until the Set or Close button is selected.

6. To grant or revoke SELECT or UPDATE object permissions to specific columns in a table or view, click on the Column Level Permissions box to display the columns of the selected table or view (see fig. 6.9). As with the other objects, to grant or revoke SELECT or UPDATE permissions on a column by column basis, either add or remove checks in the appropriate boxes.

Figure 6.9

Users can be assigned permissions to individual columns in tables and views.

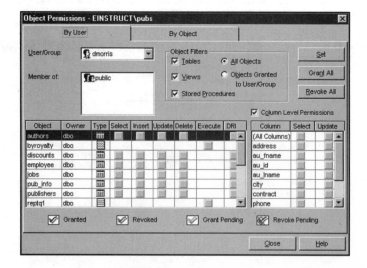

Tip

If you need to restrict users from accessing selected columns from a table, it is easier from an administrative point-of-view to create a view of the table (which includes only the necessary columns) than it is to set security on a column by column basis on a table. This not only saves the DBA time, it enables users to do a SELECT * from the view. If a view is not used, then the user would be unable to use a SELECT * from the table because he would not have permissions to all of the columns in the table.

Granting and Revoking Object Permissions Using Transact-SQL

To create, grant, or revoke object permissions using Transact-SQL, follow these steps:

1. Log in to SQL Server using the appropriate database role (SA, DBO, DBOO). Refer to the earlier sections of this chapter to check which database role you need to log in as in order to be able to grant object permissions.

2. From the SQL Query tool (or similar tool), select the database whose permissions you want to change.

3. To grant object permissions, use this syntax:

   GRANT {ALL [PRIVILEGES] [*column_list*] **|** *permission_list* **[***column_list***]}**

   ON {table_name [(column_list)]

   | view_name [(column_list)]

   | stored_procedure_name}

   TO {public | *name_list***}**

   [WITH GRANT OPTION]

where

column_list is a list of the columns, if any, that are to have their own individual permissions;

permission_list is a list of object permissions, and where ALL refers to all possible object permissions;

name_list is a list of all group names or database users to whom you want to grant object permissions, and where public refers to the built-in public database group;

WITH GRANT OPTION adds to the capability to grant the specified permission to the grantee.

Example:

GRANT SELECT, INSERT ON table_name TO jknox, jnelson

4. To revoke object permissions, use this syntax:

REVOKE [GRANT OPTION FOR]

{ALL [PRIVILEGES] | *permission_list*} **[(***column_list***)]**

ON {table_name [(*column_list***)]**

| view_name [(*column_list***)]**

**| stored_procedure_name |
extended_stored_procedure_name}**

FROM {public | *name_list*}

[CASCADE]

where

permission_list is a list of object permissions, and where ALL refers to all possible object permissions;

column_list is a list of the columns, if any, that have their own individual permissions;

name_list is a list of all group names or database users for whom you want to revoke object permissions, and where public refers to the built-in public database group;

GRANT OPTION FOR revokes the ability to give the permission to another user, but leaves the user with the permission still granted;

CASCADE revokes WITH GRANT privileges that were granted by a specified user.

Example:

REVOKE SELECT, INSERT ON table_name FROM jknox, jnelson

5. Execute the query, and the specified permission(s) are granted or revoked.

SQL Enterprise Manager can be used to view current permissions at any time. In addition, the sp_helprotect stored procedure can be used to view permissions. Used without any parameters, it displays a complete listing of permissions for a database.

If you ever need to drop and then later recreate an object, you may first want to save the object's permissions. Whenever an object is dropped, it loses any associated permissions. The easiest way to save an object's permissions is to create an SQL script of the object's permissions by using the Objects, Generate SQL Scripts drop-down menu and then choosing the Permissions option. This enables you to recreate a script that can be used to set the same permissions on a newly created object.

Exercises

Exercise 6.1: Granting and Revoking Statement Permissions Using SQL Enterprise Manager

Exercise 6.1 steps you through the process of granting and revoking statement permissions by using SQL Enterprise Manager. This exercise uses the Pubs sample database included with SQL Server, and assumes that you have completed the exercises in Chapter 5. This exercise should take less than 10 minutes to complete.

1. Load SQL Enterprise Manager.

2. From the Server Manager window, click on the plus sign next to the name of your SQL Server. The server name is highlighted and the server's folders are displayed below the server name.

3. Open the databases folder by clicking on the plus sign next to the folder. The databases are displayed.

4. Right-click on the Pubs database and choose Edit. The Edit Database dialog box appears.

5. Click on the Permissions tab. The Edit Database Permissions dialog box appears, which lists all the database users and groups for the current database, along with the available statement permissions.

6. To grant a statement permission to an individual database user or group, click on the appropriate box. A green check appears in the box, which indicates that the granted permission is pending, and will not become effective until this dialog box is exited by clicking on the OK button. When you return to this screen, the check will turn blue to indicate that the permission is currently in effect.

   To revoke a statement permission from an individual database user or group, click on the appropriate box with a blue check. A red circle with a slash through it appears to indicate that the revoked permission is pending, and will not become effective until the OK button is clicked. When you return to this screen, the blue check and red circle will disappear, and the box will be empty.

7. After granting or revoking statement permissions, click on the OK button, and the permissions will be granted or revoked as appropriate.

For more information, refer to the section "Granting and Revoking Statement Permissions Using SQL Enterprise Manager," earlier in this chapter.

Exercise 6.2: Granting and Revoking Statement Permissions Using Transact-SQL Statements

Exercise 6.2 steps you through the process of granting and revoking statement permissions using Transact-SQL statements. You will be using the SQL Query tool from SQL Enterprise Manger to perform this exercise. Alternatively, this same exercise can be performed using ISQL/W. This exercise uses the Pubs sample database included with SQL Server, and assumes that you have completed the exercises in Chapter 5. This exercise should take less than 10 minutes to complete.

1. Load SQL Enterprise Manager.

2. Load the SQL Query tool by selecting Tools, SQL Query Tool from the drop-down menu.

3. From the DB drop-down menu, choose the Pubs database.

4. To grant a statement permission to a database user, from the SQL Query tool type the following:

GRANT CREATE TABLE TO TFRANKLIN

5. To revoke a statement permission from a database user, from the SQL Query tool type the following:

REVOKE CREATE TABLE FROM TFRANKLIN

6. To execute either query, click on the Execute Query button on the toolbar, and the specified permission is granted or revoked.

For more information, refer to the section "Granting and Revoking Statement Permissions Using Transact-SQL," earlier in this chapter.

Exercise 6.3: Granting and Revoking Object Permissions Using SQL Enterprise Manager

Exercise 6.3 steps you through the process of granting and revoking object permissions using SQL Enterprise Manager. This exercise uses the Pubs sample database included with SQL Server, and assumes that you have completed the exercises in Chapter 5. This exercise should take less than 10 minutes to complete.

1. Load SQL Enterprise Manager.

2. From the Server Manager window, click on the plus sign next to the name of your SQL Server. The server name is highlighted and the server's folders are displayed below the server name.

3. Open the databases folder by clicking on the plus sign next to the folder. The databases are displayed.

4. Click on the Pubs database, choose Object, Permissions from the drop-down menu, and the Object Permissions dialog box appears. This dialog box has two views: the By User and the By Object views. This exercise assumes you will be using the By Object view, which is currently displayed.

5. Select the name of the object whose permissions you want to change. To do this, click on the Object drop-down box and select the appropriate object. The current permissions for this object on a per user and group basis are displayed.

6. To grant an object permission to an individual database user or a group, click on the appropriate box. A green check appears in the box to indicate that the granted permission is pending, and will not become effective until the Set or Close button is selected.

   To revoke an individual object permission from an individual database user or a group, click on an appropriate box with a blue check. The red circle with a slash through it indicates that the revoked permission is pending, and will not become effective until the Set or Close button is selected.

7. To grant or revoke SELECT or UPDATE object permissions to specific columns in a table or view, click on the Column Level Permissions box to display the columns of the selected table or view. As with the other objects, to grant or revoke SELECT or UPDATE permissions on a column by column basis, either add or remove checks in the appropriate boxes.

8. When you are finished granting or revoking object permissions, click on Close, and all your changes will come into effect.

For more information, refer to the section "Granting and Revoking Object Permissions Using SQL Enterprise Manager," earlier in this chapter.

Exercise 6.4: Granting and Revoking Object Permissions Using Transact-SQL Statements

Exercise 6.4 steps you through the process of granting and revoking object permissions using Transact-SQL statements. This exercise uses the Pubs sample database included with SQL Server, and assumes that you have completed the exercises in Chapter 5. This exercise should take less than 10 minutes to complete.

1. Load SQL Enterprise Manager.

2. Load the SQL Query tool by selecting Tools, SQL Query Tool from the drop-down menu.

3. From the DB drop-down menu, choose the Pubs database.

4. To grant an object permission to a database user, from the SQL Query tool type the following:

   GRANT SELECT, INSERT ON AUTHORS TO TFRANKLIN

5. To revoke an object permission from a database user, from the SQL Query tool type the following:

   REVOKE SELECT, INSERT ON AUTHORS FROM TFRANKLIN

continues

Exercise 6.4: Continued

6. To execute either query, click on the Execute Query button on the toolbar, and the specified permission is granted or revoked.

For more information, refer to the section "Granting and Revoking Object Permissions Using Transact-SQL," earlier in this chapter.

Review Questions

The following questions will test your knowledge of the information in this chapter.

1. Which of the following barriers must users pass before they are allowed to actually access data in an SQL Server database?

   A. Login ID security

   B. Database user ID security

   C. Permission security

   D. Standard Security

2. Which of the following are used by SQL Server to specify which users are permitted to use which objects, and what they are allowed to do with those objects?

   A. Access Tokens

   B. Database user IDs

   C. Login IDs

   D. Permissions

3. A database user, Anna, wants to create a new table in an SQL Server database. She has come to the SA to ask him to grant her the ability to create a new table. What kind of permission must the DBA grant her?

   A. Object

   B. Statement

   C. NTFS

   D. Access

4. When Maria tried to access the vendor table in the sales database, she received an "access denied" message. This was the first time she had ever tried to access this table. In order for her to be able to access this table, what kind of permission must be assigned to her by the SA?

   A. Object

   B. Statement

   C. NTFS

   D. Access

5. Sara has always been able to access all of the data stored in the marketing database, no matter which table the data was located in. Her boss has asked her to produce a new report using the data stored in the production database. Although she can successfully log in to SQL Server, and even log in to the production database, she consistently receives an "access denied" message when she tries to access tables in the production database. She is sure that she has a database ID for the production database. What could be preventing her from accessing the data in the production database?

   A. Sara's database ID password has expired.

   B. Sara's login ID password has expired.

   C. The production database has become corrupt and will not allow her, or any user, into the tables.

   D. Although Sara may have been given a database user ID to access the production database, she may have never been granted the necessary permissions to access any tables in it.

6. Which one of the following Transact-SQL statements cannot be granted to database users?

   A. DUMP TRANSACTION

   B. CREATE RULE

    C. DISK INIT

    D. CREATE PROCEDURE

7. Megan is an SQL database developer and needs to be able to create a new database in order to create a new client/server application. She is not an SA. What must the DBA do to give her the ability to create a new database on a currently existing database device?

    A. Megan must be granted both the DISK INIT and CREATE DATABASE statement permissions.

    B. Megan must be granted the CREATE DEVICE, CREATE DATABASE, and CREATE TABLE statement permissions.

    C. The DBA, acting as the SA, must create the new database device, and then the DBA must grant Megan the CREATE DATABASE statement permission.

    D. The DBA, acting as the DBO, must create the new database device, and then the DBA, acting as the SA, must grant Megan the CREATE DATABASE statement permission.

8. Devin has been given the CREATE DATABASE statement permission in the production database. Devin is not the SA. The production database is almost out of room and needs to be expanded. Who has the necessary permission to increase the size of the database?

    A. Only the SA may increase the size of the production database.

    B. Only Devin may increase the size of the database.

    C. Either Devin or the SA may increase the size of the database.

    D. Databases may not be expanded. Instead, a new database must be created, and the data from the smaller database moved to the new, larger database.

9. Sandra was recently given a variety of object permissions to access payroll data in the payroll database. She is able to view and change data, but seems to be unable to add any new records. Which object permission is she missing?

   A. UPDATE

   B. SELECT

   C. CHANGE

   D. INSERT

10. Debbie is the SA of the SQL Server, Jenny is the DBO of the inventory database, and Becky is the DBOO of the vendor table. Ted needs access to the vendor table in order to produce some reports. Who is able to fulfill Ted's request? Select two.

    A. Debbie

    B. Becky

    C. Jenny

    D. Ted

11. Meg is the DBOO of both the inventory and vendor tables in the production database. Sally, another database developer, wants to create a new table in the production database. When Sally attempts to create the new table, she is denied access. She then asks Meg to give her permission to create a new table, but when Meg attempts to give Sally the necessary permission, she is prevented from giving Sally access. The SA is currently unavailable. How can Sally go about creating the table?

    A. Meg can alias herself as the DBO of the database, which will give her the ability to grant Sally the necessary permission.

B. Sally can alias herself as the DBO of the database, which will give her the ability to grant herself the necessary permission.

C. Sally can use Transact-SQL statements, instead of using SQL Enterprise Manager, to create the database. This will work because permissions only affect Transact-SQL statements, not SQL Enterprise Manager.

D. Sally will just have to wait, as only the SA or the DBO of the database are able to grant Sally the necessary permission to create a new table.

12. Veronica, the DBO of the financial database, wants to mirror the device on which the database resides onto another hard disk for improved fault tolerance. When she executes the DISK MIRROR Transact-SQL statement, she is denied permission to perform this task. How can she mirror her database?

A. Veronica must ask the SA to create the disk mirror for her, as only the SA is permitted to execute the appropriate statement.

B. Veronica must ask the SA to give her the necessary permission to execute the appropriate statement.

C. Database devices cannot be directly mirrored; only databases can be mirrored.

D. Veronica needs to ask the DBOO of the objects within the database to give her the necessary permission to execute the appropriate statement.

13. The DBO of the production database wants to add a new table to the financial services database. When she attempts to create the table using the CREATE TABLE statement, she is denied permission to create the table. What is the most likely reason for her being unable to create the new table?

    A. Only the SA of a database is able to create a new table.

    B. The DBO of the production database is not the DBO of the financial services database.

    C. Only the DBOO of the financial services database is able to create a new table using the CREATE TABLE statement.

    D. She needs to use SQL Enterprise Manager instead of the CREATE TABLE statement.

14. Debbie has been aliased into the samples database as the DBO, where she creates a new stored procedure. Debbie is not an SA. Later, the SA removes the dbo alias from Debbie's login ID, but does create a new database user ID for Debbie in the samples database. When Debbie tries to execute the stored procedure, she is denied permission. Why?

    A. Only an SA can execute a stored procedure.

    B. Debbie has not been given permission to execute the stored procedure.

    C. Only the DBO of a database can execute a stored procedure.

    D. Only the DBOO of a stored procedure can execute a stored procedure.

15. The SA is currently the DBO of the payroll database. A database developer, Evan, asks the SA if he can become the DBO of the database instead, as it would make his job easier. The

SA tells Evan that it is impossible to give Evan ownership of the database. Evan mumbles something under his breath about the SA's dress habits and then sulks away. Is Evan justified in his behavior?

A. Yes. The SA is wrong. The ownership of a database can be changed from the SA to Evan, assuming the SA agrees to perform the task.

B. Yes. The SA is right, but the SA could have been more considerate and have offered Evan some other ways to make his job as a database developer a little easier.

C. No. The SA is right. Database ownership cannot be transferred.

D. No. The SA is right, at least technically. Although a database cannot be reassigned, it can first be dropped, and then re-added using a script under a new owner's name.

16. The DBOO of most of the tables in the technical database has discovered that the current size of the database is too small, and that the database needs to be enlarged. The DBOO executes the ALTER DATABASE statement, but is denied permission to perform this task. Why isn't the DBOO permitted to increase the size of the database?

A. Databases cannot be enlarged.

B. Only the SA can enlarge a database.

C. Only the DBO of a database can enlarge it.

D. Only the SA or the DBO of a database can enlarge it.

17. The SA has granted Megan the necessary permission to create a new database. Megan creates a new database named toys and then gives Sally permission to INSERT, UPDATE, SELECT, and DELETE data into objects. Sally logs in to the database and attempts to create a new table, the first table in the database, but is denied permission. Why is she unable to create a new table?

    A. Only the SA can create a new table.

    B. Only the DBO can create a new table.

    C. Only the DBOO can create a new table.

    D. Sally has not been given the necessary permission to create a new table.

18. Sara is the DBOO of the parts table. Beverly, the DBO of the database that contains the parts table, tries to delete the parts table using just the DROP TABLE statement, but is denied access. Why can't Beverly delete an object that was created in a database she owns?

    A. Only the DBOO of an object may delete the object.

    B. By default, only the DBOO of an object may delete the object. Beverly can delete the table, however, if she impersonates the DBOO by using the SETUSER statement.

    C. Only the SA of an SQL Server can delete any object or database.

    D. Beverly's permission to drop tables has been revoked by the SA.

19. The SA wants to transfer ownership of the cars table from Megan to Phillip using SQL Enterprise Manager, but seems unable to complete this task. What could be the problem?

    A. Only the DBOO of an object can transfer the ownership of an object.

    B. Only the DBO of a database can transfer objects stored within a database.

    C. SQL Server prevents anyone from transferring ownership of an object.

    D. Only an NT Server administrator can transfer the ownership of an object to another user.

20. Morgan has been given permission by the DBO of the database to create new tables, and he has created the compass table. Later, the DBO decides that the compass table needs to be altered, and tries to alter it using the ALTER TABLE statement, but is denied permission. What could cause this problem?

    A. Only an SA can alter a table.

    B. Only the DBOO of an object can alter an object.

    C. Tables cannot be altered.

    D. Tables must first be dropped before they can be altered.

21. Veronica belongs to a database group that has been assigned only the UPDATE, SELECT, DELETE, and INSERT permissions. Later, the DBO of the marketing database grants Veronica the CREATE TRIGGER and DROP TRIGGER permissions, while leaving her in the marketing group. What are Veronica's effective permissions within the marketing database?

    A. Veronica's individual permissions override her group permissions.

    B. Veronica's group permissions override her individual permissions.

    C. Veronica now has both the permissions from her group membership and her individual permissions.

    D. A user cannot be assigned both group and individual permissions.

22. The SA has assigned the public group the SELECT permission only, has assigned the data_entry group the INSERT and UPDATE permissions, and has assigned the managers group the DELETE permission. Kim has been assigned to the managers group. What are Kim's effective permissions?

    A. DELETE only

    B. SELECT only

    C. DELETE and SELECT

    D. SELECT, INSERT, UPDATE, and DELETE

23. Leigh needs the ability to SELECT, INSERT, UPDATE, and DELETE records from a table. Currently, the public group is assigned the SELECT permission, the data_entry group has been assigned the INSERT and UPDATE permissions, and the managers group has been assigned the DELETE permission. What is the easiest way to grant Leigh the necessary permissions?

    A. Add Leigh to the public, data_entry, and managers groups.

    B. Add Leigh to the data_entry and managers groups.

    C. Add Leigh the to the public and data_entry groups, and then give her the individual permission to DELETE.

    D. Add Leigh to the data_entry group, and then give her the individual permission to DELETE.

24. Michael, Sally, and Sara all are database developers and have been working together to create a new SQL Server application. None of them is an SA or a DBO, but they are the DBOOs of the objects they have created in the new financial services database. Most recently, Michael created a new table. Then Sally created a trigger for the table. Then Sara created a stored procedure that referenced the table that contained the trigger. Later, the SA assigns Peter the EXECUTE permission on the stored procedure. When Peter tries to execute the stored procedure, however, he is not able to, due to a conflict of permissions. In order for Peter to execute the stored procedure, what additional permissions must he have?

    A. The SA must also assign Peter the appropriate permissions to both the table and the trigger that the stored procedure references.

    B. The DBO of the database must assign Peter the appropriate permissions to both the table and the trigger that the stored procedure references.

    C. Because of the broken chain of ownership, Peter will never be able to receive the necessary permissions to execute the stored procedure.

    D. The only way Peter will ever be able to execute the stored procedure is if Michael, Sally, and Sara all grant Peter the necessary permissions in order to execute the stored procedure.

25. In a new database, the SA creates a new table. Later, the DBO of the same database creates a stored procedure that references the same table. A database user named Ted needs to have the necessary permission to execute the stored procedure. Does this example indicate a broken chain of ownership, and if so, how would it be possible for Ted to execute the stored procedure?

    A. This situation is a broken chain of ownership because objects in the database were created by more than one person. The SA must grant Ted the appropriate permissions to both objects in order for him to be able to execute the stored procedure.

    B. This situation is a broken chain of ownership because objects in the database were created by more than one person. The DBOs of both objects must grant Ted the appropriate permissions to both objects in order for him to be able to execute the stored procedure.

    C. This is not a broken chain of ownership. To allow Ted to execute the stored procedure, the SA only needs to grant Ted the necessary permissions to execute the stored procedure.

    D. This is not a broken chain of ownership. To allow Ted to execute the stored procedure, the DBO of each object only needs to grant Ted the necessary permissions in order for Ted to execute the stored procedure.

26. The SA wants to grant Terri the statement permission to create a new table. Which of the following Transact-SQL statements is the correct way to grant Terri this permission?

    A. GRANT CREATE TABLE TO TERRI

    B. GRANT CREATE TABLE TO TERRI IN MARKETING

    C. SELECT TERRI FROM MARKETING

    D. SELECT GRANT TABLE TO TERRI IN MARKETING

27. Veronica, Sara, Brett, and Kristin all need SELECT permission on the vendors table in the sales database. They are the only users who ever need to access the vendors table. What is the easiest and most efficient way to grant these four users this object permission?

    A. GRANT ALL ON VENDORS TO VERONICA, SARA, BRETT, KRISTIN

    B. GRANT ALL ON VENDORS TO PUBLIC

    C. GRANT SELECT ON VENDORS TO PUBLIC

    D. GRANT SELECT ON VENDORS TO VERONICA, SARA, BRETT, KRISTIN

28. Terri, Betty, and Frank all have database user IDs in the production database. Currently, the public group has been granted the SELECT, UPDATE, INSERT, and DELETE permissions on the inventory table. The SA wants to revoke Frank's ability to delete records from the inventory table. How can the SA perform this task?

    A. REVOKE DELETE ON INVENTORY FROM PUBLIC

    B. REVOKE DELETE ON INVENTORY FROM FRANK

    C. REVOKE ALL ON INVENTORY FROM FRANK

    D. The DELETE permission cannot be removed for Frank because he belongs to the public group.

Review Answers

1. A, B, C

2. D

3. B

4. A

5. D

6. C

7. C

8. C

9. D

10. A, B

11. D

12. A

13. B

14. B

15. A

16. D

17. D

18. B

19. C

20. B

21. C

22. C

23. D

24. A

25. C

26. A

27. C

28. B

Answers to Test Yourself Questions at Beginning of Chapter

1. *Statement permissions* enable users to execute specific Transact-SQL statements that are used to create database objects, or to back up databases and transaction logs. Before a user can create a new table in a database, for example, he would have to be granted the necessary statement permission. *Object permissions* determine what a user may do to a preexisting database object. Before a user could view data in a specific table, for example, he would have to be granted the necessary object permission. See the section titled "Assigning User Permissions."

2. By default, the SA has all permissions for all databases managed by SQL Server. The DBO by default has all permissions on the databases it owns. The DBOO by default has all permission on the objects it owns. Users by default do not have any inherent permissions. The only permissions users have are the permissions explicitly granted to them by the SA, DBO, or DBOO. See the section titled "Understanding the SQL Server Permission Hierarchy."

3. You need to grant Veronica the following object permissions on each of the three tables using either SQL Enterprise Manager or by using the GRANT Transact-SQL statement: DELETE, INSERT, UPDATE, and SELECT. See the section titled "Object Permissions."

4. As the DBA, your job of assigning permissions will be made more difficult than necessary because the various database objects are owned by more than one DBOO. If you want to assign a user permission to an object that depends on another object owned by a different DBOO, you will have to assign specific permissions to each object, not just the first object in the chain of objects. See the section titled "Understanding Ownership Chains."

5. After getting over the shock that a developer actually asked your advice, here is the advice you give him. You suggest that even though all of the developers already have login IDs and database user IDs, you want to alias all the developers into any new databases as the DBO, instead of using their database user IDs. This ensures that all database objects are owned by the same DBOO (in this case, the DBO), which will make the job of assigning permissions much easier because there will be no broken chains of ownership to deal with. See the section titled "How to Prevent Broken Ownership Chains."

Chapter 7

Server Alert Processing and Task Scheduling

SQL Server 6.5 provides facilities that enable automatic notification of system events, and automated processing for daily, repetitive maintenance tasks such as database backup. In this chapter, you'll gain experience in setting up system alerts to monitor critical server activity, and scheduling routine tasks for automated processing.

As always, this chapter begins with a list of the exam objectives relating to the topic at hand, moves on to the chapter pretest, offers valuable information directly addressing the objectives as well as additional relative discussion topics, and finishes with exercises, chapter review questions, and finally, answers to both the chapter review questions and the chapter pretest questions.

This chapter focuses on alert processing and task scheduling. It helps you prepare for the exam by addressing and fully covering the following objectives:

 Objectives

- ▶ Identify the role of the msdb database

- ▶ Identify the role of SQL Executive Service

- ▶ Identify the conceptual relationships among the Schedule service, the msdb database, and the Windows NT Event Log

- ▶ Set up alerts

- ▶ Set up tasks

Test Yourself! Before reading this chapter, test yourself to determine how much study time you will need to devote to this section.

1. Name two tables in the msdb database that are used to maintain task and alert information.

2. What stored procedure is used to obtain information about scheduled tasks?

3. How can alerts be integrated with an SNMP network management system?

4. What role does the msdb database play in SQL alert processing functionality?

5. What are two SQL task types?

Answers are located at the end of the chapter...

What Are Alerts and Tasks?

In order to better understand the capabilities of SQL Server's alerting and scheduling functions, it is important to understand exactly what is meant by each of these terms. Following are complete definitions:

▶ **SQL Server Alerts.** Alerts are events or actions that can be defined to be executed when specified criteria is met. For example, an administrator might define an event that performs a Dump Transaction command when a database transaction log is detected to be 80 percent full. The alert detects the full log condition and executes a defined task or action once this condition has been detected.

▶ **SQL Server Tasks.** Tasks are events or actions, defined by an administrator, to occur at predefined times or dates. A simple example might be a database backup task, scheduled to occur nightly at 10pm.

Alerts are reactive, in response to a given event or situation, while tasks are proactive, used to plan specific activity for an upcoming date/time. Alerts and tasks are maintained using the SQL Server administrative account *sa*.

SQL Alerting/Scheduling Components

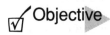 SQL alert processing and tasks scheduling capability is comprised of three overall components:

▶ The msdb database

▶ The SQL Executive Service (Scheduler)

▶ The Windows NT Event Log/SQL Server Error Log

Each of these components performs a specific function in terms of alerting and scheduling functionality. In short, the common data processing metaphor of "Input-Processing-Output" can be applied to the function performed by each SQL alerting component (see fig. 7.1).

Figure 7.1

*The SQL Alerting/
Scheduling
Components.*

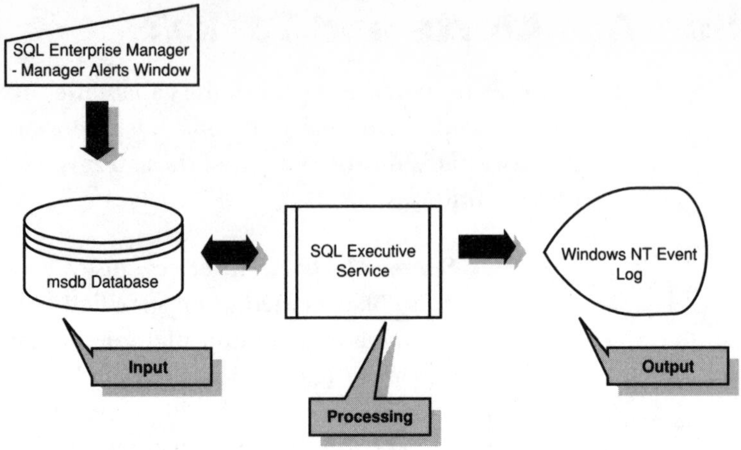

Now examine each in greater detail.

The msdb Database

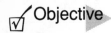

The msdb database can be likened to the Input function for the SQL alerting system. This database is used to store details about all scheduled tasks, alerts, and e-mail operator information for the given SQL Server. This includes not only user-defined tasks such as database backups, but also events related to SQL 6.5 database replication.

Similar to the Master, TempDB, and Model system databases, the msdb database is created by default when installing SQL Server.

The following two sections illustrate the database device and configuration of the msdb database. While this database is created automatically during installation, it is important to understand which system devices it utilizes. The following section also provides details about the database tables used to store alert and event information.

Device Configuration

The msdb database is initially created on the same drive where the Master database is installed. The database is allocated as 6 MB on the disk devices, as illustrated in table 7.1.

Table 7.1

The msdb Database Device Configuration		
Logical Device Name	Physical File Name	Size
MSDBData	\MSSQL\DATA\MSDB.DAT	6 MB
MSDBLog	\MSSQL\DATA\MSDBLOG.DAT	2 MB

msdb System Tables

Within the msdb database, there are five (5) user tables that maintain information for scheduled events and alerts. These tables and their respective purposes are indicated in table 7.2.

Table 7.2

msdb Database Tables Used for Alerting and Task Scheduling	
Table Name	Description
sysalerts	The primary SQL Server alert table contains a single entry for each alert defined by the SQL administrator.
systasks	This table contains a single entry for each scheduled task, such as a database backup or a SQL database replication event.
sysoperators	For each scheduled task or alert event, an e-mail operator can be defined for notification via e-mail or pager. This table contains an entry for each operator defined on the server.
sysnotifications	This table contains the actual test message that the operator will receive upon notification that an alert situation has been detected. This notification can be either the text of an e-mail message or text sent via an alphanumeric pager.
syshistory	This table contains an entry for each scheduled task or event that has occurred on the server. More importantly, the table contains information on the outcome of an event, such as whether or not an error was generated or the execution was successful.

Note   An *operator* is known to SQL server as the destination where notifications will be routed, once an alert has been processed. See the section "Operators" later in this chapter for more detailed information.

 Note   The msdb database is no different from other system databases in the fact that entries can be added, modified, or deleted, via standard Transact-SQL using ISQL/W. This makes it possible to maintain numerous alert entries across multiple servers, via standardized SQL scripts. However, if you've just begun to explore SQL alerting capabilities, it is probably best to stick with the provided graphical tools discussed later in this chapter.

The SQL Executive Service

 **Objective**   The SQL Executive Service is essentially the Processing component of SQL Alerting services (see fig. 7.2). The SQL Executive serves as the scheduling engine that executes tasks and processes alerts defined in the msdb database.

Figure 7.2

The SQL Executive Service is the processing engine for all alerts and tasks.

In order for alert processing to take place, the SQL Executive service must be started on the given server. This can be accomplished in a number of ways:

▶ Select Start from the pop-up menu when right-clicking the SQL Executive icon in the Server Display window in SQL Enterprise Manager.

- ▶ Select the SQL Executive Service in the SQL Service Manager and double-click the green light on the stoplight icon.

- ▶ Select Services from the Windows NT Control Panel and click the Start button for the SQL Executive service.

- ▶ Invoke the NET START SQLEXECUTIVE command from a Windows NT command prompt.

 Tip

> Event processing can be quickly disabled on a server simply by stopping the SQL Executive service. This is useful in situations where it is necessary to temporarily stop events from being scheduled, without the need to manually disable individual events in the msdb database.

Windows NT Event Log

The Windows NT Event Log is the Output component of SQL Alert Processing. All SQL Server events and alerts are reported in the Windows NT (Application) Log (see fig. 7.3) and in the SQL Server Error Log. This includes system events generated by SQL Server as well as user-defined alerts and the results of scheduled tasks.

Figure 7.3

Information on processed alerts and scheduled tasks is viewed in the NT Application Log.

Date	Time	Source	Category	Event	User	Computer
8/23/97	1:30:16 PM	MSSQLServer	Backup	17045	N/A	DELLXPS
8/23/97	12:57:45 PM	MSSQLServer	ODS	17060	N/A	DELLXPS
8/23/97	12:57:45 PM	MSSQLServer	ODS	17060	N/A	DELLXPS
8/23/97	12:57:44 PM	MSSQLServer	ODS	17056	N/A	DELLXPS
8/23/97	12:25:28 PM	MSSQLServer	Server	17055	N/A	DELLXPS
8/23/97	12:25:28 PM	MSSQLServer	Server	17055	N/A	DELLXPS
8/23/97	12:25:27 PM	MSSQLServer	ODS	17056	N/A	DELLXPS
8/23/97	12:25:27 PM	MSSQLServer	ODS	17056	N/A	DELLXPS
8/23/97	12:25:27 PM	MSSQLServer	Kernel	17055	N/A	DELLXPS
8/23/97	12:25:27 PM	MSSQLServer	Kernel	17055	N/A	DELLXPS
8/23/97	12:25:25 PM	MSSQLServer	Kernel	17055	N/A	DELLXPS
8/23/97	12:25:23 PM	MSSQLServer	Server	17055	N/A	DELLXPS
8/23/97	12:25:22 PM	MSSQLServer	Server	17055	N/A	DELLXPS
8/23/97	12:25:21 PM	MSSQLServer	Kernel	17055	N/A	DELLXPS
8/23/97	11:39:23 AM	MSSQLServer	Server	17055	N/A	DELLXPS
8/23/97	11:39:23 AM	MSSQLServer	Server	17055	N/A	DELLXPS
8/23/97	11:39:22 AM	MSSQLServer	ODS	17056	N/A	DELLXPS
8/23/97	11:39:22 AM	MSSQLServer	ODS	17056	N/A	DELLXPS
8/23/97	11:39:22 AM	MSSQLServer	Kernel	17055	N/A	DELLXPS
8/23/97	11:39:22 AM	MSSQLServer	Kernel	17055	N/A	DELLXPS
8/23/97	11:39:20 AM	MSSQLServer	Kernel	17055	N/A	DELLXPS
8/23/97	11:39:18 AM	MSSQLServer	Server	17055	N/A	DELLXPS
8/23/97	11:39:17 AM	MSSQLServer	Server	17055	N/A	DELLXPS
8/23/97	11:39:16 AM	MSSQLServer	Kernel	17055	N/A	DELLXPS
8/17/97	7:55:27 PM	MSSQLServer	Kernel	17055	N/A	DELLXPS
8/17/97	7:18:48 PM	MSSQLServer	Server	17055	N/A	DELLXPS

Event Viewer - Application Log on \\DELLXPS (Filtered)

Log   View   Options   Help

This functionality is due to the fact that SQL Server is installed with the option Windows NT Event Logging enabled by default. This option is configured through the SQL Server setup program in the Set Server Options section. Disabling this option will prevent alert messages from appearing in the NT Event Log; however, messages will still be logged in the SQL Server Error Log.

Now that you understand the foundation of SQL alerting and event processing, examine the actual components themselves, starting with SQL Alerts.

SQL Alerts

Using SQL Alerts, an administrator is able to define actions or events based on specific SQL criteria. This enables the administrator to proactively respond to conditions that might disrupt SQL Server availability or potentially compromise data. Alerts can be defined to monitor and act upon situations such as the following:

▶ Dumping a database transaction log before it is full

▶ Monitoring database allocation to ensure adequate space, and generating an alert when free database space is low

▶ Monitoring for fatal hardware errors that may affect database integrity

▶ Generating alerts when a user initiates a query for which he has insufficient privileges to execute

▶ Generating an alert when specific user-defined error messages are found in the SQL Server Error log

When an alert is generated, an administrator can define an appropriate action to be executed. The two specific actions that the administrator can choose to take are found in table 7.3:

Table 7.3

SQL Alert Action Types	
Type	Description/Use
CmdExec	This action type enables any command file or executable file (*.EXE) to be invoked on the NT server. This action is useful for integrating third-party tools or custom applications when alerts are generated.
TSQL	The TSQL action types invoke standard Transact SQL commands such as queries or stored procedures. These action types are common for situations where specific database actions are required based on the generated alert.

Now that you understand what makes up an alert in SQL Server, take a look at how to define and manage alerts on a given server.

Defining Alerts

 Objective

The primary interface for defining alerts is the SQL Enterprise Manager. Alerts are defined from the Manage Alerts window, which is displayed when you select the Alerts/Operators option from the Server menu, or click the Alerts tool button, which looks like an exclamation point. Note that SQL Server is installed with sample alert entries already defined (see fig. 7.4).

Figure 7.4

The Manage Alerts window in SQL Enterprise Manager.

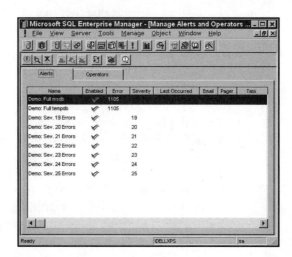

Like many other functions within the Enterprise Manager, the Manage Alerts window simply provides a graphical interface for the sp_addalert stored procedure, which is the actual method used to add alert entries in the msdb database.

When defining alerts, you must provide information for three overall sections. These are outlined in table 7.4.

Table 7.4

SQL Alerts—Required Information	
Section Name	Description
Alert Definition	This section determines whether the alert will monitor for specific error numbers, or for any error for a specified severity level. Alert Definition also determines that database which will be monitored.
Response Definition	Indicates the tasks to execute (if any) and additional user-defined messages that will be sent in addition to the text of the detected error message. This information is included in the Windows NT Application Log, or optionally as an e-mail or pager text message.
Operators to Notify	This section determines the server operator or support personnel that will be notified of the alert, either via e-mail or pager. Operators must be first specified in the Manage Operators window before alerts can be specified with operator information.

To define an alert, the following procedure is used:

1. From the SQL Enterprise Manager, connect to the desired server in the Server Display Window. Once connected, select Alerts/Operators from the Server menu.

2. Once the Manager Alerts window is displayed, select the Add Alert option from the File menu, or click the leftmost tool button for New Alert. The New Alert window appears (see fig. 7.5).

Figure 7.5

The New Alert window.

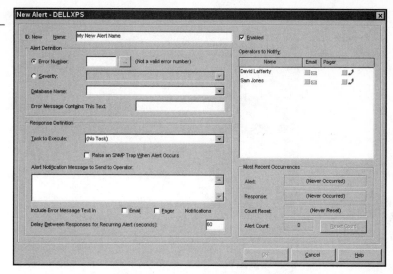

3. Enter a name for the alert in the Name field. Verify that the alert is enabled by checking the Enabled field.

4. In the Alert Definition section, determine whether the alert will monitor for a specific number of errors or for all errors of a specified severity.

5. When selecting Error Number for the alert type, click the browse button to display the Manage SQL Server Messages window (see fig. 7.6). Enter the required text in the Message Text Contains field or click the Find button to display all possible SQL Server system messages.

Note

In addition to configuring alerts based on predefined system messages, it is possible to define specific user messages for which alerts can also be generated. To define a message, select the Messages option from the Server menu in the SQL Enterprise Manager. From the Manage SQL Server Messages window, click the New button. Enter the error number, severity, and the message text and click OK (see fig. 7.7). Keep in mind that you'll have to code your application to call the user-defined message, such as using the RAISERROR command, in order for the alert to detect the error condition.

Figure 7.6

The Manage SQL Server Messages window.

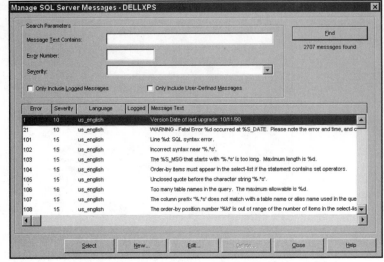

Figure 7.7

User-defined error messages can be added for alert processing.

6. Highlight the desired message from the list and click Select to return the New Alert Window.

7. When defining alerts to monitor all messages of a given severity level, select the required severity from the Severity field pull-down box.

8. Select the required database name to monitor from the Database Name pull-down box.

9. In the Response Definition section, enter a task for execution in the Task to Execute field. If no task execution is desired, select the option for no task.

Note

When you are defining a task to execute, previously defined tasks will appear in the drop-down list in the Task to Execute field. New tasks be defined on the fly by selecting New Task, which will open the New Task window. (See the "Adding Tasks" section of this chapter for additional information.)

10. Select the Raise an SNMP Trap option if desired. This will generate an alert event that will be reported to standard SNMP network management products. Note that TCP/IP and SNMP support must be installed on the NT server in order to support this functionality.

11. Enter additional text in the Alert Notification Message window. This text is displayed in addition to the system message text in the Windows NT Application Log.

12. Select the option to include the message text in a notification either in operator e-mail or in a text pager message. If both of these options are unchecked, the message text is displayed only in the Windows NT Application log.

13. Certain SQL system errors can recur repeatedly once an error condition is detected. One example might be a server in which the number of open objects needs to be increased. To control the number of alerts that are generated for a repetitive error message, enter the amount of seconds to delay alerts in the Delay Between Responses for Recurring Alerts field. This option is especially important to guard against potentially repeated e-mails or pager messages in a short period of time.

14. If the alert will be forwarded via e-mail or pager message to a specified operator, select the appropriate action for the given operator by checking either the E-mail or Pager field next to the operator's name. If no operators have been defined previously, no names will be displayed in the Operators to Notify section. (See the section in this chapter called "Operators" for additional information on adding operators.)

15. Click the OK button to complete the entry and add the alert to the msdb database.

The Manage Alerts/Operators window will display an entry for the newly defined alert. Information about the alert type, notification actions, and number of times the alert have occurred are displayed.

 Tip

> Alert entries can be displayed in their native format in the msdb database by executing the sp_helpalert stored procedure using ISQL/W in the msdb database. This method is useful for obtaining alert information without using the SQL Enterprise Manager.

Alert Maintenance

After an alert has been defined, it may be necessary to modify its criteria or temporarily disable it from being executed. Alert maintenance is performed in a similar fashion as that defined earlier: by using the SQL Enterprise Manager. The following sections elaborate on the maintenance of alerts.

Editing Alerts

To edit an existing alert, access the Manage Alerts/Operators window in the SQL Enterprise Manager. Highlight and double-click the desired alert to display the Edit Alert window. This window is identical to the Add Alert window. Modify the appropriate information and press the OK button to complete the required changes.

Alerts can also be updated by using the ISQL/W tool and by executing the sp_updatealert stored procedure in the msdb database. This procedure is also useful in situations where it is necessary to rename existing alerts.

Enabling/Disabling Alerts

An important consideration in defining alerts is that not all alerts will be required at all times. In certain situations, it may be necessary to temporarily disable (or enable) alert processing. Overall, there are three methods that can be used to disable alerts:

- ▶ Disable the alert using the Enable/Disable option

- ▶ Delete the alert from the msdb database

- ▶ Stop the SQL Executive service

Although each of these methods is acceptable, each one accomplishes a slightly different result. Using the Enable/Disable option makes it possible to disable a specific alert (or alerts). This method is recommended as an alert can be disabled while retaining its definition in the msdb database.

Deleting an alert will accomplish the same result, but the alert information will be lost from the msdb database. In order to again enable the alert, all information will have to be manually reentered.

Shutting down the SQL Executive service is useful for quickly disabling all alert processing for the given SQL Server. However, since the SQL Executive is the primary scheduling engine, all scheduled task operations will be stopped as well.

To enable or disable specific events using the Enable/Disable option, perform the following steps:

1. Access the Manage Alerts/Operators window in the SQL Enterprise Manager.

2. Highlight and double-click the desired alert, or select the Edit Alert tool button, which is indicated by an exclamation mark and a magnifying glass.

3. Deselect the Enabled option and click the OK button. When the Manage Alerts/Operators window is again displayed, there should no longer be a check mark in the Enabled field for the given event.

Alerts can also be disabled using the sp_updatealert stored procedure and specifying 0 for the enabled parameter. Entering a 1 in this parameter reenables the alert.

Deleting Alerts

Deleting specified alerts is a fairly straightforward operation. From the Manage Alerts/Operators window, highlight the desired alert and press Delete. Acknowledge the verification pop-up by selecting Yes and the alert will be deleted. This action removes the corresponding entry from the sysalerts table in the msdb database.

Alerts are also deleted by using the sp_dropalert stored procedure in the msdb database, from within the ISQL/W tool.

 Tip

To modify only the operator information for an alert, or only the notification method (pager or e-mail), the sp_updatenotification stored procedure can be executed from the msdb database. Additionally, the sp_dropnotification stored procedure will quickly modify an alert so that an operator is not notified.

Operators

Two primary benefits of SQL Server alerts are the capabilities to proactively provide notification of error conditions before they become critical, and to ensure a timely response in the event that a critical failure does occur.

These capabilities are is made possible by integrating alerts with notifications sent to an Operator. An operator is known to SQL Server as the destination where notifications will be routed after an alert has been processed (see fig. 7.8).

Figure 7.8

The Manage Operators display in SQL Enterprise Manager.

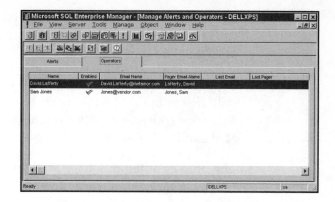

SQL Mail Operator Requirements

In order to configure SQL alerts to be sent to an operator, SQL server requires integration with a compatible e-mail system such as Microsoft Exchange or the Windows NT mail client. This integration is accomplished using the SQL Mail Service within SQL Server. SQL Mail enables SQL Server to generate messages via the mail *API (application programming interface)* set, or *MAPI (mail application programming interface)*. Before operators can be configured, you must configure the SQL server as a mail client to the Exchange Server or Windows NT post office. In most SQL implementations today, Microsoft Exchange is commonly used as the client of choice for the SQL Server.

 Tip

While using MS Exchange integration with SQL server is the most common and preferred method, smaller environments may require the use of the built-in NT mail application. Consult the SQL Server Books Online for additional information on the specific installation requirements for SQL Mail integration with an NT mail post office.

SQL Mail can be configured for use with Exchange by following these steps:

1. Log on to the NT server with the same domain account as that which the MSSQLServer service is started with. This is important to ensure that the appropriate NT registry settings

are configured for the SQL Server service. Additionally, the e-mail administrator must define a mailbox for the MSSQLServer domain account.

2. Install the Microsoft Exchange client for Windows NT as indicated in the Exchange installation procedures. If MS Exchange is already installed on the NT server, access the Mail and Fax icon from the Windows NT Control Panel.

3. The profile configuration for SQL Server must be set up with the following information services installed:

   Microsoft Exchange Server

   Personal Address Book

   When prompted for the profile setup, either during a new installation or when defining a new profile by selecting Add from the Show Profiles button in the Mail/Fax setup, do not configure personal folders or other services in the profile that SQL Server will use. This ensures that the delivery location is properly setup for the SQL Server mailbox (see fig. 7.9).

4. Once the Exchange client has been installed, verify mail send/receive capability by using the Exchange client software, while logged on to the NT server and using the same domain account as the MSSQLServer service. This will ensure mail functionality prior to configuration of SQLMail.

5. From the SQL Server Tools program group, start the SQL setup program and select Set Server Options from the SQL Server Options window and click Continue.

6. From the Select Server Options window, click the Mail Login button. This will display the Exchange Login Configuration window. Enter the profile name created in step 3 above, and click Continue.

7. If SQL Mail functionality is required immediately upon SQL Server startup, select the Autostart Mail Client option.

8. Click the Continue button to complete the configuration changes and exit the SQL Setup program.

9. Start the SQL Enterprise Manager and connect to the required SQL Server.

10. From the Server menu, select SQL Mail and select Start. After the SQL Mail service has successfully been started, the SQL Mail icon in the Server Display Window should change from red to green.

If you encounter problems in starting the SQL Mail service, consult the SQL Books Online for information on troubleshooting SQL Mail problems.

 Tip

After Exchange has been installed on the NT server, the SQL Mail configuration option will display a window prompting for the Exchange profile information that will be used for SQL Mail. Normally, the configuration option will prompt for the path to an existing Windows NT post office. This is because the Exchange installation has modified the NT registry information that controls SQL Server mail functionality.

Figure 7.9

MS Exchange Profile prompt in SQL Mail configuration.

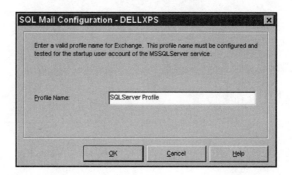

SQL Mail Operator Pager Requirements

Operator pager requirements are similar to those of notification in general, in that e-mail connectivity must be established in order to forward the alert information to the operator.

To use paging functionality in SQL Server, it is necessary to install third-party paging software that can be integrated with Microsoft Exchange or the Windows NT Post Office. This essentially provides an alternative e-mail address for an operator that specifies a pager phone number. When mail is sent to this alternative address, the paging software reroutes the request to the appropriate modem for dialout.

Without paging software in place, it is possible to route SQL alert messages only via e-mail.

Adding Operators

Operators are defined on the SQL Server using the SQL Enterprise Manager, Manage Alerts, and Operators window (see fig. 7.10). Operator information is added as a row in the sysoperators table in the msdb database.

Figure 7.10

Defining operator information in SQL Enterprise Manager.

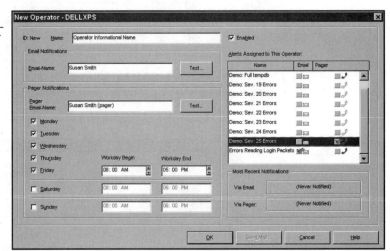

To define an operator, use the following procedure:

1. Start the SQL Enterprise Manager. From the Server menu, select the Alerts/Operators option or click the Manage Alerts/Operators tool button, which resembles an exclamation point.

2. From the File menu, select the New Operator option.

3. Enter a name for the operator in the Name field. This name is informational only and determines the name to be displayed in the Manage Operators window. Make sure that the

Enabled option is selected to ensure that the newly defined operator is immediately available for alerting purposes.

4. In the E-mail Notification section, enter the e-mail name for the desired user.

5. To test e-mail functionality, click the Test button. This will generate a test mail message to the selected user.

6. In the Pager Notification section, enter the pager e-mail address for the given operator. Click the test button to route a test message to this address. (Note that third-party paging software must be installed to support this functionality.)

7. Select the appropriate option to indicate on which days of the week that the selected operator will be notified of SQL alerts.

8. Using the scroll indicators, select the time of day for the operator's workday to begin and end. This option enables multiple operators to be defined so that alerts are routed to different personnel based on the time of day, such as first, second, or third shift operator coverage.

9. In the Alerts Assigned to Operator section, all previously defined alerts for the given SQL Server are displayed. Click the E-mail and/or Pager option next to the desired alert to determine the appropriate notification action for the operator when the alert condition is detected.

10. Click OK to complete the addition of the new operator.

At this point, the dependencies between SQL alerts and operators are clear. To effectively exploit operator notification, it is best to ensure that the required alerts are first defined on the server.

 Tip

Remember that operator information is defined only in the msdb database of the server selected in SQL Enterprise Manager. This means that in order for operator information to be

continues

consistent across all servers in the enterprise, it is necessary to define an operator on each and every SQL server.

An easy way to address this problem is to use the object transfer tool in SQL Enterprise Manager. This tool makes it possible to transfer the entire sysoperators table from the msdb database on one server, to any required SQL Server.

From the Tools menu, select the Database/Object Transfer option. In the Database/Object Transfer window, select the source server, source database (msdb), destination server, and destination database (msdb). In the Advanced Options section, deselect the option to transfer all objects and click the Choose Objects button. Select the sysoperators table from the Add/Remove Objects window (see fig. 7.11) and click Add. Click OK to return to the Database/Object Transfer window and then click the Start Transfer button.

Using this method, a single server can be designated as the one containing the master operator list. This information can then easily be transferred to all servers, ensuring consistent operator information.

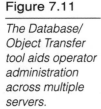

Figure 7.11

The Database/ Object Transfer tool aids operator administration across multiple servers.

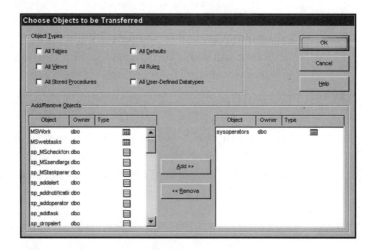

An alternative method for adding operator information without using SQL Enterprise Manager is to execute the sp_addoperator SQL stored procedure. This procedure can be executed using the ISQL/W tool and requires that the appropriate parameters be included as indicated in the SQL Books Online. Each parameter is essentially the same information indicated when adding operators using SQL Enterprise Manager.

This method is also useful for easily creating Transact-SQL files that add consistent operator information to multiple NT servers.

Editing Operators

Editing operator information is a fairly straightforward operation and can be accomplished one of two ways. Like most other SQL administrative tasks, operators can be maintained either using SQL Enterprise Manager or by executing the proper SQL stored procedure.

To edit operator information using SQL Enterprise Manager, select Alerts/Operators from the Server menu. This will again display the Manage Alerts and Operators window. Click the Operators tab to display the Operators window. Highlight the operator and double-click to display the Edit Operator window. Modify the appropriate information and click the OK button. Alternatively, you can select the Edit Operators tool button, which is indicated by the combined fireman hat/magnifying glass icon.

Using ISQL/W, operator information can be modified using the sp_updateoperator stored procedure. The syntax of the sp_updateoperator procedure is indicated as follows:

```
sp_updateoperator name [, new_name] [, enabled] [, email_address]
[, pager_number] [, weekday_pager_start_time]
[, weekday_pager_end_time] [, saturday_pager_start_time]
[, saturday_pager_end_time] [, sunday_pager_start_time]
[, sunday_pager_end_time] [, pager_days]
```

Suppose you want to modify an operator's pager number using sp_updateoperator. To complete this change, only the operator's name and information to be changed is required: in this case, pager_number. The required command would be

```
sp_updateoperator @name = 'operator name', @pager_number = 'new
pager number'.
```

All other information for the given operator would remain unchanged.

Deleting Operators

Deleting an operator removes the corresponding entry from the sysoperators table in the msdb database. Using the SQL Enterprise Manager, select Alerts/Operators from the Server menu to display the Manage Alerts/Operators window. Select the Operator tab to display the Operator window. Highlight the required operator and press Delete, or click the Delete Operator tool button indicated by the fireman hat covered by the X.

As is the case with editing operator information, these entries can be deleted natively using Transact-SQL, using the sp_dropoperator stored procedure. To delete an operator using this method, start the ISQL/W tool and log in to the SQL Server. In the query window, enter the sp_dropoperator command with the required operator's name, such as the following:

```
sp_dropoperator 'David Lafferty'
```

Execute the query using the Execute icon or by pressing Ctrl+E. This will permanently remove the corresponding operator entry from the sysoperators table.

 Tip

Remember that when an operator is deleted, notifications of alerts that were assigned to that operator may go unnoticed. Before deleting the operator, it is helpful to record which alert entries were assigned to that operator, so that they can be reassigned to another operator for subsequent alerting.

An alternative to deleting operators is to temporarily disable an operator's alerts. This has the added benefit that operator information is maintained in the sysoperators table. In the event that it is necessary to again reassign an operator to a set of alerts, the operator entry can again be enabled, without the need to redefine all the operator's information.

Operators are enabled or disabled by checking the Enabled box next to the operator name in the Operators window, from Manage Alerts/Operators in SQL Enterprise Manager.

Alert Engine Options

Implementing a successful alerting strategy for SQL Server relies on the capability to ensure that critical system events and alerts are always handled. To aid in this capability, the SQL Server alerting engine provides the means by which failsafe options can be defined for the given server. These options enable configuration of the following failsafe actions:

▶ Sending unhandled or failed pager/e-mail notifications to a specified failsafe operator.

▶ Forwarding unhandled SQL alerts and events to the Windows NT Event log for a single, centralized SQL Server.

▶ Forwarding all events of a specified severity to the Windows NT Event log of a single, centralized SQL Server.

Alerts can go unhandled for a variety of reasons, both system generated and user-generated. Suppose, for example, that an administrator defines a 24-hour pager coverage schedule between multiple operators, but inadvertently leaves a time period where no operators are assigned to receive pager or e-mail notifications. This is one situation in which having a failsafe operator defined would ensure that alerts during that time period are not unnoticed.

Unhandled alerts also can be caused by failures with the e-mail system or by incorrect operator e-mail or pager addresses.

Additionally, the SQL Alert engine can be configured to forward alerts of a given severity level to a remote or central SQL server. Using this capability, you can define a centralized alerting strategy that processes alerts from multiple servers and logs them in the NT Event log of a single SQL server.

Alert engine options can be modified using the following steps:

1. Start SQL Enterprise Manager and select the Alerts/Operators option from the Server menu. This displays the Manage Alerts window.

2. Click the Alert Engine Defaults button indicated by the Car with the open hood icon. This will display the Alert Engine Options window with the Fail-Safe tab visible (see fig. 7.12).

Figure 7.12

SQL Alert Engine Options window.

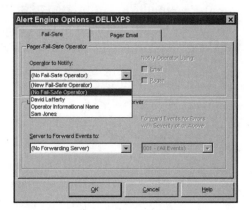

3. In the Pager Fail-Safe Operator Section, select an operator from the pull-down list in the Operator to Notify field. A new operator can be defined, if necessary, by selecting the entry for the New Fail-Safe Operator entry. This will display the New Operator window, where the required information can be entered.

4. Specify either pager or e-mail as the notification method for the operator by choosing the Pager or E-mail check box, or both.

5. In the Unhandled SQL Server Event Forwarding section's Server to Forward Events To field, select the server to forward events to from the pull-down box. If the required server is not available in the list, one can be added by selecting the New Forwarding Server. This will display the SQL Enterprise Manager Register Server window, so that the server can be registered for use with the SQL Executive service for alert processing.

6. If required, select the level of severity at which the events are to be forwarded to a remote SQL server. Limiting the alerts that are forwarded to those of a certain level of severity is useful to control the amount of network traffic resulting from the forwarding of SQL alerts.

7. Press the OK button to complete the alert engine configuration.

Another function of the Alert Engine Configuration window enables you to control and define the format of text for pager and e-mail messages generated by the alerting system. This is accomplished by configuring the template that is used by the alerting engine (see fig. 7.13). The pager/e-mail template enables the customization of various message aspects, as indicated in table 7.5.

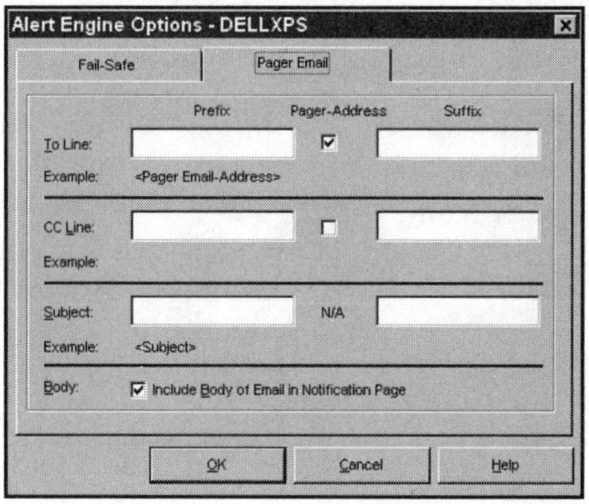

Figure 7.13

Pager/e-mail template options.

Table 7.5

Pager/E-mail Alert Template Attributes	
Attribute	Description
To Line Prefix	Determines static text that appears prior to the address in the To line of the e-mail or pager message. Some examples might be "Primary Operator—<operator name>" or "Location Name—<operator name>."
To Line Suffix	Determines static text that appears after the address in the To line of the e-mail or pager message.
CC Line Prefix	Similar to the To line; determines static text that precedes information in the CC line of the message.
CC Line Suffix	Determines text displayed at the end of the CC line.
Subject Prefix	When defining failsafe operators, SQL server automatically uses this field to precede the message subject with "Fail-Safe" to distinguish the message from normal messages. Similarly, user-defined information can be specified to accomplish that same purpose for normal alert notifications.
Subject Suffix	Determines text that appears immediately after the subject line.
Include Body Text	Deselecting this option is useful in limiting the amount of text message included in the notification. This can be a factor with text-pager systems that limit the number of characters or amount of data that can be sent. When deselected, only the subject line is sent. Selecting this option includes notification text in the message body.

With alerts and operators out of the way, let's examine the other aspect of SQL alerting and scheduling functionality.

Task Scheduling

In addition to alerting and notification, task scheduling comprises the final component of the SQL 6.5 alerting and scheduling engine. SQL Server provides the capability to schedule tasks for automated, unattended operation.

One of the primary benefits of using SQL task scheduling rather than third-party scheduling packages or the NT system scheduler (AT.EXE) is that SQL task scheduling provides integration of task history and execution results with both the NT Event log and SQL server error log. Additionally, task history information can be maintained for a specific period of time in the msdb database (see fig. 7.14).

Figure 7.14

The SQL Server task list.

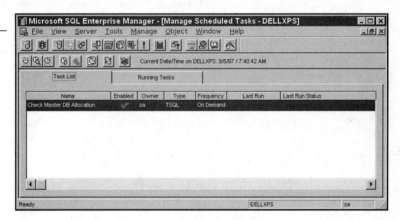

A user-defined task can be configured as a response action to a detected alert. For example, if an alert has been defined to detect when a database transaction log reaches 70 percent full, the alert could be set up to automatically execute a task to issue a Dump Transaction command.

Additionally, SQL server database replication exploits the use of the SQL Server scheduling engine exclusively. Task scheduling provides the foundation that makes automatic replication possible. This means that even without any user-defined tasks on a system, a SQL Server participating in database replication is utilizing the SQL Server task-scheduling engine.

The upcoming sections discuss the concept of task scheduling in greater detail.

Task Types

There are five (5) overall types of tasks available, each of which is used for specific processing functions. These task types and their uses are outlined in table 7.6.

Table 7.6

SQL Task Types

Task Type	Description
TSQL	This task type indicates that a native Transact-SQL command or query is to be executed. These tasks are typically simple to set up; the required SQL statements can be entered directly in the command field in the task definition. No external components are required.
CmdExec	This task type represent commands that will be executed by the Windows NT Operating System, such as command (*.CMD) or executable (*.EXE) files. These tasks execute under the security context of the SQLExecutiveCmdExec NT account. This enables these tasks to be executed by users other than the SQL Server sa account. CmdExec tasks are useful for executing external third-party or user-developed programs at predefined intervals.
LogReader	The LogReader is one of three task types used to perform SQL Server database replication. These tasks are automatically set up when you define a database replication model. This task type reads the database transaction log to determine entries that are candidates for replication.
Distribution	Distribution tasks are another type of task used in SQL replication and are scheduled on the replication distribution server. Distribution tasks make transactions available for replication on subscribing SQL servers.

Task Type	Description
Sync	Sync tasks are the third replication task type; these tasks initiate the initial commands necessary to synchronize database information that is defined for replication.

Adding Tasks

Adding tasks inserts a corresponding entry in the systasks table in the msdb database. This entry contains all attributes of a given task, such as task name, type, and schedule. After a task has been executed, information on the results of its execution, as well as its execution time, date, and duration, are entered in the syshistory table. Figure 7.15 illustrates the SQL task definition window in SQL Enterprise Manager.

Figure 7.15

New SQL task definition window.

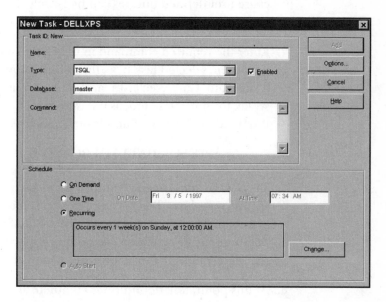

Like almost every other aspect of SQL alert information, the primary method for adding tasks is through SQL Enterprise Manager. A task must be first defined, and then scheduled. This can be accomplished using the following steps:

1. From SQL Enterprise Manager, select the Scheduled Tasks option from the Server menu.

2. The Task Scheduling window is displayed, showing the task list for the given server. To add a new task, click the New Task button, which is the leftmost button on the toolbar, indicated by the clock icon.

3. The New Task window appears. There are two sections of information to be completed: task ID and attribute information, and the required scheduling for the defined task. Enter a name for the task in the Name field.

4. Ensure that the task is enabled for scheduled execution by selecting the Enabled check box.

5. Select the task type from the pull-down list in the Type field.

6. Select the required database that the task will be executed against. This is especially important for TSQL task types because user-defined queries can be largely dependent on the database structure.

7. Enter the required command in the Command field. Depending on the selected task type, this information is fundamentally different. CmdExec tasks most often require the correct syntax for the command, as if it were directly executed from the Windows NT Command Prompt, such as in the following:

    C:\APPS\SQL\DATA\MYPROG.EXE

    TSQL tasks require query information such as EXEC sp_MyProcedure 'Test', 'Parameter2'. Replication task types are normally created automatically by SQL Server when you define replication. These tasks require specific information that determines the execution characteristics of the task.

8. At this point, task definition is complete and can now be scheduled. In the Schedule section choose whether the task's schedule will be On Demand, One Time, or Recurring.

9. Click the Add button to complete the addition of the task.

There are three scheduling methods that can be used when defining tasks:

▶ **On Demand Tasks.** These tasks require no additional scheduling information to be defined. They are executed only by using the sp_runtask stored procedure, or by clicking the Run Task button in the Task List window in Enterprise Manager.

▶ **One Time Tasks.** These are executed only once—at the specified time and date specified in the Add Task or Edit Task dialog box.

▶ **Recurring Tasks.** Recurring tasks are executed at the specified time and date interval shown in the Task Schedule window, which is displayed when you click Change in the Add Task or Edit Task window.

To configure time and date information for a recurring task, click the Change button in the Add Task or Edit Task window to display task scheduling options (see fig. 7.16). Specify the required execution interval and frequency (day, week, or month) and the start and stop dates for the task (if required) and click OK.

Figure 7.16

The advanced task scheduling dialog box.

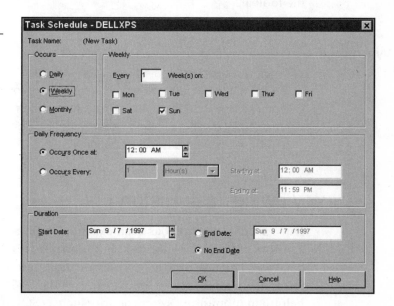

Editing Tasks

Once a task has been defined, modifying its properties is fairly straightforward.

For example, suppose you want to modify a task from a One Time to an On Demand execution type. This can easily be accomplished from the SQL Task list by selecting Scheduled Tasks from the Server menu in SQL Enterprise Manager. Highlight the desired task and double-click it to display the Edit Task window. Alternatively, click the Edit Task tool button indicated by the combined clock and magnifying glass icon. Change the schedule type from One Time to On Demand and press OK.

This will modify the task properties and the corresponding task information in the systasks table in the msdb database.

Deleting Tasks

Tasks are easily deleted by highlighting the task in the SQL Task List window and pressing the delete key, or by selecting the Delete Task tool button indicated by the combined clock and "X" icon in the toolbar.

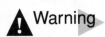 **Warning**

Remember that an alert can be defined to execute a user-defined task once the alert condition has been detected. Deleting the scheduled task may cause an error for any alerts that try to execute the deleted task. As an alternative, you can temporarily disable a task by accessing the Edit Task window and deselecting the Enabled option.

Viewing Task History

Once a scheduled task has been executed, SQL Server maintains a history of the task's execution in the syshistory table of the msdb database. The task history provides an audit trail of activity performed by a given task or set of tasks (see fig. 7.17). This can be helpful in monitoring system activity such as SQL database replication. This information is maintained until the administrator manually deletes it, or when the conditions set by the task engine options (see the next section for additional information) have been met.

Figure 7.17

SQL Server task history.

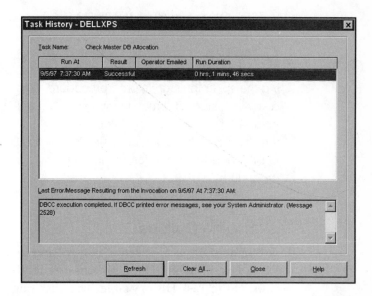

Task history information is only available after the task has been executed at least one time. Task history indicates run duration as well as any results generated from SQL system commands such as Dump Database, DBCC (CHECKDB), or any user-defined messages generated using the RAISERROR or sp_logevent commands. Additionally, task history information indicates whether or not an operator has been notified via pager or e-mail for the task, if one was assigned. To view task history information, use the following steps:

1. From SQL Enterprise Manager, access the SQL Server task list by selecting the Scheduled Tasks option from the Server menu.

2. Highlight the required task and click the Task History tool button, indicated by the blank pages covered with a clock face icon.

3. The Task History window will appear. Each line (or row) in the task history window indicates the results for subsequent executions of the given task.

4. To clear a task's history information, click the Clear All button. This permanently removes all entries from the syshistory table for the given task.

5. Click OK to return to the Task List window.

 Tip

Using ISQL/W, a task history can also be displayed by executing the sp_helphistory stored procedure. This procedure displays history information for a selected task by using any number of possible criteria, such as Task Name, Task ID, or the severity of the selected task. Consult the SQL Books Online for additional information on specific syntax for this procedure.

Task Engine Options

Task Engine options are used to control and manage the size of the Task History table. These options essentially control the size, in rows, of the Task History table. The Task Engine options are accessed via the Task Engine Options tool button from the Task List window in SQL Enterprise Manager. This icon is indicated by the open car hood icon. Figure 7.18 illustrates the Task Engine Options dialog box.

Figure 7.18

SQL Server Task Engine options.

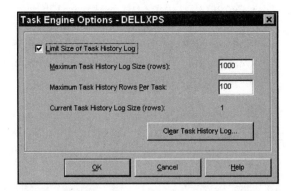

To limit the size of the Task History table, check the Limit Size of Task History Log option and specify the number of rows to be maintained in the Maximum Task History Log Size field. This setting affects the task history for all scheduled tasks on the given server. Modify the value for Maximum Task History Rows per Task to limit entries only for a specific task. Click OK to complete the option changes.

When the Limit Size option is not selected, there is no limit on the size of the Task History table. This can cause the msdb database to become completely full, leading to additional maintenance requirements. For this reason, enforcing task history limits is recommended.

Alternative Task Maintenance Methods

In certain situations, it may be necessary to modify and schedule tasks without using SQL Enterprise Manager. This can be especially useful in situations where support or operations personnel do not have access to the Enterprise Manager tool.

Table 7.7 summarizes the SQL stored procedures that comprise methods for task maintenance using the ISQL/W tool.

Table 7.7

SQL Task Maintenance Stored Procedures	
Procedure Name	Function
sp_addtask	Used for adding tasks to the server schedule.
sp_updatetask	Used for modifying task information such as the task's scheduled execution type or e-mail operator notification.
sp_runtask	Used for executing a given task. This is most often used for tasks configured as On Demand execution, or for temporarily overriding a scheduled task's normal execution time or date.
sp_droptask	Deletes the specified task.
sp_helptask	Displays information about the specified task.
sp_helphistory	Displays execution history for one or more tasks.
sp_purgehistory	Removes information from the syshistory table for one or more tasks.

Exercises

The following exercises help you to understand the relationship between operators, alerts, and tasks, by posing an example scenario. Each exercise builds on the scenario to reinforce the topics learned in this chapter.

 Note For the purposes of these exercises, operator e-mail information is indicated; however, functionality is not tested or used.

You have been assigned the task of automating backups of the msdb database for the XYZ Company. Because of operational requirements, this database must be backed up after 12am, Monday through Friday.

Each time the backup is executed, an operator (David Jones) is to be notified via e-mail. If the backup encounters an error in which the backup device is off-line, David Jones must be paged. Failures of the backup must also be logged in the company's SNMP management system. David has a fairly long workday of 7am to 6pm, and he works Monday through Saturday.

In order to ensure that all server events are processed, David's manager (Fred Smith) has asked to be configured as a failsafe operator.

Once you have created the backup job, Fred Smith would like the job run immediately to ensure that it runs properly. As part of this verification, you are to determine the execution duration for the backup task.

Exercise 7.1: Defining an Operator

In this exercise, you'll define an operator who will be notified when given alerts have been detected. It is usually best to define operators first because they can be configured for alert events and scheduled tasks. The duration for this exercise is approximately 10 to 15 minutes.

1. Start SQL Enterprise Manager. From the Server menu, select Alerts/Operators.

2. Click the Operators tab. From the File menu, select New Operator.

3. Enter the operator name **David Jones** in the Name field.

4. Ensure that the Enable option is selected.

5. In the E-Mail Name field, enter David's e-mail address **JonesD**.

6. In the Pager E-mail Name field, enter David's pager e-mail address **JonesD(pager).**

7. Configure the workday as required. Select the check box next to each day that David Jones works.

8. Modify the workday hours for David. Remember to set up hours for Monday through Friday, as well as Saturday. His workday is 7am to 6pm

9. Click the OK button to add David as a SQL operator.

See the earlier "Adding Operators" section in this chapter for additional information.

Exercise 7.2: Defining a Scheduled Task

In the example, it was indicated that due to operational requirements, the database had to backed up Monday through Friday after 12am. In this exercise, you'll define the required task. This exercise should take approximately five to ten minutes to complete.

1. Select the Scheduled Tasks option from the Server menu in SQL Enterprise Manager. The Task List window appears.

2. From the File menu, select New Task.

3. In the Name field, enter the name **MSDB Database Backup (Temp Device).**

continues

4. In the Type field, select the TSQL task type. Ensure that the Enabled option is selected.

5. In the Database field, select the msdb database from the pull-down list box.

6. In the Command field, enter the following command: **dump database msdb to disk = 'c:\mssql\data\msdb.dmp with init, stats'**.

7. Set up the schedule required for this task. Remember that the backup must run after 12am Monday through Friday, and before 11pm on Saturday. Select the Recurring task type and click the Change button.

8. In the Occurs section, select Weekly. In the Weekly section, verify that the task is set to execute Every (1) Week. Select the check boxes for Monday, Tuesday, Wednesday, Thursday, and Friday.

9. In the Daily Frequency section, select the required time, such as 12:30a.

10. Click the OK button to return to the Add Task window.

11. Click the Option button to display the Task options. In the Notifications section, select David Jones from the pull-down list of e-mail operators.

12. Click the On Success option. This will ensure that David is notified each time the task is executed.

13. Click the OK button to return to the Add Task window.

14. Click Add to add the task to the server's task list.

See the "Adding Tasks" section earlier in this chapter for details on defining scheduled tasks.

Exercise 7.3:   Defining an Alert

The example indicated that each time the backup is executed, an operator (David Jones) is to be notified via e-mail. If the backup encounters an error where the backup device is offline, David Jones must be paged. Failures of the backup must also be logged in the company's SNMP management system.

In this exercise, you'll configure the required alerting options to meet the above requirements. This exercise should take approximately 10 minutes to complete.

1. Select the Alerts/Operators option from the Server menu in Enterprise Manager. This will display the Alerts window.

2. From the File menu, select New Alert.

3. In the Alert Name field, enter **Backup Device Off-Line**. Make sure that the Enabled option is selected.

4. In the Alert Definition section, click Error Number and click the Browse button. This will display the Manage SQL Server Messages window.

5. In the Message Text Contains field, enter **Can't open dump device**. This will display SQL system error 3201 in the Message window.

6. Click Select to choose the message text and return to the New Alert window.

7. In the Database Name field, select the msdb database from the pull-down list.

8. In the Response Definition section, check the option to Raise an SNMP Trap when Alert Occurs.

9. In the Operators to Notify section, select David Jones's pager as the assigned notification for this alert.

10. Click OK to complete definition for the new alert.

See the earlier section titled "Defining Alerts" for more information.

Exercise 7.4: Configuring Alert Engine Options

In the example, it was indicated that David's manager (Fred Smith) was to be configured as a failsafe operator. In this exercise, you'll modify alert options to configure a failsafe operator. This exercise should take approximately 10 minutes to complete.

1. Select the Alerts/Operators option from the Server menu in Enterprise Manager. This will display the Alerts window.

2. From the File menu, select Alert Engine Options. The Fail-Safe tab in the Alert Engine Options window is displayed.

3. In the Operator to Notify field, select New Failsafe Operator. This will display the New Operator window.

4. In the Name field, enter David's Manager's name: **Fred Smith**.

5. In the E-mail Name field, enter Fred Smith's e-mail address: **SmithF**.

6. Enter Fred Smith's pager address in the Pager E-mail Name field: **SmithF(pager).** Ensure that the Pager option is selected for notification.

7. Click OK to return to the Alert Engine Options window.

Refer to the earlier section "Alert Maintenance" for additional information on modifying alert engine options.

Exercise 7.5: Running a Task

In the example, David's manager asked that the newly defined task be executed immediately to ensure that it is configured properly. In this exercise, you'll manually run a scheduled task. The duration to complete this exercise is approximately five minutes.

1. From the Server menu in SQL Enterprise Manager, select the Scheduled Tasks option.

2. Highlight the msdb database backup task created in Exercise 7.2.

3. From the File menu, select Run Task.

4. After you see the message that the task has started successfully, click the Running Tasks tab to verify that the backup task is active.

5. From the File menu, select the Refresh button periodically until the task is no longer displayed in the Running Tasks window.

The earlier "Adding Tasks" section discusses task execution in greater detail.

Exercise 7.6:   Viewing Task History

In the example, it was noted that the task execution duration was to be determined. In this exercise, you'll view task history information, which contains the run duration. This exercise should take approximately five minutes to complete.

1. From the Server menu in SQL Enterprise Manager, select the Scheduled Tasks option.

2. Highlight the msdb database backup task.

2. From the File menu, select Task History.

3. Verify the result for the most recent entry in the task history is Successful. Note the execution duration for the task in the Run Duration column.

Refer to the earlier "Viewing Task History" section for more details on viewing task history.

Review Questions

The following questions will test your knowledge of the information in this chapter.

1. Which three components comprise the SQL Server alerting/scheduling services?

    A. SQL Executive, msdb database, NT Event Log

    B. SQL Executive, SQL Server, msdb database

    C. msdb database, NT Event Log, SQL Server

    D. None of the above

2. Which database contains all information for SQL Server scheduled events and tasks?

    A. MASTER

    B. TEMPDB

    C. MSDB

    D. SYSTASKS

3. Which database table contains SQL alert information?

    A. SYSALERTS

    B. SYSTASKS

    C. ALERT_INFO

    D. SYSEVENTS

4. What is the difference between an alert and a task?

    A. There is no difference.

    B. An alert is executed in response to certain criteria; a task is executed at a predefined time/date.

    C. An alert can only be generated based on system events, whereas a task can be generated based on any user-defined event.

    D. None of the above.

5. What service must be running in Windows NT in order for alert and event processing to take place?

    A. The alerter service

    B. The messenger service

    C. The SQL task service

    D. The SQL Executive service

6. Which table contains information on task history?

    A. syshistory

    B. sys_task_enum

    C. sys_task_audit

    D. systaskhist

7. How many user tables in the msdb database are used for alert and task processing?

    A. 7

    B. 5

    C. 2

    D. None

8. Which alert action type enables tasks to invoke NT programs?

    A. NTSQL

    B. TSQL

    C. CMD_SQL

    D. CmdExec

9. Alerts are defined using which SQL Server utility?

    A. The SQL Alert Manager tool

    B. The SQL Enterprise Manager

    C. ISQL/W

    D. None of the above

10. Which SQL stored procedure is used to define alerts?

    A. sp_newalert

    B. sp_definealert

    C. sp_addalert

    D. sp_cralert

11. Which of the following statements is true regarding SQL alerts?

    A. SQL alerts can only be executed upon encountering a system-generated message in the SQL Error Log.

    B. SQL alerts can be executed based on system messages or user-defined messages in the SQL Error Log.

    C. User-defined SQL alerts can be executed based on system messages in the NT Event Log only.

    D. None of the above.

12. Which component provides for PROCESSING of SQL alert and event information?

    A. The msdb database

    B. MSSQLSERVER

    C. SQL Executive

    D. SQL Alert Engine

13. Choose the method for disabling processing for a given alert, without deleting alert information.

    A. Select the Enable/Disable option for the alert.

    B. Run the sp_disablealert stored procedure.

    C. Stop the SQLAlert service.

    D. None of the above.

14. Which SQL stored procedure is used to delete an alert?

    A. sp_killalert

    B. sp_dropalert

    C. sp_delalert

    D. sp_updatealert (using the DEL option)

15. Which of the following statements is true regarding operators?

    A. Alert notifications can be forwarded to operators with no additional server software or configuration required.

    B. Alert notification to operators requires configuration of a compatible e-mail system.

    C. Operators are automatically defined when NT accounts are set up.

    D. None of the above.

16. What is the benefit of defining a failsafe operator for a given server?

    A. To prevent "holes" in coverage hours

    B. To easily configure a single operator for all alert notifications

    C. To set up an operator to be notified for alerts configured with the failsafe option

    D. None of the above

17. Which component provides for INPUT to the SQL Server alerting system?

    A. The SQL Executive Service

    B. The msdb database

    C. The SQL Server Service

    D. The Master database

18. Failsafe operators are defined using which of the following methods:

    A. From SQL Enterprise Manager, select Manage Operators from the Server menu and click the Fail-Safe tool button.

    B. From the Manage Alerts/Operators window, click the Operators tab, double-click the required operator, and select the Fail-Safe option.

    C. Select Alerts/Operators from the Server menu in SQL Enterprise Manager. Click the Alert Engine Defaults tool button in the Manage Alerts/Operators window.

    D. None of the above.

19. Which component provides for OUTPUT from the SQL Server alerting system?

    A. The msdb database

    B. The SQL Executive Service

    C. The SQL Task History window

    D. None of the above

20. Which SQL task type enables execution of Transact-SQL commands?

    A. NTSQL

    B. TSQL

    C. CMD_SQL

    D. CmdExec

21. Which SQL stored procedure is used to modify information for a given operator?

    A. sp_updateoperator

    B. sp_changeoperator

    C. sp_modifoperator

    D. sp_operator

22. Which database table contains entries for the notification message the e-mail or pager operators will receive?

    A. sysoperators

    B. sysalerts

    C. systasks

    D. sysnotifications

23. Which of the following statements is true of SQL task scheduling?

    A. Provides for integration of task history and execution results into the NT Event Log and SQL Server Error Log

    B. Requires that the SQL Executive Service is running

    C. Provides for integration of task history and execution results only in the NT Event Log

    D. A and B

24. Which SQL stored Procedure is used to view a specific task's execution history?

    A. sp_viewhistory

    B. sp_taskinfo

    C. sp_helptask

    D. sp_helphistory

25. Which database table contains entries for each alert defined on a specific server?

    A. sysoperators

    B. sysalerts

    C. systasks

    D. sysnotifications

26. What method can be used to disable all event processing for a server without deleting information from the msdb database? (Choose all that apply.)

    A. Stop the SQL Executive service.

    B. Run the sp_disabletasks SQL stored procedure.

    C. Disable each alert and scheduled task by deselecting the Enable option in the appropriate Manage window in SQL Enterprise Manager.

    D. Reset the status of the msdb database to disabled.

27. Operator paging notification is made possible by which of the following?

    A. The SQL Executive service

    B. Third-party paging software

    C. The installed e-mail package

    D. None of the above

28. Which SQL account can modify SQL alert and task information?

    A. The admin account

    B. The operator account

    C. The sa account

    D. None of the above

29. Name the three scheduling methods that can be used when defining tasks.

    A. Active_Recurring, OnDemand, Single Execution

    B. OnDemand, One Time, Recurring

    C. System Recurring, One Time, User Generated

    D. None of the above

30. What other facility use of the task-scheduling engine?

    A. SQL Server replication

    B. The SQL Error Logging facilit

    C. No other facilities use this feature

    D. None of the above

Review Answers

1. A

2. C

3. A

4. B

5. D

6. A

7. B

8. D

9. B

10. C

11. B

12. C

13. A

14. B

15. B

16. A

17. B

18. C

19. D

20. B

21. A

22. D

23. D

24. D

25. B

26. A, C

27. B

28. C

29. B

30. A

Answers to Test Yourself Questions at Beginning of the Chapter

1. systasks maintains entries for each defined scheduled tasks. Sysalerts is used to maintain entries for defined alerts. See table 7.2 for additional information.

2. The sp_helptask SQL stored procedure is used to obtain information about schedule tasks on a given server. (See table 7.7.)

3. When an alert is defined in the Manage Alerts/Operators window of SQL Enterprise Manager, the option to raise an SNMP trap can be selected. This will forward an alert to any standard SNMP network management system. Look at the "Defining Alerts" section for additional information.

4. The msdb database provides input to the SQL alert processing engine (the SQL Executive Service). In short, the each entry in the systasks or sysalerts table represents a single scheduled task or alert. Refer to figure 7.1.

5. Two types of tasks are TSQL, or Transact-SQL, and CmdExec tasks. TSQL tasks are used to invoke SQL commands in response to a detected alert condition. CmdExec tasks are useful for executing external Windows NT-based programs. See the "Task Types" section for additional information.

Chapter 8

Managing Data

This chapter covers the most important things that a database administrator (DBA) has to do. Failure to accomplish these tasks could be a serious career-limiting move.

The primary duty of any database administrator is to manage data, which involves three primary duties:

▶ Backup

▶ Recovery

▶ Import/export

The duties of backing up the database are crucial to the health and well being of both the database and the database administrator. Knowing what to expect during database recovery makes the recovery process go more smoothly. Import/export tasks are crucial for loading data from foreign sources, as well as for some reporting tasks.

As always, this chapter begins with a list of the exam objectives relating to the topic at hand, moves on to the chapter pretest, offers valuable information directly addressing the objectives, as well as additional relative discussion topics, and finishes with exercises, review questions, and answers to both the review questions and the chapter pretest questions.

This chapter focuses on data management. It helps you prepare for the exam by addressing and fully covering the following objectives:

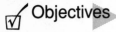 **Objectives**

- ▶ Identify the functionality of dynamic backup.

- ▶ Create a Dump device.

- ▶ Perform a database dump.

- ▶ Perform a striped backup.

- ▶ Identify how automatic recovery works.

- ▶ Dump a transaction log.

- ▶ Load a database dump.

- ▶ Identify the appropriate recovery scenario to use.

- ▶ Identify the best uses for the dumping command and the loading command in managing data.

- ▶ Identify the best uses for BCP when managing data.

Test Yourself! Before reading this chapter, test yourself to determine how much study time you will need to devote to this section.

1. Which command is used to back up a database to tape?

2. What is a database Dump device and how does it differ from a normal data device?

3. Can users be actively using a database during a full backup?

4. Casey has a database that is taking too long to back up to her tape drive. What backup technology can be employed to make use of additional tape drives on the same server?

5. How does SQL Server figure out the status of databases on startup?

6. What does the BCP command do?

7. James has a user database that has been marked suspect by recovery. What steps does he take to restore his database?

8. Nick needs to copy a database from an SQL Server running on a DEC AlphaServer to an Intel-Based Compaq Proliant. His plan is to back up the database, copy the backup to the Proliant, and load it. Why won't this work?

9. Shirley has scheduled transaction log dumps to occur every two hours during business hours with the following command:

```
dump transaction mydb to mydbtrandump with init
```

Assuming that *mydbtrandump* is a disk device, what is wrong with using this command?

Answers are located at the end of the chapter...

Backing Up Databases

Database backup is the process of creating offline copies of data. Database backup is done to facilitate disaster recovery, as well as to move data from one server to another. The process of backing up a database involves copying all of the data from the database onto a disk or tape. The primary reason for backing up databases is disaster recovery. Having good backups saves data and keeps database administrators from losing their jobs when their data goes bad.

Database backup can be can be done using two techniques. An *online backup* is a backup that is created from within SQL Server and is done while the SQL Server service is running. Online backup is the most common type of backup used with SQL Server.

Offline backup is done with Windows NT or a third-party backup package. Offline backup requires that the SQL Server services are stopped. When the SQL Server services are running, the files are in use and cannot be backed up. Stopping the SQL Server services allows the device files to be backed up. Because offline backup is a very simple process that does not involve SQL Server, it is not covered on the exam and is only mentioned in this chapter as an alternative to online backup. The rest of this section focuses on online backup strategies and procedures.

Dump Database: How It Works

SQL Server databases are backed up with the DUMP DATABASE command. Database backups are commonly referred to as *dumps*. When a bucket of water is dumped, there is no more water in the bucket. Fortunately, when SQL Server dumps a database, it is just making a copy of the database; the name "dump" is a misnomer. The DUMP DATABASE command starts at page 0 of the database in question and proceeds through the database, writing each page out to the Dump device.

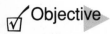 Objective

What happens when the backup is busily backing up the database and a user needs to write to a page that hasn't been backed up yet? The technology that resolves this issue is called *dynamic*

backup. Before the user request can write to a page that has not been backed up yet, the dump process is notified that a page is needed to record a user's input. The dump process takes note of where the page is, jumps ahead to back up the pages involved in the write, and then jumps back to where it left off before. When it reaches the written data in its normal course of backup, it just skips over it.

It can be inferred from the description of dynamic backup that the database backup process should probably be run when database use is at a minimum. This is usually the case, especially since database dumps are normally preceded or followed by database diagnostics, which put a strain on the CPU load and can cause extensive page locking.

 Note

> Database diagnostics should be run either immediately preceding or immediately following a database dump. If the diagnostics are run prior to the dump, it is easy to certify that the database backup was done when the database was in a clean state. If the diagnostics are done after the dump, any changes made by the diagnostics are kept in the backup file. The option is usually decided on by the temperament of the database administrator. See Chapter 12, "Troubleshooting," for more information about database diagnostics and object integrity verification.

How are databases backed up when there are users on the system? Part of the database is the *transaction log*, which is a continuing record of every operation done on the database since the last time either the database or the log were dumped. When backups need to be completed during working hours, the transaction log is usually backed up instead. This provides recovery on a finer scale than the normal nightly backup.

The process could be implemented like this: At midnight the database is backed up. At 10 AM, noon, 2 PM, 4 PM, and 6 PM, the transaction log is backed up.

Using this example backup schedule, if the database were to crash at 4:30 PM, the database dump would be loaded, the 10 AM, noon, 2 PM, and 4 PM transaction log dumps would each be loaded in the correct order, and then the database would be restored up to where it was at 4 PM. The data entered from 4 PM to 4:30 PM would be lost, but that's a small loss compared to losing the entire day's data. At the same time, the data from 4:00 to 4:30 PM may be recoverable, as well; recovery is discussed in depth in a later section.

Note that each transaction log has to be loaded in order. SQL Server places a time stamp in each transaction log dump to prevent dumps from loading in the wrong order. It helps to think of the transaction log as a list of instructions about what happened to the database since the last dump. When the transaction logs are reloaded, the reload process simply goes through and reads each instruction and performs the specific operation, whether it is to add or remove rows, update pages, or anything else. If the instructions were done in the wrong order, there may be a row that needs to be updated that does not exist yet. That is why the dumps have to be read in the correct order.

It may also help to compare loading a transaction log dump to putting together a bicycle from a book of instructions. If the instructions were done out of order, the bicycle would probably not work. If the process for installing the chain were attempted before the rear wheel was in place, for example, the instruction could not be carried out.

Each databases is backed up separately. For recovery purposes, usually the Master, Msdb, and Model databases are dumped, along with all of the non-system databases on a daily basis. The TempDB and Pubs databases are ignored because they can easily be regenerated after recovery. Normally, Master is backed up nightly because it is convenient and because the Master database is usually pretty small compared to user databases.

The Master database should be backed up whenever it is changed. The Master database is changed by any operation that changes, adds or moves databases, devices, logins or configuration options.

This is the quick and easy way to remember it for the exam. For the more difficult items to remember, note that when any of the following system stored procedures or commands are run, the database should be backed up:

- ▶ sp_configure

- ▶ DISK INIT, DISK RESIZE, sp_dropdevice

- ▶ sp_addsegment, sp_extendsegment, sp_dropsegment

- ▶ CREATE DATABASE, ALTER DATABASE, DROP DATABASE

- ▶ DBCC SHRINKDB

- ▶ sp_addumpdevice, sp_dropdevice

This is the list according to the Microsoft System Administrator's guide that ships with SQL Server, but it may not be a complete list. The list presents you with a good idea of what types of commands cause Master to be changed. Becoming very familiar with the system tables in Master will help a DBA to discern which commands cause modifications to Master. In general, backing up Master on a nightly basis, in addition to whenever it is changed, will prove to be very convenient during disaster recovery.

After backing up databases, running database diagnostics is a good idea. Microsoft recommends that the following be run on every database that is being backed up right after the backup has completed, or prior to the backup:

```
DBCC CHECKDB(<databasename>)
DBCC NEWALLOC(<databasename>)
DBCC CHECKCATALOG(<databasename>)
```

In practice, DBCC CHECKDB can take 18 to 24 hours for larger databases, so this may not be a practical procedure to accomplish on a nightly basis.

That is the theory of how databases are backed up. Next is a look at the syntax and operations used to back up databases.

Backup Operations Overview

There are two steps to backing up a database or transaction log. First, create a place to put the data—this can either be a place on disk where the data will go or a tape device. Either way, it is called a *dump device*. A dump device is not a data device. It can't be used to store data for active use. It is simply where backups go.

The second step is to dump the database, which is done using either the DUMP DATABASE syntax or by using the graphical interface in SQL Enterprise manager. Both methods are covered here because both are covered on the exam.

Creating Backup Devices

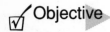 Backup devices are locations where data is dumped by SQL Server. There are two main types of dump devices. Disk dump devices are stored on disks. These are usually hard disks, but dumps can be done to floppy. Tape dump devices are dump devices that are mapped to specific tape drives. The tape drive must be accessible from Windows NT; all of the drivers must be loaded by Windows NT before the drive will be available.

Regardless of type, backup devices are created in a query tool by using the sp_addumpdevice. Note that there are only two *d*'s in the middle. The syntax for the command is as follows:

```
sp_addumpdevice {'disk' ¦ 'diskette' ¦ 'tape'}, 'logical_name',
'physical_name' [, {{cntrltype [, noskip ¦ skip [,
media_capacity]]} ¦
{@devstatus = {noskip ¦ skip}}}]
```

The first argument is the device type. Logical Name is the name of the device that will be used by SQL Server and by the backup commands.

Physical Name is the path to the device. For local disk devices, use names such as C:\MSSQL\BACKUP\DUMP.DAT. To dump across the network, use names such as \\OtherServer\DUMPS\DUMP.DAT. For local tape devices, the full path for the tape device must be specified, which is usually \\.\tape0 for the first tape device.

Cntrltype is ignored in SQL Server 6.5, but was the controller type in SQL Server 4.21.

The Skip or NoSkip parameter specifies how ANSI tape labels should be handled. See the upcoming sidebar "Labels, Labels Everywhere" for more information.

The Media_Capacity argument is also ignored by SQL Server 6.5. If the Cntrltype and Media_Capacity arguments are skipped, then the Skip and NoSkip are supplied by using the explicit argument @DevStatus=. See the sidebar "Stored Procedure Parameters" in Chapter 2 for more information on skipping parameters.

That said, the most common command used is something like the following:

```
sp_addumpdevice "disk", "PubsDBDump",
"C:\MSSQL\BACKUP\PUBSDBDUMP.DAT"
```

This command tells SQL Server to make a dump device, that it will be kept on disk, and that commands will refer to it as PubsDB-Dump.

To use the Skip or NoSkip labels while leaving out the optional parameters for media capacity and controller type, use the following syntax:

```
sp_addumpdevice "tape", "PubsDBTapeDump", "\\.\TAPE0", @DevStatus
= Skip
```

This will create the tape device and allow ANSI labels to be skipped.

The sp_addumpdevice command does not make any files. It simply tells SQL Server where to make files when the dump is done. While the database is dumping, the files are in use and cannot be used. As soon as the dump process completes, the files are available and can be backed up to tape or copied to another server.

To add dump devices by using SQL Enterprise Manager, use the following steps:

1. Start SQL Enterprise Manager.

2. Expand the server the device is to be created on.

3. Expand the Backup Devices folder.

4. Right-click on the Backup Devices folder.

5. Choose the New Backup Device option from the popup menu.

6. Type in the name for the new backup device (see fig. 8.1). This will be the logical name for the device used in future commands.

Figure 8.1

The New Backup Device screen.

7. Edit the location for the device as needed. This should be the path and file name of the device file if it is to be a disk device, or the name of the tape drive if it is a tape backup device.

8. Choose Create when the options are all set.

The new dump device should appear in the Backup Devices section of Enterprise Manager.

Dumping Databases to Single Devices

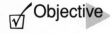

A database can be dumped either to a single device or to multiple devices simultaneously. Dumping a database to a single device means that the entire database dump is placed into a single database device. When a database is dumped to multiple devices, it is striped across the devices. The striped backup feature was introduced in SQL Server 6.0 as a way to dump large databases to multiple tape devices quickly. In this section the syntax involved in dumping a database to a single device is covered, and the next section covers the differences in syntax between a single device backup and a striped backup.

Databases are dumped to devices with the Dump Database command, which starts the process of backing up the specified database to the specified dump device. The command syntax looks
like this:

```
DUMP DATABASE {dbname ¦ @dbname_var}
    TO dump_device [, dump_device2 [..., dump_device32]]
[WITH options [[,] STATS [ = percentage]]]
```

The dbname or @dbname_var arguments are for holding either a
specific name of a database or a string variable if the dump is being executed in a script. The dump_device is the logical name of
the device being dumped to. A new feature in SQL Server 6.5, the
WITH STATS = option, provides feedback on how far along the
database dump has progressed. There are also other options, such
as INIT, which causes any existing dumps to be overwritten. The
default is to append the current dump to any existing dumps in
the dump device. This can cause some very long and confused
files to be generated. The UNLOAD or NOUNLOAD options will
either force a tape drive to rewind and eject or to not rewind or
eject. Finally, there are expiration intervals, ExpireDate and RetainDays. *ExpireDate* is the date when the backup can be overwritten. *RetainDays* is the number of days that must pass before the
backup can be overwritten.

Usually, the command will look something like the following:

```
dump database pubs to PubsDBDump with init
```

Dumping a database to a single database device does not involve
too much. In addition, dump devices don't even have to be created beforehand. SQL Server provides the capability to dump to a
specified file, making it optional to create dump devices. An example of that syntax follows:

```
dump database pubs to DISK="c:\mssql\backup\pubsdbdump.dat"
```

This provides some flexibility in dump device locations.

At first glance this seems to contradict the statement that database
devices have to be created before a database can be dumped.
Although a dump technically could be done every day to a

dynamically created device, it is usually not accepted standard practice to do so. Think of a database device as an extra piece of documentation in the process of performing a database dump.

In order to dump to a tape drive, make sure the backup is not overwritten for two weeks, and to rewind and eject the tape when the backup is complete, use a command such as this:

```
dump database pubs to TAPE="\\.\TAPE0" with INIT, UNLOAD,
RETAINDAYS=14
```

Where to Dump Databases

The questions of where to dump databases and where to create database devices are important to answer. Here are some guidelines:

Be consistent. Scattering devices and changing naming standards for devices causes confusion. Remember that the only time it will really be important to know where everything is will be when doing recovery, and the situation will be tense enough without having to worry about which files go where.

Stick with the SQL Server directory tree where possible. Usually, the \MSSQL\BACKUP directory is used for dump devices and the \MSSQL\DATA directory is used for data devices. Creating these structures on all of the logical drives on a server makes finding files much simpler.

Whatever decisions are made, be sure they are extensively documented not only to answer the "where" questions but also the "why" questions.

To backup (dump) databases using SQL Enterprise manager, follow these steps:

1. Start SQL Enterprise Manager.

2. Expand the server the database is on.

3. Expand the Databases folder.

4. Right-click on the database to be backed up.

5. Choose Backup/Restore from the popup menu. The screen shown in figure 8.2 appears.

Figure 8.2

*The Database
Backup/Restore
window.*

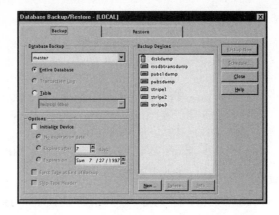

6. Choose the backup devices to use in the backup by clicking on them in the Backup Devices list.

7. Choose Initialize Device if the device should be initialized before use.

8. Choose Backup Now to start the backup immediately or Schedule to run the backup at a later time.

Dumping Tables

SQL Server 6.5 introduces the ability to dump single tables to a dump device. It had been impossible to dump or load single tables. Now it is possible to back up or restore a single table from backup.

The syntax for backing up and restoring single tables is very similar to the syntax for backing up and restoring an entire database, with the word "Table" substituted in for "database."

Keep in mind that foreign key constraints and any other programmed logic that keeps the data in the table meaningful can be lost by this process.

In other words, there may be foreign keys that don't match and other kinds of problems. If logical data consistency is extremely important, then this is not a good backup scheme to employ. If it is easy to discover and fix problems with logical concurrency in the database, however, this may be an easier, more economical way to back up data because less data can be backed up.

SQL Server cannot back up or restore individual tables that have columns with text or image data types, or tables that are published for replication.

Striped Backups

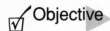 **Objective**

In order to speed the backup process, especially to tape backup systems, striped backup technology was created. The striped backup involves backing the database up to multiple devices at the same time. This speeds the backup process because the disk drive being dumped from usually outruns any tape drive very comfortably. Up to 32 devices can be dumped to simultaneously. The syntax is the same as the previous syntax, but the dump devices are placed in a comma delimited list:

```
dump database pubs to pubsdbdump1, pubsdbdump2, pubsdbdump3
with init
```

This command would dump the database out to three devices and would initialize each device prior to using it. If these devices are tape devices, it is a good idea to make sure the tapes are clearly labeled on the outside with the name of the database and the position in the stripe set.

Other options, such as the SKIP and NOSKIP options, are still active when using a striped backup. Syntax for striped and single device backups is nearly the same, the only difference being the list of devices in a striped backup.

Labels, Labels Everywhere

Many of the backup-related commands in SQL Server refer to labels. There are SKIP and NOSKIP options, and many commands have arguments such as VOLUME = for specifying volume labels. So what are these labels?

Well, unfortunately there isn't a nifty label printing program for making paper labels to stick on the tapes. A tape label is a piece of data at the beginning of the tape that contains a serial number (Volume ID), the expiration date or retention period, and the name of the program that made the tape. The labels are part of an ANSI standard, so any program that is ANSI-compliant should be able to recognize what kind of tape it is and determine whether the tape can be overwritten.

The SKIP and NOSKIP options specify whether the label should be read and used. If SKIP is specified, then the label is read and promptly ignored, allowing any tape to be overwritten regardless of when the tape expires. NOSKIP guarantees that the label will be read, if present, and that SQL Server will abide by any restrictions placed by the label.

 Warning

SQL Server is very picky about which tapes it will overwrite and which it won't, regardless of the labels. For best results, only use tapes that are either new or have been used with SQL Server before. Tapes that have been used by the Windows NT Backup program or any third-party program won't be overwritten by SQL Server, which will complain of a device error. To employ a used tape with SQL Server, use Windows NT Backup to erase the tape first.

Striped backups are very handy for speeding up the backup process and will also make restoring from tape much quicker. Keep in mind, however, that the use of a striped backup multiplies the number of tapes to store and track. Be prepared to handle the logistics of the decision to use striped backups, such as purchasing, storing, and tracking more tapes.

To create a striped backup in SQL Enterprise Manager, follow these steps:

1. Expand the Databases folder.

2. Right-click on the database to be backed up and choose Backup/Restore from the popup menu. The screen shown in figure 8.3 appears.

3. Use Shift-Click and Control-Click to choose multiple devices to back up.

4. Choose Backup Now to start the backup.

Figure 8.3

The Database Backup/Restore window with multiple dump devices chosen.

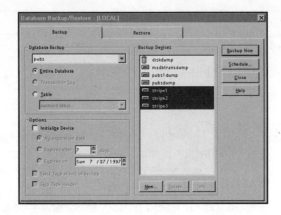

Transaction Logs and Automatic Recovery

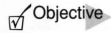

To understand the transaction log, you must understand something about how SQL Server really works. In other words, what really happens when the following sample command is executed:

```
Insert into Authors (au_id, au_lname, au_fname, phone, address,
city, state, zip, contract)
values ("123-45-6789", "Doe", "John", "800 555-1212", "2121 Codd
Drive", "Pinehurst", "KS", "66221", 1)
```

The following steps explain it:

1. SQL Server decides how it is going to execute the query. In this case, it will write a row at the end of the Authors table and update any indexes as necessary.

2. SQL Server writes the operations it is going to do into the transaction log.

3. SQL Server reads in the pages effected by the command.

4. SQL Server updates the pages.

5. SQL Server writes a completed flag into the record in the transaction log. This is called *committing the transaction.*

Periodically, a process called the *Checkpoint* runs and makes sure that all of the pages in memory that have changed and had their transactions committed since they were read from disk are written back to disk. At this point, a record is added to the transaction log. Any committed items in the log that occur before the checkpoint record have already been written to disk, and any items in the log after the checkpoint have not been written to disk.

The record of what the SQL Server did to insert the row is still stored in the transaction log. If the SQL Server were to go down after step 2 and before step 5, then, when SQL Server started up, it would roll back the transaction as part of automatic recovery.

Automatic recovery is the process that SQL Server starts when the service is started. After a database is opened, the automatic recovery process reads the transaction log for a database and looks for the last checkpoint record. Any item in the transaction log after the last checkpoint has not been written to disk yet. Of the pages that haven't been written to disk, there are committed transactions and uncommitted transactions. Each committed transaction is *rolled forward*, meaning it is written to disk as if it had been checkpointed. If the server were to go down after step 5 but before a checkpoint, the transaction would be rolled forward. Each transaction that has not been committed is *rolled back*, and the entire transaction is wiped out. This would have happened if the server had gone down. It is normal for some transactions to roll forward and some transactions to roll back in the normal course of starting the server.

Checkpoints occur at a time interval specified in the configuration option for *recovery interval*. This option can be set just like any other database option by using sp_configure or by using the server configuration in the SQL Enterprise Manager (see fig. 8.4). The recovery interval setting determines how long it will take for SQL Server to recover in case the server goes down ungracefully. The checkpoint interval is the same as the recovery interval and defaults to 5 minutes.

Every database has its own transaction log. Transaction logs can be stored either in the same device as the database or they can be placed in a separate device. If the transaction log is placed in a device separate from the rest of the database, the transaction log can be backed up separately. If the database is stored in the same device as the log, the database cannot be backed up separately.

Figure 8.4

The Server Configuration/Options dialog box. Notice that the default recovery interval is five minutes.

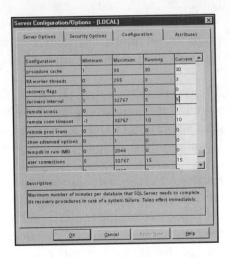

Transaction logs contain the information necessary to recover a database to a point in time. A transaction log backup takes less time and requires less space than a full database backup, so a transaction log dump can be done while users are hammering away at the database with minimal user impact. By taking periodic transaction log backups, a database can be recovered closer to the time of data loss, reducing the amount of lost data.

When backing up a transaction log, there are two important facts to keep in mind. First of all, each transaction log has to be kept in order to achieve recovery. In other words, if the database were dumped at midnight, and the server went down at 4 PM, then all of the transaction log dumps between midnight and 4 PM would be required to recover the databases. Be careful not to overwrite the dumps. Also remember that if the transaction log is truncated, the database has to be dumped again in order to start using transaction log dumps for recovery.

In addition to being used as a backup mechanism, dumping the transaction log also clears out all of the completed transactions, which prevents the log from filling up. If the log fills up, then it is necessary to truncate the transaction log. Truncating the log means removing the transactions that have been completed without copying them to a dump device. If the transaction log is dumped, it means that the database is no longer recoverable from future transaction log dumps until the database is dumped again.

In other words, if the log fills up, it is wise to immediately dump the database so it will be back in a recoverable state by using transaction logs.

Transaction logs cannot be dumped if the database and log are on the same device. Transaction logs cannot be dumped if the database option called "trunc. log on chkpt" is turned on (see fig. 8.5). This option truncates the log whenever a checkpoint process occurs. It is useful in databases that don't see a lot of activity and won't be using transaction logs for recovery. If the database has a high volume of activity, the effect of dumping the log every five minutes would be detrimental to performance.

Figure 8.5

The Edit Database Options screen.

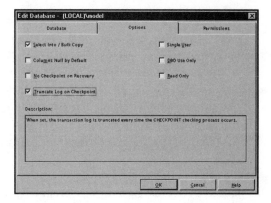

The options shown in figure 8.5 are the options on the model database. These options carry on to newly created databases. This screen can be found by double-clicking on a database name in the databases folder in SQL Enterprise Manager.

If the Select Into/Bulk Copy option is turned on in the database, the transaction log cannot be backed up. Non-logged operations may occur by chance in the database when this option is on. Non-logged operations, such as the Select Into statement or fast bulk copy, do not put entries into the transaction log, which means that any rows added using these statements would not be included in a transaction log dump and that any dumps that would occur would almost definitely cause database corruption. As a result, SQL Server does not allow the backup to occur.

So far, the theory behind how database transaction log dumps occur has been discussed. Now a look at the practical side of the transaction log dump.

Backing Up the Transaction Log

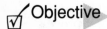 Transaction logs are dumped out to dump devices the same way databases are dumped out to dump devices. First the dump device is created, either with SQL Enterprise Manager or with the sp_addumpdevice system stored procedure, and then the transaction log is dumped. There are two different command structures for dumping the log. To back the log up to a dump device, use this syntax:

```
DUMP TRANSACTION {dbname ¦ @dbname_var}
     [TO dump_device [, dump_device2 [..., dump_device32]]]
[WITH {TRUNCATE_ONLY ¦ NO_LOG ¦ NO_TRUNCATE} {options}]
```

The dbname or @dbname_var parameters work the same as in the dump database command. Transaction log dumps can be striped, but this is very rare. The following command is the most often used:

```
dump transaction pubs to pubstransdump with noinit
```

This appends a dump of the transaction log to the dump device pubstransdump. This is useful for keeping multiple copies of the transaction log on disk while dumping to the same device.

 For transaction log dumps, it is fairly common to append dumps to the same file. Usually, it follows a schedule where the log is dumped during the day and the dump device keeps growing, and then, at the end of the day, the dump is placed on tape and the dump device file is removed from the disk to begin a new day.

Transaction log dumps can also be done with SQL Enterprise Manager and the following steps:

1. Start SQL Enterprise Manager.

2. Expand the server containing the database to back up.

3. Expand the Databases folder.

4. Right-click on the database to back up.

5. Choose Transaction Log from the Database Backup frame. If this option is greyed out, it means the transaction log cannot be backed up because it is on the same device as the data.

6. Choose options, such as Initialize Device, as desired.

7. Choose the backup device from the Backup Devices list or click the New button to create a new backup device.

8. Choose the Backup Now button to start the backup immediately or use the Schedule button to schedule the backup.

To truncate the transaction log, use the WITH TRUNCATE_ONLY, NO LOG options on the truncate statement. When truncating the log, the dump device is not specified because no dump device is needed. The following command is a typical command to truncate a transaction log:

```
dump transaction pubs with no_log, truncate_only
```

This empties out all the committed transactions from the log. Keep in mind that if the log is filling up because of one extended and currently running transaction, dumping the log will not clear out the entire log, just the parts that have already been committed, and chances are the log won't get any more available space.

To truncate the log using SQL Enterprise Manager, follow this procedure:

1. Start SQL Enterprise Manager.

2. Expand the server that contains the log to be truncated.

3. Expand the Databases folder.

4. Right-click on the database and choose Edit.

5. Click on the Truncate button to truncate the log.

Note

Occasionally, the numbers available on the Edit screen mentioned in this procedure show negative numbers. This does not indicate a problem with the database. Do not take any drastic actions because the numbers are negative. It is a normal bug in the SQL Server software that doesn't report sizes correctly. Don't worry about it. Sometimes it reports zero space available. If that doesn't seem possible, it is probably wrong. The numbers in the edit window are extremely unreliable. Microsoft has reported that installing Service Pack 3 for SQL Server will fix the problem. If Service Pack 3 is not installed, use the DBCC UPDATEUSAGE(<database>) command to fix the usage statistics.

Dumping the transaction log periodically is required to maintain the database. Fortunately, dumping the database also causes the transaction log to be cleared of committed transactions, but if the log is not large enough to handle a full day of work, it becomes critical to monitor the size of the log and make sure it is being dumped frequently enough to ensure continued operation. Transaction log dumps are a very good reason to use SQL Mail to monitor the server. If the transaction log dump does not come in on time, monitoring provides the ability to fix the problem before it affects users.

Loading Databases and Transaction Logs

Objective

The counterpart to dumping a database is loading a database. Databases are loaded from backup devices. The section covers the load process from a conceptual standpoint, and then digs into the syntax and technique of loading databases.

Database loads are an important part of disaster recovery, as well as providing a means to copy data from one server to another in a clean and efficient format. First, a look at the theory behind loading a database or transaction log, then an in-depth look at the syntax of the commands.

In order to load a database or transaction log, the administrator must have complete and exclusive use of the database. Setting the DBO Use Only flag on the database can accomplish this. This step is only necessary when there are users trying to use the database that is about to be loaded. The database into which you are loading does not necessarily have to be empty. Any data in the current database will be lost during the load process.

Database loads work by starting at page 0 of the database and page 0 of the dump, and by copying data from the dump file directly into the database. If the dump file skips around because portions of the database were in use at the time, then the load skips around as well. For this reason, a database dump can only be loaded into a database that is the same size or larger than the source database. If the destination database were smaller than the source database, the pages being restored to may not exist in the destination database. Dumping and reloading cannot be used to shrink a database.

Transaction log loads work by simply loading the transactions one at a time into the database. The transaction logs do not load if there has been any activity in the database between the transaction log that is currently in the system and the one that has been loaded.

The LOAD DATABASE command looks nearly identical to the DUMP DATABASE discussed earlier. Most of the options still look and work the same.

Devices, Segments, and Other Unpleasant Subjects

A lot of mention has been made of devices, device fragments, and segments. It is important to understand what's going on with each of these terms, and why they are such a thorn in the side of the recovery process.

Data devices are where SQL Server stores live data on the disk. They can be thought of as a mapping between a logical device name and the name of a file on disk. All a device does is

continues

provide SQL Server with a way to access data that is already on disk.

All data in a database is on a segment. User defined segments have fallen by the wayside with the advent of disk array hardware. By default, there are three segments in each database:

▶ **System segment.** Contains the system tables and system stored procedures for the database, except for the *syslogs* table.

▶ **Log segment.** Contains only the *syslogs* table, which is the transaction log.

▶ **Default segment.** Contains all the user data, by default.

Segments are used to place data onto devices. In other words, the log segment is placed onto a set of devices, and then the syslogs table is placed onto the segment.

Fragments are allocation pieces of devices. If a database is created to use all of a device, for example, then the device and database are both expanded by 500 MB to add some space; there is one device, three segments, and two fragments of the database. Every time the database size is changed on a single device, a new fragment is added to the database.

When databases are loaded from a dump file, it is critical that the devices, segments, and fragments map exactly to the source database. Failure to do this will result in a bad database load in the worst case and lost space in the best case. Fragmentation of a database is not checked prior to loading.

This raises two issues. How is fragmentation avoided to prevent this administrative hassle from occuring, and how can the segment, fragment, and device information be discovered to make rebuilding the database possible?

Fragmentation is avoided by making the devices big enough in the first place. Disk space is cheap on a production server compared with the rest of the price of the server. Figure out how big the database needs to be, then double it. The objective is to make the devices big enough that fragmentation won't become very complex until after the database administrator retires or rolls onto a new project.

Segment, fragment, and device information is found in the master database in the sysusages table. The following query from the Administrator's Companion documentation in SQL Server 6.5 shows database fragmentation:

```
select segmap, size from sysusages
    where dbid =
        (select dbid from
sysdatabases
            where name = "mydb")
```

Substitute the name of the database to check in for *mydb*. This results in a good solid segment map of the database. There are two columns. The first represents the type of allocation. Allocations with a number 3 are data allocations—in other words, allocations for the default segment. Allocations with a 4 are allocations for log space. When rebuilding devices, rebuild them in the same order specified in the table.

That is a lot of work. Microsoft decided to make it easier with the sp_help_revdatabase function, which reads the sysusages table and creates all the DISK INIT statements and all of the database creation statements, making this an extremely valuable procedure. Some database administrators even print the results of this procedure and hang them up in the office so they are always close by and easy to find.

Disaster Recovery

Now that all the pieces are in place to ensure a good backup of the data, it's time to cover the process of recovery. This includes going through the recovery scenarios and step-by-step instructions on how to recover from different problems. The first step in disaster recovery is determining which disaster occurred.

To have a successful recovery, it is important to have the correct information at hand, such as the following:

▶ The exact layout of the devices used on the server, which can be found by using the sp_help_revdatabase system stored procedure, which can be found in the master device. This gives not only the exact layout of the databases and devices, but also the script necessary to re-create every device and database correctly.

▶ A document that contains the locations of every backup tape in the organization, along with what is on the label of the tape.

▶ The *exact* character set and sort order of the database. Use sp_helpsort if necessary.

▶ A document that goes through each of the disaster recovery scenarios and includes information about how to identify which scenario applies to a given situation.

An SQL Server can suffer only a finite number of disasters, and each disaster has a recovery scenario that corresponds to it. The disaster recovery scenarios are divided according to what is not working and what backups are available. For each scenario, there is a scenario description followed by step-by-step instructions on how to recover from the scenario. These scenarios are general enough to cover every database recovery incident, yet specific enough to be followed. All of the disasters that can occur on an SQL Server and their resolutions are covered. Each scenario will have its own section.

Many of the scenarios are chained together. If the master database plus one other user database were lost, for example, first follow the procedure for recovering master, then follow the procedure for recovering user databases. Also keep in mind that the procedures should be followed after the source of the disaster is found and fixes are put into place. If the cause was a drive failure, the procedure assumes that the drive has been replaced.

These scenarios use the term *lost*. A lost database or a lost device can be the result of fire, theft, hardware failure, sprinkler system failure, natural disaster, or the undesired interface of a jumbo jet with an office building. A device or database can be lost in the following situations:

▶ The server is turned on, and SQL Server won't start. The error log says the master device is suspect.

▶ When trying to access a database, SQL Server returns an error saying the device is suspect. Figure 8.6 shows an example of a suspect database in SQL Enterprise Manager.

▶ After walking into the server room, it is determined that the server isn't in the server room or anywhere else.

▶ Flames and "Police Line—Do Not Cross" tape are the new decor of the office building, and the tail of a jetliner is seen sticking out of the server room window.

▶ The server was last seen floating down what used to be Main Street.

Figure 8.6

The Pubs data-base has been marked as sus-pect here in the Server Manager window.

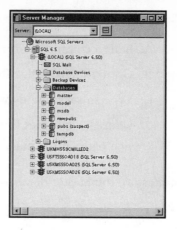

These are just some of the ways to determine that there may be a problem with the database server. In the case of the last three, backups stored off site will be the key to a successful restore.

Scenario 1: Master Database Lost, Backup Available

 If the Master database is lost and a backup is available, the proce-dure is to restore the Master database from backup and restart the server. During auto-recovery, the server goes through the newly restored Master database and finds all the other databases. Follow-ing is an outline of the recovery technique used to get the server running again after this type of disaster:

1. Create a new Master database by doing the following:

   A. Start SQL Setup.

   B. Continue to the Microsoft SQL Server 6.5—Options screen.

   C. Choose Rebuild Master Database.

   D. Choose the correct character set and sort order.

   E. Rebuild the Master database.

2. Start SQL Server in single-user mode:

    A. Start a command prompt.

    B. Go to the \MSSQL\BINN directory.

    C. Type **sqlservr -m -d\<master device path\>**

       where -m specifies single user mode, and \<master device path\> is the path to the device created in step B.

3. Restore the Master database from the backup:

    A. Start a command prompt.

    B. Go to the \MSSQL\BINN directory.

    C. Run type **isql -Usa -P** to start the command line ISQL utility.

    D. Use sp_addumpdevice to add a dump device for the Master database. Here's a reason to learn all of this command line SQL. Make sure to type **go** after typing the command to add the dump device. The go" command makes the command line ISQL execute the batch. The batch just sits in memory until a "go" is reached.

    E. In the ISQL utility, load the database using the following command:

```
load database master from <device>
```

      where *\<device\>* is the name of the device created in step D.

    F. After the Master device finishes loading, the SQL Server will shut down.

At this point, the SQL Server Master database has been restored, and SQL Server can be started normally. If the Master database is the only device lost, then this is the end of the recovery scenario. If other devices were lost, continue on to Scenario 3.

Scenario 2: Master Database Lost, No Backup Available

If the Master database was lost due to a corruption problem, and there is no backup of the Master database available to load from, the only option is to re-create the Master database, relink in all the devices, and restart the server. All the logins and settings will have to be reset by hand. Here's a step-by-step process on how to recover from this scenario:

1. Promise always to back up the Master database from now on.

2. Create a new Master database, using step 1 from Scenario 1. It is critical that the sort order and character set be absolutely correct.

3. Start SQL Server in single user mode, using step 2 from Scenario 1.

4. Relink each of the database devices in order. It is critical that the exact size of each device be known from the *sp_help_revdatabase* statement. If the output from this stored procedure is available, it is very simple to restore the databases. Run Disk Reinit for each segment:

```
Disk Reinit
    name = 'logical name',
    physname = 'physical name',
    vdevno = virtual device number,
    size = size
```

The information for using this is all found in the DISK INIT statements in the output from sp_help_revdatabases. It is an identical syntax to that used in the DISK INIT statement. Be sure to type **go** after each DISK REINIT statement so it will take effect. Keep in mind that this has to be done for each segment and each device in the database before going on to step 5.

5. Run DISK REFIT. Then use go to make the refit take. This commits the changes. Then type **checkpoint** and **shutdown** to stop SQL Server.

6. When SQL Server starts back up, it will have no configuration information and no security information. All the logins will have to be created and all the memory, open object, and other configurations will need to be reset.

Scenario 3: Data Devices of User Database Lost, Transaction Log Lost

If a user database is lost, you must know how to restore it from backup. If the transaction log is available, follow the steps in Scenario 4 first, then come back to this scenario to finish the job. Here are the steps to restore a user database:

1. Check to make sure the database is actually suspect.

   A. In SQL Enterprise manager, expand the server, then expand the Databases server. If the database is suspect, it will display Suspect next to the database. If it doesn't, right-click on the Databases folder and choose Refresh.

   B. In a query tool, execute the following query:

   ```
   Select name, status from sysdatabases
        where status = status & 256
   ```

   This query returns the name and status of any suspect databases. The Status field contains the status of the database. This is a bitmask field, in which each bit has a different meaning. The bit in the eighth place (the 256's bit) is the suspect bit and will be set to 1 if the database is suspect.

2. If the database has not been marked suspect, it should be dropped with the Drop Database command.

3. If the database has been marked suspect, it is necessary to use a different procedure to drop the database. A dbcc command called DBCC DBREPAIR is used as such:

   ```
   dbcc dbrepair(<database name>, dropdb)
   ```

Substitute the name of the database to be dropped into the command. Yes, the command really is dbrepair to drop a database.

4. It is also a good idea to drop the devices involved. Make sure that the information is available to create the devices again with all the correct segment information. The use of sp_help _revdatabase is recommended here to speed up the process. Use the script created by sp_help_revdatabase to create the devices and the database.

5. After the database is created, load the database using the Load Database command. The syntax used for loading a database would look like the following:

```
Load Database <database name> from <dump device>
```

6. Apply the transaction log dumps, if available, using the Load Transaction statement:

```
Load Transaction <database name> from <dump device>
```

7. Run DBCC CHECKDB() on the database to make sure that the database is consistent.

Scenario 4: Data Devices of User Database Lost, Log Intact, Backups Available

If the data devices of a user database are destroyed, but the transaction log for the user database is still intact, it may be possible to restore the database to the moment of failure by using a special option with the Dump Transaction command. This involves dumping the transaction log for the user database to a dump device and following the procedure outlined in Scenario 3. Here are the steps to recover partial data from a transaction log:

1. With the database marked suspect and prior to dropping the database, run the following dump transaction statement:

```
Dump Transaction <database name> to <dump device> with
no_truncate
```

2. Use Scenario 3 to restore the database.

3. Load the transaction log dump saved in step 1 as the last transaction log dump.

This is not a "sure thing" technique, but more of a "nice thing" technique. It is always worth a shot and can't do any harm. It may just save some data if the data device was corrupted but the transaction log device was OK.

Disaster Recovery Scenarios: Conclusion

That's the sum of the things that can happen during database recovery. By stringing these scenarios together, a database can be recovered from backup. Make sure that the master and the other databases are backed up and backed up clean, or none of these processes will work. Being prepared for a disaster is the best prevention.

Importing and Exporting Data

There are many instances where it is desirable to copy data from SQL Server to either another SQL Server or to another tool. Some shops use data import and export to provide a query server to reduce the load of ad-hoc queries on the production database server. It is sometimes necessary to put large quantities of data out into files for use in spreadsheets or for people to take on the road for analysis. Having multiple copies of a database also provides an extra level of redundancy for data recovery.

Getting data from one SQL Server to another or moving data between SQL Server and another product can involve some tricky maneuvering. There are two ways to import or export data from SQL Server. The method of choice is to load a database dump. This is simple, direct, and fast. There are also a lot of restrictions on loading data from database dumps. The other method is to use the Bulk Copy Program (BCP). The BCP utility is an outstanding tool, not because of a great interface, but because of the tremendous throughput that can be achieved.

Using Database Dumps for Import/Export

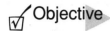

Database dumps and loads are used for two very important purposes in managing data. Most importantly, database dumps are used to handle database backup for the purposes of recovery. Another important purpose of a database dump is to provide data redundancy.

One of the key questions a database designer must answer is whether a database is to be used for data entry, data query, or a mixture of both. Databases used strictly for data entry will have a minimal number of indexes on them to reduce the overhead of insert and update operations. Databases used for data query, on the other hand, tend to be heavily indexed to provide quick response for returning data. Databases set up for a mixture of both tend to have performance problems until the proper balance is struck. One way to avoid this problem is to maintain a query server independent of the data entry server. The query server can be loaded nightly and indexed more heavily than the data entry server, providing good query response time without causing an impact on data entry operations.

By using the database dump and load capabilities in SQL Server, it is possible to efficiently dump and restore a database quickly, and reliably automate the process. Database dumps provide an excellent means for managing data in this way. Because a database dump is a very exacting process, there are some very strict conditions on using database dumps to copy data from server to server:

1. Windows NT is running on the same hardware platform on both SQL Servers. Moving data from an Intel box to a MIPS or ALPHA platform is not supported and absolutely will not work.

2. Both SQL Servers are running exactly identical character sets and sort orders.

3. The database segment and fragmentation map are identical on both servers. However, the target database can be larger than the source database, if desired.

Assuming all of these conditions are met, feel free to use the dump and load commands to handle all data import and export needs. To perform these types of operations, there are some logistical decisions to be made, such as the following:

1. Will the database be copied from one database to another database on the same server or will the data be copied to another server?

2. If the data is going to another physical SQL Server, is there any risk of violating the three conditions?

3. Will the dump be sent to disk or will there be a tape involved? If dumping to disk, have adequate preparations been made to handle the amount of data being dumped? If sending the dump to tape, it is important to consider how the tape will get from one machine to another (if necessary) and the tape's capacity.

4. What precautions will be made for users who are in the database at the time of the load? Remember, a load will not start if users are in the database.

After these decisions are worked out, create dump devices and use the Dump Database command to dump the data. Remember the dump device does not have to be on the local server; it can refer to a network share. Create a dump device on the target SQL Server. This provides a place for SQL Server to use when loading data. Then use the load database command to load the dump into the target database.

Warm Spare Servers

A warm spare server is a server that contains an exact duplicate of a production database usually restored from dump files on a continuous basis. This is the equivalent of the process used to move data from a data entry server to a query server, but taken to the level of transaction log backups. It is a good example of how to use database dumps to manage data. Every night the entire database is backed up to disk, the dump file is copied over, and the resulting dump loaded onto the warm spare server. Periodically through the day, the transaction log on the production server is dumped; copied to the warm spare server and loaded as well.

This technique is called *warm spare* because it is a warmed up machine, but it cannot go into production immediately. Usually, if the production server were to crash, the warm spare server would be assigned the computer name of the production server, certain options would be reset, and the server would be rebooted. At that point, all of the users would be back online. After the problem with the production server is found, all of the resetting of options and rebooting would take less than 5 minutes.

These are options that need to be set on the warm spare server's database:

▶ DBO Use Only

▶ No Chkpt on Recovery

The warm spare cannot be used by any users because if the server is in use when the database or transaction logs need to load, the loads will fail, causing the warm spare not to have data that is current enough. The DBO Use Only flag prevents users from tampering with the database while it is a backup.

The No Chkpt on Recovery prevents a checkpoint record from being written into the transaction log when the warm spare server is rebooted for maintenance. Because there is no write activity on the warm spare, no checkpoint records are added to the transaction log. Unfortunately, during the bootup process of SQL Server, a checkpoint record is written to every database after it has been recovered. Setting the No Chkpt on Recovery option prevents the checkpoint record from being written.

Warm spares provide a cheaper alternative to the hot sparing and clustering technology promised, but do not provide the up-to-the-transaction latency capabilities of upcoming clustering technologies.

Bulk Copy Program (BCP)

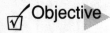

The Bulk Copy Program utility is a command line program that loads data into SQL Server or pulls data out of SQL Server. It handles multiple input formats, multiple output formats, and is almost ridiculously fast. Unlike the database dump and load routine discussed in the previous section, BCP operates on a table-by-table basis. If there are thirty tables to be exported, then BCP will be run thirty times.

The BCP utility is a holdout from the Sybase SQL Server days when the server ran on a Unix platform. The syntax of BCP will look familiar to anyone who is familiar with Unix utilities such as tar or cpio. Because it does have Unix roots, it is important always to remember that all of the command line options are case sensitive.

BCP runs on a wide variety of platforms, including Windows NT, Windows 95, and DOS. It is not installed by default when the 16-bit Windows utilities are installed, but the DOS utilities do install BCP, and so do the Windows 95 and Windows NT versions. One of the keys to good performance of BCP is to keep the data file off of the same drive as the SQL Server database device being used. This dramatically speeds BCP. BCP runs fastest on the server where the database is, provided the data file is on a different physical disk than the database. The next best solution is to load the data from a workstation on the network, with the data file stored on the workstation. The worst case is to have the file stored on the server, read to a workstation, and put back on the server.

The utility runs in two directions, in and out. When the *in* direction is chosen, data is read from a file and put into SQL Server. With *out*, data is read from a table in SQL Server and placed into a file.

When BCP is copying data in, it uses all defaults specified on the table, so if a field isn't specified in a record and there is a default on the field, the default will be used. However, triggers, constraints, and rules are not applied to data that comes in via BCP.

First you'll take a conceptual look at how the bulk copy utility works by examining the two types of copy in (fast and slow) and then the process of copying data out. Then you'll take a look at the syntax and actual operational use of BCP.

Fast and Slow BCP

When using BCP to copy data into a table, there are two possible modes, fast and slow. There is no command line switch for "run fast" or "run slow." Rather, if the following conditions are met, BCP runs in fast mode; otherwise it runs in slow mode:

1. The Select Into/Bulk Copy option is turned on in the target database.

2. The target table has no indexes.

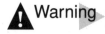 **Warning**

> Fast BCP is not logged. The data is copied directly into the table without additions to the transaction log. It is imperative when running fast BCP that the database is backed up immediately following the BCP.

If either of the conditions are not met, the result will be a logged, or slow, BCP. The difference in performance between fast and slow BCP is usually about 50 percent. This includes the time needed in fast BCP to drop and rebuild indexes.

Fast BCP works by not logging each row insert in the transaction log. Instead, fast BCP allocates each 2 KB data page used. This results in much lower transaction log volume, but maintains the transactional integrity of SQL Server. If the BCP were to fail, the allocation of the pages would fail, and those pages wouldn't be part of the new table.

Using BCP to Export Data

When exporting data, BCP can only be used to export an entire table. By using the -F (first row) and -L (last row) commands, it is possible to limit the number of rows written into the data file, but the number of columns cannot be changed.

Fortunately, BCP can export from either a table or a view. Views can be thought of as virtual tables. A view is created by defining a SELECT query. BCP can use views that contain joins or any other type of limitation, except for grouping and sorting. So data can be filtered by using BCP, but only if BCP is actually exporting from a view. The view being used can limit the number of rows being returned, change the format of the rows, or even join to other tables.

To look at this technique a little more closely, consider the following view in the Pubs database:

```
Create View vAuthorTitles as
    select convert (char(15), au_lname) au_lname,
convert(char(10), au_fname) au_fname,
                            convert(char(30), title) title
from authors, titleauthor, titles
        where authors.au_id = titleauthor.au_id
            and titles.title_id = titleauthor.title_id
```

After running this command in a query tool, the view can be queried like this:

```
select * from v_AuthorTitles
```

This results in three columns of output: the authors' last names, their first names, and the books they wrote. If multiple authors collaborated on a single book, there will be a line for each author relating them to the book in question. The following shows what the data would look like if the BCP command were used to copy the data out of the v_AuthorTitles view as created previously:

```
au_lname          au_fname    title
--------------    ---------   -------------------------------
Green             Marjorie    The Busy Executive's Database
Bennet            Abraham     The Busy Executive's Database
O'Leary           Michael     Cooking with Computers: Surrep
MacFeather        Stearns     Cooking with Computers: Surrep
Green             Marjorie    You Can Combat Computer Stress
Straight          Dean        Straight Talk About Computers
del Castillo      Innes       Silicon Valley Gastronomic Tre
DeFrance          Michel      The Gourmet Microwave
```

```
Ringer            Anne       The Gourmet Microwave
Carson            Cheryl     But Is It User Friendly?
Dull              Ann        Secrets of Silicon Valley
Hunter            Sheryl     Secrets of Silicon Valley
Locksley          Charlene   Net Etiquette
MacFeather        Stearns    Computer Phobic AND Non-Phobic
Karsen            Livia      Computer Phobic AND Non-Phobic
Ringer            Anne       Is Anger the Enemy?
Ringer            Albert     Is Anger the Enemy?
Ringer            Albert     Life Without Fear
White             Johnson    Prolonged Data Deprivation: Fo
Locksley          Charlene   Emotional Security: A New Algo
Panteley          Sylvia     Onions, Leeks, and Garlic: Coo
Blotchet-Halls    Reginald   Fifty Years in Buckingham Pala
O'Leary           Michael    Sushi, Anyone?
Gringlesby        Burt       Sushi, Anyone?
Yokomoto          Akiko      Sushi, Anyone?

(25 row(s) affected)
```

To use BCP to extract the data, use the following syntax:

```
bcp pubs..vAuthorTitles out AuthorTitles.csv -c -t, -r\r\n -Usa -P
```

This syntax results in the following screen output:

```
D:\WINNT\Profiles\cmille02\Desktop>bcp pubs..vAuthorTitles out
AuthorTitles.csv
-c -t, -r\r\n -Usa -P

Starting copy...

25 rows copied.
Network packet size (bytes): 4096
Clock Time (ms.): total =     20 Avg =       0 (1250.00 rows per
sec.)

D:\WINNT\Profiles\cmille02\Desktop>
```

This command creates a comma delimited file that contains the author's name and title.

Using BCP to Import Data

The bulk copy program is also used to copy data into SQL Server. To import data using BCP, it is important to prepare a location for the data to land, which means either creating a table or using an existing one. BCP does create tables; it can only put data into tables that already exist. Try to make the columns in the table the same order as the columns in the file being imported.

When using BCP to import data, it is usually best to use tables that do not have indexes. As a rule of thumb, it is usually faster to drop the indexes on a table and re-create them when the import is going to add more than thirty percent of the rows in the table. For example, for a 5,000-row table, if more than 1,500 rows are being imported, it is probably faster to drop and rebuild the indexes than to leave them on. Like any other performance-tuning operation, there is a balance of art and science happening, so experiment a bit for the best results.

When BCP is importing data, it reads in a block of data, parses it into fields, and inserts the data into the target table. If there is a failure in parsing the individual fields or the end of record, an error is registered. By default, a single error in the file will stop BCP, but that can be adjusted by using the command line options shown in the next section. The parsing of the data is done differently depending on the data format used.

Using BCP to Read Different Data Formats

Because the Bulk Copy Program can be used to bring in data from other SQL Servers or from almost any other source, BCP was written to handle a variety of data formats. BCP is very flexible in what types of data it can read. SQL Server has a native format that it uses for copying tables from one server to another. Most mainframe data sources use a fixed-width data format, where every column is a specified width. Most PC-based systems use delimited data, where a comma or tab is usually used to separate fields of data. This section covers the different data formats that BCP can use. In the next section, you'll take a look at the BCP command line, which is where BCP determines which data format will be used.

BCP runs with three different types of data:

► Native format data

► Character delimited data

► Fixed-width data or column-delimited data

Native format data is used when copying from one SQL Server to another. Native format is the fastest format available. It handles data conversions quickly and is more space efficient because each character field is prefixed with a number representing how long the field is. This is more efficient than using a fixed-width file.

Character delimited data has fields separated by a character or string of characters. This is normally used for comma or tab de-limited files. Be very careful when choosing delimiters in order not to choose a delimiter that appears in the data in the file. With software that allows any character to be a delimiter, choose a com-bination of two or more uncommon symbols, such as the curly braces ({}) or the carat (^) to delimit the file. An example of char-acter delimited data:

```
Burton,Joseph,1232 West User Drive,Almont,CA
Charles,Bill,3393 East Avenue,Peculiar,MO
```

Fixed-width data, or column-delimited data, uses columns to sepa-rate data. Each line of text in the file contains one record, and each field in the record is a fixed number of bytes wide. Here is the same sample of data in a fixed-width format:

```
Burton    Joseph   1232 West User Drive   Almont    CA
Charles   Bill     3393 East Avenue       Peculiar  MO
```

To optimize the operation of fast BCP during copy in operations, use native format when possible. The second choice is character-delimited format. If character format isn't available, then use fixed-width format. The reason is simple. Native format produces the smallest files because of the way it handles numbers and char-acter fields. Character format produces nice delimited files that are smaller than fixed width files. Fixed-width files are the least desirable choice simply because the files are larger than normal. If slow BCP is being used, it really doesn't matter which format is used because the bottleneck will be in SQL Server instead of in the data load portion of BCP. In the next section, you'll learn how to choose the different data format options on the BCP command line.

The BCP Command Line

The BCP utility uses a variety of command line switches to accomplish the tasks of importing and exporting data. The BCP utility is a command line utility and is run from a command prompt, not from within a query tool. Here are the parameters for BCP, which are available by typing **BCP** /? at the command prompt:

```
bcp dbtable {in ¦ out} datafile
        [-m maxerrors] [-f formatfile] [-e errfile]
        [-F firstrow] [-L lastrow] [-b batchsize]
        [-n native type] [-c character type] [-q quoted identi-
fier]
        [-t field terminator] [-r row terminator]
        [-i inputfile] [-o outputfile] [-a packetsize]
        [-E explicit identity] [-U username] [-P password]
        [-S server] [-v version] [-T trusted connection]
```

The parameters are defined as follows:

▶ *dbtable.* The name of the table in SQL Server being operated on. It is specified in the format *database.user.table,* which can be abbreviated to *database..table* when the user executing BCP owns the table or when the table is owned by the DBO (database owner).

▶ **{in | out}.** Direction of transfer. Transfer direction "in" will copy data from a file into SQL Server. Transfer direction "out" will copy data from a table or view in SQL Server out to a file.

▶ *datafile.* Name of the file being operated on.

▶ **-m** *maxerrors.* Specifies the number of errors that can occur before BCP aborts the transfer.

▶ **-f** *formatfile.* Name of the format file. Format files help define the columns in a column-delimited file.

▶ **-e** *errfile.* Name of the file to write errors to. Will produce a text output file that can be read with Notepad.

▶ **-F** *Firstrow,* **-L** *Lastrow.* The first and last row to be processed. If the first row contains column headings, for example, use "-F 2" to skip the first row. The lastrow argument is normally used for testing large imports. Use it to read in the first few hundred or thousand rows to make sure the import is working correctly before reading in millions of rows.

▶ **-b** *batchsize.* Determines how many rows are written between commits. By default, all of the rows to be inserted are placed in one transaction. If the next to the last row causes the error count to be exceeded, then the whole load will fail. By using a batchsize parameter with the "Truncate Log On Checkpoint" database option, large database loads can happen with less risk of the log filling up. Even fast BCP logs each extent that it uses.

▶ **-n** *native type.* If this flag is present, BCP will assume that the file format is the Native format. Should not be used with the -c flag, which denotes character delimited data.

▶ **-c** *character type.* Denotes the file will be a character-delimited file. Generally, if this flag is used, the -t and -r options are also used.

▶ **-q** *quoted identifier.* Flag that turns on the use of quoted identifiers. This means that any identifier can be used as a table or column name as long as it is in double quotes ("").

▶ **-t** *field terminator,* **-r** *row terminator.* The -t flag determines what characters will appear between columns in the data file. The -r option determines what characters appear between rows. The available characters are all alphanumeric characters plus symbols, and special characters and their representations (see table 8.1).

Table 8.1

Special Characters Used with BCP

Character	Representation	ASCII Code
Carriage Return	\r	13
Linefeed/New Line	\n	11
Tab	\t	9

▶ **-i** *inputfile,* **-o** *outputfile.* Used to redirect input and output to the program. The file specified by -i should be the input required to fill in the options requested by the BCP program. The -o outputfile will contain the messages normally displayed to the screen by BCP.

▶ **-a** *packetsize.* This is the DB-Library packet size. It is used to determine packet length of the DB-Library packets and takes some tuning. Most people don't even bother with it unless there is a long WAN link between the BCP program and the server.

▶ **-E explicit identity.** Used when the file being imported has numbers in the identity column that should be imported directly. The default is to ignore the numbers in the identity column and put in numbers based on the seed and current value of the identity column in the table. Note that leaving out the identity column will not work because of a bug in SQL Server 6.5 BCP.

▶ **-u** *username.* Specify the name of the user to be log in to BCP with. For BCP out, the user must have select permissions on the table. For BCP in, the user must have insert permissions. Defaults to "sa."

▶ **-p** *password.* Specify the password of the user specified in the -u argument. If this is left out and the -T is not specified, BCP will prompt for a password.

▶ **-S** *server.* Specify the name of the server the BCP should use.

▶ **-v** *version.* BCP will return what version of BCP is running.

▶ **-T trusted connection.** BCP won't bother with asking for user logins or passwords and will use integrated security for validation.

Running BCP

BCP runs by default in column-delimited mode. Using the -c or -n switches shuts off the column-delimited mode. When using BCP in column-delimited mode, BCP will prompt for certain information for each column to be imported, including the name of the field in which to put the data, the length of the field, the prefix length, and the type. The name of the field is the name of the table where the data should land. Length of the field is the length, in bytes, that the data takes up in the data file. The prefix length should be ignored and set to 0. Prefix length is used for processing special types of native format files. The data type is the type of the data coming in.

BCP does a fairly good job at guessing data into the correct data type. For example, it can interpret the character string 12/31/1971 and the string December 31, 1971 correctly, along with many other variants. However, the string 19711231 will not convert and will cause an error. See the following sidebar, "Using Scratch Tables to Clean Data," for more information on data conversion.

Using Scratch Tables to Clean Data

Although the BCP utility is great at loading data, sometimes it cannot handle the data type conversions that are required to pull data in from the huge array of different sources. Almost every database or data storage program ever written has its own way of storing dates, for example. Although BCP does a great job at handling many different date formats, it cannot handle every possible combination of day, month, and year. In addition, programs have been written that perform little or no validation of the type of data being stored in certain fields, so it becomes impossible to reliably import numeric data because a mischievous user has put character data into numeric fields and the program never figured it out.

A few different ways to get around data problems do exist. One is to write a

continues

program in a programming language, such as C, to scan the data files and correct formatting problems. Another is to use a user query tool, such as Microsoft Access, to read the data into its native format and the use linked tables to write the data into SQL Server. Writing a C program requires a fairly good programmer who can solve the problem. Using a tool such as Microsoft Access requires much less thought and planning, but the resulting process is much slower than BCP.

Another solution is to use BCP to pull the data into tables that are all character fields, and then write SQL scripts to clean it up and insert it into production tables. There are two downsides to this approach. It can require an extensive knowledge of Transact-SQL,

and it requires more disk space to hold the temporary data.

The idea is fairly simple. Create a table that has the same field names as the production table, but the same field order as the data file. For each column in the table, make sure it is a character field and that the column width is appropriate for the data being stored. Use BCP to import the data, and then write Transact-SQL scripts to take the data out of the scratch tables and to insert it into the production tables.

This seems like a lot of work, but considering that BCP can read data in at thousands of rows per second, and that Microsoft Access can be as slow as 20 records per second, the time to develop these solutions is fairly well spent.

Here are some examples of running BCP. To run BCP to read in a comma delimited file into the Finance database, the following command could be used:

```
bcp finance..importdata in finance.dat -c -t, -r\r\n -Sfinserv -
Usa -P
```

To use a format file to read into the same table:

```
bcp finance..importdata in finance.dat -f finance.fmt -Sfinserv -
Usa -P
```

The use of the -f switch means that SQL Server will not prompt for row definitions. If we needed to read in a file that was delimited by the tab character, the BCP command line would look like this:

```
bcp finance..importdata in finance.txt -c -t\t -r\r\n -Sfinserv -
Usa -P
```

There will be some more examples of how to use BCP in the chapter exercises. Because this is a process that is best learned by doing, it is recommended that you try these examples out.

BCP provides output in the form of either the number of rows processed or the completion of a single batch of data. If a batchsize is not specified, then output is presented every 1,000 rows with the number of rows that have been processed so far. If a batchsize is specified, then BCP displays a message after each batch is processed; unfortunately it is the same message over and over, so it is difficult to gauge progress.

Using Format Files

Format files are used by BCP to handle automating the bulk load process. Normally, the BCP command line is used for handling native mode or character mode data transfers; however, the a format file can allow more flexibility.

A format file defines which columns in the data file go into which columns in the table. The data file and table are not specified and have to be defined on the command line. The first two rows of a format file specify the version of SQL Server, and therefore BCP, that is being used. The second row contains the number of columns being imported. From the third row on, each line contains the following data:

- ▶ Column number in the source data file

- ▶ Data type, usually SQLCHAR for character fields

- ▶ Prefix length, always zero

- ▶ Field length

- ▶ End of field delimiter

- ▶ Column number in the target table

- ▶ Name of column

If both the data field length and field delimiter are specified, then the column will include data up to the field delimiter, unless there is no field delimiter in the length of characters specified in the data field length column, in which case the data field length would be used.

A sample data file and the format file that would be used follows:

```
Burton     Joseph     1232 West User Drive     Almont    CA
Charles    Bill       3393 East Avenue         Peculiar  MO
```

If the BCP utility were given a table with the columns shown in this minitable, BCP would produce output following the table to make the format file:

Field	Type	Length
lname	char	10
fname	char	10
address	char	25
city	char	10
state	char	2

```
Enter the file storage type of field lname [char]:
Enter prefix-length of field name [0]:
Enter length of field lname [10]:
Enter field terminator [none]:

Enter the file storage type of field fname [char]:
Enter prefix-length of field fname [0]:
Enter length of field fname [10]:
Enter field terminator [none]:

Enter the file storage type of field address [char]:
Enter prefix-length of field address [0]:
Enter length of field address [25]: 0
Enter field terminator [none]:

Enter the file storage type of field city [char]:
Enter prefix-length of field city [0]:
```

```
Enter length of field city [10]:
Enter field terminator [none]:

Enter the file storage type of field state [char]:
Enter prefix-length of field state [0]:
Enter length of field state [2]:
Enter field terminator [none]:
```

The format file would look like the following:

```
6.0
5
1       SQLCHAR   0    10      " "      1      lname
2       SQLCHAR   0    10      " "      2      fname
3       SQLCHAR   0    25      " "      3      address
4       SQLCHAR   0    10      " "      4      city
5       SQLCHAR   0    2       "\r\n"   5      state
```

Note

Always make sure there is a blank line at the end of a format file. Each line has to have a carriage return at the end of it, and if there is no blank line at the bottom of the file, the last line in the format file would not have a carriage return at the end of it.

The format files are flexible enough to handle extra data in the file, as well as handling extra columns in the destination table. For extra data in the file, simply put a line in the format file that has the correct file column number, type, prefix, length, and delmiter. For the table column number, put in a zero. For the name of the column, make something up. It cannot be the name of a column already in the table, and it cannot be blank, but it can be any other legal SQL Server identifier. Tradition is to use the word *foo*.

To skip columns in the database, make sure that the length for that column is set to 0. So in the format file, the length of the field is 0, but everything else reflects the normal settings. If a data file in the format of the previous sample data file came in, but was missing the address field, for example, the format file would look like the following:

```
6.0
5
1       SQLCHAR     0     10      " "         1     lname
2       SQLCHAR     0     10      " "         2     fname
3       SQLCHAR     0     0       " "         3     address
4       SQLCHAR     0     10      " "         4     city
5       SQLCHAR     0     2       "\r\n"      5     state
```

If a data set came in that was comma delimited rather than row delimited, a format file could still be used. The format file would look just like the first sample format file, but would have commas between the double quotes.

Hints for Successful Data Loading with BCP

It is very simple to use BCP to produce some outstanding results. Follow these hints for a smoother path to success when using BCP to load a lot of data:

1. Make sure the Select Into/Bulk-copy switch is set correctly. Fast BCP will not happen if this switch is not turned on.

2. If using the Select Into/Bulk-copy option, make sure to shut it of when BCP is done and then dump the database.

3. To improve performance, make sure the data file being processed and the database aren't on the same physical device.

4. Make sure there are no indexes on the target table.

5. Use defaults to fill in fields in case of null. Remember, defaults will work during BCP, but triggers, constraints, and rules will not.

6. Use the batch size parameter correctly. If an all-or-nothing import is desired, don't use a batch size. If fast BCP is not possible and the data set is sufficiently large, then batch size will need to be used along with the truncate log on checkpoint to prevent the log from filling up. In most cases for fast BCP, it is best to skip using a batch size and just allow the whole file to either succeed or fail. If it succeeds, it will all commit at once. If it fails, it is usually faster to fix the error and start from scratch than to attempt to manually remove all of the data that is already imported and start over again.

Exercises

Exercise 8.1:   Creating a Dump Device

In this exercise, two dump devices are created. The first one is created by using commands and the SQL Query tool. The second is created using the SQL Enterprise Manager. This exercise should take about five minutes.

1. Open a SQL Query tool, such as ISQL/W, or use the Tools/ SQL Query Tool menu option in SQL Enterprise Manager.

2. You'll be creating a disk dump device for the Pubs database called PubsDump that will reside in \MSSQL\BACKUP. Type the following command, replacing the *d:* with the drive letter that SQL Server is installed on:

```
sp_addumpdevice 'disk', 'pubsdump',
'd:\mssql\backup\pubsdump.dat'
```

3. Use the Execute button (or press Ctrl+E) to execute the query.

4. The SQL Query tool should respond with `'Disk'` device added.

5. Close the SQL Query tool and open SQL Enterprise Manager if it is not already open.

6. Expand the server that the device is to be created on.

7. Right-click on the Backup Devices folder.

8. Choose New Backup Device from the popup menu.

9. In the Name box, type **pubs1dump**.

10. Verify that the location box contains the directory that the dump device should be created in: D:\MSSQL\BACKUP\ pubs1dump.DAT.

11. Expand the Backup Devices folder. There should be at least three backup devices, DiskDump, Pubs1Dump, and Pubs-Dump.

continues

Exercise 8.1: Continued

For more information on this exercise, please refer to the section titled "Creating Backup Devices."

Exercise 8.2: Performing a Database Backup to a Single Backup Device

In this exercise, the Pubs database is dumped by using SQL Query tool commands and by using the graphical interface provided by SQL Enterprise Manager. This exercise assumes that you have completed Exercise 8.1 and have the dump devices created. The exercise should take about 10 minutes.

1. Open a SQL Query tool, either ISQL/W or the one in SQL Enterprise Manager.

2. Verify that the target dump device exists by typing **sp_helpdevice** and executing the query. There should be a row returned that shows the PubsDump device.

3. Dump the Pubs database to the PubsDump device using the following command:

```
dump database pubs to pubsdump with init
```

4. Execute the dump query.

5. The query tool should respond with the following message:

```
Database 'pubs' (209 pages) dumped to file <1> on device 'pubsdump'
```

The number of pages dumped may vary based on the amount of data in the Pubs database.

6. Verify that the backup occurred by using the following command:

```
load headeronly from pubsdump
```

After executing this query, there should be one row indicating that the Pubs database was dumped to the device.

7. Use the following command to append another database dump to the PubsDump device:

```
dump database pubs to pubsdump
```

The results of this command should be the following:

```
Database 'pubs' (209 pages) dumped to file <2> on device
'pubsdump'
```

Notice that the file number is <2>. This means it is the second dump in the file.

8. Use the following command to verify the PubsDump backup device contains two database dumps:

```
load headeronly from pubsdump
```

This should return the following output:

Dumptype	Database	Striped	Compressed	Sequence	Volume	Devicetype
1	pubs	0	0	1	SQL001	2
1	pubs	0	0	2	SQL001	2

```
(2 row(s) affected)
```

Note that many of the columns were truncated to make this more readable; the point is that there are now two dumps of the same database inside the same dumpfile.

9. Close the query tool and SQL Enterprise Manager if necessary.

10. Expand the server that contains the database to be backed up.

11. Expand the Databases folder.

12. Right-Click on the Pubs database and choose Backup/Restore from the popup menu.

13. Verify that the Pubs database is selected, that the Initialize Device checkbox is on, and that the Pubs1Dump device is chosen in the Backup Devices list.

continues

Exercise 8.2: Continued

14. Click the Backup Now button.

15. Choose OK at the Backup Volume Labels window.

16. Watch the pretty blue bar go across the screen.

17. Choose OK at the Backup of Database "Pubs" Completed message box.

18. Click on the Close button.

19. Expand the Backup Devices folder.

20. Expand the Pubs1Dump device and notice that the single backup is in place.

21. Expand the PubsDump device, which was used earlier. Note that there are two databases in the device.

22. Close SQL Enterprise Manager.

More information on this topic can be found in the section "Dumping Databases to Single Devices."

Exercise 8.3: Performing a Striped Backup

This exercise will be done with a SQL Query tool and completed with the graphical interface in SQL Enterprise Manager. This exercise should take about 10 minutes.

1. Open a SQL Query tool.

2. Create three disk dump devices, Stripe1, Stripe2, and Stripe3, by using the following commands:

```
sp_addumpdevice 'disk', "stripe1",
"d:\mssql\backup\stripe1.dat"
go
sp_addumpdevice 'disk', "stripe2",
"d:\mssql\backup\stripe2.dat"
go
sp_addumpdevice 'disk', "stripe3",
```

```
"d:\mssql\backup\stripe3.dat"
go
```

The SQL Query tool should return with the following:

```
'Disk' device added three times.
```

3. Use the following command to stripe a backup of the Pubs database across all three dump devices:

```
dump database pubs to stripe1, stripe2, stripe3
```

The results should be similar to the following:

```
Msg 4035, Level 10, State 1
Database 'pubs' (66 pages) dumped to file <1> on device
'stripe3'.
Msg 4035, Level 10, State 1
Database 'pubs' (76 pages) dumped to file <1> on device
'stripe1'.
Msg 4035, Level 10, State 1
Database 'pubs' (71 pages) dumped to file <1> on device
'stripe2'.
```

4. Verify the database dump on the devices by running the following command on each device:

```
load headeronly from stripe1
```

5. Close the query tool and open SQL Enterprise Manager if necessary.

6. Expand the server to be used.

7. Expand the Backup Devices folder and verify that the devices that were created in step 2 are present. If they are not, right-click on the Backup Devices folder and choose Refresh to make them appear.

8. Expand the Databases folder.

9. Right-Click on the Pubs database and choose Backup/ Restore.

continues

Exercise 8.3: Continued

10. Verify that the Pubs database is chosen and that the Initialize Device checkbox is checked.

11. Choose the Stripe1 through Stripe3 database devices by clicking on Stripe1 and then holding the Shift key down and clicking on the Stripe3 device.

12. Choose OK at the Backup Volume Labels window.

13. Watch the pretty blue bar go across the Progress window.

14. Choose OK at the Backup Progress message box.

15. Click on the Close button on the Backup/Restore window.

16. Expand the Stripe*x* devices. Note that each one shows two different database dumps in the device, even though the devices were initialized prior to the second dump. This happens because the entries in this interface are not from the headers in the file, but rather from a file that keeps a history of what has been dumped to the device. This interface has no bearing on the reality of what is in the backup device currently.

For more information on this topic refer to the section "Striped Backups."

Exercise 8.4: Dumping the msdb Database and Transaction Log

In this exercise, the database msdb is dumped by using a temporary device to prepare for the dumping of the transaction log, using a SQL Query tool. Then the transaction log is dumped by using the graphical interface in the SQL Enterprise Manager. The msdb database is being used instead of the pubs database because the pubs transaction log is on the same device as the data; the pubs transaction log, therefore, cannot be backed up. In addition, many of the qualifications of the Dump Transaction command will be explored. This exercise can be done in about 25 minutes.

1. Open a SQL Query tool.

2. Create a dump device called msdbTransDump by using the following command:

```
sp_addumpdevice 'disk', 'msdbtransdump',
"d:\mssql\backup\msdbtransdump.dat"
```

The query tool should respond with the following:

```
'Disk' device added.
```

3. Use the following command to dump the transaction log:

dump transaction msdb to msdbtransdump with init

The result should be an error message:

```
DUMP TRANsaction is not allowed while the trunc. log on
chkpt. option is enabled: use DUMP DATABASE, or disable the
option with sp_dboption.
```

4. Disable the truncate log on checkpoint option with the following command:

sp_dboption "msdb", "trunc. log on chkpt.", false

The result should be the following:

```
"CHECKPOINTing database that was changed."
```

5. Run the command in step 3 again. This should result in another error message:

```
DUMP TRANsaction is not allowed because log was truncated or
DUMP DATABASE was never run. Must run DUMP DATABASE.
```

6. Dump the msdb database to a temporary device by using the following command:

dump database msdb to disk="d:\mssql\backup\msdbdump.dat"

This should result in a message similar to the following:

```
Database 'msdb' (621 pages) dumped to file <1> on device
'd:\mssql\backup\msdbdump.dat'.
```

continues

7. Dump the transaction log by using the command in step 3. The resulting message should be similar to the following:

```
Database 'msdb' log(3 pages) dumped to file <1> on device
'msdbtransdump'.
```

8. Close the SQL Query tool and open SQL Enterprise Manager, if it is not already open.

9. Expand the server to be used.

10. Expand the Databases folder.

11. Right-click on the msdb database and choose Backup/Restore from the popup menu.

12. Verify that the msdb database is chosen and that the Initialize Device checkbox is *not* checked.

13. Choose the Transaction Log radio button in the Database Backup frame.

14. Choose the msdbtransdump device.

15. Click on the Backup Now button.

16. Choose OK at the Backup Volume Labels window.

17. Watch the pretty blue bar go across the screen.

18. Choose OK at the Backup Progress message box.

19. Close the Database Backup/Restore window.

20. Verify the backup by expanding the Backup Devices folder and the msdbtransdump backup device. There should be two transaction log backups in place.

For more information on backing up transaction logs, refer to the section "Transaction Logs and Automatic Recovery," earlier in this chapter.

Exercise 8.5:   Loading a Database Dump

In this exercise, you will create a new database device for the pubs database and load the dump created in Exercise 8.2 by using a SQL Query tool. The database dump will be loaded again using the SQL Enterprise Manager to show how that procedure is carried out. This exercise should take about 10 minutes.

1. Start the SQL Query Tool.

2. Create the device for the new copy of the pubs database. To determine the size of the pubs database, use the sp_helpdb stored procedure. The pubs database is 3 MB, or 1,536 pages. The device could be created with the following command:

```
DISK INIT name = 'pubsdev',
            physname = "d:\mssql\data\pubsdev.dat",
            size = 1536,
            vdevno = 3
```

Note that the vdevno parameter may need to be increased. If the DISK INIT fails because the vdevno is already in use, increment the vdevno and try again.

3. Create the database, Newpubs, in which to load the pubs database. This can be done with the following command:

```
create database newpubs on pubsdev = 2
```

And should return the following result:

```
CREATE DATABASE: allocating 1024 pages on disk 'pubsdev'.
```

4. Load the database from the dump file created in Exercise 2 by using the following command:

```
load database newpubs from pubs1dump
```

This loads the database and returns the following string:

```
Warning, file <1> on device 'D:\MSSQL\BACKUP\pubs1dump.DAT'
was dumped from database 'pubs'.
```

continues

This warning is issued because the database was originally called Pubs and was loaded into a database with a different name.

5. Close the query tool and open SQL Enterprise Manger, if it is not already open.

6. Expand the server.

7. Expand the Databases folder. If the newpubs database is not listed, right-click on the Databases folder and choose Refresh from the popup menu.

8. Right-click on the NewPubs database and click on Backup/ Restore from the popup menu.

9. Click on the Restore tab.

10. Click the From Device button.

11. Choose the Pubs1Dump device.

12. Click on the Restore Now button.

13. Watch the pretty blue bar go across the screen.

14. Accept the Restore Progress message.

15. Click on the Close button.

16. Browse through the Newpubs database to ensure that it was loaded properly.

Please refer to the section "Loading Databases and Transaction Logs," earlier in this chapter, for more information.

Exercise 8.6: Using BCP to Export Data

In this exercise, you will use the BCP program to export data from a table in the pubs database to a text file. This exercise should take about 15 minutes to complete.

1. Open a command shell by running the Command Prompt icon.

2. Run the following command to export data from the Authors table to the file data.txt:

```
bcp pubs..authors out data.txt -c -t, -r\r\n -Usa -P
```

If the SQL Server is not on the computer this is being run on, add an -S *server* argument, replacing the parameter *server* with the name of the computer running SQL Server. BCP will run and exit with a message of how many rows were copied.

3. Examine the output file with notepad by typing the following:

```
start notepad data.txt
```

The result should be a nicely formatted comma delimited text file.

4. Close notepad.

For more information on this topic, refer to the section "Bulk Copy Program(BCP)," earlier in this chapter.

Review Questions

The following questions will test your knowledge of the information in this chapter.

1. Assuming the dump devices have been properly created, which of the following commands could be used to successfully dump the Pubs database to do a striped dump to the dump devices Pubs1, Pubs2, and Pubs3?

    A. Dump database Pubs to Pubs1, Pubs2, Pubs3 with striping.

    B. Dump database Pubs to Pubs1-3.

    C. Dump database Pubs to Pubs*.

    D. Dump database Pubs to Pubs1, Pubs2, Pubs3 with init.

2. The Recovery Interval configuration object determines which of the following:

    A. How often SQL Server performs garbage collection to recover allocated and unused memory.

    B. How often SQL Server removes tombstoned records.

    C. How long SQL Server can take to open a database when the server is restarted.

    D. How often SQL Server will take to recover from a network error.

3. Juan needs to back up his database. He follows this procedure:

    1. Juan starts the Windows NT Backup Program.

    2. He chooses the drive that contains the SQL Server data devices.

    3. Then, he chooses to back the drive up to tape.

Which of the following are true about this procedure?

A. This procedure will enable Juan to recover from a server crash.

B. This procedure will enable Juan to recover from a server crash, but there are more efficient ways of accomplishing the same goal.

C. This procedure will back up Juan's databases, but they cannot be used for data recovery.

D. This procedure is totally useless for backing up the data in Juan's databases.

4. Juan needs to back up his database. He follows this procedure:

1. Using SQL Enterprise Manager, Juan creates one disk dump device for each database.

2. Using SQL Enterprise Manager, Juan dumps each backup device to its own dump device.

3. Using the Windows NT Backup program, Juan backs up the directory where the dump devices are located.

Which of the following is true about this procedure?

A. This procedure will enable Juan to recover from a server crash.

B. This procedure will enable Juan to recover from a server crash, but there are more efficient ways of accomplishing the same goal.

C. This procedure will back up Juan's databases, but they cannot be used for data recovery.

D. This procedure is totally useless for backing up the data in Juan's databases.

5. Jacques is attempting to recover a database from a good backup. He has already correctly created the new database devices and correctly created the database. He has loaded the database dump into the new database. He is attempting to load a transaction log dump file, and keeps getting messages about the dump file being out of sequence.

   Which of the following could *not* be a cause of this error?

   A. Jacques is attempting to load the dump files in the wrong order.

   B. Users on the SQL Server are writing data to the database before the transaction log has been loaded.

   C. The Select Into/Bulkcopy option was turned off on the source database.

   D. Jacques specified with init instead of with noinit on the DUMP TRANSACTION statement.

6. Susan needs to read a million records in from a data file produced on a mainframe. Which of the following techniques would work best?

   A. Use the BCP command in a SQL Server query window to read the data into SQL Server.

   B. Use the LOAD DATABASE command in a SQL Server query window to read the data into SQL Server.

   C. Use the BCP command from a command prompt to read the data into SQL Server.

   D. Use the BCP command to load a format file into the SQL Server.

7. The CHECKPOINT process accomplishes which of the following:

   A. Assures that SQL Server processes haven't locked up.

   B. Assures that new data in the SQL Server cache is periodically written to disk.

C. Executes database maintenance routines to make sure the database is not corrupted.

D. Ensures that the number of connected users has not exceeded the software license.

8. George needs to ensure that SQL Server cannot overwrite the tapes he is using for backup for three weeks. Which of the following backup commands will meet this requirement?

A. Dump database Pubs to TapeDump with expiredate = 21.

B. Dump database Pubs to TapeDump with retaindays = 21.

C. Dump database Pubs to TapeDump with label.retaindays = 21.

D. Dump database Pubs to TapeDump with Skip.

9. Which of the following are true about having the Truncate log on Checkpoint option turned on for a database?

A. All of the records in the transaction log will be removed whenever the checkpoint process occurs.

B. All of the inactive transactions will be cleared from the transaction log when a checkpoint occurs.

C. This option makes the Dump Transaction command cause an error.

D. This option causes a performance degradation on busy databases.

10. Which of the following are messages in the SQL Server Error Log that indicate that a number of transactions were rolled back?

A. Normal messages for Automatic Recovery

B. Indicators of possible hardware problems

C. Indicators of corrupt data

D. An indication that SQL Server needs to be reinstalled

11. Which two of the following conditions will prevent the DUMP TRANSACTION statement from executing successfully?

    A. The Truncate log on Checkpoint option

    B. Users submitting transactions to the database

    C. The database and log being on the same device

    D. The creation of a new table in the database

12. Which two of the following are cause for an immediate backup of the Master database?

    A. Creation of a new device

    B. Creation of a new index in a user database

    C. Creation of a new user in a user database

    D. Creation of a new login ID

13. Why is Fast BCP is faster than Slow BCP?

    A. The -M Fast option is turned on in the BCP command line.

    B. There is reduced logging of incoming data.

    C. The indexes are updated in a more efficient manner.

    D. The data being imported must be column delimited.

14. Over the weekend, Wanda's SQL Server computer had a hard disk failure on the hard disk containing the Master device. Unfortunately, Wanda does not have a backup of the Master device. What can she do to get the server back up and running?

    A. Nothing. If the Master database is lost, the server cannot be recovered.

    B. Use the SQL Server setup program to build a new Master database.

C. Use the bldmaster program to create a new Master database.

D. Copy the Master database from the SQL Server 6.5 CD.

15. Which of the following is important for rebuilding the Master database?

    A. Character Set

    B. Sort Order

    C. Sizes and Locations of Devices

    D. All of the above

16. Which of the following will empty the transaction log without creating a backup?

    A. DUMP TRANSACTION msdb WITH NO_LOG

    B. DUMP TRANSACTION msdb WITH EMPTY_LOG

    C. DUMP TRANSACTION msdb WITH TRUNCATE_ONLY

    D. DUMP TRANSACTION msdb TO msdb_dev

17. Which of the following can be used to drop databases that have been marked as suspect?

    A. DBCC DROPDB()

    B. DROP DATABASE

    C. DBCC DBREPAIR()

    D. sp_dropdatabase

18. Julie needs to move data from one SQL Server to another. The servers are both Digital AlphaServers running Windows NT 4.0 and SQL Server 6.5. They are both using the same character set, sort order, and network libraries. Which of the following is the best method for accomplishing this task?

    A. BCP each table out of the source server using character delimited mode, re-create the tables on the destination server, and import the data using BCP.

    B. BCP each table out of the source server using native mode, re-create the tables on the destination server, and import the data using BCP.

    C. BCP each table out of the source server using native mode. Use BCP to copy the data back onto the destination server.

    D. Use the DUMP DATABASE command to copy the data off of the destination server. Use the LOAD DATABASE command to load the data back in.

19. BCP is installed by default with the SQL Server client on which of the following systems?

    A. Windows 95

    B. Windows NT

    C. MS-DOS

    D. Windows 3.1

20. Which of the following will prevent Fast BCP?

    A. Triggers on the destination table

    B. Rules on the destination table

    C. Defaults on the destination table

    D. None of the above

21. BCP can copy data out of which of the following objects?

    A. Tables

    B. Views

    C. Output of a stored procedure

    D. Query output

22. Josie needs to create a database dump device on her SQL Server. The dump device should output to a disk file on her server's D: drive in the \MSSQL\BACKUP directory. Which of the following commands will accomplish this task?

    A. `sp_adddumpdevice "MyDumpDevice",`
       `"D:\MSSQL\BACKUP\MYDUMP.DAT"`

    B. `sp_addumpdevice "MyDumpDevice",`
       `"D:\MSSQL\BACKUP\MYDUMP.DAT"`

    C. `sp_addumpdevice "disk", "MyDumpDevice", "D:\",`
       `"MSSQL\BACKUP\MYDUMP.DAT"`

    D. `sp_addumpdevice "disk", "MyDumpDevice",`
       `"D:\MSSQL\BACKUP\MYDUMP.DAT"`

23. Which of the following are advantages of dynamic backup?

    A. Enables users to use a database while it is being restored

    B. Enables users to use a database while it is being backed up

    C. Enables SQL Server to process transactions during backup

    D. Enables SQL Server to dump to changing dump devices

Review Answers

1. D

2. C

3. D

4. A

5. C

6. C

7. B

8. B

9. B, C, D

10. A

11. A, C

12. A, D

13. B

14. B

15. D

16. C

17. C

18. D

19. A, B, D

20. D

21. A, B

22. D

23. B, C

Answers to Test Yourself Questions at Beginning of the Chapter

1. The DUMP DATABASE command is used to back databases up to tape. This is covered in the section "Dump Database: How It Works."

2. A database dump device is used to send output from the DUMP DATABASE command. It is not an online device, and it stores no data that can be directly accessed by the user. It is created with the *sp_addumpdevice* system stored procedure. For more information, read the section "Creating Backup Devices."

3. Yes. This is part of the SQL Server dynamic backup functionality. See the section "Dump Database: How It Works" for more info.

4. Striped backups, which are covered in the section "Striped Backups," allow multiple dump devices to be used to increase backup throughput.

5. The Automatic Recovery process determines the status of databases when SQL Server starts. See the section "Transaction Logs and Automatic Recovery" for details.

6. The BCP command is used to export data from SQL Server and to import data into SQL Server. See the section titled "Bulk Copy Program (BCP)" for more information.

7. James had better be looking for his backup tapes. The section "Disaster Recovery" would be very handy reading for him, also.

8. Database dumps are not portable across different processor architectures. See the section "Using Database Dumps for Import/Export" for more details.

9. The with init clause causes each subsequent backup to overwrite the previous backup. Unless all of the transaction log dumps are available, the logs cannot be loaded. See the section "Transaction Logs and Automatic Recovery" for more details.

Chapter

Replication

9

It is often necessary in an enterprise to distribute data to more than one location, whether it is in the same office, building, city, or country. Several methods of distributing this data to multiple locations exist. Some of these methods include the following:

▶ Backing up the data to removable media, sending the media to the destination, and restoring the data

▶ Exporting the data to a file, transferring the file by some means, and importing the data from the file

▶ Executing remote stored procedures to gather up the data and place it in its appropriate location

▶ Replication

The first option can fail if the media has any errors reading or writing, or if it is lost by the courier. The second option might fail if any data does not conform to a general record format (image data, for example), if there is a conflict between the data and the delimiter chosen, or if the import and export specifications are not identical. Executing remote stored procedures is a better way to distribute the data, but it is difficult to keep track of which data has changed in order not to retransmit the same set of data repeatedly.

Instead of these options, replication uses safer techniques to get the data from one place to another. Replication is the process that reproduces data from a table in the source database to a table in the destination database. Through the use of a publisher/subscriber metaphor, the replication process uses servers that play the publishing, distributing, and subscribing roles to transfer the data from one place to another. In addition, at least one database on the distributing server is dedicated solely to the replication process. The way that replication distributes data has advantages over the other methods in that it is fault-tolerant and can raise or lower the amount of data that is distributed, as well as the frequency in which the data is distributed from source to destination.

It is fault-tolerant in that instead of actually replicating the data, it re-creates the Transact-SQL statements (INSERT, UPDATE, and DELETE) that created the data in the source database. Because there is no external media, there is no chance that it will be lost by the courier. There is no file to be corrupted or mangled in the process of importing and exporting due to the fact that replication bypasses the import and export specifications and creates the actual statements necessary to create the data. Replication transfers data in its native format, thereby negating the possibility that the data will have a conflict with the delimiter. It is a method by which data and schema are transferred from a source database to a destination database where it becomes read-only. This allows for the retrieval of various amounts of data without contention in the original database, which is then free to be modified. The data to be replicated can be transferred either at specified intervals or continuously as it is modified, depending upon the manner in which it is set up.

In addition to modifying the frequency with which the data is transferred, the administrator can choose to replicate smaller sets of filtered data or the complete set of data. The source database might replicate its data to any number of destinations, as well as be a destination database for another source database.

Replication is also a method of data distribution. It corresponds to a data consistency grouped simply as loose consistency. *Loose consistency* is defined as a distributed data process that might have a time lag involved between the instant that the data in the original table is modified and the data in the destination table that is updated to make the two copies of data identical. It is not guaranteed that the copies of the data in the source and destination tables are identical at all moments in time in loose consistency models. Instead, loose consistency models can operate over nearly any communication link, whether it is a modem, local area network (LAN), wide area network (WAN), or databases connected across the internet that do not always have a constant connection to each other.

The other consistency model is known as *tight consistency*. Although this model has the benefit of identical data in all locations simultaneously, it requires much more intricate hardware. Some of this hardware can be high-speed LANs or other connections that allow high volumes of data to be transferred nearly instantaneously. The cost is less scalability and reduced database availability.

In order for you to understand replication and do well on that aspect of the exam, this chapter addresses and covers in detail each of the objectives centered around replication, as outlined in the following section, "Objectives."

As always, this chapter begins with a list of the exam objectives relating to the topic at hand, moves on to the chapter pretest, offers valuable information directly addressing the objectives, as well as additional related topics, and finishes with exercises, chapter review questions, and answers to both the chapter review questions and the chapter pretest questions.

This chapter focuses on replication. It helps you prepare for the exam by addressing and fully covering the following objectives:

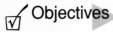 Objectives

- ▶ Identify prerequisites for replication

- ▶ Configure the servers used for setting up replication

- ▶ Set up various replication scenarios

- ▶ Implement replication

- ▶ Schedule a replication event

- ▶ Recognize the situations in which you must perform manual synchronization

- ▶ Identify the system tables that are used in replication

- ▶ Resolve setup problems

- ▶ Resolve fault-tolerance problems and recovery

Test Yourself! Before reading this chapter, test yourself to determine how much study time you will need to devote to this section.

1. Name the prerequisites for replication that must be set up.

2. Name the valid replication models.

3. How can data be published?

4. In what way might servers perform roles in a replication relationship?

5. In order to recover replication what must be completed?

6. How are replication events set up?

7. When must synchronization be performed?

8. What issues must be resolved while planning replication?

Answers are located at the end of the chapter...

An Overview of Replication

Before replication can be discussed, certain terms used to describe replication components must be defined. The components of replication can be categorized in several ways.

The major components of replication are the publisher, distributor, and subscriber. The *publisher* is the SQL Server that provides the data to be distributed. The SQL Server that receives the modifications the the data found on the publisher is referred to as the *subscriber*. The *distributor* serves as a holding bin for the data modifications from the publisher and transmits the modifications to the subscriber. Each of these terms can refer to either the database or the server itself; that is, "subscriber" might refer to the subscribing server or to the database that receives the modifications.

The smaller components of replication are publications and articles. *Articles* are the basic unit of replication. They contain references to the base table that is marked for replication, the destination table, as well as information on how the data will be replicated. Publications are groups of articles that are bound together by the administrator. This group of articles might be synchronized initially as one unit. Synchronizing a group of articles as one unit aids in maintaining referential integrity if the articles are grouped correctly in a common publication. Articles within publications can be likened to pages of a chapter within a larger book, which contains information.

Identify Prerequisites for Replication

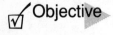 Before replication can be implemented, it must be planned out by addressing several issues:

- ▶ Replicating appropriate data
- ▶ Choosing a replication model

- ▶ Selecting destinations for data

- ▶ Deciding where the work of distributing the data should be done

Replicating Appropriate Data

In most situations, not all of the data in the publishing database needs to be replicated to the subscribing database. Replicating unneeded data not only consumes time and resources, it also reduces available network bandwidth for applications and other operations. It is important, therefore, to adequately analyze which sets of data need to be replicated.

An example of this is a corporate data warehouse. The warehouse might not need all of the information contained in the individual sites, but rather the summarized data for the activity at each site for each week.

Choosing a Replication Model

The general replication models fit a variety of situations, such as distributing data from a central location to multiple satellite locations or from the satellite locations to the central location. Proper planning of which replication model to use conserves resources and reduces maintenance tasks.

The use of an incorrect replication model can result either in too much data being distributed to inappropriate locations on its way to its correct destination or data that might not make it to its correct destination at all.

By applying the corporate data warehouse model to this issue, you can see that if the warehouse is not a subscriber for each of the satellite locations, it can never receive the data that it should. By the same token, if each of the satellite locations serves as a publisher, subscriber, and distributor for the same data, it is possible that one site might get another's data, which is not a desirable effect.

Selecting Destinations for Data

When selecting destinations for modified data, it is important to consider how each will use the data. If the site needs the data but will modify it as well, then either replication is not the desired method of distributing the data or a more intricate replication implementation design is in order. If the destination needs the data on a real-time basis, replication might not function up to required specifications because it used a loose consistency model as its basis. However, if the data on the destination database will not be modified and only a subset of the entire set of data is needed, then replication can be a good fit for the situation.

The corporate data warehouse that executives use weekly to gather statistical data for reporting and marketing decisions is a good example of an application of replication. The requirement that the data be reviewed weekly allows the loose consistency model to work in favor of the requirements. The use of the data strictly for reporting purposes allows the data to be read-only so that it will stay synchronized with the original data. The warehouse serves as a central repository for the summarized data for each of the satellite sites.

Deciding Where the Work of Distributing the Data Should Be Done

One of the components of the replication process is to distribute the commands that perform the data modifications. The distribution server must have enough resources available to store the commands, as well as to transmit them to the destination. If the publishing server is already functioning at a high capacity, it might be better to put the distribution process on a different server. Another factor is the distance between the publishing server and the distribution process and the reliability of the distribution server. In the case that a link between servers might be unreliable, the distributor should be put at a central point between the servers that has a reliable connection to both.

Configure the Servers Used for Replication

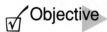Objective

After you have determined the prerequisites for replication, the servers that are to participate in replication relationships must be properly configured.

Servers and Networks

Because the data is to be distributed between servers across some form of a network, it is necessary to ensure that both the servers and network are configured properly. Following are the basic concepts that need to be addressed in terms of this pre-replication configuration:

▶ Memory

▶ Permissions

▶ Verifying server communication

▶ Compatibility between servers

One of the first concerns is the amount of memory on each server. Variable amounts of memory are required, depending upon the replication roles that the server will play. For servers that function only as publishers or subscribers, the minimum amount of memory required is 16 MB of RAM. If the server will function as a distributor of any kind, the minimum server memory configuration required is 32 MB of RAM with 16 MB allocated for use by SQL Server. These are the bare minimum levels that SQL Server requires in order to function, albeit poorly. The amount of memory allocated to SQL Server should be raised, depending upon the work load and the desired performance level.

Another area of concern is that of permissions. Replication uses the underlying NT file system for a variety of functions, whether it is formatted with File Allocation Tables (FAT) or NT File System (NTFS). SQL Server must have a working directory set up for its use for synchronization files as a publisher. The default is \MSSQL\REPLDATA, but this could change, depending upon the directory in which the administrator installs SQL Server.

In order for replication to work between servers, each server must both know about other servers it is interacting with and be able to communicate with them.

The normal process of setting up the replication servers involves registering the servers with Enterprise Manager. Any of the servers can be registered before the replication setup process begins or during the setup process. The administrator must register the servers prior to enabling publishing, subscribing, or distribution between them.

Often, the replication publisher and destination are in different Windows NT Server Domains, which brings about a need for additional setup steps. One such need is that replication requires a trust relationship across the domains to handle connections and communication. When the servers participating in the relationship are in the same domain, the trusts are implicitly set up, and no additional work needs to be done in this area.

Communication between domains utilizing trust relationships is an issue when the servers are in different domains. The only protocols that currently allow trusted connections are Named Pipes and Multiprotocol. Therefore, if the servers are in different Windows NT Server domains, you must take care to ensure that the servers use one of these protocols; otherwise, the servers might not be able to communicate and distribute data modifications.

Note

Another issue with the servers is the sort order and character set that the servers use. To ensure consistent results from queries of replicated data, all of the servers in the replication relationship should use the same character set and sort order.

Devices and Databases

After the appropriate servers are set up and the appropriate network protocols have been implemented, the data devices and databases on each server participating in the replication relationship can be set up. Before this actually takes place, an analysis process must be performed to determine actual space requirements. The general formulas for this analysis follow:

$RS \times Art \times Pub \times DI$ (for the database)

and

$RS \times Art \times PUB \times DI \times TC$ (for the transaction log)

The components for this formula are the following:

▶ Storage space for raw data (RS)

▶ Multiples of the storage space per publication (Pub) and article (Art)

▶ Storage space to contain the data for the interval defined by the replication frequency (DI)

▶ Storage space to contain the transaction commands for each article in the log (TC)

The raw storage space that the data occupies under peak operating conditions must be determined so that the data devices that contain the databases and transaction logs can be created with sufficient storage space.

The amount of storage space allocated for each table must be multiplied by the number of times that the table's data is to be replicated so that sufficient space can be allowed for copies of all of the data that is to be contained in the distribution database. When this amount is determined, it must be multiplied by the number of intervals that the data will persist before being archived or deleted.

Finally, space for the Transact SQL Commands must be figured into the equation to take into account the log space used by the syntax portion of the commands.

After these requirements are determined, the data devices, as well as the databases, can be created. A traffic jam could ensue if the analysis is done improperly.

Following is a scenario that points out the way the storage space should be calculated with the following parameters:

1. The server replicates data in a publication containing one article to six subscribers.

2. Normal data activity is determined to be 15 MB per day with 7 MB of log space required for transactions because only the data is required, rather than the entire Transact-SQL command.

3. Data is replicated weekly with previously replicated data discarded after a time period of one week.

In the formula for the database storage size, the variables are 15 (RS), 14 (DI), 1 (ART), 1 (Pub), and 6 (TC). DI has a value of 14 because the data persists for 7 days times 2 weeks. TC has a value of 6 because the commands must be repeated once for each subscriber.

Proper analysis gives rise to the following figures: 15 MB per day multiplied by 7 days equals 105 MB per week, which must be multiplied by 2 to take into account that the data will persist for 1 week after the changes are propagated to each server, which equals 210 MB of data. Using the same functions, the amount of log space required seems to be 98 MB. A common mistake would be to make the database 210 MB of data and the log 98 MB, without taking the number of publishers into account, but in this case, the log size must be multiplied by the 6 publishers, bringing the total size needed to 588 MB to ensure that transactions are not dropped prematurely.

This process must be applied to each of the servers in the replication relationship so that appropriate amounts of storage space are available in the following areas:

▶ Transaction log for the publishing database for each publishing server

▶ Transaction log for the distribution database

▶ Destination database

In the case that the distribution database or the subscription database does not exist, they must be created with appropriate storage space in mind.

Users

Just as SQL Server requires logins and users for the server and database to receive data modifications, user accounts must also be created. The user accounts must have certain privileges to perform modifications.

SQL Server uses a service called the SQL Server Executive to perform the majority of work. The user account that SQL Executive uses must have all of the privileges of an administrator on the server. The easiest way to accomplish this task is to make the account a member of the Administrator user group by using the User Manager application in Windows NT. Because the SQL Server Executive is actually an NT Service, the account must be granted the right to Log On As A Service. Other options that should be assigned to the account in order to simplify maintenance tasks later follow:

▶ Password Never Expires

▶ User Cannot Change Password

Setting the password never to expire prevents the possibility that all SQL Server activity will stop after a certain period of time when the password normally would expire, preventing the SQL Server Executive service from logging in and performing its normal tasks.

If the User Cannot Change Password option is enabled, the user under that account cannot log in and change the password. When the password is changed, the SQL Server Executive needs to have its password changed to match; otherwise, the login will fail and the service will fail to start.

After the user has been created, the number of connections must be increased. SQL Server replication requires that the maximum number of connections be set to the maximum number of normal user connections in addition to the log reader and two connections for each distributor/subscriber combination for each publisher. For example, a server that replicates 2 databases to 3 subscribing servers, each with 50 users, requires that the number of connections be set to 114 to include 50 normal connections, 1 log reader connection, and 6 distributor/subscriber connections, totaling 57 connections for each database. If the maximum number of connections is set to below this number, one or more users will be not be allowed to log in because the replication processes will already be using the last set of connections.

Data Sources and Target

The setup of the data source and target is one of the final steps in preparing for replication. Issues to consider are the destination database type and the setup of the tables that serve as the source for the data modifications. For the tables to be published, they must first be modified to contain a primary key. If the table has already been defined, the administrator can use the Manage Table function of SQL Enterprise Manager to declare the primary key, or the ALTER TABLE statement from a query window or in an I/SQL session.

If the destination database is a non-SQL Server database, then the replication is no longer homogeneous. Heterogeneous replication involves communicate through Open Data Base Connectivity (ODBC) drivers. These drivers must conform to the following specifications:

▶ ODBC Level-1 compliant

▶ 32-bit and thread-safe

▶ The distribution process must be executed on one of the following platforms: Intel, Power PC, Alpha, or MIPS

▶ Capable of handling transactions

▶ Supports the data definition language (DDL)

▶ Cannot be read-only

If the ODBC Driver is not 32-bit and thread safe, it is executed in 16-bit application space and runs the risk of being blocked or mangled by a misbehaving 16-bit application. The driver must be capable of handling transactions simply because there can be more than one Transact SQL Statement in a replicated transaction. If the driver is not capable of handling transactions, there is no guarantee that it will handle multiple statements correctly.

Replication creates and alters schema for the destination tables depending upon synchronization options and creation scripts; the driver must therefore provide these commands with data definition language support.

If the driver connects to the destination database a read-only workspace, no data modifications can be made that will halt the replication process.

Setting Up Various Replication Scenarios

The various schemes that administrators use to implement replication generally correspond to a combination of one or more general replication models. Four of the most commonly used replication models are central subscriber, central publisher, central publisher with remote distributor, and multiple publishers of one table. The two less commonly implemented models are downloaded data and publishing subscriber models. Each has its own individual characteristics. Applying an incorrect replication model to a situation where replication has been chosen to distribute data can turn the normally positive benefits of replication into a maintenance and implementation nightmare. Each of the four common models and an appropriate example of each is covered next.

Replication Model Types

To apply the appropriate replication model to formulate a solution, the administrator must be aware of the advantages and disadvantages of each replication model. The following four subsections discuss each in detail.

Central Publisher

As shown in figure 9.1, only one server in this model performs the role of the publisher. It serves as the source for all of the data to be distributed and is the default replication option in Microsoft SQL Server. In addition to performing this role, it also performs the task of the distribution server. It distributes the data to any number of subscription servers.

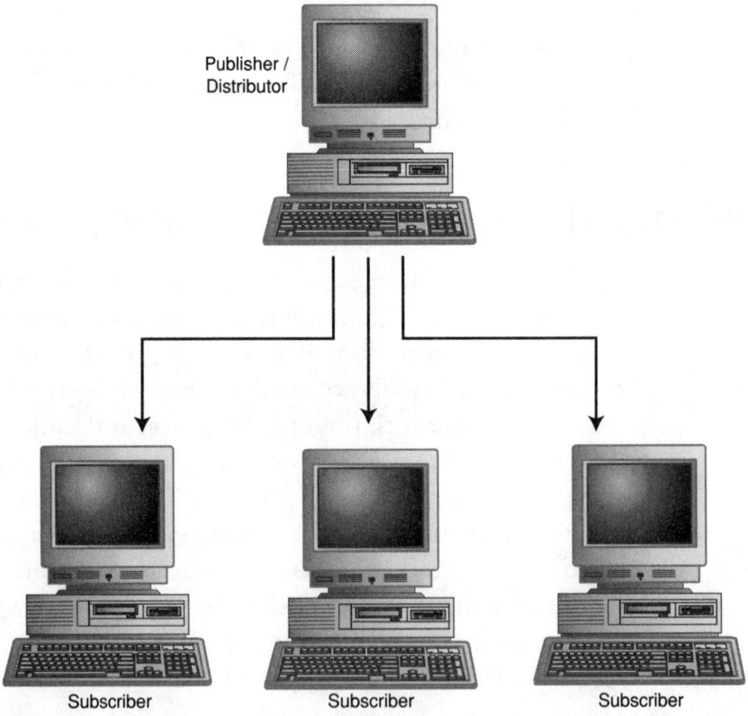

Figure 9.1

The central publisher model.

Publisher / Distributor

Subscriber   Subscriber   Subscriber

Satellite locations such as local libraries serve as good examples for the central publisher replication model. When a person is searching through the library catalog for a particular title, chances are good that the search extends beyond the local library. The local library catalog then serves as a subscriber to the Library of Congress, which is the publisher and distributor. The master list of titles is kept on the Library of Congress server and replicated down in parts to the individual library servers. The next time the title is the subject of a search, the title is already found on the local catalog.

Central Publisher with Remote Distributor

In some instances, the publisher server might have an above average work load—when it acts concurrently as a file server, for example. In this case, the administrator can choose to offload the work of distributing the data to the subscribing servers to another server (see fig 9.2). This configuration is referred to as central publishing with remote distribution. The distributor might be on the same LAN, on a WAN, or across the Internet. As long as the two servers can communicate, the distribution process proceeds normally, which reduces the amount of storage space required on the publishing server, but also requires that another complete server be brought online.

Figure 9.2

Central publisher with remote distributor.

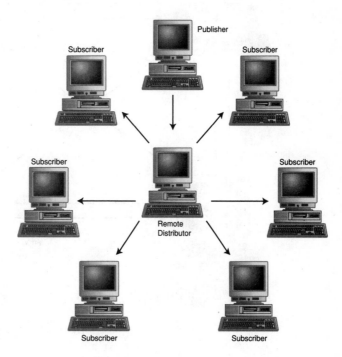

Multiple Publishers of One Table

Multiple publishers of one table is the most complicated model of the general categories. In this scenario, each server serves all of the functions of the three roles: publisher, distributor, and subscriber, as shown in figure 9.3. The servers are all interconnected and receive, as well as send, data from a common table. More attention must be paid to defining ownership rules for data in this model. Unlike the central subscriber model, the database cannot be placed with read-only permissions because the data can be modified from any of the connected servers. Instead, the design must provide a method for each server to update its own data but leave the remaining data as read-only. This model comes closest to fully implementing a fully distributed data set across all of the sites.

Figure 9.3

Multiple publishers of one table.

Publisher /
Distributor /
Subscriber

Publisher /
Distributor /
Subscriber

Publisher /
Distributor /
Subscriber

Publisher /
Distributor /
Subscriber

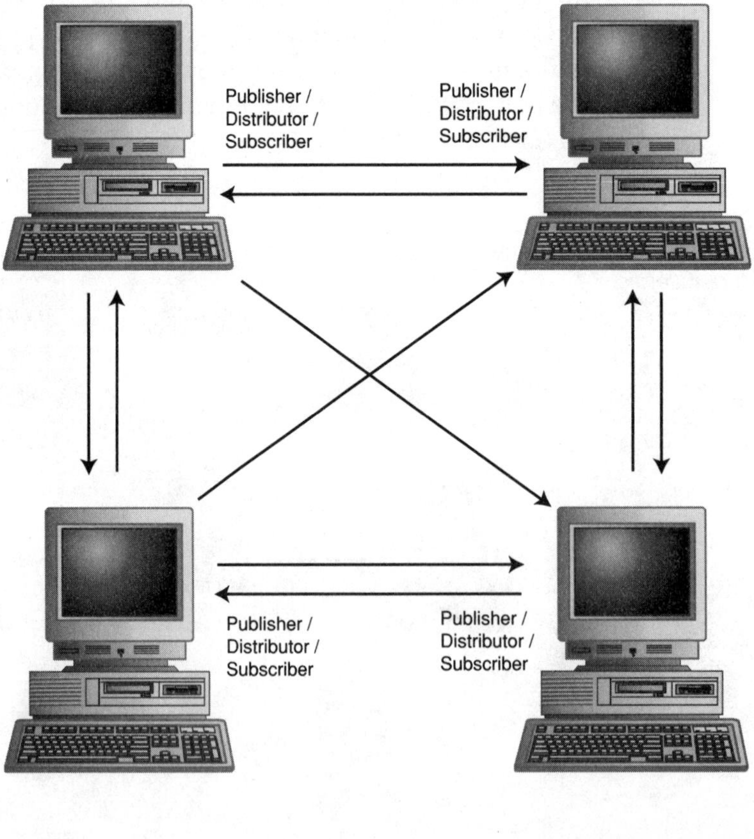

The multiple publishers of one table replication model can be appropriately applied to the task of customer maintenance across an enterprise. In this case, each site keeps track of its own customers in a table that is scheduled for replication. This table contains the information about the customer, as well as a column identifying the site originating the change. The data is replicated to each site allowing the same data about a customer to be retrieved locally. When a change is made to a customer's data at the site the customer was created, the change is replicated across the enterprise. Because the column exists with the originating site, code can be written on each server to give only the repl_subscriber process permission to update information with another site ID.

Central Subscriber

The central subscriber model is used in cases where one target database receives data and changes from a number of sites, as shown in figure 9.4. It is normally used to generate corporate data warehouses or other enterprise-wide reporting databases. This model requires a bit more analytical work because the issue of ownership of data comes into play. If the implementation of this type of replication model is not done correctly, data could be overwritten by similar data from other sites.

Note

The destination database should not allow the replicated data to be modified because replication only happens in one direction, from the source to the destination. Data that is changed in the destination has *no* effect upon the original data. Changing this read-only data can cause errors to occur if that particular set of data is to be updated by a change in the source database.

Tip

Set permissions on the destination database (subscriber) to read-only instead of putting the database in read-only mode. Otherwise, the replication processes will not be able to add or modify the data to be replicated!

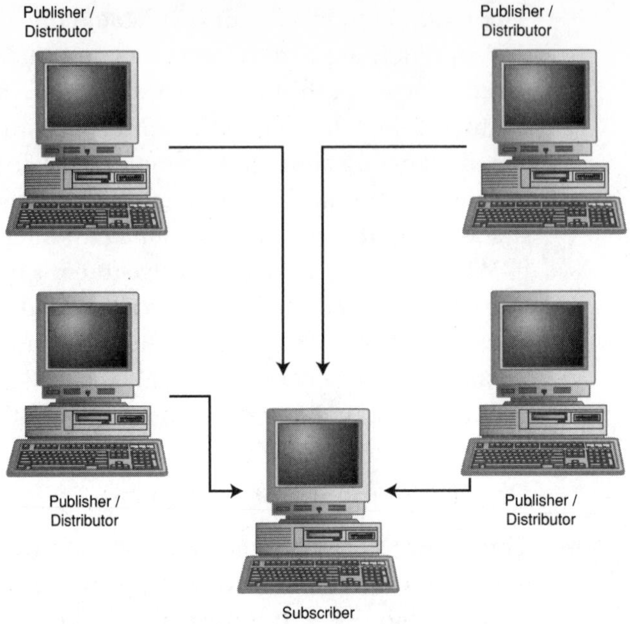

Figure 9.4

Central Sub-scriber.

Subscriber

A good example of this type of replication model is a corporate data warehouse for a manufacturing plant. In this case the individual factories' servers play the roles of the publishing and distribution servers. As they create their normal products, they use up supplies. A record of the supplies that they use is kept on the server, as well as the amount of pieces produced. When replication runs, this information is sent to the corporate headquarters to the central subscriber. At corporate headquarters, the individual in charge of ordering supplies takes a look at the amount for each supply. If the amount in inventory is less than a predetermined quantity, this individual calls the plant and reminds them to order additional supplies for that plant. When the supplies arrive, the clerk at the plant updates the number in inventory. On the other side of the central office, executives run reports correlating trends in products and usage of supplies. With this information, they can forecast the individual plant's supply and production needs.

Setting Up Each Type of Scenario

The basic set up procedure for each scenario is the same: the publishing server(s) must be setup, the distribution server(s) must be set up, and the subscribing server(s) must be set up. The main differences are the order of operations and the connections between the servers. The following sections show the setup for each of the models in turn. The actual process that the steps involve is discussed later in the chapter.

Central Publisher

The process to set up a Central Publisher replication model is very similar to the Central Subscriber model with the order modified in the following manner:

1. Set up the publishing server to run SQL Server.

2. Create the data devices on the publishing server.

3. Create the publishing database.

4. Install replication on the publishing server with the distribution database on the same server.

5. Create the publications and articles.

6. Set up the subscribing server to run SQL Server.

7. Create the data devices on the subscribing server.

8. Create the subscribing databases.

9. Register the subscribing server with the publishing server.

10. Enable publishing to the subscription server.

11. Subscribe to the publications.

12. Synchronize the publications.

Steps 6 through 12 must be completed for each of the subscribing servers that participate in the replication relationship. This model requires substantially less work because the publications need only be set up once instead of for each publishing server in the central subscriber model.

Central Publisher with Remote Distributor

Due to the fact that the distributor is no longer in the same server as the publisher, the following additional steps are required for central publisher with remote distributor:

1. Set up the publishing server to run SQL Server.

2. Create the data devices on the publishing server.

3. Create the publishing database.

4. Set up the distribution server to run SQL Server.

5. Create the data devices on the distribution server.

6. Install replication on the distribution server with a local distribution database.

7. Register the distribution server with the publishing server.

8. Install replication on the publishing server using the remote option. Select the distribution server for the remote option.

9. Create the publications and articles.

10. Set up the subscribing server to run SQL Server.

11. Create the data devices on the subscribing server.

12. Create the subscribing databases.

13. Register the subscribing server with the publishing server.

14. Register the subscribing server with the distribution server.

15. Enable publishing to the subscription server.

16. Subscribe to the publications.

17. Synchronize the publications.

Steps 10 through 17 must be completed for each of the subscribing servers that participate in the replication relationship. Although this model requires more work than the central publisher model with local distribution, the tradeoff of the additional horsepower on the distribution server frees up the publishing server so that more work can be accomplished.

Multiple Publishers of One Table

The multiple publishers of one table model requires more caution to ensure that it is set up correctly. The following steps are required to set up this model:

1. Set up the server to run SQL Server.

2. Create the data devices on the server.

3. Create the publishing database, which is also the subscribing database.

4. Install replication on the server with a local distribution database.

5. Create the publications and articles.

6. Register each of the subscribing servers.

7. Enable publishing to each server.

8. Subscribe to the publications on each of the servers.

9. Synchronize all publications.

Steps 1 through 5 must be completed for each of the subscribing servers that participate in the replication relationship. Because these steps are repetitive, it is easier to make a mistake and leave at least one of the servers out of a publisher/distributor/subscriber relationship. It is for this reason that special care must be taken to plan this model, check that each step is completed, and ensure that relationships exist between all of the servers.

Central Subscriber

In order to set up the central subscriber replication model, the steps must occur in the following order:

1. Set up the subscribing server to run SQL Server.

2. Create the data devices on the subscribing server.

3. Create the subscribing database.

4. Create the publishing server.

5. Create the data devices on the publishing server.

6. Create the publishing databases.

7. Register the subscribing server with the publishing server.

8. Install replication on the publishing server and choose the distributor.

9. Enable publishing to the subscription server.

10. Create the publications and articles.

11. Subscribe to the publications.

12. Synchronize the publications.

Steps 4 through 12 must be completed for each of the publishing servers that participate in the replication relationship.

Implement Replication

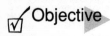 Before replication can be implemented, the administrator must be cognizant of the various roles that a server can play, and how to set up each of them.

Replication is implemented by using a publisher/subscriber metaphor. Any SQL Server that is set up for replication performs one or more of the following roles:

▶ Publication server

▶ Distribution server

▶ Subscription server

In addition to the roles that each server plays, further down the hierarchy are publications, articles, and subscriptions.

Recognizing the Role of the Publication Server (Publisher)

A publication server performs several tasks. It contains and maintains the source database for data and schema. It transfers changes and original data to the distribution server.

The following subsections explain how to enable publishing servers and databases, modify distribution options for each server, and create and manage publications and articles.

Enabling Publishing Servers and Databases

A component of setting up the publishing server is choosing which servers it will be replicating to. As shown in figure 9.5, Enterprise Manager provides a dialog box accessible under the Server menu by choosing Replication Configuration, Publishing.

Figure 9.5

Enabling publishing to subscribers via the Replication - Publishing dialog box.

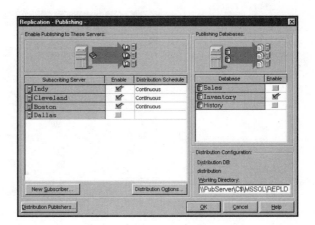

In this example, the servers at Indy, Cleveland, and Boston are permitted to subscribe to PubServer's publications. The check box beside the Inventory database indicates that publications can be created in the inventory database, but not the Sales or History databases. Here, the directory used for synchronization files and special replication commands is set to \\PubServer\C$\SQL65\REPLDATA. Because the field is not long enough to display the entire path, it truncates it at SQL65 in the display, but not the actual string.

Modifying Distribution Options for Each Server

After the servers that are permitted to subscribe have been set, each server is defaulted to receive modifications continuously after 100 transactions have occurred. If a different frequency of distribution is needed, the administrator must set the distribution options for each of the subscribers that is different from the default. Figure 9.6 shows the dialog box that pops up when the Distribution Options button is clicked from the Subscriber dialog box. Here, the administrator has chosen to transmit data modifications to Boston after every 10 transactions. In addition to modifying the number of transactions to occur before transmission, the administrator can choose to transmit at scheduled intervals rather than continuously. The amount entered in the Retention Period After Distribution (hours) box determines how many hours after the transaction is applied to the subscription database that the transaction information is retained in the distribution database.

Figure 9.6

The Distribution Options dialog box.

Because the replication model can be expressed in terms of publishers, distributors, and subscribers, the model is further fleshed out by publications and articles.

Managing Publications

The publisher is the source of all the data that will be replicated, and, as such, it is important to analyze and set up the publication server correctly. Publications are specific to the database in which they are created; multiple publications can therefore be created with the same name in different databases. This allows great flexibility in switching the source of the data from the subscriber's side. The price for this flexibility is that a publication might contain articles from only one database, but multiple publications can be defined in each database on the publication server. Figure 9.7 shows the dialog box that displays the existing publications for a server.

Figure 9.7

The Manage Publications dialog box.

SQL Enterprise Manager provides mechanisms to easily set up publication and articles. These mechanisms are found under the Manage menu by selecting Replication, Publications. After a name is entered for the publication, the articles that is contains must be chosen (see fig. 9.8).

Figure 9.8

Creating publications in the Articles tab of the Edit Publications dialog box.

The application provides for each publication three customizable methods, which follow:

▶ Security

▶ Replication Frequency

▶ Synchronization

Security

At times, the administrator might want to specify that a publication can be subscribed to only by selected servers. In this case the administrator chooses the security method of the publication and marks it Restricted To, which makes the publication invisible to any server that is not selected to be marked for access. Otherwise, the default security method for publications is Unrestricted, which makes the publication accessible by any server that can communicate with the publication server (see fig. 9.9).

Figure 9.9

The Security tab of the Edit Publications dialog box.

Replication Frequency

The replication frequency method determines when and how data can be modified (see fig. 9.10). If transaction-based replication is chosen, each transaction that occurs can be retrieved from the transaction log by the log reader process and sent to be applied by the distribution process. The other option is to replicate by scheduled table refreshes. As per the name, each article contained in the publication can transfer its complete set of data to be mirrored in the destination table at scheduled intervals. In addition to the data being replicated, the administrator can choose to have the actual schema replicated at all. In this case, the server switches to very loose consistency because no modifications to the publisher's data are replicated between the time that a refresh occurs and the next scheduled refresh.

Figure 9.10

*Replication fre-
quency.*

Synchronization

The initial method of synchronization, as shown in figure 9.10, must be determined before a subscribing server creates a subscription.

The first method is implemented by a bulk data copy operation using the native format. The advantage of this method is speed—no translation is required—but the cost is that the architectures must be identical and the servers be SQL Server. The second method trades speed for compatibility by translating the data to character strings and is referred to by character format mode.

The administrator can also set the synchronization schedule. At the scheduled interval, the publishing table will update each of the subscribers to the most current snapshot of data. This automatic synchronization incurs a reasonably high level of overhead for the publishing server and the network itself because all of the data must be brought forward. Because of this, administrators would not want a synchronization event to occur in the middle of peak database activity. By scheduling this during low activity periods, such as after normal usage hours, this problem is avoided. Proper scheduling also ensures that at certain intervals, the data will be mirrored, tightening the consistency according to the frequency.

Users other than the database owner can publish tables for replication and maintain ownership of their tables. This method is referred as owner qualifying the table name. It allows the data from the table in the publishing server to be replicated in the subscribing server.

In cases where complex operations are to be performed, the administrator setting up the article can choose to use column names in SQL statements. Although it increases network traffic by increasing the length of each INSERT statement generated from the transaction log, it ensures that the data to be inserted will fill the appropriate columns in the destination table.

Managing Articles

The base component of the replication model is an article. The article is composed of a table, or subset of a table. Although articles have their own properties, they cannot be published for replication by themselves. In addition, the underlying table must have a primary key defined.

 Note

Due to the way that Microsoft SQL server handles the entries in the transaction log, the replication processes must have a serialized entry point on which to modify data. The primary key in the table normally fulfills this.

Articles can be created from any set of data in a table and grouped or partitioned in certain ways. If the data is grouped by table columns such that one or more columns is not replicated, the article is referred to as being *vertically partitioned* (see fig. 9.11). This grouping is useful when replicating from one table to another table that does not include all of the columns in the source table.

Another method of partitioning is known as *horizontal partitioning* (see fig. 9.12). Servers that subscribe to articles that are horizontally partitioned receive only a subset of the rows. In Microsoft SQL Server T-SQL, a WHERE clause is provided in the filter clause for the article, whether it is a SELECT, DELETE, or UPDATE statement.

Figure 9.11

*Vertical Partition-
ing.*

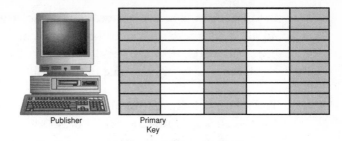

Publisher

Primary
Key

Primary
Key

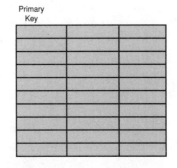

Subscriber

Figure 9.12

*Horizontal parti-
tioning.*

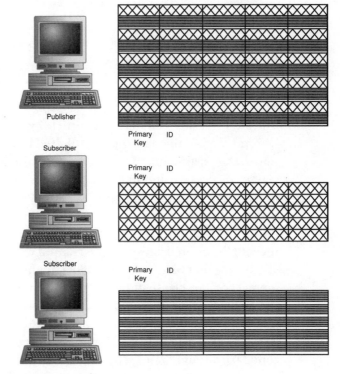

Publisher

Primary   ID
Key

Subscriber

Primary   ID
Key

Subscriber

Primary   ID
Key

Because it is sometimes necessary to replicate groups of data that do not conform to vertical or horizontal partitioning, articles can be partitioned both ways. In addition, each grouping method can be placed in a separate article in the publication list.

The unit one layer up from the article is referred to as a *publication*, which is a group of articles bound together under a common label. In any given database, there can be any number of publications. Publications are the units that subscribing servers use to retrieve and modify the data. When a publication is subscribed to, the subscription server receives the data from all of the articles bound inside the publication.

Note

In Microsoft SQL Server, synchronization occurs at the publication level, effectively mirroring the data from the underlying articles as a group. It is therefore advisable to group related tables into a single publication so that referential integrity is assured.

Articles have both general options and advanced options to further tune their settings.

General Options

The administrator can define an article by selecting the table to be replicated. If the data must be filtered by row, some type of horizontal partitioning must be defined by including a filter clause. Vertical partitioning is used when not all of the columns need to be replicated. In figure 9.13, the Belts_table article in database Inventory on publisher PubServer is an example of both horizontal and vertical partitioning. The blank box at the right of the length row indicates that the column will not be replicated. It also means that the destination table might not contain this column. The filter clause indicates that only the rows in which the site_id column has a value of 200 will be replicated. This is a clue that this article is part of a multiple publishers of one table replication model. The normal default for an article is neither horizontal partitioning nor vertical partitioning.

Figure 9.13

Create Article (General).

Articles can be specialized further in terms of what kinds of modifications to the tables will be replicated. The administrator can choose to have any combination of modifications active for replication by changing the status on the Scripts tab of the Articles dialog box. The default replication mechanism is to replicate INSERT, UPDATE, and DELETE modifications to the table. In the case that a modification on a group of commands is undesirable, the administrator clicks the circle next to the custom field of the command and inputs "NONE," which indicates that the article will not replicate these modifications. In addition to specifying a binary replicate, or not replicate, the administrator has the option to set up a stored procedure that exists on the subscribing database that executes when a command is found. The stored procedure takes each of the replicated columns as parameters and can perform any operation that a normal stored procedure is capable of performing. Figure 9.14 shows that a procedure named update_belt_inventory will run when an update modification is applied to the subscribing database. If the administrator did not want modifications from INSERT statements to be replicated, the Custom option next to INSERT would be selected and the word "NONE" would be entered in the text box.

Figure 9.14

Create Article (Scripts).

The last of the general options for articles is the creation script. SQL Server Enterprise Manager defaults this to the path specified in the setup for the distribution files with the table name and a .SCH extension. The administrator can override this value, but must be careful that the file exists and that read permission is allowed on the login account that SQL Server is using.

The creation script is used when synchronizing the destination table for the first time or when the administrator manually initiates the synchronization process. As shown in figure 9.15, the creation script performs a T-SQL statement that creates the destination table. This table has only the columns that are replicated. The script is normally generated when the administrator clicks the Generate button on the Create Article dialog box.

Figure 9.15

Edit Creation Script.

When the Generate button is clicked, the next dialog box contains settings that affect the manner of synchronization (see fig. 9.16). The first group of settings affects the actions of the destination database when the destination table already exists. If the administrator does not want any activity taken (rows deleted, table data truncated, or the table dropped) then the Do Nothing option should be selected. If the data must be exact but there are triggers on the destination table that must be kept to ensure other operations such as referential integrity, then the Truncate Table can be selected. When there are no triggers or the work done by the triggers is duplicated elsewhere, the DROP TABLE option is a good fit for a synchronization option. If the table participates in a multiple publisher of one table replication model, the only reasonable option is the DELETE DATA using Restriction Clause. When this is set up correctly, it ensures that even when a synchronization event occurs, only that server's data is modified rather than all of the table data.

Figure 9.16

Auto-Generate Sync Scripts.

As shown in figure 9.16, there are a number of other options for the synchronization scripts:

▶ Transfer Clustered Index

▶ Transfer non-Clustered Index

▶ Convert UDDT to Base Datatype

▶ Include DRI-PK

The Transfer Clustered Index appends a definition of a clustered index on the destination table if it exists to the synchronization script. If the non-clustered indices are desired as well, the Transfer non-Clustered Index diamond should be toggled on. In the case that user-defined datatypes (UDDT) have been defined for a table but have not necessarily been created in the destination database, the Convert UDDT to Base Datatype checkbox should be filled to ensure that errors do not occur in the initial table create because the UDDT does not exist in the target database. The final option, Include DRI-PK, allows the replication of Primary Keys, Foreign keys, and other constraints on the source table to be created in the destination table, as well.

Advanced Options

There could be an instance in which the filter clause might not be as simple as a field's value being compared to a constant. In this case a stored procedure that is created in the publication database can be used to determine whether a row will be replicated. The procedure must be of the following form, where *sql_statement* is replaced by a Transact-SQL statement that peforms filtering on a row by row level:

```
IF sql_statement RETURN 1, ELSE RETURN 0
```

For example:

```
If DATENAME(month, getdate()) = "July" RETURN 1 ELSE RETURN 0.
```

This filter is executed for each record in the transaction log for the replicated table. To minimize the overhead cost of this operation, this filter should be as simple as possible.

Recognizing the Role of the Distribution Server (Distributor)

The distributor contains the distribution database and is responsible for storing the changes it receives to the published data in the distribution database. It then forwards the data to the servers that are subscribing to the publication.

Before anything can be replicated, the distribution database must be created. Figure 9.17 shows the Install Replication Publishing dialog box from SQL Server Enterprise manager that pops up during this portion of replication installation. This dialog box is accessible from the Server Manager window of SQL Enterprise Manager through the Server menu by choosing Replication Configuration, Install Publishing.

Figure 9.17

*Creating the
distribution data-
base.*

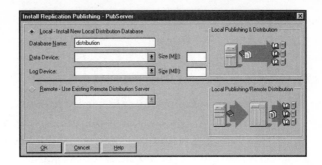

The default option for Enterprise Manager is to set up the distribution database on the local publication server. Although the
database can be placed on any data device and log device, it is
suggested that the database and log be placed on separate devices
in case one gets corrupted. The size of the database and log
should be at least the size of all the original data with additional
space available to take in account the increased commands replication creates in the log.

The distribution server is responsible for several functions:

▶ Retrieving the data from the publishing server

▶ Storing the changes

▶ Applying the changes to the subscription server

▶ Keeping track of what changes have been processed

Retrieving the Data from the Publishing Server

The default for replication in SQL Server utilizes the same server
for both the publishing server and the distribution server, which
makes retrieving the data much simpler. On the same server, the
log reader process can read the data out of the transaction log in
the source database.

In the case of the remote distributor model, however, additional
steps are required. First, the server must be able to connect to the
server by using Named Pipes or the IP address, usually. When the
distribution server knows the location of the publishing server, it
must be given at least SELECT permission. This is normally not a
problem because most installations use an administrator account

of some sort. At this point the log reader process takes over and retrieves the data.

Storing the Changes

When a subscriber initiates a subscription, an ID is created in the distribution database corresponding to the destination database. After the command is picked up by the log_reader, it is stored in the distribution database. A job is then attached both to the command and to the subscriber's ID.

Applying the Changes to the Subscription Server

After the job has been separated and stored in the distribution database, the distribution server initiates a repl_subscriber process, which establishes a connection to the destination database on the destination server. This process actually retrieves the commands from the distribution database storage space and applies them to the destination database.

Keeping Track of What Changes Have Been Processed

After repl_subscriber applies the change to the destination database, it updates the status of the command and the entire job to a success or failure. If there is a failure, the task entry on the distribution server is updated to reflect the failure and the error that occurred.

Due to the manner in which the modifications are retrieved, manipulated, and forwarded to the subscription server, the distribution server incurs a large amount of overhead. For this reason, the distribution server is required to have a minimum of 32 MB of RAM with a minimum of 16 MB allocated to SQL Server, or it will not run.

 Tip

If the distribution database will be used heavily, put the distributor on a separate server from the publishing database.

Recognizing the Role of the Subscription Server (Subscriber)

The subscriber is the target database for the published data. It holds a copy and receives any changes from the publishing server that are forwarded by the distribution server.

In addition to the various partition methods and grouping of articles in publications, mechanisms are in place to change how the subscribing server gets the data.

Pull and Push Subscriptions

The first mechanism is the issue of how the subscriptions will be administrated, and how servers can request that bands of data be replicated and synchronized.

When the subscriptions are set up on the publishing server's side, the subscription is known as a *push* subscription. This server gathers up all of its data and the appropriate modifications and pushes it down the link to all of the subscribing servers. A push subscription has the advantage of consolidated administration across multiple servers at the same time. There are two caveats, however:

▶ The administrator of this type of subscription must have sa permissions on each of the subscribing servers.

▶ The data cannot be selectively gathered by the subscribing servers; each time a synchronization event occurs, all of the data will be replicated again.

The other type of subscription is a *pull* subscription, which requires that the subscribing server take the administrative role after the publication has been created on the publishing server. With pull, the subscribing server can request certain articles or that the entire publications be synchronized at any given time without all of the data needing to be replicated. Also, the administrator can determine which publications to subscribe to by selecting publications from a master list on the publisher.

Extended Replication

The second mechanism for the subscribing server is found in Microsoft SQL Server's extended replication capabilities. With the extended replication commands, it is possible to publish data to non-SQL Server databases, including Microsoft Access, Oracle, and any other ODBC-compliant database. This capability allows SQL Server to interconnect and share data in environments where mixed databases are present. It also allows the distribution of data to areas such as a small Microsoft Access database on a laptop for use in the field.

Schedule a Replication Event

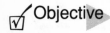 In order to enable replication, replication events must be set up (scheduled) before the process can begin.

Replication Events

Replication requires two basic events: the initial synchronization of all articles in a publication, and the manual synchronization to ensure that the copies of the data match the original.

The initial synchronization event is normally set up under two circumstances. The first is when the publishing server creates a push subscription to a publication. This event requires the administrator on the publishing server to have administrator rights on the subscribing server.

The administrator selects the servers that will receive the push subscription first, as shown in figure 9.18. The push subscription sets up a synchronization task on the publishing server based upon the options set on the article (see fig. 9.19), which are found in the dialog box displayed when the server is selected.

Figure 9.18

Selecting a subscriber in the Publication Subscribers dialog box.

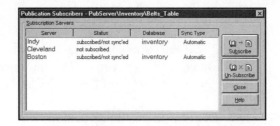

Figure 9.19

Selecting a synchronization option in the Manage Article dialog box.

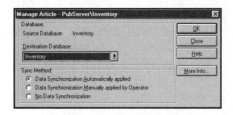

The first option, Data Synchronization Automatically Applied, should be selected when SQL Server should automatically synchronize the schema and data of the destination table with the published table. This option does all of the work to set up the task and enable it in the background and is the default synchronization method.

Select the second option, Data Synchronization Manually Applied by Operator, when the administrator will initiate the synchronization task manually. Manual synchronization requires the administrator to retrieve the schema and data files from the distribution server first. After the files have been retrieved, the schema and data of the subscribed table must be manually synchronized with that of the published table. When this is completed, the administrator informs SQL Server that the synchronization is complete.

 Note

The administrator must be careful when selecting manual synchronization because it might affect the data replicated to the destination database. The reason is that when the synchronization job becomes the next job in the distribution database queue, the entire replication process is suspended until the manual synchronization is carried out and SQL Server is informed that the synchronization is complete.

Using Task Manager

After the events are planned out, the administrator can use the Task Manager in SQL Enterprise Manager to finish setting up the replication tasks. The replication tasks take three forms:

▶ **Distribution.** Makes the modifications to the destination database as specified by the publication options.

▶ **LogReader.** Picks up the information from the transaction log on the publishing database and places it into the distribution log as a job.

▶ **Sync.** Initializes the target tables and brings the destination table up to be an exact data copy of the published table. Sync tasks are the replication tasks that an administrator can normally set up and execute.

Recognize the Situations in Which Synchronization Must Be Performed

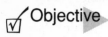 Objective

Under normal circumstances there are two circumstances in which synchronization must be performed:

▶ Before replication starts

▶ To ensure exact copies

Before Replication Starts

In order for replication to begin automatically, the source and destination tables must be synchronized, whether manually or automatically. If this is not done, none of the transactions will replicate because SQL Server will not have a starting point (reference point) with which to begin.

Ensuring Exact Copies

If at any point the administrator wishes to ensure that the source and destination tables are the same, a synchronization task is the easiest way to complete this. After synchronization has been completed, the tables will be duplicates of each other.

Other Situations That Require Synchronization Be Performed

The only other situation that requires that synchronization be performed is after recovery from backup after a failure. Other situations in which synchronization must be performed are during disaster recovery, when a new server subscribes to a publication, or when an article in a publication changes.

During disaster recovery, all subscriptions must be terminated, the databases restored, and then the process of creating articles, publications, and subscriptions must be completed. Because of this rebuild process, synchronization is necessary to restart replication.

When a new server or database creates a subscription, the tables might not be exact copies. Either way, replication must go through a synchronization process to create a common point of reference in order to continue to make data modifications to the destination database.

To change the way an article replicates its data, the subscriptions must also be terminated and rebuilt. This process is similar to the work done in disaster recovery in that all of the subscriptions must be re-created, but the database restoration step can be omitted.

Identify the System Tables That Are Used in Replication

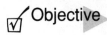 Objective

The system tables that replication uses are located in the servers that serve in the publishing, distributing, and subscribing roles.

System Tables in the Publisher

The system tables that are found in the publisher are as follows:

- ▶ sysobjects
- ▶ syspublications
- ▶ sysarticles
- ▶ syssubscriptions

The sysobjects table contains a category field, in addition to its normal role of containing rows for each object in the database. The field is set by replication for each object involved in replication when an article is created and on the initial subscription to the article.

One row for each of the publications that the publication server is publishing is found in the syspublications table.

The sysarticles table contains one row for each of the articles that the publication server is publishing.

The associations between the Ids of published articles and the Ids of all of the subscription servers that expect to receive the modified data from the article are found in the syssubscriptions table.

System Tables in the Distributor

The system tables that are found in the distribution database are as follows:

- ▶ MSjobs
- ▶ MSjob_commands
- ▶ MSjob_subscriptions
- ▶ MSsubscriber_info
- ▶ MSsubscriber_ jobs
- ▶ Mssubscriber_status

The MSjobs table stores one entry for each of the transactions stored in the distribution database.

One entry for each command that is associated with a transaction located in the MSjobs table is placed in the MSjob_commands table. Each of these transactions can contain many commands.

The MSjob_subscriptions table contains asssociations between subscribers with articles. (This is actually subscriber-side information that is maintained in the distribution database.)

SQL Executive uses information found in the MSsubscriber_info table to pass jobs to their destination.

The MSsubscriber_ jobs table contains cross-references between subscribers and the commands that subscriber needs to receive.

Status information for the individual batches of transactions sent to subscribers is contained in the Mssubscriber_status table.

System Tables in the Subscriber

Depending upon the number of jobs (transactions) that have been processed, the MSlast_job_info table can exist. If jobs have been processed, the table exists and contains the job ID of the last job (from a batch) that was successfully applied. The name of the publication, article, and description of each job that is waiting in the distribution queue while it is paused awaiting manual synchronization is also stored in this table.

Resolve Setup Problems

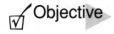 While setting up replication, the administrator might run into issues on the publishing, distributing, and subscribing servers.

Resolving Setup Issues on the Publisher

Common issues found during Setup on the publishing server follow:

- ▶ Replication does not install

- ▶ The publisher cannot publish a database

- ▶ The publisher cannot set up a push subscription

To resolve the problem of being unable to install replication on the publisher, make sure that the server has at least 16 MB of memory, which is the minimum amount that replication requires if the server does not additionally perform the role of distribution. If the amount of memory is at least 16 MB, then the problem could lie either in a corrupted registry or insufficient rights. If these issues cannot be resolved, then SQL Server might need to be reinstalled completely.

If a database cannot be published, check the Replication-Publishing option under the Server menu. If the box to the right of the database is unchecked, then the database will be unable to publish tables.

When a situation arises that a push subscription cannot be set up for a server, first make sure that the server is registered and that you have administrator rights on it. If this is the case, then check the Replication-Subscribing options for the target server. Be sure that the server can receive data modifications from the publishing server.

Resolving Setup Issues on the Distributor

Common issues found in set up on the distribution server follow:

- ▶ Replication does not install

- ▶ Data modifications are not making it to the subscriber

- ▶ The server cannot be used as a remote distributor

To resolve the problem of being unable to install replication on the distributor, make sure that the server has a minimum of 32 MB of memory, which is the minimum amount to memory that replication requires to use the server as a distributor.

If data modifications are not making it to the subscriber, determine whether the LogReader task is having a problem or the Distribution task is having a problem using Task Manager in SQL Enterprise Manager. Replication requires that both of these processes be active and running in order to get data modifications to the subscriber. If one of the tasks has stopped, fix the problem found in the error text and restart the process.

If the server cannot be used as a remote distribution server, the problem is usually one of two things. The server might not be registered on the publishing server. Verify this and correct the problem if the server is not registered. The other problem is that the distribution server is not set up to be a remote publisher. Change the status of the server under Replication-Distribution options.

Resolving Setup Issues on the Subscriber

Common issues found in set up on the subscription server follow:

▶ Cannot subscribe to publications

▶ The initial synchronization fails

▶ The server cannot be used as a remote distributor

If the subscriber does not seem to subscribe to publications on a publishing server, check to see whether the publisher is indeed publishing. Once verified, make sure the publisher is publishing to the subscribing server. If this also checks out, make sure the publication in question is not restricted to exclude the subscription server.

If the initial synchronization fails, the problem could either be conflicting data or a task not executing properly. Use Task Manager to verify that the syntax of the task is correct. If the syntax is correct, examine the data and the synchronization options to make sure they are appropriate.

When a server is not letting you use it as a remote distributor, the most common cause is that the option that makes it act as a remote distributor is not selected in the Replication-Distribution dialog box. Verify that the server is allowed to serve as a remote distributor for the server in question under the Distribution Publishers button on the Replication-Publishing dialog box.

Resolve Fault-Tolerance Problems and Recovery

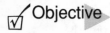 Objective

Although replication has built-in error checking and is fault tolerant, errors do occur sometimes; therefore, the administrator should have a recovery plan. The recovery plan will change depending upon which role the server with the error plays (publisher, distributor, or subscriber).

Recovery Plans for the Publisher

The transaction log of the publisher keeps all of the replicated transactions in it until they are replicated. Therefore, the a database dump of the publishing server, along with the log and a backup of the distribution database, is the key to recovery. Because the two are linked with transactions, both parts are necessary to recover. If the dump of the distribution database does not match the log of the publishing database, replication will attempt to continue with a mismatched entry point and will fail.

If the transaction log of a published (replicated) database continues to fill and absolutely must be truncated, unsubscribe all subscribers of that database. This enables you to truncate past the oldest distributed transaction. After this is completed, make another backup of both the publisher and the distributor so that recovery is possible later.

Recovery Plans for the Distributor

Until a transaction is applied to each of the subscribers that is to receive it, the transaction is retained in the distribution server. In addition, the transaction ID is preserved in the MSjobs table of the distribution database. This ID serves as a pointer to the publisher's transaction log, which points to the transaction that was successfully transferred into the database last.

For distribution to resume from any point, the distribution server must contain a valid reference to a transaction in the publisher's log. The two databases should therefore be dumped at a point at which all activity is minimized and the log is quiescent.

Recovery Plans for the Subscriber

Because of the nature of the subscribing database, it is the easiest of the three to recover. The simplest way is to restore the database from a dump and resynchronize each of the publications. This ensures that the transaction IDs are reset and that further transactions will continue.

Exercises

The setup of the exercises found in this chapter is slightly different from those found in other chapters in the book. This structure matches logically the nature of the subject matter at hand.

Exercise 9.1: Implementing the Appropriate Replication Model

Your company has six sites that require common data distributed across them with the following specifications:

Sites A, B, C, and D all perform customer maintenance for additions, updates, and deletions, with the provision that each site can only update the customers that it adds.

Sites A, B, C, and D also perform real-time online transaction processing for the company and cannot afford to slow down processing of transactions to transmit data to the corporate server at Site E.

The company has provided Site F to act as a temporary storage repository for the transaction information from each site along its way to Site E.

The customer data must be distributed to sites A, B, C, and D such that each site can see each of the other site's customers.

Describe the replication models used to solve this situation.

Answer:

Because each site will be modifying the data, the best model for this situation is the multiple publishers of one table model for the customer table. The need to have the results transmitted as close to real time as possible is a reason to offload the work of the distribution onto server F. Therefore A, B, C, and D use E as a remote distribution server to which F is a subscriber.

Exercise 9.2: Troubleshooting

Servers A and B have just been set up with 16 and 32 MB of memory, respectively, and SQL Server has just been installed. Replication must occur between the two servers that are in the same Windows NT Domain on the Inventory database on the Widgets table.

Neither server can currently replicate to the other one. Which way will replication take place and what are the steps necessary to correct this problem?

Answer:

First register Server B on Server A, and Server A on Server B through SQL Enterprise Manager. Because Server B has 32 megabytes of memory, it is the only server that can act as a distributor. Therefore, set up Server B as a local distributor to itself and a remote distributor for Server A. Enable publishing on both Inventory databases to the other server. Create a publication containing the Widgets table as an article. Subscribe to both publications. Initiate the synchronization task and the process is complete. Replication will take place in both directions.

Review Questions

The following questions test your knowledge of the information in this chapter. For additional questions, see MCP Endeavor and the Microsoft Roadmap/Assessment Exam on the CD-ROM that accompanies this book.

1. What are the minimum memory levels in megabytes for the publisher, distributor, and subscriber respectively?

   A. 16, 16, 16

   B. 32, 32, 32

   C. 16, 32, 32

   D. 16, 32, 16

2. Choose two or more correct reponses. Replication can be installed on which platforms?

   A. Macintosh

   B. Intel

   C. Unix

   D. Alpha

3. Choose two or more correct responses. Replication requires which components?

   A. Synchronization of publisher and subscriber

   B. Synchronization of publisher and distributor

   C. Articles and pathways

   D. Publications and databases

4. What kind of a metaphor is typically used to describe replication?

   A. push/pop

   B. child/parent

   C. commands/transactions

   D. publisher/subscriber

5. Replication corresponds to which of the following categories?

   A. loose consistency

   B. rapid distribution

   C. tight distribution

   D. ANSI standard based

6. What is the smallest unit of replication?

   A. table

   B. article

C. publication

D. synchronization process

7. Which of the following is an appropriate and neccessary choice when planning replication?

    A. Establishment date

    B. Synchronization time

    C. Replication model

    D. ODBC Driver

8. If the publisher has an above average workload, which of the following should be moved to another server?

    A. Publishing database

    B. Synchronization database

    C. Subscribing database

    D. Distribution database

9. The account SQL Server logs into Windows NT under must have permission to access which of the following?

    A. The Internet

    B. Working directory

    C. Shared directories

    D. NT Timer services

10. Choose two or more correct responses. For optimum replication, the servers involved must share which of the following?

    A. An sa password

    B. Sort order

    C. Publications

    D. Character sets

11. Which of the following is the general formula for space requirements for a database?

    A. $RS \times Art \times Pub \times DI$

    B. $RS \times Art \div Pub \div DI$

    C. $Pub \times DI \div RS \times Art$

    D. $DI \div RS \times Art \times Pub$

12. The user account that SQL Server uses generally must be a member of which Windows NT Group?

    A. Users

    B. Backup Operators

    C. Power Users

    D. Administrators

13. Which of the following is in appropriate option to set on the user account for a SQL Server?

    A. Password Never Expires

    B. User Can Use Dialup Networking

    C. User Can Change Password

    D. User Is The Primary Administrator

14. Choose two correct responses. Heterogeneous replication requires that the ODBC Drivers conform to which of the following?

    A. ODBC Level 2 compliance

    B. ODBC Level 1 compliance

    C. Support of the schema definition language

    D. Capability to handle transactions

15. Which of the following is one of the general replication models?

    A. Central downloader

    B. Publishing distributor

    C. Downloaded data

    D. Central repository

16. Which of the following is the most complicated replication model?

    A. Downloaded data

    B. Multiple publishers of one table

    C. Publishing subscriber

    D. Publishing distributor

17. If the implementation of the central subscriber model is not completed correctly, what might happen?

    A. Data will be doubled.

    B. Data might be corrupted.

    C. Data might be overwritten.

    D. Data might be tripled.

18. A corporate data warehouse is probably a good fit for which replication model?

    A. Publishing subscriber

    B. Central subscriber

    C. Central publisher

    D. Multiple publishers of one table

19. What is the default number of transactions that will occur before replication distributes the modifications?

    A. 1

    B. 10

    C. 100

    D. 1000

20. Two of the ways that a publication can be customized are which of the following?

    A. Synchronization

    B. Consistency

    C. Replication frequency

    D. Partitioning

21. The administrator of the publication can choose which two methods of synchronization?

    A. Truncate table

    B. Bulk copy native

    C. Bulk copy character

    D. No synchronization

22. Which two of the following are ways in which an article can be partitioned?

    A. Vertically

    B. By odd columns

    C. By even rows

    D. Horizontally

23. A filter clause is used to do which of the following?

    A. Vertically partition a publication

    B. Vertically partition an article

    C. Horizontally partition a publication

    D. Horizontally partition an article

24. Choose two correct responses. How are creation scripts created?

    A. Manually by the administrator

    B. When the generate button is clicked

    C. When the option button is clicked

    D. When the New Article button is clicked

25. Choose two correct responses. How does the remote distribution server communicate with the publisher?

    A. Multiprotocol

    B. Named Pipes

    C. An IP address

    D. IPX/SPX

26. Who sets up Push subscriptions?

    A. The publishing administrator

    B. The subscribing administrator

    C. The distribution administrator

    D. The system account

27. Who sets up Pull subscriptions?

    A. The publishing administrator

    B. The subscribing administrator

    C. The distribution administrator

    D. The system account

28. Replication tasks are composed of which of the following? (Choose all that apply.)

    A. Sync

    B. Dump

    C. LogReader

    D. Distribution

29. Which two system tables of the following are used in replication?

    A. syspublications

    B. sysobjects

    C. syscolumns

    D sysarticles

30. Which databases are required to be restored in order to re-start replication as part of a disaster recovery process?

    A. The publisher

    B. The subscriber

    C. The distributor

    D. The Master database

Review Answers

1. D

2. B, D

3. A, D

4. D

5. A

6. B

7. C

8. D

9. B

10. B, D

11. A

12. D

13. A

14. B, D

15. C

16. B

17. C

18. C

19. C

20. A, C

21. B, C

22. A, D

23. D

24. A, B

25. B, C

26. A

27. B

28. A, C, D

29. A, D

30. A, B, C

Answers to Test Yourself Questions at Beginning of the Chapter

1. The prerequisites for replication that must be set up are servers, networks, databases, devices, users, data-sources and data. See "Configure the Servers Used for Replication."

2. Valid replication models are central publisher, central publisher with remote distributor, central subscriber, multiple publishers of one table, downloaded data, and publishing subscribers. See "Replication Model Types."

3. Data can be published in its entirety by rows or by columns. See "Managing Articles."

4. A server can play the roles of publisher, distributor, or subscriber. See "Implement Replication."

5. To restore replication after disaster recovery, all publications and subscriptions must be dropped, the publishing, distribution, and subscribing databases must be restored, and the publications and subscriptions re-created and synchronized. See "Resolve Fault-Tolerance Problems and Recovery."

6. Replication events are set up by using Task Manager in SQL Enterprise Manager. See "Schedule a Replication Event."

7. Synchronization must be performed when initial subscriptions are made, when the administrator wants to ensure that the copies of data are exact, or after disaster recovery. See "Recognize the Situations in Which Synchronization Must Be Performed."

8. The issues that must be resolved when planning replication are that appropriate data is being replicated, the proper model is chosen for replication, appropriate destinations are selected to receive the modifications, and where the work of distributing the data is completed. See "Identify Prerequisites for Replication."

Chapter 10

Connectivity and Network Support

SQL Server is all about connectivity. The capability of client computers to access data regardless of network protocol or client architecture makes SQL Server excel in the database management system field. Very few other database management servers can handle the breadth of protocol support in SQL Server.

In addition, SQL Server offers support for making calls into the Windows NT operating system and other services by using extended stored procedures. These extended stored procedures give SQL Server the capability to interact with its environment and with other server architectures.

As always, this chapter begins with a list of the exam objectives relating to the topic at hand, moves on to the chapter pretest, offers valuable information directly addressing the objectives, as well as additional relative discussion topics, and finishes with exercises, chapter review questions, and answers to both the chapter review questions and the chapter pretest questions.

This chapter focuses on connectivity and network support. It helps you prepare for the exam by addressing and fully covering the following objectives:

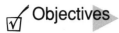 Objectives

- ▶ Set up support for network clients by using various network protocols

- ▶ Install an extended stored procedure

Test Yourself! Before reading this chapter, test yourself to determine how much study time you will need to devote to this section.

1. Josie is the database administrator for a new SQL Server. The predominant protocol on her network is IPX/SPX, used by the network workstations to communicate with Novell Netware file servers. Which network libraries should Josie install on the server?

2. Mark is using SQL Server on a network consisting of clients using Net-BEUI and TCP/IP. Most of the other servers on the network are using TCP/IP. Mark is planning to use integrated security. Which network libraries should Mark install on the server?

3. Bob is trying to add support for TCP/IP Sockets to a network client. He has filled out the server name and DLL name. What should Bob put into the Connection String field?

4. Explain how SQL Server extended stored procedures are executed in the process space of SQL Server.

Answers are located at the end of the chapter...

Set Up Support for Network Clients by Using Various Network Protocols

☑ Objective ▶ SQL Server supports most of the popular network protocols today, including TCP/IP, IPX/SPX, and NetBEUI, without requiring any additional software. SQL Server's support for these protocols relies heavily on Windows NT support. There is very little server-side setup for any network protocol because the Windows NT operating system handles most of the details. Server-side network functionality is implemented in network libraries, or net-libs, which provide extensibility to the network interface. If Microsoft wants to add support for a new protocol, they need only to write a new net-lib and distribute it.

On the client side, however, SQL Server requires a bit more to handle network protocols. Because SQL Server is not usually included by most directory protocols, it is important that the client know some type of a network address for the server. In the case of IPX/SPX or NetBEUI this is usually the server name. In the case of TCP/IP, this is the TCP/IP address or the server name, assuming that the naming services are up and running correctly.

First, this section covers how to set up server and client-side network libraries. Then each protocol (to be supported) is covered, along with how to install and configure each on Windows NT, how to install and configure each on the client, and how to configure the server network libraries. The IPX/SPX, TCP/IP, Banyan-VINES SPP, AppleTalk ADSP, and DEC Net protocols are covered here, too. The "multiple protocol" network libraries are then covered. These are the Named Pipes and Multi-Protocol libraries that are network protocol independent, but dependent upon Windows NT services. These specific protocols are covered because they come with SQL Server and because they are the ones covered on the exam.

Installing Server-Side Network Libraries

The server-side network libraries are installed by using SQL Setup as follows:

1. Start SQL Setup.

2. Click on Continue to accept the title screen.

3. Click on Continue to accept the fact that SQL Server has already been installed.

4. Choose the Change Network Support radio button (see fig. 10.1).

Figure 10.1

Choose Change Network Support here and then Continue to advance to the Select Network Protocols dialog box.

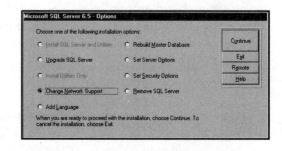

5. Choose Continue to start the Select Network Protocols dialog box.

6. Click in the check box for each network protocol to be installed (see fig. 10.2).

Figure 10.2

The Select Network Protocols dialog box.

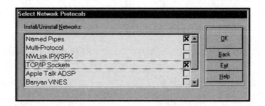

7. Fill out the parameters for each chosen network protocol. (Parameters for each protocol are discussed in more detail in the upcoming sections that address each network protocol separately.)

8. Click the Exit to Windows NT button to complete the setup.

9. Start the SQL Service Manager application.

10. Stop and restart SQL Server.

Changing network support is usually very simple. Keep in mind this procedure does not include the process to install the correct network protocols in Windows NT.

Configuring Client-Side Network Libraries

Libraries are configured on the client computer using the SQL Client Configuration utility, except on DOS clients, where it is configured manually. DOS clients aren't covered here because of the complexity involved in setting them up and because the exam doesn't ask any questions about DOS client network protocols. By default, the Named Pipes and Multi-Protocol libraries should be ready to use. Other protocols, such as IPX/SPX or TCP/IP Sockets, should be configured using the SQL Client Configuration utility.

The SQL Client Configuration Utility configures three different areas of connectivity. The first area (the first tab) concerns how the DBLibrary layer will handle special characters. The first check box, Automatic ANSI to OEM, changes how ANSI characters are mapped to characters in the operating system's character set (see fig. 10.3). This box is usually checked. The Use International Settings implies that the DBLibrary should use the separators specified in the Control Panel/International Settings applet. These settings include currency marks, decimal separators, and thousands separators.

Figure 10.3

The DBLibrary tab of the SQL Server Client Configuration Utility.

The second tab of the SQL Client Configuration Utility is Network Library (see fig. 10.4), which enables you to choose the default network library. The default network library is the library that will be used if no other library is selected for the particular server being connected to. If a particular server requires a different network protocol, it will be set up on the Advanced tab. The default protocol is used unless it is overridden by settings on the Advanced tab.

Figure 10.4

The SQL Client Configuration Utility, Net Library window. Notice the valuable version information in the bottom half.

 The Net Library tab also provides the capability to check which versions of network libraries are currently installed on the client. Version numbers and names of libraries change when you choose different libraries in the drop-down list. This can be valuable information for fixing problems with network connectivity.

The third tab on the SQL Client Configuration Utility is Advanced (see fig. 10.5), which is not very user-friendly and must be used with care to avoid very confusing and inconsistent results. The Advanced tab is used to link a specific server with a specific network library and parameters for that library.

In the case of figure 10.5, the server computer, ukmh559cmille02, is to be connected to by using the TCP/IP sockets library, and the address is the local host address of 127.0.0.1.

Figure 10.5

The Advanced tab is used to show links between a client and a specified server.

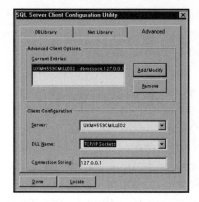

To use the Advanced tab to create specific mappings between a server and a network protocol, do the following:

1. Type the name of the server in to the Server drop-down combo box.

2. Use the DLL Name combo box and choose the network library to be used.

3. Type the connection string for the particular network library. This varies from library to library. For TCP/IP it is the IP address of the server. For IPX/SPX, it is the service name of the server.

4. Click on the Add/Modify button. Failure to click the Add/Modify button causes changes to be lost.

To edit settings already present in the Current Entries box:

1. Choose the setting to modify from the Current Entries box.

2. Click on the Add/Modify button.

3. Make the changes you need to make to the Server Name, DLL, or Connection String. If the server's TCP/IP address has changed, for example, edit the connection string to reflect the new address.

4. Click on the Add/Modify button to save changes.

The truly "user-unfriendly" part of this process is that if after making changes you were to exit before saving, the utility would exit without prompting to save the settings first. This is very annoying.

IPX/SPX Support

IPX/SPX is the protocol used by Novell Netware networks. It is a routable protocol with non-assignable addresses. In other words, each computer has a numeric address, but that address is not one the administrator has to choose. The address usually is the hardware address of the network interface card (NIC) in the computer. IPX/SPX is a definite client and server model. Servers on the network make themselves known using the Service Advertising Protocol (SAP). Each server broadcasts its existence to the rest of the servers. Clients cannot advertise services because they do not have the SAP loaded.

Two components must be installed when IPX/SPX with Windows NT is used. Microsoft's IPX/SPX-compatible protocol, the NWLink protocol, is installed first. NWLink enables the server to communicate with the client computers on the network. The Gateway Services for Netware (GSNW) must be installed as well. The GSNW provides Windows NT with access to the SAP. The SAP provides the Windows NT Server with the capability to advertise itself to other computers on the network.

After installing the proper protocols and services, it is important to install the network libraries into SQL Server. Follow the procedure outlined in the "Installing Server-Side Network Libraries" section and choose the NWLINK IPX/SPX option. The parameter for NWLINK IPX/SPX is the name of the server as it will be advertised on the Netware network—this is the *service name*. The name of the computer is usually used here, and it is the default. If it is desirable to have the server name be different on the Novell network, this option accomplishes the task. Be sure to stop and restart the SQL Server service to make the protocol load correctly.

To install and configure the client software, first install the IPX/SPX protocol on the client computer. This can take the form of the real mode drivers, which are loaded in CONFIG.SYS, AUTOEXEC.BAT, and STARTNET.BAT, or it can take the form of a Windows 95 or Windows NT protocol stack and client services. Check the documentation provided by your network administrator on the types of protocols used on your network. Some companies use drivers provided by Novell, some use drivers provided by Microsoft, and some use a mixture of both or even third-party drivers.

After installing the protocol, take a few minutes if possible to connect to a file server on the Netware network. If you succeed at connecting to the the file server, you have an excellent indication that the protocol stack is working correctly. If the test fails, there may be a problem with the network protocols that should be diagnosed before attempting to connect to SQL Server.

After the network protocols are installed, be sure to use the SQL Client Configuration Utility on each client to configure the client-side network libraries. If all of the SQL Servers on the network are going to be using IPX/SPX to connect, then choose IPX/SPX as the default protocol on the Net Library tab. Otherwise, follow the instructions in the preceding section, "Configuring Client-Side Network Libraries," for entering an exception by using Advanced tab. In the Connection String text box, enter the name of the SQL Server. It should be the same name as was entered when setting up the NWLink IPX/SPX network library on the server.

TCP/IP Support

TCP/IP is the primary protocol in use in large companies today. It scales well and is easy to route. By using the Dynamic Host Configuration Protocol (DHCP), it becomes very easy to allocate IP addresses to client computers, making network management much simpler (see fig. 10.6). TCP/IP uses a unique address for every computer. This address, the *IP address*, is four numbers, each greater than 0 but less than 256, which are separated by periods. An example of an IP address would be 192.3.2.1.

Figure 10.6

The TCP/IP Properties window on Windows NT 4.0. This computer was enabled for DHCP, so the network supplies it with an address.

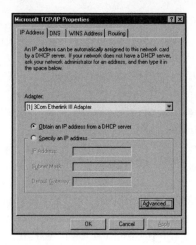

By using either the Window Internet Naming Service (WINS) or the Domain Naming Service (DNS), computer names can be attached to the IP addresses. These names are usually the "friendly" names of the servers, which usually correspond to the Windows NT Server names.

To install the TCP/IP services onto the SQL Server, follow the procedure outlined in the "Installing Server-Side Network Libraries" section and choose the TCP/IP Sockets option. The parameter for this library is the socket number. Save a lot of time and frustration by using the default socket number. A *socket number* is a number that specifies which service is being requested by a particular network request. For example, electronic mail services use a different socket than SQL Server does. The sockets are standardized by an international standards body to ensure that multiple socket numbers are not assigned to the same port. By using the default socket, the socket number does not usually have to be configured for any client software. The default socket for SQL Server is 1433. To see other socket numbers, look in the file \WINNT\SYSTEM32\DRIVERS\ETC\SERVICES.

In order to connect to a server from a client computer, it is important to know either the name or the IP address of the computer that is running SQL Server. If all of the SQL Servers on the network are going to be using TCP/IP sockets, then go to the Net Library tab and choose TCP/IP Sockets for the default protocol.

On the Advanced tab, enter the name of the server in the Server Name box, choose TCP/IP Sockets from the drop-down list, and type either the name of the server or the IP address for the server in the Connection String box. Note that the server name will be used by the client to access the server and is not necessarily related to the name of the server.

Banyan-VINES SPP Support

Support for the Banyan-VINES network on Windows NT is provided by Banyan. The protocol must be obtained from Banyan and installed according to their instructions. This provides access by Windows NT to the Banyan-VINES network.

After installing support for Banyan on the Windows NT computer, install the server-side network libraries for SQL Server. Follow the instructions given in the "Installing Server-Side Network Libraries" section and choose Banyan-VINES. The parameter for this network library is the PC-Based Service Name, which is laid out as ServiceName@Group@Org. Choose OK to save the choice and do not forget to stop and restart SQL Server to start the Banyan-VINES libraries.

Client-side setup is very similar to the client setup for Named Pipes. First, set up the client as a Banyan-VINES client and ensure that it can connect to Banyan-VINES servers. Follow the instructions provided by your network administrator to do this, and then configure the connection to SQL Server with the SQL Client Configuration Utility. Use the Net Library tab on the utility to set Banyan-VINES to be the default protocol if all of the SQL Servers will be using Banyan-VINES. Otherwise, use the Advanced tab. Put the name of the server in the Server Name box, choose Banyan-VINES from the drop-down list, and type the complete service name in the Connection String box.

AppleTalk ADSP

To use AppleTalk to enable Macintosh computers to connect to SQL Server, first install File Services for Macintosh on the

Windows NT computer. This will install enough of the AppleTalk protocol to be a server on the AppleTalk network. Installation is handled through the Control Panel in the Networks applet, just like installing any other network service.

In the server-side network libraries, use the instructions in the "Installing Server-Side Network Libraries" section. Check the box next to AppleTalk ADSP to enable the library. The parameter for the library is the AppleTalk Service Object Name, which is usually the server name. The zone is not specified because the local zone is always used.

Unfortunately, Microsoft does not supply ISQL/W for the Macintosh, so it is a little more difficult to experiment with the protocol on a Macintosh than the typical PC protocols. However, there is a protocol included with SQL Server to test the ADSP protocol setup. Copy the file DBMSADSN.DLL into the \MSSQL\DLL directory of another Windows NT Server on the network that is running Services for Macintosh. The SQL Client Configuration utility can then be used in the normal fashion to connect using ADSP—by selecting it on the Advanced tab. Do not attempt to use this method for connecting from ISQL/W on the computer running SQL Server because loopback connections are not supported with the library.

Support for DEC Net

The DECNet from DEC is supported very similarly to how Banyan-VINES is supported. First, install a DEC-supplied protocol stack onto the Windows NT computer. This protocol is a package that is usually available directly from Digital. Follow Digital's instructions for installation.

Follow the procedure outlined in the "Installing Server-Side Network Libraries" section and choose the DECNet Sockets option to install the server side of the network libraries. The server-side network library requires as a parameter a DECNet socket object ID. Socket IDs must be unique on a network, so be sure to check with the system administrator to find a unique socket identifier.

Also, any numeric socket IDs should be prefaced with the pound sign (#) to designate them as numeric sockets and not just a string of numbers.

The client side is configured like the other client-side libraries. Install and configure the client computer to use DECNet according to the standard on the network as provided by the network administrator. Use the Net Library tab on the utility to set DEC-Net Sockets to be the default protocol if all of the SQL Servers will be using DECNet Sockets. Otherwise, use the Advanced tab. Put the name of the server in the Server Name box, choose DECNet Sockets from the drop-down list, and type the complete Socket Object ID in the Connection String box.

That concludes the setup and details of the protocol-specific libraries. Now take a look at the protocol-independent libraries: Named Pipes and Multi-Protocol.

The Named Pipes and Multi-Protocol Libraries

The Named Pipes and Multi-Protocol libraries are a little different from the other server-side network libraries. They are not libraries that work with a specific protocol; rather, they work with established, non-protocol—specific network communications mechanisms. The Multi-Protocol library uses RPC to communicate between the client and the server, and Named Pipes uses SMB, or Server Message Blocks, for communications.

Both of these protocols rely on Windows NT to provide network security. All incoming connections must be validated against the Windows NT server, which means either every user must have a Windows NT account or the guest account should be enabled on the server. The reason is simple. The Named Pipes protocol is essentially using a file-like structure on the server for passing messages. The use of this type of a structure requires a server password. The RPC used by the Multi-Protocol library provides high security, including encrypted passwords. This is a very secure system, but requires the user to have a Windows NT account to handle some of the workings of security.

The Named Pipes protocol requires a parameter that is the name of the pipe to be used. By default, the pipe is \\.\PIPE\SQL\QUERY. The "\\." means to use the current computer. "\PIPE\SQL\QUERY" is the name of the pipe and can change.

The Multi-Protocol library is the simplest server-side library to configure. There is no parameter entry for the Multi-Protocol library. The Multi-Protocol library automatically works with IPX/SPX, TCP/IP, or NetBEUI protocols without any additional configuration.

That is the extent of the network protocol discussion. The network-specific protocols and the network-independent ones that use RPC were covered. Now it is time look at how SQL Server can interact with the operating system and the outside world using Extended Stored Procedures.

Installing Extended Stored Procedures

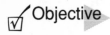

Extended stored procedures are calls from SQL Server into a dynamic link library on the server. These calls are normally used to do things that SQL Server cannot, such as running Windows NT commands, handling Windows NT security, or editing the registry.

Extended stored procedures are written with the SQL Server Open Data Services libraries. Most of the third-party extended stored procedures focus on connectivity between SQL Server and other database systems.

Installation of extended stored procedures is done with the sp_addextendedproc system stored procedure, which takes as arguments the function name and the name of the DLL file. To drop an extended stored procedure, use sp_dropextendedproc, which takes as its parameter the name of the stored procedure.

Both of these procedures affect the sysobjects and syscomments tables. Extended stored procedures should only be placed in the Master database. Extended stored procedures can only be added by the system administrator (sa).

To use an extended stored procedure, start a query window and type the following to return a directory listing of the current directory on your server, most likely the C:\WINNT\SYSTEM32 directory:

```
xp_cmdshell "dir"
```

You can add to this command line just like the dir command when used in the command shell.

To examine how extended stored procedures exist and how they can be rebuilt, use the sp_helpextendedproc stored procedure. When trying any of these experiments, use a stored procedure that isn't critical to operation of the server, such as the HTML generating stored procedures. Here's an example:

```
sp_helpextendedproc "xp_makewebtask"
```

To drop the extended stored procedure, use sp_dropexendedproc:

```
sp_dropextendedproc "xp_makewebtask"
```

To add the extended stored procedure back in, use the data from the sp_helpextendedproc executed earlier to get the name of the DLL; in this case the DLL is called XPSQLWEB.DLL. The command to put the procedure back follows:

```
sp_addextendedproc "xp_makewebtask", "XP_SQLWEB.DLL"
```

Thoroughly test all extended stored procedures prior to adding them to production servers. Keep in mind that extended stored procedures run as dynamically linked libraries and not as separate processes, which means that the extended stored procedures execute in the same memory space and with the same security context as SQL Server. SQL Server does keep close tabs on all extended stored procedures and watches for access violations. If an access violation occurs, SQL Server terminates the extended stored procedure. Access violation checking is a complex process and may result in some memory being accessed by the extended stored procedure that shouldn't be, which is why it is very important to test extended stored procedures thoroughly.

In addition, be aware of who can run the extended stored procedures. Extended stored procedures run in the security context of the server. If the stored procedure can create Windows NT user accounts, for example, then any user who can run the stored procedure automatically can create whatever user accounts the SQL Server service account can.

The only procedure that violates the rule of security contexts is the xp_cmdshell procedure, which has a special server option assigned to it, which is in the Server Options tab in SQL Enterprise Manger. The option is called Use SQLExecutiveCmdExec for Non SAs. If turned on, any user who is not a system administrator who has the ability to run xp_cmdshell can run it in the security context of the SQL Executive process instead of in the security context of SQL Server. The security on the SQL Executive service's account can then be properly adjusted so prying users cannot do things such as create administrator accounts.

To create an administrator account from the command line, type **net help user** at the Windows NT command prompt. It provides complete instructions for creating a user account from the command prompt.

Exercises

Exercise 10.1:   Installing the TCP/IP Sockets Library on the Server

The TCP/IP Sockets library is probably the most widely used library after Named Pipes and the Multi-Protocol library. Take a look at how the installation of TCP/IP Sockets is done. It is typical of how all the protocols are installed. This exercise should take about 15 minutes.

1. Start the Control Panel, Networks applet.

2. Check to see whether the TCP/IP protocol is installed. On Windows NT 3.51, it is listed in the large list box on the Networks applet. For Windows NT 4.0, it is listed on the Protocols tab of the applet.

3. If TCP/IP is not installed, install it. For Windows NT 3.51, choose Add Software, then add TCP/IP. Insert disks as instructed. For Windows NT 4.0, choose Add on the Protocols property sheet and add the TCP/IP protocol.

4. Configure the TCP/IP protocol. Choose an address that won't conflict with any other IP addresses on the network. Try to use a static address instead of a DHCP-assigned address.

5. After rebooting, open a command prompt. Run IPCONFIG to determine the network address of the server. Write this down.

6. Start SQL Setup. Choose Continue until you get to the Microsoft SQL Server 6.5 - Options dialog box.

7. Choose Change Network Support and click on Continue.

8. Check the check box next to TCP/IP Sockets to select it.

9. Click on OK to continue.

continues

10. SQL Setup prompts you for the Named Pipe name if Named Pipes is still chosen as a network library. Choose Continue to accept the default.

11. SQL Setup prompts for the TCP/IP Socket Number. Choose Continue to accept 1433, the default socket number.

12. SQL Setup installs the chosen network library, then informs you that you must restart SQL Server for the changes to take effect.

13. Start the SQL Service Manager. Stop SQL Server if it is running, wait a few seconds, then start it again. Close the SQL Service Manager.

For more information, check the section "Installing Server-Side Network Libraries."

Exercise 10.2: Installing Support for TCP/IP Sockets on a Client

This exercise can either be done on the SQL Server or on another computer on the network. This exercise assumes that TCP/IP is installed on the computer being used as a client. The client computer should be running either 16-bit Windows, Windows 95, or Windows NT. This exercise also assumes that the client software for SQL Server has already been installed. If it has not, it can be installed by running the Setup program in the \i386 directory on the CD-ROM for 32-bit Windows clients, or the Setup program in the \CLIENT directory for 16-bit Windows users. This exercise should take about 25 minutes.

1. Start a command prompt.

2. "Ping" the address of the SQL Server by typing **Ping**, followed by the IP address, which was noted in step 5 in the preceding exercise. The result should be four ping responses, each with timing information. If you get either a "Host Unreachable" or "Bad IP address" message, TCP/IP is most likely not configured correctly on the client.

3. Start the SQL Client Configuration Utility on the client computer.

4. Choose the Advanced tab.

5. Type the name of the server in the Server Name box. The name doesn't actually have to be the same as that of the server; it is what you want to use when referencing the server on this particular client computer.

6. Choose TCP/IP Sockets from the DLL Name drop-down list.

7. Type the IP address of the server into the Connection String field.

8. Click the Add/Remove button to commit the changes.

9. Start ISQL/W on the client computer.

10. Type the server name entered in step 5.

11. Put in sa for the login id.

12. Put in the password if necessary.

13. Click on the Connect button to connect ISQL/W to the server.

14. Assuming the connection succeeded, you are presented with a query window for the master database on your server.

15. If the connection did not succeed, check the IP address on the server and in the SQL Client Configuration Utility.

For more information on this exercise, see the section "Set Up Support for Network Clients by Using Various Network Protocols."

Exercise 10.3: Extended Stored Procedures

In this exercise, you will examine, drop, and rebuild an extended stored procedure. You will use the xp_makewebtask extended stored procedure. If the server you use for the exercise uses the

continues

Exercise 10.3: Continued

HTML-generation utilities that come with SQL Server, you may want to double-check your backup of the Master database or choose a different stored procedure for this exercise. This exercise should take about 10 minutes.

1. Open a SQL Query Tool and connect to your server.

2. Verify that the Master database has been selected.

3. Use the following stored procedure to retrieve a list of the available extended stored procedures:

```
sp_helpextendedproc "xp_makewebtask"
```

This returns the name of the extended procedure and the name of the DLL it uses.

4. Execute the following query to see the extended stored procedures in the sysobjects table:

```
select * from sysobjects where type = "X"
```

This should return a list of names and other information about all of the extended stored procedures, but it does not return the names of the DLL files involved with the extended stored procedures.

5. Use the following command to drop the extended stored procedure:

```
xp_dropextendedproc "xp_makewebtask"
```

6. Use the following command to bring the extended stored procedure back:

```
xp_addextendedproc "xp_makewebtask", "xpsqlweb.dll"
```

For more information, see the section "Installing Extended Stored Procedures."

Review Questions

The following questions test your knowledge of the information in this chapter.

1. Which of the following is true about client-side network libraries?

    A. They form the entire protocol stack for the client computer.

    B. They sit between the SQL Server client software and the network protocols.

    C. The TCP/IP protocol must be loaded for SQL Server to function properly.

    D. Directory or name services are required on the network for the client libraries to be configured properly.

2. What is the Advanced tab on the SQL Client Configuration Utility used to do?

    A. Configure the local workstation's TCP/IP address.

    B. Override default network library settings.

    C. Create specific settings for different servers.

    D. Configure the network library to run under IPX/SPX.

3. Abby's SQL Server is running on a network with Novell Netware servers and clients. She has configured the NWLink IPX/SPX protocol on the server and installed the appropriate network libraries, but the clients still cannot connect to her server. What is the most likely problem?

    A. The network is down.

    B. A router is not configured properly to pass NetBEUI traffic.

    C. SQL Server and Windows NT cannot run on Novell networks.

    D. The Gateway Services for Netware service is not loaded.

4. Joey has a SQL Server that is participating in a network with both Windows-based PC clients and Macintosh systems. He wants to provide Appletalk access to his Macintosh computers and also TCP/IP connectivity to the PC clients. Which of the following does *not* have to be loaded to provide this support?

   A. File Services for Macintosh

   B. TCP/IP protocol for Windows NT

   C. TCP/IP Network Library

   D. Multi-Protocol Network Library

5. The Multi-Protocol network library has which two of the following features?

   A. Encrypted passwords

   B. Communications through named pipes

   C. Addressable network protocol socket switching

   D. Uses Remote Procedure Calls to transfer data

6. Extended stored procedures are what? (Choose two.)

   A. Stored procedures that use an extended command set

   B. Links into DLL files

   C. Used to drop and create tables

   D. Used to integrate with the operating system and other third-party products

7. Extended stored procedures are linked when using which of the following methods?

    A. Editing system tables

    B. Using the sp_addextendedproc stored procedure

    C. Using the Create Extended Procedure command

    D. Extended stored procedures cannot be added, only procedures that come with SQL Server are allowed

8. The Named Pipes server-side network library uses which communications mechanism to transfer data?

    A. Remote Procedure Calls

    B. TCP/IP Sockets

    C. NetBEUI Sockets

    D. Server Message Blocks

9. Which of the following is used to add server-side network libraries?

    A. The SQL Setup program

    B. The SQL Server Configuration Utility

    C. The sp_addserverlibrary stored procedure

    D. The Windows NT Network Control Panel

10. After installing a new network library, which of the following must take place?

    A. The server computer must be rebooted.

    B. The SQL Server has to be stopped and restarted.

    C. The network components on the server have to stop and restart.

    D. The SQL Executive must stop and be restarted.

Review Answers

1. B

2. C

3. D

4. D

5. A, D

6. B, D

7. B

8. D

9. A

10. B

Answers to Test Yourself Questions at Beginning of the Chapter

1. Josie should use the IPX/SPX network library. Although the Named Pipes or Multi-Protocol libraries would also work, they would require Windows NT accounts in addition to SQL Server logins. See the section "IPX/SPX Support" for more information.

2. Mark should definitely use the Multi-Protocol network library. Integrated security means everyone will already have a Windows NT account, so it is not a problem. See the section "The Named Pipes and Multi-Protocol Libraries" for more details.

3. The Connection String field for TCP/IP sockets is the TCP/IP address of the SQL Server computer. See the section titled "TCP/IP Support" for more information.

4. Extended stored procedures are executed in the process space of the SQL Server, and the SQL Server monitors them to prevent access violations and shuts down the stored procedure if there is a problem. For more information, see the section "Installing Extended Stored Procedures."

Chapter 11

Tuning and Monitoring

This chapter discusses various options available to the system administrator for tuning and monitoring SQL Server. The administrator can monitor the system to determine problem areas, record benchmarks, and evaluate trends. From this, a course of action can be determined. Once it is implemented, new benchmarks can be taken to compare to the old benchmarks. If the difference in benchmarks does not provide the desired result(s), another course can be determined.

An improperly tuned SQL Server can become a burden to the server, the network, and its users. It can also affect the performance of other applications residing on the same server. Tuning enables the administrator to configure SQL Server to be optimized for the environment in which it resides, as well as for the work it must perform. The environment includes the network, and the server on which it is installed. The work it must perform is determined by the applications that require its services.

As always, this chapter begins with a list of the exam objectives relating to the topic at hand, and then moves on to the chapter pretest. Next, it offers valuable information that directly addresses the exam objectives, and includes additional related discussion topics. The chapter concludes with exercises, chapter review questions, and answers to both the chapter review questions and the chapter pretest questions.

This chapter focuses on tuning and monitoring SQL Server, and helps you prepare for the exam by addressing and fully covering the following objectives:

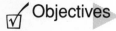 **Objectives**

▶ Identify the benefits of installing TempDB database in RAM

▶ Configure the number of worker threads

▶ Select the appropriate settings for read ahead

▶ Select the appropriate settings for locks

▶ Monitor log size

▶ Tune and monitor physical and logical I/O

▶ Tune and monitoring memory use

▶ Set database options

▶ Update statistics

Test Yourself! Before reading this chapter, test yourself to determine how much study time you will need to devote to this section.

1. What is the proper syntax for configuring memory to 8 MB?

2. How much memory is allocated to SQL Server during installation on a machine with 64 MB of RAM?

3. What is the proper syntax for configuring TempDB to run in 2 MB of RAM?

4. What command would you use to optimize an index on a table?

5. What is the default value assigned to the procedure cache configuration option?

Answers are located at the end of the chapter...

Identifying the Benefits of Installing TempDB in RAM

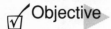 **Objective** *TempDB* is a temporary storage area that SQL Server sets aside for the creation of work tables and temporary tables. SQL Server creates work tables in TempDB when it needs intermediate results, such as when an ORDER BY or GROUP BY is requested. Developers can create temporary tables in TempDB for purposes such as reducing the number of joins in a query, or to hold the results of a query that will be added to or used by another query.

New with SQL Server v 4.2 is the capability to store TempDB in RAM. With this new feature, the entire size of TempDB is allocated in RAM when SQL Server is started, and so any tables created in TempDB are readily available for use. This can greatly improve the speed with which SQL Server can process queries requiring work tables, as well as the speed of stored procedures which create and use temporary tables.

Place TempDB in RAM by using either Enterprise Manager's Server Configuration/Options window or the following sp_configure syntax executed from an ISQL session.

```
sp_configure "tempdb in RAM", 2
```

This installs a 2 MB TempDB in RAM.

The caveat here is that the space needed for TempDB must be available at the time SQL Server is started; if the memory is not available, SQL Server will not start. A problem like this will most likely arise only on a machine that is not fully dedicated to SQL Server. If the machine is not dedicated, when SQL Server is shut down and then brought back up, other processes on that server may have snatched up the additional memory that is needed for TempDB. If you encounter this situation, you must shut down the offending process before you restart SQL Server.

Note TempDB has a default install size of 2 MB. This space or any other space is defined for your TempDB will not be a part of the memory allocated for SQL Server. It will take memory away from NT, and therefore may cause a degradation in performance for NT and/or other processes on that server. For a further discussion on how SQL Server uses memory, see the section on "Tuning and Monitoring Memory Use" later in this chapter.

Configuring the Number of Worker Threads

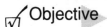**Objective** *Worker threads* refers to the threads, an independent unit of work, available to SQL Server to handle user requests. If the number of user connections is less than the number of worker threads, each user connection gets its own thread. At the point that the number of user connections surpasses the number of worker threads, thread pooling occurs, and the next thread to complete its task is assigned multiple user connections to service. The user connections sharing a thread may notice decreased throughput. The users continue to share threads until the number of user connections drops below the maximum worker thread count.

Note When all the worker threads are in use and thread pooling begins, SQL Server writes a message to the error log stating that the worker thread limit has been reached.

The maximum number of worker threads available to SQL Server is configurable using the sp_configure option "max worker threads." Note that this option defaults to 255, with a minimum value of 10 and a maximum value of 1024. You should configure the max worker threads option to allow one thread per user connection. The syntax resembles the following:

```
sp_configure "max worker threads", 300
```

Selecting the Appropriate Settings for Read Ahead

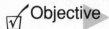 Objective

Read Ahead technology began with SQL Server 6.0, and is also referred to as Asynchronous Read Ahead, RA, and Parallel Data Scan. In short, Read Ahead attempts to provide the data needed by the query before SQL Server looks for the data. Read Ahead is capable of performing this service for large queries and table scans because when data is being read in sequentially, Read Ahead can predict which data the query requires next. The Read Ahead Manager can be configured to optimize the role it plays on the server. The following is a list of the configuration options available for the Read Ahead Manager:

▶ RA Cache Hit Limit

▶ RA Cache Miss Limit

▶ RA Delay

▶ RA Pre-fetches

▶ RA Slots per Thread

▶ RA Worker Threads

Use the command sp_configure to change these options, as shown in the following example:

```
sp_configure "RA cache hit limit", 200
```

RA Cache Hit Limit

The *RA cache hit limit* is the number of times the Read Ahead Manager finds the data needed in the cache. After the specified number of hits, the read ahead request is canceled because it is not needed. The default value for RA cache hit limit is 4. The minimum value is 1, and the maximum is 255. You should not need to change this value from the default unless your Primary Support Provider suggests the use of another value.

RA Cache Miss Limit

The *RA cache miss limit* is the number of times the query does not find the data it needs in the data cache. At that point, a read ahead request is made. If this value is set to 1, a Read Ahead request is made every time data is read from disk, leading to poor system performance. The default value is 3, the minimum value is 1, and the maximum is 255. You should not need to change this value from the default unless your Primary Support Provider suggests the use of another value.

RA Delay

The *RA delay* is the time in milliseconds that the read ahead process is delayed after the initial request. This delay is used to prepare the RA Manager. The default value is 15, the minimum is 0, and the maximum is 5000. Use the default value on Symmetric Multiprocessor (SMP) machines.

RA Pre-fetches

The *RA pre-fetch* value specifies how many extents (8 pages) the RA Manager reads before it becomes idle. The default value is 3, with a minimum value of 1, and a maximum of 1,000.

RA Slots per Thread

The *RA slots per thread* value represents the number of slots per thread that RA Manager manages. Each Read Ahead request is assigned to a slot in a thread. The default value is 5, the minimum value is 1, and the maximum is 255.

RA Worker Threads

The *RA worker threads* value represents the available number of threads for Read Ahead Manager. The number of slots multiplied by the number of threads represents the total number of requests RA Manager can handle. A message is written to the error log if the number of requests exceeds the number of configured slots. The default for RA worker threads is 3, the minimum is 0, and the maximum is 255.

An Example of the Read Ahead Process

With the available options in mind, it's time to step through the process by taking a look at the following example:

A client makes a large sequential request, and SQL Server looks at the data cache to try to satisfy the request. If the data isn't there, it has to be retrieved from disk, which counts as a cache miss. SQL Server then looks to the data cache again for the next bit of information. If it's not there again and the server has to perform disk I/O to retrieve it, that counts as another cache miss. When the number of cache misses equals the configured parameter RA cache miss limit, a request is made to the Read Ahead Manager. The Read Ahead Manager then assigns the task to the next available slot in the next available thread. If all the slots are being used, a message is written to the error log stating the condition. Otherwise, the assigned slot reads in an extent to the data cache. The RA pre-fetch value is checked. Once this value is met by the slot, the Read Ahead Manager becomes idle until it is needed again.

Selecting the Appropriate Settings for Locks

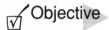

SQL Server issues *locks* to prevent users from interfering with each others' work, and there are several types of locks. A *shared lock* is usually acquired by read operations. Write operations use *exclusive locks*. An *update lock* is like a shared lock and is used during the first part of an update while information is being read in. If a lock is held on a series of 8 pages, that is an extent lock. *Extent locks* are used during CREATE, DROP, and some INSERT and UPDATE operations. An *intent lock* specifies the intent to gain a shared or exclusive lock.

Locks can be viewed by using either the command sp_locks or the SQL Server tool Enterprise Manager. In Enterprise Manager, the Current Activity window, shown in figure 11.1, is used to display a list of the current connections to SQL Server. The information displayed includes who is connected, which database they are connected to, the activity in progress (INSERT, SELECT, and so on), the type of lock being used, and any blocking that occurs.

Figure 11.1

The Current Activity window of Enterprise Manager.

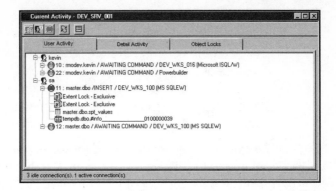

SQL Server returns an error message if you run out of available locks. If this occurs, you can configure the number of available locks by using sp_configure with the locks option. The minimum is 5000 (also the default) and the maximum is 214748364. The syntax resembles the following:

```
sp_configure locks, 10000
```

If your only concern were ensuring that the system never ran out of locks, you would want to use the maximum value available. However, each configured lock, used or not, comes with a penalty of 32 bytes of SQL Server memory consumed. Therefore, if you must significantly increase the number of locks available for your SQL Server, you may also need to increase the amount of memory allocated for SQL Server.

Monitoring Log Size

Objective

The *transaction log* is used to hold uncommitted actions on the database. When a checkpoint or truncate is issued on the transaction log, all committed transactions up to the first uncommitted transaction are removed from the log, freeing up space for more transactions.

Note

If a transaction is left uncommitted for an extended period of time, this could cause the transaction log to fill up. All committed transactions up to this open transaction would be removed by a checkpoint, but the log would continue to fill up

continues

after the checkpoint. So, even if all the other transactions in the log were committed, a checkpoint would not be able to remove any of the committed transactions until this open transaction was committed. Thus, it is important to make sure that all transactions are either committed or rolled back.

You can use Performance Monitor to keep track of the use of the transaction log. There are two counters that can be used to monitor the SQLServer-Log object: Log Size (MB) and Log Space Used (%). Performance Monitor provides a graphical representation of these counters for the transaction log (see fig. 11.2).

Figure 11.2

The Performance Monitor.

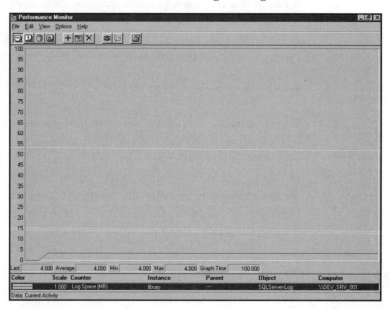

You can also use Performance Monitor to set up an alert when the transaction log reaches a certain percentage. Add an alert by means of the Add to Alert dialog box. Choose the SQLServer-Log object and Log Space Used (%) counter. Decide the level at which you would like to see the alert, and what program you would like to have run when the alert occurs.

Alternately, the system stored procedure sp_spaceused with syslogs as the object name (sp_spaceused syslogs) can be used to obtain the space allocated for syslogs as well as the space currently being used.

In addition, the command DBCC OPENTRAN returns information on the oldest open transaction in the log. This could be an uncommitted transaction, a runaway process, and so on. If necessary, use the SPID (process ID) returned from this command to KILL the offending transaction.

Other DBCC commands that provide similar information are DBCC CHECKTABLE (SYSLOGS) and DBCC SQLPERF (LOGSPACE).

Tuning and Monitoring Physical and Logical I/O

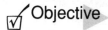 Objective

As a rule, you want to minimize you physical I/O (read/writes to disk), and maximize your logical I/O (read/writes to memory), for the simple reason that accessing memory is much quicker than accessing a disk. For the purpose of providing quicker query response, SQL Server makes use of two caches: the procedure cache, and the data cache. It also provides the administrator with counters that can be monitored by means of the Performance Monitor. These counters, which are discussed below, enable the administrator to obtain an idea of how much physical I/O is being performed versus logical I/O.

Physical I/O

Physical I/O refers to disk input and output performed. Use Performance Monitor to view the amount of disk I/O being performed.

 Note

diskperf -y must be run before you can obtain any disk performance information. You will also need to restart the server.

In Performance Monitor, the counters PhysicalDisk: % Disk Time and PhysicalDisk: Disk Queue Length provide a graphical representation of the disk I/O being performed:

▶ **PhysicalDisk: % Disk Time.** Refers to the percentage of time that is being spent accessing the disk.

▶ **PhysicalDisk: Disk Queue Length.** Shows the number of I/O operations that are waiting to be performed.

The amount of disk I/O performance can be adjusted by using one or more of the following techniques to bring more of the data into memory before it is needed:

▶ Adjust the configuration for Asynchronous Read Ahead. (Refer to "Selecting the Appropriate Settings for Read Ahead" earlier in this chapter.)

▶ Adjust the amount of memory available to SQL Server for the data cache and procedure cache. (See "Logical I/O.")

▶ Place TempDB in RAM. (Refer to "Identifying the Benefits of Installing the TempDB in RAM" earlier in this chapter.)

▶ Obtain faster or higher-quality disk/disk controllers.

Logical I/O

Logical I/O refers to accessing information already in memory. SQL Server keeps two kinds of caches:

▶ Data cache

▶ Procedure cache

Data Cache

The *data cache* holds the data that SQL Server reads when it performs disk I/O. When a command is issued to the server, such as a SELECT statement, SQL Server looks at the data cache first to see whether the information needed to satisfy the query is already there. If not, SQL Server must read it in from disk. The larger the data cache, the better the chance that it contains the necessary data. Use Performance Monitor to determine if the size of the data cache is appropriate by means of the following three counters:

- ▶ SQLServer: Cache Hit Radio

- ▶ SQLServer: I/O - Lazy Writes

- ▶ Memory: Page Faults/sec

The *SQLServer: Cache Hit Radio* counter represents the percentage of time that the data SQL Server needed was found in the data cache. You want to make sure that this number stays consistently high (greater than 85 percent). If it does not, the data cache is probably too small. You can allocate more memory to SQL Server, which in turn causes the data cache to have more memory.

The *SQLServer: I/O - Lazy Writes* counter is used to view the number of pages per second that the Lazy Writer has to move out to disk. Optimally, this counter hovers at 0. Otherwise, the Lazy Writer is performing too much disk I/O, which indicates that the data cache is too small.

A *page fault* occurs when a virtual page is not found in memory and must be retrieved from disk. The *Memory: Page Faults/sec* counter displays the number of times this occurs per second. If this counter is greater than 0 a good portion of the time, Windows NT does not have enough memory allocated for the page. You can approach this problem in one of several ways: take the memory from SQL Server, which takes it from the data cache and procedure cache, or move some of the other processes to another server.

Procedure Cache

The *procedure cache* is an area of SQL Server memory used to hold trees and query plans that have recently been used or are currently in use by SQL Server. If a user requests that a stored procedure be executed, SQL Server looks at the procedure cache to see if the procedure is already available in memory. If it is already in use by another user, SQL Server must create another instance of the procedure in the procedure buffer, which holds the actual instructions. If the procedure is not found in the procedure cache, however, SQL Server must retrieve it from the disk.

You can configure the size of the procedure cache by means of the Procedure Cache Configuration option with sp_configure. This specifies the percentage of SQL Server memory that the procedure cache should use. The default is 30 percent, the minimum is 1, and the maximum is 99. Note that when a greater percentage of memory is allocated for the procedure cache, the memory is taken from the data cache. So, unless the data cache is too large, more memory should be allocated to SQL Server as a whole at the same time as the procedure cache size is adjusted. Microsoft recommends the following calculation for determining the appropriate size for the procedure cache:

Procedure Cache = (Maximum Concurrent Users) × (Size of Largest Plan) × 1.25

The following counters for the SQLServer-Procedure Cache object are helpful in determining the appropriate size of the procedure cache, and can be viewed using Performance Monitor:

▶ **Max Procedure Buffers Active %.** This counter indicates the percentage of buffers that were active at least once during the monitored time span.

▶ **Procedure Buffers Active %.** This counter indicates the percentage of buffers that are currently active.

▶ **Max Procedure Buffers Used %.** This counter indicates the percentage of buffers that were used during the monitored time span.

▶ **Procedure Buffers Used %.** This counter indicates the percentage of buffers that are currently active.

▶ **Max Procedure Cache Active %.** This counter indicates the percentage of the procedure cache that was active at least once during the monitored time span.

▶ **Procedure Cache Active %.** This counter indicates the percentage of the procedure cache that is currently active.

▶ **Max Procedure Cache Used %.** This counter indicates the percentage of the procedure cache that was used during the monitored time span.

▶ **Procedure Cache Used %.** This counter indicates the percentage of the procedure cache that is currently used.

▶ **Procedure Cache Size.** This counter indicates the current size of the procedure cache. If other SQL Server processes need the slots allocated for the procedure cache, the cache may shrink.

Tuning and Monitoring Memory Use

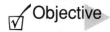

SQL Server requires a portion of the memory from the server on which it is installed. It uses this memory to hold the procedure cache, data cache, and overhead. The *overhead* includes locks, user connections, and code. SQL Server takes what is needed from the memory pool to satisfy its overhead. After that, the value in the configuration option "procedure cache" is used to determine the size of the procedure cache. If the value is 30 (the default), for example, 30 percent of the remaining SQL Server memory is allocated for the procedure cache. The remaining memory is then used for the data cache.

When it is installed on the server, SQL Server is allocated a certain amount of memory. If the server has 32 MB or more of memory, SQL Server is initially given 16 MB. If the server has less than 32 MB, SQL Server is given 8 MB. Use the counters in Performance Monitor to determine if the allocated memory is appropriate. Note that DBCC MEMUSAGE can also provide valuable insight. If necessary, use sp_configure or Enterprise Manager to configure the amount of memory allocated to SQL Server.

Using Performance Monitor to Monitor Memory Use

Certain counters in Performance Monitor are helpful in determining the correct setting for SQL Server memory:

▶ **SQLServer: Cache Hit Ratio.** This counter represents the percentage of time that the data SQL Server needed was found in the data cache. You want make sure this number stays consistently high (greater than 85 percent). If it does not, the data cache is probably too small. You can allocate more memory to SQL Server, which in turn causes the data cache to have more memory.

▶ **SQLServer: I/O - Lazy Writes.** This counter is used to view the number of pages per second that the Lazy Writer has to move out to disk. Optimally, this counter should hover at 0. Otherwise, the Lazy Writer is performing too much disk I/O, indicating that the data cache is too small.

▶ **SQLServer: I/O - Page Reads/sec.** This is the total number of physical page reads performed in a second. Physical reads consume much more time than logical reads. If this number is consistently high, you may benefit from increasing the size of the data cache by increasing total memory for SQL Server, or by lowering the procedure cache percentage.

▶ **Memory: Page Faults/sec.** A page fault occurs when a virtual page is not found in memory and must be retrieved from disk. This counter displays the number of times this occurs per second. If this counter is greater than 0 a good portion of the time, Windows NT does not have enough memory allocated for the page. The needed memory may be taken from SQL Server, which takes it from the data cache and procedure cache. Alternately, move some of the processes on the server to another server.

Using DBCC MEMUSAGE to View Memory Information

Issue the command DBCC MEMUSAGE to obtain information on memory usage for SQL Server. DBCC MEMUSAGE returns a report of the following information:

▶ Configured memory size

▶ Overhead size

▶ Top 20 items in the data cache

▶ Top 20 items in the procedure cache

The overhead is broken down into certain factors such as locks, connections, and code. The information provided for the procedure cache includes the number and size of query plans and trees currently stored.

Configuring Memory Size Using sp_configure

The amount of memory allocated to SQL Server is configured by means of the "memory" configuration option for the system stored procedure sp_configure. Memory is specified in 2 K pages. The new memory value does not take effect until the server is shut down and restarted.

Configuring Memory Size Using Enterprise Manager

Enterprise Manager can be used to configure memory through a GUI interface. The Configuration option on the Server menu causes the Server Configuration/Options window to open. The Configuration tab displays all the configuration options with the minimum, maximum, running, and current values. You can use the current value column to set the value to be assigned to the configuration option. Some options take effect when OK or Apply is clicked, and some do not change until the server is shut down and restarted.

Here, you can change the memory value to the desired number of 2 K pages. Click OK and the Server Configuration/Option window disappears. The server needs to be shut down and restarted for this value to take effect. Use the Stop/Pause/Start Server button to perform this task.

Setting Database Options

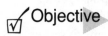 SQL Server database options effect the way in which SQL Server operates in its environment, and how it handles its workload. These options include variables such as the amount of memory allocated to SQL Server, the number of user connections

permitted, and the amount of time SQL Server waits for a connection to a remote server. SQL Server database options can be set by using either the sp_configure command or Enterprise Manager.

Changing Configuration Values Using sp_configure

sp_configure can be used from an ISQL session and has the following syntax:

```
sp_configure ['config name'][,config value]
```

If no configuration name is specified, a list of the current values for each option is displayed. If you specify a configuration name, the current value for that option is displayed. If both parameters are supplied, the configuration option is changed to the new configuration value. Any user can run sp_configure with zero or one parameter, but only system administrators can run it with both parameters.

Following a value change using sp_configure, the RECONFIGURE command must be executed for the change to take place. The RECONFIGURE command has the following syntax:

RECONFIGURE [WITH OVERRIDE]

The WITH OVERRIDE is necessary only if the Allow Updates configuration value is changed to 1.

Changing Configuration Values Using Enterprise Manager

Enterprise Manager supplies a GUI interface for viewing and updating configuration values. Inside Enterprise Manager, choose Configuration from the Server menu to display the Server Configuration/Options window, shown in figure 11.3. From here, use the current value column to change a configuration option value. If the option is dynamic, the value takes immediate effect when either Apply or OK is clicked. *Dynamic* in this sense means that the server does not have to be shut down and restarted in order for the value to take effect.

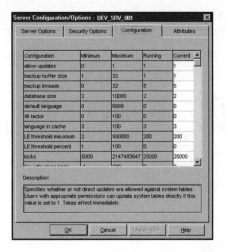

Figure 11.3

The Server Con-figuration/Options window.

When SQL Server is installed, each option is configured to its default value. Normally, you would not want to change the default values unless, through monitoring your SQL Server, you determine that a change to one or more options is necessary in order to obtain your SQL Server's desired level of performance.

Configuration Options

Table 11.1 illustrates the configuration names and their minimum, maximum, and default values. In the first column of the table, the padlock icon signifies advanced options, which are those options that are displayed only when the Show Advanced option is set to 1. The running man icon in the same column marks those options that are dynamic. The word NEW in this column indicates which options are new with SQL Server 6.5.

Table 11.1

	Configuration Name	Minimum	Maximum	Default
NEW	Affinity Mask	0	2147483647	0
	Allow Updates	0	1	0
	Backup Buffer Size	1	10	1

continues

Table 11.1 Continued

Configuration Name	Minimum	Maximum	Default
Backup Threads	0	32	5
Cursor Threshold	-1	2147483647	100
Database Size	1	10000	2
Default Language	0	9999	0
Default Sortorder ID	0	255	52
Fill Factor	0	100	0
Free Buffers	20	524288	204
Hash Buckets	4999	265003	7993
Language in Cache	3	100	3
LE Threshold Maximum	2	500000	200
LE Threshold Minimum	2	500000	20
LE Threshold Percent	1	100	0
Locks	5000	2147483647	5000
Logwrite Sleep (ms)	-1	500	0
Max Async IO	1	255	8
Max Lazywrite IO	1	255	8
Max Text Repl Size	0	2147483647	65536
Max Worker Threads	10	1024	255
Media Retention	0	365	0
Memory	1000	1048576	4096
Nested Triggers	0	1	1

	Configuration Name	Minimum	Maximum	Default
	Network Packet Size	512	32767	4096
	Open Databases	5	32767	20
	Open Objects	100	2147483647	500
	Priority Boost	0	1	0
	Procedure Cache	1	99	30
	RA Cache Hit Limit	1	255	4
	RA Cache Miss Limit	1	255	3
	RA Delay	0	500	15
	RA Pre-Fetches	1	1000	3
	RA Slots per Thread	1	255	5
	RA Worker Threads	0	255	3
	Recovery Flags	0	1	0
	Recovery Interval	1	32767	5
	Remote Access	0	1	1
NEW	Remote Conn Timeout	-1	32767	10
	Remote Login Timeout	0	2147483647	5
NEW	Remote Proc Trans	0	1	0
	Remote Query Timeout	0	2147483647	0
	Resource Timeout	-1	2147483647	100
	Set Working Set Size	0	1	0
	Show Advanced Option	0	1	1

continues

Table 11.1   Continued

	Configuration Name	Minimum	Maximum	Default
	SMP Concurrency	-1	64	1
 	Sort Pages	64	511	64
 	Spin Counter	1	2147483647	10
	TempDB in Ram (MB)	0	2044	0
	User Connections	5	32767	20
NEW	User Options	0	4095	0

 = Advanced option    = Dynamic option   NEW = New with 6.5

Affinity Mask

The affinity mask value specifies which processors are used by the SMP SQL Server. It is a bit mask where each "on" bit represents the processor to be used. The processor numbering starts at 0, and the first bit represents processor 0.

Allow Updates

When set to 1, this option allows changes to the system tables in the Master database. Changes to the Master database should not be made directly, but rather through system stored procedures. However, if you need to make a change, do so very carefully. If you make an invalid change, SQL Server may not start.

Backup Buffer Size

This option specifies the number of 32 page sets to use as a buffer for database dump and load operations.

Backup Threads

This is the number of threads used during database dump and load operations that involve parallel striping.

Cursor Threshold

This number is used to determine if the keyset for a query should be generated synchronously or asynchronously. The server estimate the size of the result set and checks it against this value. If the value is greater than the estimate, the keyset is generated synchronously; otherwise, it is generated asynchronously. Note that it is faster to generate small result sets synchronously.

Database Size

This is the size (in megabytes) used to create a new database when the size is not specified in the CREATE statement.

Default Language

This is the ID of the default language for SQL Server. U.S. English is 0.

Default Sortorder ID

This is the ID of the sort order set up as the system default.

Fill Factor

This is the percentage of fullness of each page when SQL Server creates an index on a table containing data, unless a different percentage is specified in the CREATE INDEX statement. The default value of 0 means that full pages are created, but it is not the same as a fill factor of 100. A fill factor of 100 should only be used on read-only tables.

Free Buffers

Free buffers is the number of buffers Lazy Writer should keep available for use by SQL Server. This value is automatically reconfigured each time the amount of memory allocated to SQL Server changes, and represents five percent of the memory.

Hash Buckets

This is the number of buckets to use for hashing pages. If the number specified is not a primary number, the closest primary number is used.

Language in Cache

This is the maximum number of languages to be stored in the language cache.

LE Threshold Maximum

This is the maximum number of page locks that can be held before the lock becomes a table lock. This is referred to as Lock Escalation.

LE Threshold Minimum

This is the minimum number of page locks that have to be held before a table lock occurs. A table lock does not occur in this case until the LE threshold percent is also exceeded.

LE Threshold Percent

This is the percentage of page locks that have to occur before a table lock is issued. This is a percentage of page locks versus pages on a table.

Locks

This is the maximum number of locks that can be held at any one time. Note that each configured lock uses 32 K of memory whether it is needed or not.

Logwrite Sleep (ms)

This is the time in milliseconds that the logwrite waits to write to the log. This is set to allow time for more information to gather in the buffer so that fewer writes need to be processed.

Max Async IO

This is the maximum number of asynchronous I/O operations at any one time.

Max Lazywrite IO

This is the maximum number of I/O operations that can be performed by the Lazy Writer at any one time. It cannot be configured greater than max async IO.

Max Text Repl Size

This specifies the maximum size of any data added to a text or image column that is being replicated.

Max Worker Threads

This specifies the number of threads to make available to SQL Server. When there are more connections than threads, a single thread handles the requests of multiple connections. This is referred to as thread pooling.

Media Retention

This is the number of days you plan to retain a backup. If the number specified is greater than zero, SQL Server issues a warning if you attempt to reuse a media within the specified number of days.

Memory

This is the size, in 2 K pages, of memory allocated for SQL Server.

Nested Triggers

This option, when set to 1, enables the nesting of triggers.

Network Packet Size

This is the default size to use for network packets.

Open Databases

This specifies the maximum number of databases that can be open at a time.

Open Objects

This specifies the maximum number of objects that can be open at a time.

Priority Boost

When this option is set to 1, SQL Server has a higher priority than other processes on the server.

Procedure Cache

This is the percentage of memory allocated to SQL Server that is allocated for the procedure cache. The amount of memory given to procedure cache is calculated once SQL Server takes the memory it needs for overhead such as code, locks, and , (comma) connections. The size of the allocated memory can fluctuate if SQL Server needs more room for overhead.

RA Cache Hit Limit

This limit is the number of times the Read Ahead Manager finds the data needed in the cache. After the specified number of hits, the read ahead request is canceled because it is not needed.

RA Cache Miss Limit

The RA cache miss limit is the number of times the query does not find the data it needs in the data cache. At that point, a Read Ahead request is made. If this value is set to 1, a Read Ahead request is made every time data is read from disk. This condition leads to poor system performance.

RA Delay

This is the time in milliseconds that the read ahead process is delayed from the initial request. This delay is used to prepare the RA Manager.

RA Pre-Fetches

This value specifies how many extents (8 pages) the RA Manager reads before it becomes idle.

RA Slots per Thread

This value is the number of slots per thread that RA Manager manages. Each read ahead request is assigned to a slot in a thread.

RA Worker Threads

This number represents the available number of threads for Read Ahead Manager. The number of slots multiplied by the number of threads represents the total number of requests RA Manager can handle. A message is written to the error log if the number of requests exceeds the number of configured slots.

Recovery Flags

If this value is 0 only minimal messages are written to the error log during recovery. The message informs you of the database name and that the recovery is taking place. If this value is one, information about each transaction and its status is recorded.

Recovery Interval

This is the time in minutes that each database needs for recovery.

Remote Access

If this option is set to 1 (the default), remote servers can access the system. If the value is 0, then they cannot.

Remote Conn Timeout

This is the amount of time (in seconds) the connection between servers can be inactive before the communication is terminated.

Remote Login Timeout

This is the amount of time (in seconds) the remote login can be inactive during a login attempt before the communication is terminated. A zero (0) means there is no time limit.

Remote Proc Trans

This specifies whether procedure calls between servers are protected by MS-DTC.

Remote Query Timeout

This is the amount of time (in seconds) the remote query can be inactive before it is terminated. A zero (0) means there is no time limit.

Resource Timeout

This is the amount of time (in seconds) to wait for a resource to be released.

Set Working Set Size

If this is set to 1, Windows NT reserves the value in memory plus the size of TempDB if it is configured to run in RAM.

Show Advanced Option

When this value is set to 1, all the advanced option settings can be displayed. When it is set to 0, they are not displayed.

SMP Concurrency

SQL Server releases the number of threads specified here for use by Windows NT. If the machine is dedicated to SQL Server, this value should be set to –1. If the machine is a uniprocessor, the value should be (and defaults to) 1. When SQL Server is installed, it autoconfigures this value to the number of processors –1, unless one of the two preceding scenarios exist.

Sort Pages

This is the number of pages each user can use for sorting.

Spin Counter

This is the number of attempts that are made to obtain a re-source. The default value is 10 on single-processor machines and 10000 on multiprocessor machines.

TempDB in RAM (MB)

If this value is anything other than 0, it specifies the size (in mega-bytes) to allocate in RAM for TempDB. If this value is 0, TempDB is not loaded into RAM.

User Connections

This specifies the maximum number of user connections to allow at any one time. Each configured connection, used or not, re-quires about 40 K of memory.

User Options

This is the value used to specify certain default user options for query-processing. See SQL Server Books Online for information on those options and their values.

Updating Statistics

 SQL Server retains certain information on key value distribution for each index. This information is then used to determine the best index to use for a query plan. If the information is old, this can cause the wrong indexes to be used and queries to slow down over time. You can run UPDATED STATISTICS to capture the current information for one or more indexes on a table. The syntax for UPDATE STATISTICS resembles the following:

```
UPDATE STATISTICS [[database.]owner.]table [index]
```

If just the table is specified, the information on all the indexes on that table is updated. If an index is specified as well, just the information for that index is updated. UPDATE STATISTICS runs automatically when an index is created on a table. You can use STAT_DATE to see when the statistics were last gathered.

If you know that a table has had a lot of activity, or that queries against a particular table are beginning to slow down, run UPDATE STATISTICS. In many cases, this greatly improves the performance of your queries. The more activity on a table, the more often this command should be run. You can schedule UPDATE STATISTICS to occur regularly on a table or tables by using Task Manager.12.

Exercises

Exercise 11.1: Deciphering Poor Query Performance

Assume that users are starting to complain that their system, which has been in production for about five months, is running too slowly. In this exercise, you will try to decipher the problem with this system. The time it takes to perform the following steps will vary.

Use the following steps to determine the cause:

1. Because the system has been in production for five months and the users are just now noticing a slowdown, the problem is more than likely on the back end (server side).

2. Users of other databases are not complaining of problems with their systems, so it is probably not a server configuration issue.

3. When you interview the complaining users, they all notice the slowdown most frequently on their heaviest-used windows and reports.

4. You open the Current Activity window in Enterprise Manager and check for blocking. Minimal blocking is occurring, so that is not the problem.

5. Finally, you look at the offending queries and notice that they all use a particular set of heavily-used tables.

6. You run UPDATE STATISTICS on those tables and check to see whether the problem still exists.

7. For the purpose of this exercise, you determine that this has in fact solved the problem and the users are happy once again. If this did not solve the problem, however, the database could be filling up (although, if it were properly designed, it should not be doing so after just five months of use).

See the section on "Updating Statistics" for more information on the UPDATE STATISITCS command. See "Selecting the Appropriate Settings for Locks" for more information on using the Current Activity window.

Exercise 11.2:   Increasing the Size of the Data Cache

In this exercise, you are going to determine that the size of the data cache is too small. You will then attempt to increase it without disturbing other properly-configured values. The time these tasks require will vary.

Use the following steps:

1. First, open up Performance Monitor and have it monitor the counter SQLServer: Cache Hit Ratio. You discover that the hit ratio for this example is hovering around 55 percent. Optimally, this ratio should be around 85 percent. Thus, the data cache needs more space.

2. You could take the space from the procedure cache rather than increasing the total memory supplied for SQL Server. To determine if this is a good solution, monitor the counter Max Procedure Cache Used % for the SQLServer - Procedure Cache object. If it shows that, when monitored during the heaviest periods, a portion of the procedure cache is not being used, some space is being wasted that the data cache could use. If this is the case, use sp_configure to adjust the procedure cache value. The extra memory then belongs to the data cache.

3. For the purpose of this exercise, assume that the procedure cache was properly configured. This means you need to allocate more memory to SQL Server as a whole. To do this, use Enterprise Manager's Server Configuration/Options window. In the current value column for the row for memory, type in the new value. Close the window by clicking OK. Then shut down the server and restart it by means of the Stop/Pause/Start Server window.

4. After the server comes back up, use Performance Monitor to monitor the Cache Hit Ratio discussed previously to make sure it now reaches the required level. Also check Memory: Page Faults/sec to make sure you did not take too much memory away from Windows NT. The counter should remain at 0 most of the time.

See the section on "Tuning and Monitoring Physical and Logical I/O" for more information on procedure and data cache configuration.

Exercise 11.3: Placing TempDB in RAM Using Enterprise Manager

In this exercise, you are going to configure SQL Server to place TempDB in RAM. You will give TempDB 4 MB of memory to use. The time this exercise takes will vary.

Follow these steps to place TempDB in RAM:

1. First, make sure that the 4 MB you want to allocate to TempDB will be available any time you may need to restart TempDB. If the memory is not available, SQL Server will not restart until the memory becomes available.

2. Open Enterprise Manager.

3. Select Configuration from the Server menu. The Server Configuration/Options window opens.

4. Find the TempDB in RAM option in the list. In the current value column for that option, type 4.

5. Click the OK button. The window closes.

6. Click on the Stop/Pause/Start button on the toolbar.

7. Stop the server and restart it.

See the section "Identifying the Benefits of Installing TempDB in RAM" for more information.

Exercise 11.4: Setting the Number of Worker Threads Using sp_configure

In this exercise, you are going to configure the number of worker threads using sp_configure instead of using Enterprise Manager. For the purpose of this exercise, you are going to set the number of worker threads to equal to the number of user connections. Time required to complete the exercise will vary.

The following steps determine the number of threads to set and configure the value:

1. Because you are using sp_configure instead of Enterprise Manager, you need to open an ISQL/W session.

2. In the IQSL/W window, type the following to retrieve the number of user connections currently configured.

```
sp_configure "user connections"
```

3. The output from this query is the number you use to configure the worker threads. Clear the Query window and type the following command, replacing config_value with the number you gathered from the previous query.

```
sp_configure "max worker threads", config_value
```

4. Now, because you have changed a dynamic configuration option, you must run the reconfigure command. Again, clear the query window and type the following:

RECONFIGURE

See the section "Configuring the Number of Worker Threads" for more information on worker threads. See the section "Setting Database Options" for more information on the configuration options.

Exercise 11.5: Configuring Read Ahead for a Typical Database

In this exercise, because you are going to change more than one value, you are going to use Enterprise Manager to configure the values. Assume that you are configuring Read Ahead for a typical database, meaning that it has no special concerns or uses as do query-only databases. Time required to complete this exercise will vary.

The following steps configure RA for a typical database:

1. Open Enterprise Manager.

2. Select Configuration from the Server menu. The Server Configuration/Options window opens.

3. Find the User Connection option in the list. Note the value in the current value column for that option. You need this value to set RA worker threads.

continues

4. Find the RA Worker Threads option. In the current value column, type the value found in step 3. This sets the number of worker threads to equal the number of user connections.

5. SQL Server documentation tells you not to change a couple of RA configuration options unless told to by your Primary Support Provider, so check those two and make sure they contain the defaults. These options are RA Cache Hit Limit and RA cache miss limit, and they should be set at 4 and 3, respectively.

6. RA Delay is fine left at its default value of 15. You just need to make sure it's set to the default.

7. RA Pre-Fetches has a default of 3, and this is the value you want to use because, in this example, your database has no special needs, such as an abnormally high number of large queries.

8. RA Slots per Thread should be appropriately set to its default value of 5. You would only want to increase this number if you had an efficient I/O system.

5. Click the OK button. The window closes.

6. Because you changed a non-dynamic configuration option, RA Worker Threads, you have to stop and restart the server. Click on the Stop/Pause/Start button on the toolbar.

7. Stop the server and restart it.

See the section "Selecting the Appropriate Settings for Read Ahead" for more information on worker threads.

Exercise 11.6: Monitoring the Log Using System Commands

In the following exercise, you are going to gather current information about the log by using sp_spaceused and DBCC OPENTRAN. Time required to complete the exercise will vary.

The following steps give you the desired information:

1. Open ISQL/W.

2. Type the following query and execute it:

   sp_spaceused syslogs

   This query returns information about the size of the log and how much space is currently used. You can use this information to determine how often you need to dump or truncate the log, and also to determine if your log size is appropriate.

3. In place of the preceding query, type the following query and execute it:

   DBCC OPENTRAN

   This command provides information about the oldest open transaction in the log. Open transactions keep other, more recently committed transactions from being purged from the log.

See the section "Monitoring Log Size" for more information.

Review Questions

The following questions test your knowledge of the information contained in this chapter.

1. How do you tell SQL Server that you want to view the advanced configuration values?

    A. sp_configure "show advanced options", 1

    B. sp_configure all

    C. SHOW_ADVANCED ON

    D. SET ADVANCED ON

2. Where does the memory come from to be used for TempDB in RAM?

    A. The memory allocated for SQL Server.

    B. The memory allocated for Data Cache.

    C. The memory for TempDB in RAM is independent of SQL Server's memory allotment.

    D. The memory allocated for Procedure Cache.

3. Which configuration option is used to set the maximum number of Read Ahead requests that can be made?

    A. Max Requests

    B. RA Requests

    C. RA Slots per Thread

    D. RA Requests per Thread

4. When does thread pooling occur?

    A. When there are too many threads sitting idle

    B. When there are more user connections than threads

    C. When Windows NT and SQL Server are fighting over the same threads

    D. When Windows NT runs out of threads

5. Which of the following are actions of the Read Ahead Manager? (Choose two options.)

    A. Anticipates a user's next request

    B. Tries to predict the result set

    C. Works best for large queries

    D. Works best for smaller queries

6. What determines the memory for the procedure cache?

    A. The size of the left-over memory

    B. The procedure cache configuration value

    C. The value in megabytes stored in the procedure cache configuration value

    D. The size of the data cache

7. What information does DBCC MEMUSAGE provide? (Choose two options.)

    A. The top 20 items in the data cache

    B. The top 12 items in the procedure cache

    C. The amount of memory allocated to SQL Server

    D. The size of TempDB in RAM

8. What happens if you specify UPDATE STATISTICS with only the table name parameter?

    A. Nothing happens

    B. Only the clustered index is updated

    C. All indexes on that table are updated

    D. Only the non-clustered indexes are updated

9. How much memory does a single connection consume?

    A. 30 K

    B. 40 K

    C. 20 K

    D. 50 K

10. What does the Performance Monitor allow the user to view? (Choose two options.)

    A. The current user list, process ids, and transaction information

    B. Information about the number of user connections

    C. Input/Output statistics

    D. The query plan for a stored procedure

11. How much memory is consumed by a configured lock?

    A. 40 K

    B. 32 K

    C. 40 bytes

    D. 32 bytes

12. Which of the following is removed from the transaction log on checkpoint?

    A. All transactions

    B. All uncommitted transactions

    C. All transactions up to the oldest uncommitted transaction

    D. All committed transactions

13. Which of the following can be used to set database options? (Choose two options.)

    A. Performance Monitor

    B. Enterprise Manager

    C. Current Activity window

    D. sp_configure

14. What is the default installation size of TempDB?

    A. 2 MB

    B. 4 MB

    C. 8 MB

    D. 16 MB

15. When does thread pooling end?

    A. When the "thread pooling" option is set to 0

    B. When the number of user connection rises above the number of worker threads

    C. When the number of worker threads drops below the number of user connections

    D. When the number of user connections drops to equal to or below the number of worker threads

16. Which of the following is not a valid configuration option for Read Ahead?

    A. RA Cache Hit Limit

    B. RA Cache Hit Ratio

    C. RA Delay

    D. RA Worker Threads

17. What SQL command is used to get a list of current locks?

    A. sp_who "locks"

    B. sp_help locks

    C. sp_locks

    D. sp_showlocks

18. What information does DBCC OPENTRAN provide?

    A. Information about all transactions in the log

    B. Information about open transactions since the specified time

    C. Information about open transactions in the log

    D. Information about the oldest open transaction in the log

19. Which of the following terms refer to a virtual page not being found in memory?

    A. Page fault

    B. Cache miss

    C. Cache fault

    D. Memory fault

20. Which of the following items determines the memory allocated to SQL Server?

    A. The value selected at installation time

    B. The value in the Memory configuration option

    C. The value in the SQL Memory configuration option

    D. Thirty percent of the memory in the server

Review Answers

1. A

2. C

3. C

4. B

5. B, C

6. B

7. A, C

8. C

9. B

10. B, C

11. D

12. C

13. B, D

14. A

15. D

16. B

17. C

18. D

19. A

20. B

Answers to Test Yourself Questions at Beginning of the Chapter

1. The syntax for configuring TempDB in RAM with a size of 8 MB is sp_configure "memory", 4096. See "Identifying the Benefits of Installing TempDB in RAM."

2. SQL Server is given a default size of 16 MB of RAM when installed on a machine containing at least 32 MB. See "Tuning an Monitoring Physical and Logical I/O."

3. sp_configure "tempdb in RAM", 2 provides the desired result of installing tempdb in RAM with a size of 2 MB. See "Setting Database Options."

4. UPDATE STATISTICS is used to optimize an index or all indexes on a table. See "Updating Statistics."

5. The procedure cache has a default value of 30, which represents the percentage of SQL Server memory allocated to the procedure cache. See "Tuning and Monitoring Physical and Logical I/O."

Chapter 12

Troubleshooting

System administrators spend some of their time troubleshooting problems with their servers, which usually involves finding, diagnosing, and resolving issues related to data, the network, or current processing. This chapter helps to tie together the rest of the information in this book about restoring databases, reading error logs, and dealing with processes—all part of the troubleshooting process.

As always, this chapter begins with a list of the exam objectives relating to the topic at hand, moves on to the chapter pretest, offers valuable information directly addressing the objectives, as well as additional relative discussion topics, and finishes with exercises, chapter review questions, and answers to both the review and pretest questions.

This chapter focuses on troubleshooting. It helps you prepare for the exam by addressing and fully covering the following objectives:

 Objectives

- ▶ Locate information relevant to diagnosing a problem
- ▶ Resolve network error messages
- ▶ Check object integrity
- ▶ Investigate a database that is marked suspect
- ▶ Restore a corrupted database
- ▶ Re-create a lost device
- ▶ Cancel a sleeping process

Test Yourself! Before reading this chapter, test yourself to determine how much study time you will need to devote to this section.

1. Bob is having a problem with his SQL Server. It doesn't seem to be starting correctly. What is a good source of information on SQL Server startup that Bob can use to diagnose the problem?

2. Ned is receiving periodic messages in the Windows NT Event Log from SQL Server that say "Error sending results to the front end." What can Ned do to resolve these errors?

3. What is the group of commands that are used to check database objects?

4. What is the impact on users when a database is marked suspect?

5. Bill has a process that is blocking other processes. When he checks the current activity on the server, he finds that there is a process that is blocking all the other users, but it is "sleeping." What can be done to this process to unblock the other processes?

6. What command is used to rebuild a database that has been corrupted?

7. What is the source of information used to rebuild lost devices?

Answers are located at the end of the chapter...

Locating Information Relevant to Diagnosing a Problem

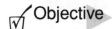 **Objective** ▶ Information used to diagnose problems is stored in several locations on the Windows NT computer running SQL Server. Each place has particular strengths and weaknesses for determining the nature of specific problems. The following areas will help you to find information to resolve problems:

- ▶ The Windows NT Event Log

- ▶ The SQL Server Error Log

- ▶ The Current Activity screen

The Windows NT Event Log

The Windows NT Event Log is one of the features that make Windows NT a good operating system to work with. It provides a centralized location for any application or part of the operating system to report informational and error messages so they can be viewed in order of occurrence. The Event Log is seen by using the Windows NT Event Viewer, which can be found in the Administrative Tools program group.

The Event Viewer divides the Event Log into three parts:

- ▶ **System log.** Includes mostly operating system events, such as logon script and account replication, Windows NT service startup and stop messages, and any hardware or device driver errors.

- ▶ **Security log.** Contains the audit log, so if auditing is turned on, the events will show up in the Security log.

- ▶ **Application log.** Contains information about different applications that are running on the server. Most of the SQL Server messages are found in the Application log. As you can see from figure 12.1, the application log shows the normal chain of events after starting SQL Server. Note that they are in reverse chronological order (most recent event first).

Figure 12.1

The Windows NT Event log, Application section.

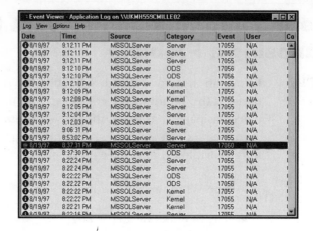

To use the Event Viewer, start the application from the Administrative Tools group. By default, it starts by displaying the event log of the local computer. To choose another computer, go to the Log menu and choose Select Computer.

For the events in the Event Log, the viewer show summary information for each event. From left to right, the columns include the following (refer to figure 12.1):

▶ **A severity icon.** Helps to show the importance of an event. There are three severity levels: information, warning, and error.

▶ **Date.**

▶ **Time.**

▶ **Source.** Shows what service caused the error to occur.

▶ **Category.**

▶ **Event number.** The message number that is included. This number is very handy when searching the knowledge base on TechNet or at Microsoft's web site.

▶ **User.** Usually set to N/A except for in the Security log.

▶ **Name of computer.**

Note   The best way to tell when the Windows NT computer was restarted is to examine the system log for Event Log messages.
Look for one that says, "The Event Log service was started."
This message appears when the server starts and is usually
the first or second message after a server starts. This message is helpful if you are trying to diagnose problems related
to automatic startup of services.

To get detailed information on an event, double-click on it or
choose the event and press Enter. The event details include a description of the event, including specific information such as the
name of the user that caused the problem or the database that is
being effected.

Some messages in the Event Log are critical, and some are safe to
ignore. When SQL Server starts, it logs a bunch of events related
to startup. Become familiar with these events so that when they
change the differences will be easier to find. The normal sequence of startup events is as follows:

1. "Mesg 17162 : SQL Server is starting at priority class 'normal' with dataserver serialization turned on (1 CPU
   detected)."

   This message means that the SQL Server executable is starting. The message varies on multiprocessor systems. If configured correctly for a multiprocessor system, it would probably
   read:

   "SQL Server is starting at priority class 'realtime' with
   dataserver serialization turned off (2 CPU's detected)."

2. "Mesg 18109 : Recovery dbid 1 ckpt (7939,33) oldest
   tran=(7939,32)"

   This message happens once for each database on the server
   and means that database 1 has successfully recovered itself.
   To see a list of database names with numbers, execute the
   following query:

   ```
   select dbid, name from sysdatabases
   ```

3. "Mesg 17026 : Using 'SQLEVN60.DLL' version '6.00.000'."

   This message is informational and describes which ODS DLL files are being loaded and provides version information on each. There will be several of these messages.

4. "Using 'SSNMPN60.DLL' version '6.5.0.0' to listen on '\\.\pipe\sql\query'."

   This event occurs for each network library installed on the server, showing the name of the DLL being used and the parameter that was supplied. This DLL is for the Named Pipes library.

This is the normal startup procedure. Items 2, 3, and 4 are interspersed until they complete. Databases recover while the DLL files are loading, and each event is recorded chronologically. The whole process runs in multiple threads, so database recovery messages are mixed in with various DLLs loading, and the DLL files load semi-independently, so they may not appear in the same order every time. The order of loading isn't important, just what got loaded and whether there are any errors involved.

Some errors are normally occurring operations. Whenever a client program terminates abnormally and is waiting for results from SQL Server, the following message is likely to show up:

Error : 17824, Severity: 10, State: 0
Unable to write to ListenOn connection '\\.\pipe\sql\query', loginname 'sa', hostname 'UKMH559CMILLE02'.
OS Error : 109, The pipe has been ended.

The key to deciphering the Error Log is understanding what each error means. Use the log carefully. Before taking any drastic action or even getting mildly concerned about an error message, look it up on the knowledge base on Microsoft's web site to get the most recent information on all of the error messages and the best ways to deal with them.

The SQL Server Error Log

The SQL Server error log is stored in a series of plain text files in the \MSSQL\LOG directory on the Windows NT computer running SQL Server. These files can be viewed in Notepad (see fig. 12.2) or by following this procedure in SQL Enterprise Manager:

1. Start SQL Enterprise Manager.

2. Expand the server to be viewed.

3. Choose Error Log from the Server menu.

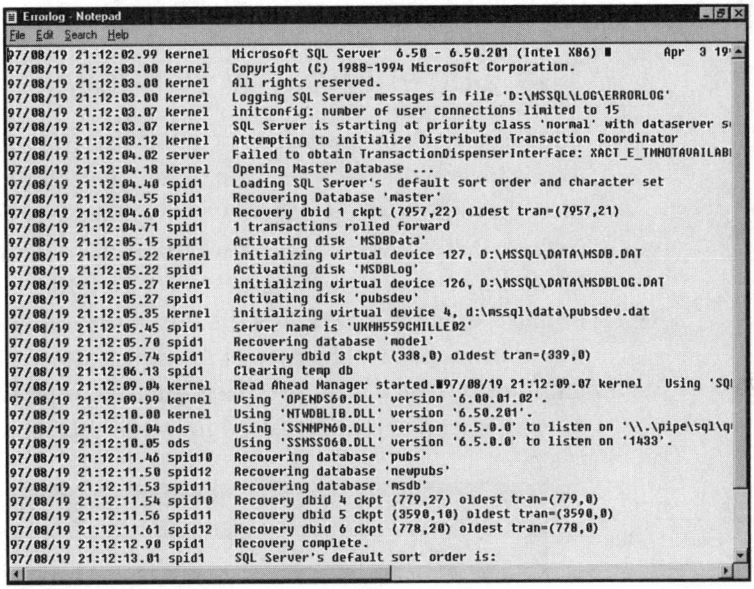

Figure 12.2

The events viewed in the SQL Server error log are shown in chronological order and start with the last server start time.

A new error log is created every time SQL Server is started. The files in the LOG directory are called ERRORLOG, ERRORLOG.1, ERRORLOG.2, and so on up to ERRORLOG.6. The ERRORLOG file is the log since the last time SQL Server was started. The ERRORLOG.1 is the previous log, and so on. Within SQL Enterprise Manager, use the drop-down box at the top to access the old error logs.

The error log contains much of the same information as the Windows NT Event Log, with two differences. The error log only contains items relevant to SQL Server, so there is no need to filter out events from other services. Also, the error log contains more details on some events, such as showing the character set and sort order descriptions on startup. Every error from SQL Server in the Windows NT Event Log is in the error log. Not every item in the error log is in the Windows NT Event log. The SQL Server error log provides a lot more detail on every event, but is much more difficult to read because there is a lot more detail in the way.

Usually, the Windows NT Event Log is monitored to help find problems with SQL Server, but the SQL Server error log is used to dig deeper and figure out exactly what happened. A good working knowledge of both is important to find out what is wrong.

The Current Activity Window

The Current Activity window in SQL Enterprise Manager shows who is logged on, what they are doing, and, most importantly, what they have locked and how many times (see fig. 12.3). The Current Activity window is critical to diagnosing and correcting problems related to locking behavior. To find the same information in a query tool requires the use of the sp_who and sp_lock stored procedures. The System Administrator (sa) always shows a lot of locks, which are the objects queried to populate the Current Activity screen and always show up when this screen is in use.

Figure 12.3

The Current Activity screen.

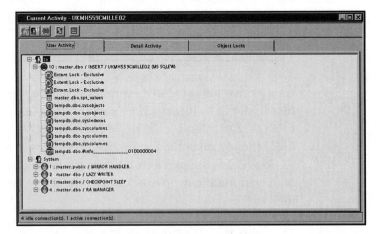

The Current Activity window has three tabs:

▶ **User Activity.** Shows each user along with what they have locked. Double-click on any user to find the last command they executed. Note that double-clicking on the connection you are using will show that you are running the dbcc input-buffer(10) command, which is used to determine the currently running command.

▶ **Detail Activity.** Shows the same information as the User Activity screen, but allows the information to be sorted in any order, instead of it being grouped by user.

▶ **Object Locks.** Shows each object that has one or more locks on it, along with how many locks are present on the object. This information is useful for detecting bottlenecks in processing where multiple users are waiting for a single page of the database.

If a user process is locking up or it becomes desirable to make the process stop holding all of the locks it is holding, choose the user connection on the User Activity tab and click on the Kill Process button on the toolbar of the Current Activity window. This kills the user's process, causing all open transactions to roll back.

To stop a user process in a query tool, use sp_who to determine the user's process id, which is the first column returned by sp_who, and then use the kill command to stop the process. To kill process number 42, type **kill 42** and then click the Execute button.

Resolving Network Errors

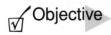 Objective

SQL Server network errors are the most common errors that are logged to the Event Log. They include errors related to client programs crashing, network configuration, and network library configuration.

The SQL Server administrator cannot do much to prevent client programs from crashing. Periodically, crashes happen because computers are not configured correctly or because some other program quits responding, and rather than trying to stop that one program, the user reaches for the reset button on the front of the case. Keep in mind, however, that some network problems might be caused by the administrator.

Users often perceive that a program has locked up if it begins to take longer than normal to retrieve data. Changes made to indexes or configuration of memory can cause SQL Server to take more time, causing the client programs to take more time to display data, which in turn causes the users simply to kill processes because they were "locked up." Watch for large batches of network errors; they may point to a problem like this.

Network errors are often caused by bad configuration on either the client side or the server side. Make sure that the "user connections" configuration is set high enough to handle the number of users connecting. The allowable amount is being exceeded when the following error occurs:

> Unable to connect. The maximum number of '15' configured user connections are already connected. System Administrator can configure to a higher value with sp_configure.

Use sp_configure or the server configuration option in SQL Enterprise Manager to configure the server to handle more connections. A good rule of thumb is to figure out how many connections there are during peak usage using either sp_who in a query tool or the Current Activity monitor in SQL Enterprise Manager, and then to add about ten percent more connections to the "user connections" configuraton.

If the client cannot connect to a server, many points of failure to check must be checked. The error message usually looks something like the following:

> A connection could not be established to NEWSERVER - [DB Library] Unable To Connect: SQL Server is unavailable or does not exist. SQL Server not found.

This specific message points to one of three possible problems. Check to make sure the SQL Server service is actually running on the specified server. Ensure that the server can be contacted on the network, and then check the SQL Client Configuration Utility.

To check the service, go to the Windows NT computer running SQL Server and log in. Go to Control Panel, Services and look for the MSSQLServer service. If it says "Started" to the right, the service is started.

To check to see whether the server can be contacted requires the use of different methods for different networks. For a TCP/IP network, open a command line and use the PING utility to check for connectivity. PING sends out network packets to an address, which are then sent back. PING measures the amount of time it takes to get from the client to the server and back. Use PING by typing **PING <*computername*>** on a Windows command line. If the name can't be found, there is likely a problem with the DNS or WINS settings on that computer. Talk to the network administrator for more details.

Checking the SQL Client Configuration Utility involves starting the utility and going through the options to find out how the client is trying to connect to the server. You can find a setting for Default Library on the Network Library tab. Make sure the default library is one of the libraries being used by SQL Server. On the Advanced tab, check to see whether communications between this client and the server have any special settings. If so, make sure these settings are correct. See Chapter 10, "Connectivity and Network Support," for more information on the SQL Client Configuration utility.

Checking Object Integrity

Checking the consistency of database objects such as tables, views, stored procedures, rules, and triggers, is an important part of maintaining a working database. Diagnostic utilities included with SQL Server, in accordance with a good backup plan (discussed in Chapter 8, "Managing Data"), are not only important to the health of the database, but to the health of the database administrator's career.

The set of diagnostics used in SQL Server are called the Database Consistency Checker (DBCC) commands, which include routines that check the data in the database to make sure that all of SQL Server's internal structures are correct. A description of most of the commands is in table 12.1.

Table 12.1

DBCC Commands and Descriptions	
Command	Description
CheckAlloc or NewAlloc	Check the allocation chains to ensure they are consistent. NewAlloc does a better job and is the newer version of the utility. It is the one that should be used the most.
CheckCatalog	Check the system tables to ensure they are consistent. Makes sure every column has a datatype, that syslogs have been checkpointed recently, and that every table should have at least one type.
CheckTable and CheckDB	CheckTable goes through a given table and all of its indexes and makes sure that it can get from one end to the other. It also makes sure that all of the links are properly recorded and that all of the indexes are functioning properly. CheckDB does the scans of CheckTable to every table in the specified database.
TextAlloc and TextAll	TextAlloc checks all of the text/image data pages for a given table and makes sure they are correct and properly linked. TextAll runs the same checks for every table in the database with text or image datatypes.
UpdateUsage	Checks to make sure that the number of rows specified in the *sysindexes* table for a given table is correct. This should be run if the stored procedure *sp_spaceused* is giving false results.

This table does not a list every DBCC command. Many of the DBCC commands have nothing to do with database diagnostics, but were placed there because DBCC supplies the developers with a convenient place to store this type of procedure. An example of this is the DBCC INPUTBUFFER(ID) command, which displays the last command executed by the supplied process id.

Microsoft recommends that DBCC CheckDB and DBCC NewAlloc are run prior to or immediately following a nightly backup. This schedule is not always practical because some of these procedures take a long time to run. The CheckDB routine, for example, can take 18 to 20 hours on very large databases. Clearly, this is not something that can be done every night. When the database becomes too large to run these diagnostics on a daily basis, they should be run as often as possible, probably on a weekly basis.

Many of these procedures, including CheckAlloc and NewAlloc, should be run at times of very low usage because they consume a lot of CPU or require locks on tables, which makes them undesirable to run during the workday. These procedures may report problems that don't exist. Whenever these commands are run and the database is not in single user mode, they return a warning that spurious errors may be found. Normally, this is run without putting the database in single-user mode, but the errors are monitored to make sure they do not occur every night.

Many of these procedures consume a lot of CPU or require locks on tables that make them undesirable to run during the day. For the most part, these tasks should be scheduled to run at periods of low activity to prevent interfering with the users.

The syntax for these procedures follows:

```
DBCC <FunctionName> (<dbname> or <tablename>)
```

For example, to run the CheckTable procedure on the authors table in the Pubs database, use the following command from within the Pubs database:

```
DBCC CheckTable (authors)
```

This would return as output:

```
Checking authors
The total number of data pages in this table is 1.
Table has 23 data rows.
DBCC execution completed. If DBCC printed error messages, see
your System Administrator.
```

The final line, which starts "DBCC Execution Completed," is normal for any DBCC command. To run the CheckDB routine on the same database, simply put in the following line:

```
DBCC CheckDB(pubs)
```

This command would result in output such as the following:

```
Checking pubs
Checking 1
The total number of data pages in this table is 4.
Table has 70 data rows.
Checking 2
The total number of data pages in this table is 4.
Table has 49 data rows.
Checking 3
The total number of data pages in this table is 10.
Table has 280 data rows.
Checking 4
The total number of data pages in this table is 1.
Table has 29 data rows.
Checking 5
The total number of data pages in this table is 24.
Table has 170 data rows.
Checking 6
The total number of data pages in this table is 2.
Table has 28 data rows.
Checking 7
The total number of data pages in this table is 1.
Table has 3 data rows.
Checking 8
The total number of data pages in this table is 1.
*** NOTICE: Notification of log space used/free cannot be
reported because the log segment is not on its own device.
Table has 20 data rows.
Checking 9
The total number of data pages in this table is 1.
The number of data pages in Sysindexes for this table was 0. It
has been corrected to 1.
Table has 88 data rows.
Checking 10
The total number of data pages in this table is 1.
Table has 3 data rows.
Checking 11
```

```
The total number of data pages in this table is 1.
Checking 12
The total number of data pages in this table is 1.
Table has 14 data rows.
Checking 13
The total number of data pages in this table is 1.
Checking 14
The total number of data pages in this table is 1.
Table has 10 data rows.
Checking 15
The total number of data pages in this table is 1.
Table has 34 data rows.
Checking 16
The total number of data pages in this table is 1.
Checking 17
The total number of data pages in this table is 1.
Checking 18
The total number of data pages in this table is 1.
Checking 16003088
The total number of data pages in this table is 1.
Table has 23 data rows.
Checking 112003430
The total number of data pages in this table is 1.
Table has 8 data rows.
Checking 192003715
The total number of data pages in this table is 3.
Table has 18 data rows.
Checking 288004057
The total number of data pages in this table is 1.
Table has 25 data rows.
Checking 368004342
The total number of data pages in this table is 1.
Table has 6 data rows.
Checking 416004513
The total number of data pages in this table is 1.
Table has 21 data rows.
Checking 496004798
The total number of data pages in this table is 2.
Table has 86 data rows.
Checking 544004969
The total number of data pages in this table is 1.
Table has 3 data rows.
Checking 592005140
The total number of data pages in this table is 1.
Table has 14 data rows.
```

```
Checking 688005482
The total number of data pages in this table is 1.
The total number of TEXT/IMAGE pages in this table is 62.
Table has 8 data rows.
Checking 752005710
The total number of data pages in this table is 2.
Table has 43 data rows.
DBCC execution completed. If DBCC printed error messages, see
your System Administrator.
```

Notice two important items in this sample output. The really low numbers—when it says "Checking 1" to "Checking 18," for example—are system tables being checked. The higher numbers would then be the system tables. Also, notice for "Checking 8" that it is probably the syslogs table and that the amount of space used could not be reported. Normally, for the CheckDB routine, the amount of free space in the logs is reported.

To reduce the amount of output resulting from these commands, use the "With No_InfoMsgs" command to eliminate the messages in the output except the error messages.

Error number 2540 may occur periodically in a database. The error message follows:

> Allocation Discrepancy: Page is allocated but not linked; check the following pages and ids: allocation pg#=%ld extent id=%ld logical pg#=%ld object id on extent=%ld (object name = %.*s) indid on extent=%ld

Error 2540 occurs when a page in the database cannot be used because the allocation chain skips over it. This is not usually a serious problem; it just means that there is one page in the database that cannot be used. If it is desirable to recover the page, run DBCC CheckDB to make sure there are no other problems, and then run DBCC FIX_AL to fix the allocation chain.

For almost any other error message, the resolution is to restore from a known clean backup. The concept of a "known clean backup" is the reason that diagnostics are run on the database every night. Without these diagnostics, it can't be known whether a database dump is clean. No reliable method exists for fixing a database that has a serious problem. Most of the time, the solution is to restore the database.

The process of dumping a database may log some errors. Most of these errors will be related to some type of a hardware error because the dump process does actually read every single used page in the database.

In the event that it is impossible to restore a non-suspect database from a known clean backup, the alternative method for keeping the data safe is to transfer the database to another server by using the Transfer option in SQL Enterprise Manager. The Transfer option automates the process of creating tables by using BCP to back up the data, re-creating tables, and loading data. If the tables can be scripted and copied out, the procedure should work very well for recovering data.

Investigating Suspect Databases

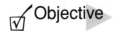 Objective

This section discusses suspect databases by first explaining how they are marked thus and then addressing various remedy methods.

When Databases Are Marked Suspect

Databases are marked suspect when the Automatic Recovery process cannot apply the transaction log to the database. This can occur because the transaction log is corrupted or because the target tables are corrupted.

It is important to figure out why a database is marked suspect. Databases are marked suspect in three cases:

▶ SQL Server cannot open the database device files either because they do not exist or because of a device failure.

▶ An error occurs when SQL Server reads the transaction log of the database being recovered, either because of a structural problem in the SQL Server data structures or because of a hardware device failure.

► An error occurs when SQL server attempts to write information ("roll forward") a transaction that was successfully read in the transaction log, but cannot due to a write error on the data device, either caused by a SQL Server data structure problem or a hardware device failure.

The most common time when SQL Server marks a database suspect is when the DBA (Database Administrator) has been out moving or changing permissions on the devices. Most of the time, the database can be put back where it was supposed to be and have the status reset to normal with the procedure outlined previously. The moral of the story is to be careful messing with database device files.

Another common failure is hardware failure. The best protection against hardware failure is redundancy. Use either Windows NT disk mirroring or SQL Server device mirroring on the Master device to make recovery easier. Use disk arrays with parity, preferably hardware implementations, to handle data devices. The ability to replace a dead drive with another with no downtime gives a DBA reason to feel great. Disk array technology allows this to happen.

The other two failure mechanisms are caused by SQL Server handling something incorrectly or by the server going down non-gracefully. Both of these are actually the same problem. SQL Server should never be affected by the server going down ungracefully. Unfortunately, it happens. So use a UPS and never kill the MSSQLServer process or just shut the computer off. Always use the Shut Down command before turning off a server.

Databases that have been marked Suspect are no longer accessible to SQL Server. SQL Server's recovery process has decided that the database is no longer a valid database and has refused to open it. This is very bad. This section addresses how to work with suspect databases to extract as much data as possible.

The whole situation comes down to this: Is there a known, clean backup of the database? If there is, use the recovery scenarios presented in Chapter 8 to recover the data. If there is no backup, use the material in this section to help recover as much of the data as possible. To prevent having to follow these operations again, immediately follow this process with an investigation into what went wrong in the backup process. Here's what is going to be covered and the steps to go through to help recover data:

▶ Attempt to recover data from the suspect database. This means fooling SQL Server into allowing you access to your database even though SQL Server doesn't like it.

▶ Attempt to recover data from transaction logs of corrupted databases. This was covered some in Chapter 8 and more detail is added here.

Attempting to Retrieve Data from Suspect Databases

A database is marked suspect by the Automatic Recovery process in SQL Server during server startup. To attempt to get access to the database again, it is necessary to mark the database as no longer suspect, and to prevent it from writing any new data into the syslogs table. You do this by turning on the capability to update system tables, changing the status of the database, turning off the capability to update system tables, and then restarting SQL Server:

1. Start a SQL Server query tool.

2. Turn on the capability to update system tables with the following:

```
sp_configure "Allow Updates", 1
go
reconfigure with override
```

The "reconfigure with override" tells SQL Server that it really should do what it is being asked to do. The Allow Updates option should be used very carefully. Editing system tables is very similar to editing the Windows NT Registry in that editing the wrong piece of data can cause severe problems.

3. Set the status bit on the table by starting a transaction and updating the sysdatabases table:

```
begin transaction
update sysdatabases set status = status ¦ 4112
    where name = "database name"
```

The status of 4112 sets the status to single-user mode and to "No Chkpt on Recovery" so the log will not be written to.

4. After executing the preceding command, make sure the change only effects one row. Then commit the transacton:

```
commit transaction
```

5. Turn off the capability to update system tables:

```
sp_configure "Allow Updates", 0
go
reconfigure
```

6. Shut down SQL Server:

```
shutdown
```

7. Start SQL Server.

This procedure should result in SQL Server starting up and not marking the database as suspect. Running DBCC CHECKDB and DBCC NEWALLOC will find the problems in the database. Use BCP or the transfer tool built in to SQL Enterprise Manager to transfer as much data out of the database as possible to reload into the new database.

In many cases, a database is marked as suspect when the transaction log is corrupt. Try using the following command to clear the transaction log and then run DBCC CHECKDB to make sure the database is OK.

```
DUMP TRANSACTION <DBNAME> WITH NO_LOG, TRUNCATE_ONLY
```

This clears the inactive portion of the transaction log. Running CheckDB afterwards can help isolate the problems associated with the database that is corrupt.

Recovering the Transaction Log of a Suspect Database

Another thing that can be done with suspect databases prior to recovering them from known clean backups is to dump the transaction log so it can be used later during recovery. If the data portion of the database was corrupted but the log part of the database is OK, it is possible to use the DUMP TRANSACTION command to back up the transaction log:

```
DUMP TRANSACTION <DBNAME> TO <DumpDevice> WITH NO_TRUNCATE
```

This dumps the transaction log out to the specified dump device. At this point, the database can be scripted, dropped, and reloaded, and then the transaction logs up to the point of the failure can be loaded.

Using the SQL Enterprise Manager Transfer Function

The SQL Enterprise Manager now comes with the built-in capability to copy a database or any object within a database to another server. This powerful capability used to be built into a separate application, the SQL Transfer Manager, but is now integrated into SQL Enterprise Manager.

The best way to describe a database transfer is to say that it scripts all of the selected objects and then runs the script on the target server. The data is copied to the target server by using BCP to copy the data out of the source server and then again to load it on the target server. This is all handled by the transfer process.

To initiate a database transfer, use the following procedure:

1. Start SQL Enterprise Manager.

2. Make sure both the target and source servers are registered. The target server is where the data is being copied to. The source server is where the data is coming from.

3. Expand the source server by clicking on the plus sign to the left of its name in the Server Manager window.

4. Expand the Databases folder.

5. Right-click on the database to transfer and choose Transfer from the popup menu.

continues

6. Verify that the Source Server and Source Database are set correctly.

7. Choose a target server and target database.

8. Set the transfer options. Copy Schema sets SQL Server so it will generate a script of all of the selected database objects. Drop Destination Objects First sets up the script so it will drop any objects in the target database with the same name. Include Dependency Objects means that all of the objects that are depended on by the chosen objects will be copied. If a table is chosen to copy and the Include Dependency Objects is chosen, for example, any rules, types, or defaults used by that table will also be transferred.

9. Choose the objects to copy. There is a Transfer All Objects check box in the Advanced Options frame. If that is what needs to be done, leave the checkbox alone and all objects will be copied. Otherwise, uncheck the checkbox and click the Choose Objects button to bring up another window to set up which objects will be copied.

10. Set the scripting options. For large transfers, turn off the Use Default Scripting Options checkbox and click on Scripting Options. Select what needs to be scripted and copied to the destination server. Usually it is a good idea to check the box labeled "Create Clustered Keys/Indexes After Data Transfer With 'Sorted Data'." This significantly cuts the amount of time necessary to copy large tables with clustered indexes. Also be sure to select the security options that are necessary. If the copy of the database should not have any users, set the options so none of the security information is copied. Click on OK when finished setting the scripting options.

11. Click on the Start Transfer button to begin the transfer immediately, or schedule it to happen later. For large databases, the transfer process takes a long time.

Keep in mind that the transfer process copies the structures and then copies the data. The indexes are all rebuilt as part of the copy in, so if there are data problems inside the indexes, they won't be problems on the target server.

Restoring a Corrupted Database

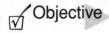 Objective

Restoring corrupted databases is a fairly easy task assuming the backups are available and easy to find. See Chapter 8 for information on making backups. To restore a corrupted database, first find the parameters of the database, drop the corrupted database, create a new database, and then load the data from backup. If you don't have a good backup, follow the steps in the preceding section, "Investigating Suspect Databases." If that doesn't help, Microsoft Tech Support may be able to give you a hand, but it's time to start evaluating options on rebuilding the data outside of SQL Server.

Finding the Parameters for the Database

The parameters for a database include which devices the database is on and how much of each device it uses in the correct order. Every time a database is expanded, even if it is expanded onto the same device, there is a new fragment created. When re-creating the database, it is important to set up the fragments correctly.

The best way to find these parameters is by using the sp_help_revdatabase stored procedure, which generates a script that can be used to re-create the devices and databases with the correct fragmentation. For this section, just use the "create database…" line, but for the next section, which is about re-creating devices, this procedure also scripts all of the device creations.

Notice that the procedure does not necessarily just create the database outright, but creates the database and then expands it using the exact same parameters as the current database was created with and later expanded by. If the database was created and then expanded onto a new device, the script will show the initial creation and then the expansion onto the new device in two steps.

If the sp_help_revdatabase stored procedure is not available, use the following procedure to determine the segment map for the database:

1. Start a SQL Query tool.

2. Using the Master database, execute the following query to determine the database id (dbid) of the suspect database:

   ```
   select * from sysdatabases wherename = <dbname>
   ```

3. Select all of the records in the sysusages table that apply to the dbid found in step 2:

```
select * from sysusages where dbid = <dbid>
```

4. Interpret the resulting data. As an example:

```
dbid    segmap   lstart   size   vstart
----    ------   ------   ----   ------
5       3        0        3072   2130706432
5       4        3072     1024   2113929216

(2 row(s) affected)
```

This data would be interpreted as a database that is 8 MB total, with 6 MB of data space (3,072 two-KB pages with a segmap value of 3) and 2 MB of log (1,024 two-KB pages with a segmap value of 4).

5. Write the Create Database statement down. In this case, it would be

```
create database msdb on msdbdev = 6 log on msdblog = 2
```

Reducing the Number of Fragments in a Database

SQL Server 6.5 introduces a new stored procedure, sp_coalesce_fragments, which helps to reduce the number of fragments in a database.

One of the problems introduced in SQL Server 6.0 came from the new capability to expand a device. This was very handy because previous to SQL Server 6.0, the only way to make more space available for SQL Server was to create a new device, resulting in many small devices, making recovery more difficult than necessary.

After the capability to extend devices was allowed, increasing numbers of DBAs used the ability to expand a device and then expand the database to use more of the same device. Even though all of the data was still contiguous, this results in two fragments.

To reduce the number of fragments in a database, use the sp_coalesce_fragments stored procedure. This procedure irons out all of the consecutive fragments on a single device into a single fragment, assuming that they are all contiguous and all belong to the same database. Recovery is made much simpler.

Because the sp_help_revdatabase stored procedure reads data only from the Master database, the procedure can be used while the target database is marked suspect. It must be used before the suspect database is removed, or the data that it uses will be gone.

Dropping the Suspect Database

Databases that have been marked suspect cannot be dropped using the Drop Database command. Two others can be used to drop them.

The sp_dbremove stored procedure is one method for removing damaged databases. This procedure takes as its parameters the name of the database and the optional dropdev argument. The dropdev argument specifies that not only should the database be dropped, but any devices that were exclusively used by the database should also be dropped and their files deleted.

The other method for removing a suspect database is to use the DBCC DBREPAIR command, which takes two parameters. The first one is the name of the database, and the second is the word "dropdb." The procedure does not work without including the second parameter, even if the parameter is always the same.

Using either command removes the database from the system tables, making the database name usable again. The next step in recovering from a suspect database is to create the database.

Rebuilding the Database

After dropping the suspect database, the next step is to rebuild the database. First, make sure that the underlying devices are stable. Then, by using the data pulled out of the sp_help_revdatabase stored procedure run back in the first step, rebuild the database. The create database and alter database steps will be used to reconstruct the database with the same segment mapping as before. Remember that the sp_help_revdatabase stored procedure produces as output a script. Simply copy and paste that script into a new query window, run it, and the new database is created.

Loading the Database

Use the Load Database command as specified in Chapter 8 to load the database. The number of pages read from the dump is reported at the end of the load. Make sure the number of pages is reasonable; it should be equal to the number of pages used in the database device that the data came from.

Re-creating Lost Devices

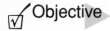 A *device* is simply a file on disk that SQL Server can use to store a database, multiple databases, or a part of a database. Devices and databases do not necessarily have a direct one-to-one correlation. In most cases, a given database is stored on two devices, commonly called a *log device* and a *database device.* Storing multiple databases on a given device is usually not done, except in the case of the master device, which stores the Master, Model, Pubs, and TempDB databases.

To rebuild a lost device, first determine the specifications of the device. Drop the old device and make sure the problems that caused the device to become lost in the first place are gone. Then create the new device.

Determining Device Specifications

Before dropping a lost device, make sure that the information needed to rebuild it is available by running the sp_helpdevice procedure in a SQL Server query tool. Note the name and size of the device so it can be re-created later. Following is the output from the sp_helpdevice procedure, with some of the columns removed for clarity.

```
device_name      physical_name              description
--------------   -------------------------  -----------------------------------------
master           D:\MSSQL\DATA\DATADEV.DAT   special, default disk, physical disk, 3 MB
low              high
--------------   --------
67108864         67110399

(1 row(s) affected)
```

The size of the device in pages can be found by taking the number in the high column, subtracting the number in the low column, and adding one—in the case of the previous example, 1,536 pages, or 3,072 KB, or 3 MB. Devices are always created to a specific number of pages, but usually to an even half-megabyte boundary. When rebuilding a device, it can always be created larger than the old device, but should never be created smaller, or the database going onto the device will not fit. If in doubt, add a few hundred pages. If 200 pages are added, that's 400 KB of disk space lost, which usually is not a big deal.

Dropping Lost Devices

Database devices are created by using the DISK INIT command. Devices are dropped by using the system stored procedure sp_dropdevice, which takes one mandatory parameter (device name) and one optional parameter (DELFILE), which will delete the file on disk after dropping the device. So, in most cases, the command will look like the following:

```
sp_dropdevice datadev, DELFILE
```

This drops the device datadev and afterwards deletes the file on disk. Failure to use the DELFILE argument causes the device to be dropped, but the file is still on disk.

If a database exists that is using the device in question, the device cannot be dropped until the database is dropped. First drop the database, then drop the device. To find out whether a device is being used by a database, follow these steps:

1. Start SQL Enterprise Manager.

2. Expand the server.

3. Expand the Database Devices folder.

4. Double-click on the device in question.

5. Read the Device Space Usage window. By moving the mouse over different bars, the contents at the bottom of the window will change to show how much space is being used on the device by a given database.

Diagnosing and Resolving Device Problems

After a device has been determined to be bad, ensure there are no hardware or software problems that could cause the device to go bad again. Reloading databases from tape and rebuilding devices is not something one wants to do on a regular basis.

If the problem was a hardware failure, make sure the hardware was replaced with an adequate substitute. If the problem was caused by an operating system error, call Microsoft and find out why the error occurred. To diagnose hardware and software problems, consult the Event Log. If there were operating system events that show errors writing to the hard disk, it's a hardware problem. If the operating system crashes with the "blue screen of death," it could be either a hardware problem or a software problem.

Devices are very simple entities. Any malfunction in a database device usually points directly to a hardware failure of some kind. In rare cases, SQL Server corrupts devices if it is not taken down gracefully. Make sure the Windows NT computer running SQL Server is always shut down before powering off the server.

Rebuilding Devices

After dropping the device and making sure the problem encountered with the old device won't happen again soon, it is time to rebuild the device. The first step in this procedure was to record the device size from the sp_helpdevice system stored procedure. Now it is time to rebuild the device. To build a device by using a SQL Query tool:

1. Use the Master database.

2. Use the DISK INIT command to rebuild the device. The command is as follows:

```
disk init name = 'Datadev',
     physname = 'D:\MSSQL\DATA\DATADEV.DAT',
     size = 1536,
     vdevno = 12,
     vstart = 67108864
```

This will rebuild the device. By using the vstart parameter, SQL Server places the device into the exact same position it was before.

Note This example should stress the importance of keeping paper records of where devices go. Most DBAs keep a paper pinup in their office of the layout of every device in the servers they are responsible for. Paper is very reassuring, even if it is never needed.

Canceling a Sleeping Process

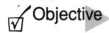

Objective Every connection in SQL Server is assigned a process ID. This identifier can be found either in the Current Activity window in SQL Enterprise Manager or by using the sp_who stored procedure in a SQL query tool. Here is the output of the sp_who command:

```
spid   status     loginame    hostname              blk   dbname    cmd
------ ---------- ----------- --------------------- ----- --------- -----------------
1      sleeping   sa                                0     master    MIRROR HANDLER
2      sleeping   sa                                0     master    LAZY WRITER
3      sleeping   sa                                0     master    CHECKPOINT SLEEP
4      sleeping   sa                                0     master    RA MANAGER
10     sleeping   sa          UKMH559CMILLE02       11    newpubs   SELECT
11     sleeping   sa          UKMH559CMILLE02       0     newpubs   AWAITING COMMAND
12     runnable   sa          UKMH559CMILLE02       0     newpubs   SELECT

(1 row(s) affected)
```

Notice that the process with system process ID (spid) of 10 is being blocked (blk) by the process with spid 11. Process 11 will block process 10 when process 11 has pages exclusively locked that are needed by process 10. Also, notice that the status of process 11 is "sleeping" and the command (cmd) is "AWAITING COMMAND," which usually means that process 11 started a transaction, updated the row, and has either stopped or is waiting user input to complete the transaction. In the meantime, the user could have gone to lunch or out for the evening and the user trying to execute process 10 would just have to wait for him or her to get back.

Situations like this are ideal for one of the DBA's favorite commands, KILL. To use the KILL command, first isolate which process is causing the problem. This is outlined in the previous paragraph. Then kill the process by executing the following command:

```
KILL 10
```

This logs an event to the Windows NT event log and gives the user who picked a bad time to go to lunch a really nasty error message. The normal response to this is SQL Server's austere error message, "This command did not return data, and it did not return any rows," meaning SQL Server completed the task and did not have any data to return. At this point, process 11 should continue running. Process 10 will have its transaction rolled back.

Programming and Administering Transactions

Transaction processing is critical to any database environment. Being able to successfully maintain logical database integrity is very important to the functionality of software. *Logical database integrity* (also known as *relational integrity*, or *RI*) is attained when all of the foreign key relationships in a database are valid. When the keys point to records that exist, the database has relational integrity.

When programs are written to use a database and insert or update records, they should encapsulate the insert or update statements inside of transactions. This helps to prevent breakdowns in the relational integrity of a database.

A key to writing programs that use databases that have relational integrity is writing transactions properly, which means that a transaction should be done as a sequence of events with no user input. In the example, one user started a transaction and went out for lunch. If the program puts up a message window to get more information before completing the transaction, nobody else can use the records involved in the transaction until the user gets back from lunch and completes the transaction.

Transactional programming is a good example of where the DBA and pro-grammer have to communicate. If a program hangs up, the DBA will know about it if it leaves transactions open because users will complain that the whole database is "locked up."

To stop a process in SQL Enterprise Manager, pull up the Current Activity window, select the process that needs to be stopped, and click on the Kill Process button on the toolbar. (The Kill Process button has a picture of a globe with a red X through it.)

If a process is running and the process is stopped, the current transaction for that process is rolled back and the process is killed. When a transaction is rolled back, it takes just as long to roll back as it took for the transaction to arrive at that point to begin with. In other words, if a transaction has been running for four hours, and it has not been blocked for a significant part of that time, it will take about four hours to roll back the transaction.

If the SQL Server is stopped during a transaction, the exact same process of rolling back the transaction will run as part of automat-ic recovery. Stopping the SQL Server, shutting down Windows NT, or simply shutting the server off will not abate this time, and will just cause other problems. If a process takes a long time to run, it takes a long time to undo.

Exercises

Exercise 12.1: Using the Windows NT Event Log

In this exercise, you will start the Windows NT Event Viewer and read through the SQL Server and Windows NT Startup events, which can be done on the computer running SQL Server, on another Windows NT computer on the network, or on a Windows 95 computer that has the Windows NT Administration tool kit installed. This exercise should take 10 to 15 minutes to complete.

1. Start the Event Viewer application. In Windows NT 3.51, this is done by opening the Administrative Tools window in Program Manager and double-clicking on the Event Viewer icon. In Windows NT 4.0, click the Start button, choose the Programs item, then the Administrative Tools item, and then Event Viewer.

2. The Windows NT Event Viewer window opens. If you aren't using the computer running SQL Server to run this, choose Select Computer from the Log menu and choose the computer from the list presented.

3. Choose System from the Log menu to display the log of system events. Look for an event from the Event Log service and double-click on it to open it. The message text should say, "The Event log service was started," and usually is the first or second message in the log during a server reboot.

4. Click on the Previou button. Keep in mind that the buttons in the Event Viewer can be considered to be labeled backwards. The Previous button advances to the next event that occurred. The Next button moves to earlier events.

5. Read the events that occured to the server during bootup. If there is ever a problem with SQL Server starting, it will be logged in here with the source Service Control Manager with data saying the MSSQLServer service failed to start. Close the Event Detail window by clicking on the Close button.

6. From the Log menu, choose Application to display the Application log, which is where most of the SQL Server events

are logged, along with the rest of the non-operating system services that are running on the server.

7. Search the log for event number 17055, with MSSQLServer listed as the source and Kernel listed as the category. Several of these will have occurred the last time SQL Server was started. Double-click on the oldest event in the log. It should display the following message:

Mesg 17162 : SQL Server is starting at priority class 'normal' with dataserver serialization turned on (1 CPU detected).

This is the first SQL Server startup message.

8. By clicking on the Previous button, examine the events that occur during SQL Server startup. These include the messages starting "Mesg 18109," which are databases being recovered, and the messages that explain which DLL files are loading and display the version numbers.

9. Click on the Close button to close the Event Detail window.

10. Choose Exit from the Log menu to close the Event Viewer.

For more information, please review the section "The Windows NT Event Log" earlier in this chapter.

Exercise 12.2:   Reading the SQL Server Error Log

The SQL Server error log contains information directly from SQL Server from the time it was last started. The error log file is a plain text file called ERRORLOG. There is no extension to the filename. The file can be opened in SQL Enterprise Manager or by using any text editor, such as Notepad. In this exercise, you will open the error log and look for some key events. The exercise should take about 10 minutes to complete.

1. Start the SQL Enterprise Manager.

2. Expand the server you want to work with by clicking the plus sign to the left of the server name.

continues

3. From the Server menu, choose Error Log.

4. The window contains the text of the error log. Notice that the top of the window contains a drop-down box with the word "Current" followed by a date and time. The date and time are the last time an event was written into the error log. By dropping down the error log, you can look at the error log from the previous time SQL Server was started.

5. Read the startup messages in the error log file. Notice that the messages that were mentioned in Exercise 10.1 as being startup messages are listed here, but there are a lot more messages here also.

6. Scroll down to the message that says "Recovery Complete." This message indicates that the SQL Server has finished the automatic recovery sequence and is almost completed with its startup routine.

7. The next few lines in the error log show the character set and sort order being used. This information is important to know if the Master database needs to be recovered (see Chapter 8 on Data Management for details about Character Set and Sort Order in recovery).

8. Close the Error Log window.

Please see the section "The SQL Server Error Log" earlier in this chapter for more information.

Exercise 12.3: The Current Activity Screen and Canceling Processes

The Current Activity window shows which processes are active and which objects are locked, which is valuable information for diagnosing the problems of clients locking up because it helps to find records that are locked. The alternate method for accomplishing this task is covered in the second part of the exercise. Both parts of the exercise should take about 15 minutes.

1. Open SQL Enterprise Manager if it is not already open.

2. Expand the server you want to look at by clicking on the + sign to the left of the server name.

3. From the Server menu choose Current Activity to open the Current Activity window.

4. The Current Activity window has three tabs: User Activity, Detail Activity, and Object Locks. The User Activity tab contains all of the users, and, by expanding each user by clicking on the + sign to the left of the user name, you can view which processes the user owns. By clicking on the + sign next to a process, you can view which objects are locked by the process.

5. Click on the Detail Activity tab to display a table. Every lock currently on the server has one line, which contains information about the process that has the lock, including the owner, the type, and the database in use.

6. Click on the Object Locks tab to display a list of the currently locked objects. Expanding each object displays a list of the users who have the object locked.

7. To kill a specified task, click on the User Activity tab, choose the task to be killed, and click on the Kill Task button on the toolbar, which has a globe with an X through it.

For more information on this topic, please see the section "The Current Activity Window."

Now take a look at how to find and stop processes by using a SQL Query tool.

1. Start a SQL Query tool.

2. Execute the command sp_who to return a list of active connections and the actions currently being done on them. Note the system process id (SPID) in the first column.

continues

Exercise 12.3: Continued

3. Execute the command kill *<number>* where *number* is the number of the process to be killed.

4. Execute sp_who to check whether the process was killed.

Please see the section "Canceling a Sleeping Process" for more information on this part of the exercise.

Exercise 12.4: Checking Object Integrity

In this exercise, you will execute DBCC commands to check the integrity of the database's internal structures. All of the exercises in this chapter are carried out against the Pubs database, but other databases can be used the same way. Be careful when using these commands on production systems during times of heavy user activity because the users may lock up. This exercise will take about 10 minutes, depending on the speed of the computer running SQL Server.

1. Open a SQL Query tool.

2. Select the Pubs database from the DB: drop-down box.

3. Execute the command "dbcc checktable(authors)" to return the following output:

```
Checking authors
The total number of data pages in this table is 1.
Table has 23 data rows.
DBCC execution completed. If DBCC printed error messages,
see your System Administrator.
```

4. Execute the same command again, this time with a new parameter:

```
dbcc checktable(authors) with no_infomsgs
```

This returns only the row of output that starts "DBCC execution completed." This parameter is frequently used to suppress informational data so it is easier to find problem data.

5. Execute the following command: dbcc checkdb(pubs). Notice that this returns the same information as in step 3, but for each table in the Pubs database.

6. Execute the following command: dbcc newalloc(pubs). The first message returned from this says:

> Database 'pubs' is not in single-user mode - may find spurious allocation problems due to transactions in progress.

This is a normal message. It is usually not necessary to place a database into single-user mode to find allocation problems, but if problems are found, it is a good idea to put the database into single-user mode and run the command again.

For more information on this topic, please see the section "Checking Object Integrity."

Exercise 12.5: Investigating a Suspect Database

In this exercise, you will mark a database as suspect and then perform actions to see what errors occur. This exercise takes about 15 minutes.

1. Start a SQL Query tool.

2. Execute the following set of commands, which will allow edits to system tables, change the sysdatabases table to mark the Pubs database as suspect, and then turn off edits to the system tables. Note that editing system tables is a lot like editing the registry and should be done with extreme caution and not done on production servers.

```
use master
go
sp_configure "allow updates", 1
go
reconfigure with override
go
update sysdatabases set status = 320 where name = "pubs"
go
```

continues

Exercise 12.5: Continued

```
sp_configure "allow updates", 0
go
reconfigure
go
```

3. Stop and restart SQL Server. The service will start.

4. In a SQL Query tool, execute the following command: use pubs. This results in the following error message:

```
Msg 926, Level 14, State 1
Database 'pubs' cannot be opened - it has been marked
SUSPECT by recovery. The SA can drop the database with DBCC.
```

5. Notice that after attempting to use the use pubs command, the current database is still not pubs.

6. Reset the database to normal mode by executing the following code:

```
use master
go
sp_configure "allow updates", 1
go
reconfigure with override
go
update sysdatabases set status = 0 where name = "pubs"
go
sp_configure "allow updates", 0
go
reconfigure
go
```

7. Stop and restart SQL Server to get the Pubs database back online.

For more information on this exercise, please see the section "Checking Object Integrity."

Exercise 12.6: Restoring a Corrupt Database

If a database as been marked suspect by recovery or if it has enough internal problems that it is not working properly, then it becomes necessary to restore the database from backup. This exercise assumes that the database was corrupted internally, but the underlying devices are still intact. This exercise will take approximately 10 minutes.

1. Execute the following query to dump the Pubs database out to disk:

```
dump database pubs to disk="c:\mssql\backup\ch12.dat"
```

2. Examine the database's structure by using the sp_help_revdatabase stored procedure, which generates a complete script for rebuilding the database. An example of the output of sp_help_revdatabase pubs follows:

```
/********1*********2*********3*********4*********5*********6**
Reverse generated at 1997/08/19  21:13:03:380
Server / Database / Default sortorder ID :
UKMH559CMILLE02 / pubs / 52
DBName                          FromLPage   ToLPage    segmap
------------------------------- ---------   -------    ------
pubs                            0           511        7
pubs                            512         1535       7
@@version:  Microsoft SQL Server  6.50 - 6.50.201 (Intel X86)
********1*********2*********3*********4*********5*********6**/
go
USE master
go
--------------- Space and Log allocations -------------
CREATE  Database  pubs
      on  master = 1  -- 512  of two Kb pages
go
ALTER   Database  pubs
      on  master = 2  -- 1024  of two Kb pages
go
------------------ DB Options -----------------
EXECute sp_dboption  pubs ,'ANSI null default'
                          , false
EXECute sp_dboption  pubs ,'dbo use only'
                          , false
EXECute sp_dboption  pubs ,'no chkpt on recovery'
                          , false
/***
```

continues

Exercise 12.6: Continued

```
EXECute sp_dboption  pubs ,'offline'
                          , false
***/
/***
EXECute sp_dboption  pubs ,'published'
                          , false
***/
EXECute sp_dboption  pubs ,'read only'
                          , false
EXECute sp_dboption  pubs ,'select into/bulkcopy'
                          , false
EXECute sp_dboption  pubs ,'single user'
                          , false
/***
EXECute sp_dboption  pubs ,'subscribed'
                          , false
***/
EXECute sp_dboption  pubs ,'trunc. log on chkpt.'
                          , false
go
------------------ sa  is  dbo ------------------
go
---
```

3. Drop the database by using the following command:

   ```
   drop database pubs.
   ```

4. Rebuild the database by using the script created in Step 2 using sp_help_revdatabase.

5. Reload the database by using the load database command:

   ```
   load database pubs from file=c:\mssql\backup\ch12.dat.
   ```

For more information, please see the section "Restoring a Corrupted Database."

Exercise 12.7: Re-creating a Lost Device

This exercise will show you how to construct a statement used to rebuild a device. This technique will work when a device other than the Master device is lost. This exercise will take about 10 minutes.

1. Start the SQL Query tool.

2. Make sure the database is set to master in the DB: drop-down list at the top of the window.

3. To find information about the device that was lost, use the sp_helpdevice system stored procedure. This procedure queries the sys-devices table. The output looks something like this:

device_name	physical_name	description	status	cntrltype	device_number low	high
diskdump	nul	disk, dump device	16	2	0	20000
diskettedumpa	a:sqltable.dat	diskette, 1.2 MB, dump device	16	3	0	19
diskettedumpb	b:sqltable.dat	diskette, 1.2 MB, dump device	16	4	0	19
master	D:\MSSQL\DATA\MASTER.DAT	special, physical disk, 25 MB	3	0	0	12799
MSDBData	D:\MSSQL\DATA\MSDB.DAT	special, physical disk, 6 MB	2	0	127 2130706432	2130709503
MSDBLog	D:\MSSQL\DATA\MSDBLOG.DAT	special, physical disk, 2 MB	2	0	126 2113929216	2113930239
pubsdev	d:\mssql\data\pubsdev.dat	special, physical disk, 3 MB	2	0	4 67108864	67110399

4. For the Pubsdev device, the device's location is "D:\MSSQL\DATA\PUBSDEV.DAT," the device number, or the vdevno, is 4, and the size of the device is 3 MB. Unfortunately, the DISK INIT command requires the device size in pages, which are 2 KB each. However, to make finding the correct number of pages easy, subtract the value in the low column from the value in the high column and add one. In this case, for the Pubsdev device, this would be 1,536 pages. Check this by multiplying by 2,048 (the number of bytes on a page) and then dividing that by 1,024 (the number of kilobytes in a megabyte) and dividing that result by 1,024 again (the number of bytes in a kilobyte) to produce the actual device size of 3 MB.

5. Rebuild the command for the DISK INIT statement. In this case, the command would be

```
DISK INIT name = "pubsdev",
      physname = "d:\mssql\data\pubsdev.dat",
      size = 1536,
      vdevno = 4
```

For more information about this chapter, please see the section "Re-creating Lost Devices."

Review Questions

The following questions will test your knowledge of the information in this chapter.

1. Joe wants to check detailed startup information for SQL Server to determine which code page is being used. Which of the following sources contain the information he is seeking?

   A. The Current Activity log

   B. The Windows NT Event log

   C. The SQL Server Error log

   D. The Windows NT Crash dump file

2. After the Windows NT Server that is running SQL Server starts, Mario notices a message on the screen that says, "At least one service or driver has failed to start." Where should Mario look for details on this error message?

   A. The Current Activity log

   B. The Windows NT Event log

   C. The SQL Server Error log

   D. The Windows NT Crash dump file

3. Barry is receiving frequent errors about running out of user connections in the SQL Server error log. What can he do to fix the problem?

   A. Purchase more licenses for SQL Server.

   B. Increase the number of connections by using the sp_configure stored procedure.

   C. Purchase more licenses for Windows NT Server.

   D. Stop the License Logging Service.

4. Jane was examining the Windows NT Event Log and noticed that there were a lot of messages about network errors while sending results to the front end. What is a likely cause of this error?

    A. There is a loose wire between the hard disks and the lighted panel on the server's case.

    B. The applications that are querying the server are either crashing or being canceled.

    C. The wrong network card is configured in Windows NT.

    D. The Master database is about to crash and should be reloaded from backup.

5. Which of the following commands should be used to track down problems in the Pubs database that involve the image data type?

    A. DBCC TEXTALLOC(pubs)

    B. DBCC CHECKDB(pubs)

    C. DBCC CHECKIMAGE(pubs)

    D. DBCC EXAMINEDBIMAGETYPES(pubs, images)

6. Which of the following will check the system tables in the Pubs database for consistency?

    A. DBCC CHECKCATALOG(pubs)

    B. DBCC CHECKDB(master)

    C. DBCC EXAMINESYSTEM(pubs)

    D. CHECKDATABASE(pubs)

7. After starting SQL Server, Bob notices that one of the databases in SQL Server was marked suspect by recovery. What does this mean for his users?

    A. They will be able to access the database normally, but should save their work often.

    B. The database will not be accessible to any users.

   C. The database will only be accessible to system administrators.

   D. The database needs to be repaired.

8. After a database has been marked suspect, which two of the following can be done to retrieve data?

   A. Nothing.

   B. The transaction log can be dumped.

   C. The database can be accessed by the database administrator.

   D. The database can be examined by the administrator to rebuild a replacement database.

9. After discovering that his database was marked suspect, Stanley needs to restore his database, Production, from backup. What is the first step?

   A. Dropping the suspect database by using the Drop Database command

   B. Loading the new database on top of the suspect one

   C. Running DBCC DBREPAIR(production, DROPDB)

   D. Rebuilding the devices using the DEVICE REBUILD command

10. Dan finds out that his database has a large number of allocation errors, which have probably been in the database for a long time. Which of the following methods will best fix the problem?

   A. Dump the database and reload it.

   B. Restore the database from a known clean backup.

   C. Export the data to another server using SQL Transfer.

   D. Use DBCC DBREPAIR() to fix the database.

11. One of the disks on Ernesto's SQL Server failed overnight. It didn't contain the Master database, but did contain one of the user databases. What stored procedure can Ernesto use to determine the size of the device?

    A. It cannot be done because the device no longer exists.

    B. sp_help_revdatabase.

    C. sp_helpdevice.

    D. sp_devicesize.

12. All of the users of Robert's server called him over lunch to report that their applications had locked up. What can Roberto use to find the process that is causing the other users to lock?

    A. The Current Activity screen

    B. DBCC FINDLOCKS()

    C. The Activity Report

    D. Queries to the sysdatabaselocks table

13. After finding the user process that locked the database, how should Robert stop the process?

    A. Robert should use the Kill Process button on the Current Activity screen.

    B. User processes cannot be stopped by administrators.

    C. Robert should turn off the user's workstation.

    D. Robert should disconnect the server from the network.

14. Which of the following is a likely cause of a connection going into a sleeping state while records are locked?

    A. The user doesn't commit a transaction before walking off for coffee.

    B. The server fails to process requests in a timely manner.

    C. Not enough server memory.

    D. Not enough user connections.

15. Which of the following types of problems is the DBCC NEWALLOC(pubs) command likely to fix?

    A. Allocation chain linkage problems

    B. Pages that are linked but not used

    C. Pages that are used but not linked

    D. None of the above

16. What is the difference between DBCC CHECKDB(…) and DBCC CHECKTABLE(…) ?

    A. DBCC CHECKDB checks allocation tables and text pages, and DBCC CHECKTABLE does not.

    B. DBCC CHECKTABLE is more thorough in how it checks tables.

    C. DBCC CHECKDB runs the exact same checks as DBCC CHECKTABLE, but it runs on all of the tables instead of just one.

    D. DBCC CHECKTABLE is used to check tables, but DBCC CHECKDB checks all of the tables on a server.

17. Why is it important to examine databases regularly for corruption?

    A. To fix problems with allocation tables

    B. To optimize databases by reducing segmentation

    C. To ensure that a database backup is clean

    D. To reduce the number of ghosted connections

18. When is it necessary to drop a database and reload it?

    A. Whenever corruption is found in the database

    B. Only when a database is marked suspect

    C. When users start getting errors that say the database is out of connections

    D. Whenever a database is out of space

19. Which of the following tables would contain data that can be used to rebuild devices?

    A. sysdatabases

    B. sysdevices

    C. sysallocations

    D. DeviceMap

20. Maurice is having a problem with his server stopping at random times during the day. Where should he start looking to find the source of his problem?

    A. The Windows NT Event Log

    B. The SQL Server Error Log

    C. The Current Activity screen

    D. The SQL Server Activity Listing

21. How is a database marked as suspect?

    A. SQL Server changes an entry in the sysdatabases table.

    B. SQL Server removes the database from the sysdatabases table.

    C. SQL Server removes all mention of the devices and database from all of the system tables.

    D. SQL Server makes a change to the registry on startup.

Review Answers

1. C

2. B

3. B

4. B

5. A

6. A

7. B

8. B, D

9. C

10. C

11. C

12. A

13. A

14. A

15. D

16. C

17. C

18. A

19. B

20. A

21. A

Answers to Test Yourself Questions at Beginning of the Chapter

1. Bob should probably use the SQL Server Error Log, found in \MSSQL\LOG, to determine the cause of startup problems. This is discussed in the first section, "The SQL Server Error Log."

2. Ned's errors are mostly transient errors caused by locking client applications. He would know that if he had read the section "Resolving Network Errors."

3. The DBCC commands (Database Consistency Check) are used to diagnose and possibly fix database consistency problems, among other things. These are discussed in the section "Checking Object Integrity."

4. When a database is marked suspect, administrators usually panic because nobody, including the administrator, can get to the data. This is covered in the section "Investigating Suspect Databases."

5. The process that is sleeping can be killed. The user that walked away for lunch probably should be killed, but that may be against the law in your area. See the section on "Canceling a Sleeping Process" for more information on the solution less likely to make the television news.

6. The sp_help_revdatabase command is used to build the scripts used to rebuild databases. It is covered in the section "Restoring Corrupted Databases."

7. Information used to rebuild lost devices is found in the sysdevices table, as mentioned in the section "Re-Creating Lost Devices."

Appendix A

Overview of the Certification Process

To become a Microsoft Certified Professional, candidates must pass rigorous certification exams that provide a valid and reliable measure of their technical proficiency and expertise. These closed-book exams have on-the-job relevance because they are developed with the input of professionals in the computer industry and reflect how Microsoft products are actually used in the workplace. The exams are conducted by an independent organization—Sylvan Prometric—at more than 700 Sylvan Authorized Testing Centers around the world.

Currently Microsoft offers four types of certification, based on specific areas of expertise:

▶ **Microsoft Certified Product Specialist (MCPS).** Qualified to provide installation, configuration, and support for users of at least one Microsoft desktop operating system, such as Windows 95 or Windows NT Server. In addition, candidates may take additional elective exams to add areas of specialization. MCPS is the first level of expertise.

▶ **Microsoft Certified Systems Engineer (MCSE).** Qualified to effectively plan, implement, maintain, and support information systems with Microsoft Windows NT and other Microsoft advanced systems and workgroup products, such as Microsoft Office and Microsoft BackOffice. The SQL Server Administration exam can be used as one of the two elective exams. MCSE is the second level of expertise.

▶ **Microsoft Certified Solution Developer (MCSD).** Qualified to design and develop custom business solutions using Microsoft development tools, technologies, and platforms, including Microsoft Office and Microsoft BackOffice. MCSD also is a second level of expertise, but in the area of software development.

▶ **Microsoft Certified Trainer (MCT).** Instructionally and technically qualified by Microsoft to deliver Microsoft Education courses at Microsoft-authorized sites. An MCT must be employed by a Microsoft Solution Provider Authorized Technical Education Center or a Microsoft Authorized Academic Training site.

For up-to-date information about each type of certification, visit the Microsoft Training and Certification World Wide Web site at http://www.microsoft.com/train_cert. You must have an Internet account and a WWW browser to access this information. You also can call the following sources:

▶ Microsoft Certified Professional Program: 800-636-7544

▶ Sylvan Prometric Testing Centers: 800-755-EXAM

▶ Microsoft Online Institute (MOLI): 800-449-9333

How to Become a Microsoft Certified Product Specialist (MCPS)

Becoming an MCPS requires you pass one operating system exam. The following list shows the names and exam numbers of all the operating systems from which you can choose to get your MCPS certification:

- ▶ Implementing and Supporting Microsoft Windows 95 #70-63

- ▶ Implementing and Supporting Microsoft Windows NT Workstation 4.02 #70-73

- ▶ Implementing and Supporting Microsoft Windows NT Workstation 3.51 #70-42

- ▶ Implementing and Supporting Microsoft Windows NT Server 4.0 #70-67

- ▶ Implementing and Supporting Microsoft Windows NT Server 3.51 #70-43

- ▶ Microsoft Windows for Workgroups 3.11-Desktop #70-48

- ▶ Microsoft Windows 3.1 #70-30

- ▶ Microsoft Windows Architecture I #70-160

- ▶ Microsoft Windows Architecture II #70-161

How to Become a Microsoft Certified Systems Engineer (MCSE)

MCSE candidates need to pass four operating system exams and two elective exams. The MCSE certification path is divided into two tracks: the Windows NT 3.51 track and the Windows NT 4.0 track. The "System Administration on Microsoft SQL Server 6.5" exam covered in this book can be applied to either track of the MCSE certification path as an elective exam.

Table A.1 shows the core requirements (four operating system exams) and the elective courses (two exams) for the Windows NT 3.51 track.

Table A.1

Windows NT 3.51 MCSE Track		
Take These Three Required Exams (Core Requirements)	Plus, Pick One Exam from the Following Operating System Exams (Core Requirement)	Plus, Pick Two Exams from the Following Elective Exams (Elective Requirements)
Implementing and Supporting Microsoft Windows NT Server 3.51 #70-43	Implementing and Supporting Microsoft Windows 95 #70-63	Implementing and Supporting Microsoft SNA Server 3.0 #70-13
AND Implementing and Supporting Microsoft Windows NT Workstation 3.51 #70-42	*OR* Microsoft Windows for Workgroups 3.11-Desktop #70-48	*OR* Implementing and Supporting Microsoft SNA Server 4.0 #70-85
AND Networking Essentials #70-58	*OR* Microsoft Windows 3.1 #70-30	*OR* Implementing and Supporting Microsoft Exchange Server 4.0 #70-75
		OR Implementing and Supporting Microsoft Exchange Server 5 #70-76
		OR Microsoft Server 4.2 Database Implementation #70-21
		OR Implementing a Database Design on Microsoft SQL Server 6.5 #70-27
		OR Microsoft SQL Server 4.2 Database Administration for Microsoft Windows NT #70-22
		OR System Administration for Microsoft SQL Server 6.5 #70-26

Take These Three Required Exams (Core Requirements)	Plus, Pick One Exam from the Following Operating System Exams (Core Requirement)	Plus, Pick Two Exams from the Following Elective Exams (Elective Requirements)
		OR Microsoft Mail for PC Networks 3.2-Enterprise #70-37
		OR Internetworking Microsoft TCP/IP on Microsoft Windows NT (3.5-3.51) #70-53
		OR Internetworking Microsoft TCP/IP on Microsoft Windows NT 4.0 #70-59
		OR Implementing and Supporting Microsoft Internet Information Server 3.0 and Index Server 1.1 #70-77
		OR Implementing and Supporting the Microsoft Proxy Server 1.0 #70-78
		OR Implementing and Supporting Microsoft Proxy Server 2.0 (#70-88)
		OR Implementing and Supporting Microsoft Internet Explorer Administration Kit for Microsoft Internet Explorer 4.0 #70-79

Table A.2 shows the core requirements (four operating system exams) and elective courses (two exams) for the Windows NT 4.0 track. Tables A.1 and A.2 have many of the same exams listed, but there are distinct differences between the two. Make sure you read each track's requirements carefully.

Table A.2

Windows NT 4.0 MCSE Track		
Take These Three Required Exams (Core Requirements)	Plus, Pick One Exam from the Following Operating System Exams (Core Requirement)	Plus, Pick Two Exams from the Following Elective Exams (Elective Requirements)
Implementing and Supporting Microsoft Windows NT Server 4.0 #70-67	Implementing and Supporting Microsoft Windows 95 #70-63	Implementing and Supporting Microsoft SNA Server 3.0 #70-13
AND Implementing and Supporting Microsoft Windows NT Workstation 4.0 in the Enterprise #70-68	*OR* Microsoft Windows for Workgroups 3.11-Desktop #70-48	*OR* Implementing and Supporting Microsoft SNA Server 4.0 #70-85
AND Networking Essentials #70-58	*OR* Microsoft Windows 3.1 #70-30	*OR* Implementing and Supporting Microsoft Exchange Server 4.0 #70-75
	OR Implementing and Supporting Microsoft Windows NT Workstation 4.02 #70-73	*OR* Implementing and Supporting Microsoft Exchange Server 5 #70-76
		OR Microsoft Server 4.2 Database Implementation #70-21
		OR Implementing a Database Design on Microsoft SQL Server 6.5 #70-27

Take These Three Required Exams (Core Requirements)	Plus, Pick One Exam from the Following Operating System Exams (Core Requirement)	Plus, Pick Two Exams from the Following Elective Exams (Elective Requirements)
		OR Microsoft SQL Server 4.2 Database Administration for Microsoft Windows NT #70-22
		OR System Administration for Microsoft SQL Server 6.5 #70-26
		OR Microsoft Mail for PC Networks 3.2-Enterprise #70-37
		OR Internetworking Microsoft TCP/IP on Microsoft Windows NT (3.5-3.51) #70-53
		OR Internetworking Microsoft TCP/IP on Microsoft Windows NT 4.0 #70-59
		OR Implementing and Supporting Microsoft Internet Information Server 3.0 and Index Server 1.1 #70-77
		OR Implementing and Supporting the Microsoft Proxy Server 1.0 #70-78
		OR Implementing and Supporting Microsoft Proxy Server 2.0 (#70-88)

Table A.2   Continued

Windows NT 4.0 MCSE Track		
Take These Three Required Exams (Core Requirements)	Plus, Pick One Exam from the Following Operating System Exams (Core Requirement)	Plus, Pick Two Exams from the Following Elective Exams (Elective Requirements)
		OR Implementing and Supporting Microsoft Internet Explorer Administration Kit for Microsoft Internet Explorer 4.0 #70-79

How to Become a Microsoft Certified Solution Developer (MCSD)

MCSD candidates need to pass two core technology exams and two elective exams. Unfortunately, the System Administration on Microsoft SQL Server 6.5 (#70-26) exam does NOT apply toward any of these requirements. Table A.3 shows the required technology exams, plus the elective exams that apply toward obtaining the MCSD.

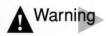 **Warning**

The "System Administration on Microsoft SQL Server 6.5" (#70-26) exam does NOT apply toward any of the MCSD requirements.

Table A.3

MCSD Exams and Requirements	
Take These Two Core Technology Exams	Plus, Choose from Two of the Following Elective Exams
Microsoft Windows Architecture I #70-160	Microsoft SQL Server 4.2 Database Implementation #70-21

Take These Two Core Technology Exams	Plus, Choose from Two of the Following Elective Exams
AND Microsoft Windows Architecture II #70-161	*OR* Developing Applications with C++ Using the Microsoft Foundation Class Library #70-24
	OR Implementing a Database Design on Microsoft SQL Server 6 #70-27
	OR Microsoft Access 2.0 for Windows-Application Development #70-51
	OR Microsoft Access for Windows 95 and the Microsoft Access Development Toolkit #70-69
	OR Developing Applications with Microsoft Excel 5.0 Using Visual Basic for Applications #70-52
	OR Programming in Microsoft Visual FoxPro 3.0 for Windows #70-54
	OR Programming with Microsoft Visual Basic 4.0 #70-65
	OR Developing Applications with Microsoft Visual Basic 5.0 #70-165
	OR Implementing OLE in Microsoft Foundation Class Applications #70-25

Becoming a Microsoft Certified Trainer (MCT)

To understand the requirements and process for becoming a Microsoft Certified Trainer (MCT), you need to obtain the Microsoft Certified Trainer Guide document (MCTGUIDE.DOC) from the following WWW site:

http://www.microsoft.com/train_cert/download.htm

On this page, click on the hyperlink MCT GUIDE (mctguide.doc) (117k). If your WWW browser can display DOC files (Word for Windows native file format), the MCT Guide displays in the browser window. Otherwise, you need to download it and open it in Word for Windows or Windows 95 WordPad. The MCT Guide explains the four-step process to becoming an MCT. The general steps for the MCT certification are as follows:

1. Complete and mail a Microsoft Certified Trainer application to Microsoft. You must include proof of your skills for presenting instructional material. The options for doing so are described in the MCT Guide.

2. Obtain and study the Microsoft Trainer Kit for the Microsoft Official Curricula (MOC) course(s) for which you want to be certified. Microsoft Trainer Kits can be ordered by calling 800-688-0496 in North America. Other regions should review the MCT Guide for information on how to order a Trainer Kit.

3. Pass the Microsoft certification exam for the product for which you want to be certified to teach.

4. Attend the Microsoft Official Curriculum (MOC) course for the course for which you want to be certified. This is done so you can understand how the course is structured, how labs are completed, and how the course flows.

Note

You should use the preceding steps as a general overview of the MCT certification process. The actual steps you need to take are described in detail in the MCTGUIDE.DOC file on the WWW site mentioned earlier. Do not misconstrue the preceding steps as the actual process you need to take.

If you are interested in becoming an MCT, you can receive more information by visiting the Microsoft Certified Training (MCT) WWW site at http://www.microsoft.com/train_cert/mctint.htm; or call 800-688-0496.

Appendix

Study Tips

B

Self-study involves any method that you employ to learn a given topic, with the most popular being third-party books, such as the one you hold in your hand. Before you begin to study for a certification book, you should know exactly what Microsoft expects you to learn.

Pay close attention to the objectives posted for the exam. The most current objectives can always be found on the WWW site http://www.microsoft.com/train_cert. This book was written to the most current objectives, and the beginning of each chapter lists the relevant objectives for that chapter. As well, you should notice a handy tear-out card with an objective matrix that lists all objectives and the page you can turn to for information on that objective.

If you have taken any college courses in the past, you have probably learned what study habits work best for you. Nevertheless, consider the following:

▶ Study in bright light to reduce fatigue and depression.

▶ Establish a regular study schedule and stick as close to it as possible.

▶ Turn off all forms of distraction, including radios and televisions; or try studying in a quiet room.

▶ Study in the same place each time you study so your materials are always readily at hand.

▶ Take short breaks (approximately 15 minutes) every two to three hours or so. Studies have proven that your brain assimilates information better when this is allowed.

Another thing to think about is this: there are three ways in which humans learn information: visually, audially, and through tactile confirmation. That's why, in a college class, the students who took notes on the lectures had better recall on exam day; they took in information both audially and through tactile confirmation—writing it down.

Hence, use study techniques that reinforce information in all three ways. For example, by reading the books, you are visually taking in information. By writing down the information when you test yourself, you are giving your brain tactile confirmation. And lastly, have someone test you out loud, so you can hear yourself giving the correct answer. Having someone test you should always be the last step in studying.

Pre-testing Yourself

Before taking the actual exam, verify that you are ready to do so by testing yourself over and over again in a variety of ways. Within this book, there are questions at the beginning and end of each chapter. On the accompanying CD-ROM, there is an electronic test engine that emulates the actual Microsoft test and enables you to test your knowledge of the subject areas. Use these repeatedly until you are consistently scoring in the 90 percent range (or better).

 Note

This means, of course, that you can't start studying five days before the exam begins. You will need to give yourself plenty of time to read, practice, and then test yourself several times.

TestPrep, the electronic testing engine on the CD-ROM, we believe is the best one on the market. While described in Appendix D, "All About TestPrep," here it's just important for you to know that TestPrep will prepare you for the exam in a way unparalleled by most other engines.

Hints and Tips for Doing Your Best on the Tests

In a confusing twist of terminology, when you take one of the Microsoft exams, you are said to be "writing" the exam. When you go to take the actual exam, be prepared. Arrive early and be ready to show your two forms of identification and sit before the monitor. Expect wordy questions. Although you have 90 minutes to take the exam, there are 61 questions you must answer. This gives you just over one minute to answer each question. This may sound like ample time for each question, but remember that most of the questions are lengthy word problems, which tend to ramble on for paragraphs. Your 90 minutes of exam time can be consumed very quickly.

It has been estimated that approximately 85 percent of the candidates taking their first Microsoft exam fail it. It is not so much that they are unprepared and unknowledgeable. It is more the case that they don't know what to expect and are immediately intimidated by the wordiness of the questions and the ambiguity implied in the answers.

For every exam that Microsoft offers, there is a different required passing score. The SQL Server Administration passing score is 730, or 73 percent. Because there are 61 questions on the exam (randomly taken from a pool of about 150), this means you must correctly answer 45 or more to pass.

Things to Watch For

When you take the exam, look closely at the number of correct choices you need to make. Some questions require that you select one correct answer; other questions have more than one correct answer. When you see radial buttons next to the answer choices, you need to remember that the answers are mutually exclusive and there is but one right answer. On the other hand, check boxes indicate that the answers are not mutually exclusive and there are multiple correct answers. Be sure to read the questions closely to see how many answers you need to choose.

Also, read the questions fully. With lengthy questions, the last sentence often dramatically changes the scenario. When taking the exam, you are given pencils and two sheets of paper. If you are uncertain of what the question is saying, map out the scenario on the paper until you have it clear in your mind. You're required to turn in the scrap paper at the end of the exam.

Marking Answers for Return

You can mark questions on the actual exam and refer back to them later. If you get a wordy question that will take a long time to read and decipher, mark it and return to it when you have completed the rest of the exam. This will save you from wasting time on it and running out of time on the exam—there are only 90 minutes allotted for the exam and it ends when those 90 minutes expire, whether or not you are finished with the exam.

Attaching Notes to Test Questions

At the conclusion of the exam, before the grading takes place, you are given the opportunity to attach a message to any question. If you feel that a question was too ambiguous, or tested on knowledge you did not need to know to work with the product, take this opportunity to state your case. Unheard of is the instance where Microsoft changes a test score as a result of an attached message. However, it never hurts to try—and it helps to vent your frustration before blowing the proverbial 50-amp fuse.

Good luck!

Appendix C

What's on the CD-ROM

This appendix is a brief rundown of what you'll find on the CD-ROM that comes with this book. For a more detailed description of the newly developed TestPrep test engine, exclusive to Macmillan Computer Publishing, please see Appendix D, "All About TestPrep."

TestPrep

A new test engine was developed exclusively for Macmillan Computer Publishing. It is, we believe, the best test engine available, because it closely emulates the actual Microsoft exam and it enables you to check your score by objective, which helps you determine what you need to study further. Before running the TestPrep software, be sure to read CDROM.hlp (in the root directory of the CD-ROM) for late breaking news on TestPrep features. For a complete description of the benefits of TestPrep, please see Appendix D.

Copyright Information and Disclaimer

Macmillan Computer Publishing's TestPrep test engine: Copyright 1997 Macmillan Computer Publishing. All rights reserved. Made in U.S.A.

Appendix

D

All About TestPrep

The electronic TestPrep utility included on the CD-ROM accompanying this book enables you to test your SQL Server knowledge in a manner similar to that employed by the actual Microsoft exam.

While it is possible to maximize the TestPrep application, the default is for it to run in smaller mode so you can refer to your SQL Server Desktop while answering questions. TestPrep uses a unique randomization sequence to ensure that each time you run the program you are presented with a different sequence of questions—this enhances your learning and prevents you from merely learning the expected answers over time without reading the question each and every time.

Question Presentation

TestPrep emulates the actual Microsoft "System Administration for Microsoft SQL Server 6.5" exam (#70-26), in that radio (circle) buttons are used to signify only one correct choice, while check boxes (squares) are used to imply multiple correct answers.

You can exit the program at any time by clicking the Exit button, or you can continue to the next question by clicking the Next button.

Scoring

The TestPrep Score Report uses actual numbers from the "System Administration for Microsoft SQL Server 6.5" exam. For SQL Server Administration, a score of 730 or higher is considered passing; the same parameters apply to TestPrep. Each objective category is broken down into categories with a percentage correct given for each of the 12 categories.

Choose Show Me What I Missed to go back through the questions you incorrectly answered and see what the correct answers are. Click Exit to terminate the application.

I n d e x